THE **COMPLETE WORKS** OF **SWAMI VIVEKANANDA**

VOLUME IX

Discovery Publisher

2019, Discovery Publisher

No part of this book may be reproduced in any form or by any electronic or mechanical means including information storage and retrieval systems, without permission in writing from the publisher.

Author: Swami Vivekananda

616 Corporate Way, Suite 2-4933
Valley Cottage, New York, 10989
www.discoverypublisher.com
edition@discoverypublisher.com
facebook.com/discoverypublisher
twitter.com/discoverypb

New York • Paris • Dublin • Tokyo • Hong Kong

TABLE OF CONTENTS

Epistles — Fifth Series   3

I — SIR	4		XXVII — MOTHER	16
II — SIR	4		XXVIII — MOTHER	17
III — SIR	4		XXIX — MOTHER	17
IV — BALARAM BABU	5		XXX — MOTHER	19
V — TULSIRAM	5		XXXI — MOTHER	20
VI — SHARAT	5		XXXII — MOTHER	20
VII — MOTHER	6		XXXIII — MOTHER	20
VIII — MOTHER	6		XXXIV — MOTHER	20
IX — MOTHER	7		XXXV — MOTHER	21
X — MOTHER	7		XXXVI — MOTHER	22
XI — MOTHER	8		XXXVII — MOTHER	22
XII — MOTHER	8		XXXVIII — MOTHER	22
XIII — MOTHER	8		XXXIX — MOTHER	23
XIV — MOTHER	9		XL — MRS. BULL	23
XV — MOTHER	9		XLI — MISS THURSBY	24
XVI — MOTHER	10		XLII — MOTHER	24
XVII — MOTHER	11		XLIII — MOTHER	24
XVIII — MOTHER	11		XXXIV — MOTHER	24
XIX — MOTHER	12		XLV — MOTHER	25
XX — MOTHER	12		XLVI — MOTHER	25
XXI — MOTHER	13		XLVII — MISS THURSBY	26
XXII — MOTHER	13		XLVIII — ADHYAPAKJI	27
XXIII — MOTHER	13		XLIX — MOTHER	27
XXIV — MOTHER	14		L — MOTHER	28
XXV — MOTHER	15		LI — MOTHER	28
XXVI — MOTHER	15		LII — MOTHER	28

LIII — MOTHER	29
LIV — MOTHER	29
LV — FRIEND	29
LVI — MOTHER	30
LVII — MOTHER	30
LVIII — SIR	30
LIX — MOTHER	31
LX — DOCTOR	31
LXI — MOTHER	31
LXII — MOTHER	32
LXIV — MOTHER	32
LXV — MOTHER	32
LXVI — MOTHER	33
LXVII — FRIEND	33
LXVIII — MRS. G. W. HALE	34
LXIX — CHRISTINA	34
LXX — MOTHER	34
LXXI — SISTER CHRISTINE	35
LXXII — ISABELLE MCKINDLEY	35
LXXIII — CHRISTINA	36
LXXIV — CHRISTINA	36
LXXV — CHRISTINA	37
LXXVI — YOUR HIGHNESS	37
LXXVII — SIR	37
LXXVIII — CHRISTINA	37
LXXIX — MRS. OLE BULL	38
LXXX — SIR	38
LXXXI — MRS. BULL	38
LXXXII — MRS. FUNKEY	38
LXXXIII — MRS. BULL	39
LXXXIV — CHRISTINA	39
LXXXV — MRS. BULL	39
LXXXVI — MISS THURSBY	40
LXXXVII — FRIEND	40
LXXXVIII — CHRISTINA	41
LXXXIX — MRS. FUNKEY	41
XC — CHRISTINA	41
XCI — CHRISTINA	42
XCII — MRS. BULL	42
XCIII — SIR	42
XCIV — MRS. BULL	43
XCV — MOTHER	43
XCVI — SIR	43
XCVII — MRS. BULL	44
XCVIII — BLESSED AND BELOVED	44
XCIX — CHRISTINA	45
C — NOBLE	45
CI — MISS NOBLE	45
CII — CHRISTINA	45
CIII — MADRAS COMITTEE	45
CIV — GENTLEMEN	46
CV — CHRISTINA	46
CVI — MRS. BULL	46
CVII — RAM RAM	47
CVIII — MISS NOBLE	47
CIX — LALAJEE	47
CX — BADRI SAH	48
CXI — MOTHER	48
CXII — MRS. BULL	48
CXIII — FRIEND	48
CXIV — SHIVANANDA	49
CXV — CHRISTINA	49
CXVI — SISTER CHRISTINE	50

CXVII — MISS NOBLE	50
CXVIII — CHRISTINA	50
CXIX — MARGARET	51
CXX — DHIRA MATA	51
CXXI — JAGMOHAN	52
CXXII — MISS MACLEOD	52
CXXIII — SIR	52
CXXIV — MISS MACLEOD / MRS. BULL	52
CXXV — MR. J. J. GOODWIN'S MOTHER	53
CXXVI — YOUR HIGHNESS	53
CXXVII — CHRISTINA	53
CXXVIII — YOUR HIGHNESS	54
CXXIX — YOUR HIGHNESS	54
CXXX — MARGOT	55
CXXXI — NIVEDITA	55
CXXXII — CHRISTINA	55
CXXXIII — RAJA	56
CXXXIV — S	56
CXXXV — MARGOT	56
CXXXVI — SIR	57
CXXXVII — MARGOT	57
CXXXVIII — CHRISTINA	57
CXXXIX — MISS MACLEOD	57
CXL — CHRISTINA	57
CXLI — CHRISTINA	58
CXLII — SISTER CHRISTINE	58
CXLIII — MOTHER	59
CXLIV — ISABEL	59
CXLV — CHRISTINA	59
CXLVI — MOTHER CHURCH	60
CXLVII — MOTHER	60
CXLVIII — CHRISTINA	61
CXLIX — CHRISTINA	61
CL — CHRISTINA	61
CLI — CHRISTINA	62
CLII — CHRISTINA	62
CLIII — MRS. BULL	62
CLIV — CHRISTINA	63
CLV — DHIRA MATA	63
CLVI — MOTHER	63
CLVII — MARGOT	64
CLVIII — MOTHER	64
CLIX — CHRISTINA	64
CLX — BRAHMANANDA	65
CLXI — CHRISTINA	65
CLXII — MARGO	66
CLXIII — JOE	66
CLXIV — CHRISTINA	67
CLXV — SISTER CHRISTINE	67
CLXVI — MARGOT	67
CLXVII — MARGOT	68
CLXVIII — MOTHER	68
CLXIX — CHRISTINA	68
CLXX — ABHEDANANDA	69
CLXXI — CHRISTINA	69
CLXXII — CHRISTINA	70
CLXXIII — CHRISTINA	70
CLXXIV — CHRISTINA	70
CLXXV — MRS. HANSBROUGH	71
CLXXVI — SISTER CHRISTINE	71
CLXXVII — MRS. HANSBROUGH	71
CLXXVIII — ABHEDANANDA	72
CLXXIX — CHRISTINA	72

CLXXX — MRS. LEGGETT	72	CXCIX — FRIEND	78
CLXXXI — CHRISTINE	72	CC — CHRISTINA	79
CLXXXII — NIVEDITA	73	CCI — CHRISTINE	79
CLXXXIII — CHRISTINE	73	CCII — CHRISTINE	80
CLXXXIV — CHRISTINA	73	CCIII — CHRISTINE	80
CLXXXV — MOTHER	74	CCIV — CHRISTINE	81
CLXXXVI — ALBERTA	74	CCV — CHRISTINA	82
CLXXXVII — CHRISTINA	74	CCVI — CHRISTINA	82
CLXXXVIII — MARGO	74	CCVII — MARGO	83
CLXXXIX — SISTER CHRISTINE	75	CCVIII — CHRISTINA	83
CXC — YOUR HIGHNESS	75	CCIX — CHRISTINE	84
CXCI — MOTHER	75	CCX — CHRISTINE	85
CXCII — SIR	76	CCXI — CHRISTINE	85
CXCIII — MARGOT	76	CCXII — CHRISTINE	86
CXCIV — CHRISTINE	77	CCXIII — SISTER CHRISTINE	87
CXCV — INTRODUCTION	77	CCXXIV — CHRISTINE	87
CXCVI — CHRISTINE	77	CCXXV — CHRISTINE	88
CXCVII — MOTHER	78	CCXXVI — CHRISTINE	88
CXCVIII — MRS. HANSBROUGH	78	CCXXVII — CHRISTINE	89

Lectures and Discourses — 92

THE WOMEN OF INDIA	94
THE FIRST STEP TOWARDS JNANA	103
BHAKTI-YOGA	110
THE MUNDAKA UPANISHAD	116
HISTORY OF THE ARYAN RACE	123

Notes of Lectures and Classes — 132

THE RELIGION OF INDIA	134
CHRIST'S MESSAGE TO THE WORLD	136
MOHAMMED'S MESSAGE TO THE WORLD	136

MOHAMMED	136
CLASS LESSONS IN MEDITATION BY SWAMI VIVEKANANDA	137
THE GITA	137
THE GITA — I	138
THE GITA — III	139
GITA CLASS	141
REMARKS FROM VARIOUS LECTURES	141

Writings: Prose and Poems — 144

THE ETHER	146
NOTES	148
LECTURE NOTES	148
MACROCOSM AND MICROCOSM	149
SWAMI VIVEKANANDA'S FOOTNOTES TO THE IMITATION OF CHRIST	149
BOOK I	149
Chapter 1	149
Chapter 3	151
Chapter 5	151
Chapter 6	151
THE PLAGUE MANIFESTO	152
ONE CIRCLE MORE	153
FACSIMILE	153
AN UNTITLED POEM ON SHRI RAMAKRISHNA	153
AN UNFINISHED POEM	153
BHARTRIHARI'S VERSES ON RENUNCIATION	154
BHARTRIHARI'S VERSES ON RENUNCIATION	154

Conversations and Interviews — 160

FIRST MEETING WITH MADAME EMMA CALVE	162
FIRST MEETING WITH JOHN D. ROCKEFELLER	162

A DUSKY PHILOSOPHER FROM INDIA	163
"WE ARE HYPNOTIZED INTO WEAKNESS BY OUR SURROUNDINGS"	165
MARRIAGE	165
LINE OF DEMARCATION	166
GOD IS!	166
RENUNCIATION	166
SHRI RAMAKRISHNA'S DISCIPLE	166
THE MASTER'S DIVINE INCARNATION	166
A PRIVATE ADMISSION	167
A GREETING	167
"THIS WORLD IS A CIRCUS RING"	167
ON KALI	167
TRAINING UNDER SHRI RAMAKRISHNA	167

Excerpts from Sister Nivedita's Book — 170

NOTES OF SOME WANDERINGS WITH SWAMI VIVEKANANDA	172
FOREWORD	172
CHAPTER I — THE HOUSE ON THE GANGES	173
CHAPTER II — AT NAINI TAL AND ALMORA	175
CHAPTER III — MORNING TALKS AT ALMORA	176
CHAPTER IV — ON THE WAY TO KATHGODAM	182
CHAPTER V — ON THE WAY TO BARAMULLA	183
CHAPTER VI — THE VALE OF KASHMIR	185
CHAPTER VII — LIFE AT SRINAGAR	187
CHAPTER VIII — THE TEMPLE OF PANDRENTHAN	189
CHAPTER IX — WALKS AND TALKS BESIDE THE JHELUM	192
CHAPTER IX — THE SHRINE OF AMARNATH	195
CHAPTER IX — AT SRINAGAR ON THE RETURN JOURNEY	197
CHAPTER IX — THE CAMP UNDER THE CHENNAARS	198

CONCLUDING WORDS OF THE EDITOR	200

Sayings and Utterances — 202

LIST OF ABBREVIATIONS	204

Newspaper Reports — 218

PART I: AMERICAN NEWSPAPER REPORTS	**220**
RESPONSE TO WELCOME	220
PARLOR TALK	221
RELIGION NOT THE CRYING NEED OF INDIA	221
THE CHICAGO LETTER	222
RELIGIONS OF INDIA	223
ALL RELIGIONS ARE TRUE SUCH IS THE MESSAGE BROUGHT FROM INDIA	223
A MESSAGE FROM INDIA	224
REINCARNATION	225
AN INTELLECTUAL FEAST	225
A PRAYER MEETING	225
ON AMERICAN WOMEN	225
ON THE BRAHMO SAMAJ	226
A WITTY HINDU	226
THE MANNERS AND CUSTOMS OF INDIA	226
HINDU PHILOSOPHY	227
TWO REMARKABLE THINGS IN THIS COUNTRY	227
HIS CRITICISM OF MISSIONARIES	228
A GOD EVERY DAY	228
VIVE KANANDA LEAVES	228
CULTURE AT HOME	229
KANANDA, THE PAGAN	229
What India Is	230

Antagonize Native Interests	230
Most Missionaries Incompetent	231
Filled the World with Bloodshed	231
AS THE WAVE FOLLOWS WAVE	232
WAYSIDE STORIES	233
A HINDOO MONK	233
KANANDA ARRIVES	233
THE MANNERS AND CUSTOMS OF INDIA	233
A LECTURE ON "INDIA AND HINDUISM"	234
AT SMITH COLLEGE, NORTHAMPTON, MASSACHUSETTS	235
A LECTURE ON INDIA AND REINCARNATION	235
LECTURE BY HINDOO MONK	235
THE BRAHMAN MONK	237
His Iterations	237
SWAMI VIVEKANANDA	238
NIRVANASHATKAM	238
THE NONSENSE OF NATIONS	239
A HIGH PRIEST OF INDIA	239
PRIEST SWAMI IN TOWN	239
His Idea of Humor	240
Views on Topics of the Day	240
Likes the Elevator	240
A WISE MAN AMONG US	240
LOVE RELIGION'S ESSENCE	241
The Student Not Satisfied	241
Love Abideth	242
THE HINDOO OPTIMISTIC	243
VIVEKANANDA'S LECTURE	243
LET INDIA ALONE	243
ABOU BEN ADHEM'S IDEAL	244

THE DOCTRINE OF THE SWAMI	244
"UNIVERSAL RELIGION"	245
VIVEKANANDA'S PHILOSOPHY	246
HEARD SWAMI TALK	247
PHILOSOPHY OF FREEDOM	247
OUT OF THE EAST	248
SAID A UNIVERSAL RELIGION IS IMPOSSIBLE	249
FOR UNIVERSAL RELIGION	249
SWAMI VIVEKANANDA	251
HINDU PHILOSOPHY	253
Conception Of The Universe In Distant India	253
CONCEPTION OF THE UNIVERSE	253
TOLD ABOUT INDIA	254
THE RELIGIOUS LEGENDS OF INDIA	255
THE SCIENCE OF YOGA	255
SWAMI VIVEKANANDA AT THE LOS ANGELES HOME	255
HINDOO MONK LECTURES	256
VEDANTISM, AND WHAT IT IS AND WHAT IT IS NOT	256
TRUE RELIGION	257
PART II: EUROPEAN NEWSPAPER REPORTS	**258**
SWAMI VIVEKANANDA ON LOVE	258
AN INDIAN ASCETIC	259
NATIVE INDIAN LECTURER AT PRINCES' HALL	259
THE CHRISTIAN COMMONWEALTH	260
AN UNIVERSAL RELIGION	260
EDUCATION	261
SPIRITUALISM AND THE VEDANTA PHILOSOPHY	261
AN OCTOBER CLASS REVIEW	262

PART III: INDIAN NEWSPAPER REPORTS — 262

A BENGALI SADHU — 262
- The Vedic Religion — 262
- The Hindu Ideal of Life — 263
- The Shradh [Shrâddha] Ceremony — 263
- Education of Women — 263
- Emancipation of the Hindus — 264

THE PARLIAMENT OF RELIGIONS — 264
PARLIAMENT OF RELIGIONS IN CHICAGO — 264
ON CHRISTIAN CONVERSION — 265
THE CENTRAL IDEA OF THE VEDAS — 265
SWAMI VIVEKANANDA ON THE SEA VOYAGE MOVEMENT — 265
A SUMMARY OF "BUDDHISM, THE FULFILMENT OF HINDUISM" — 266
INDIAN PHILOSOPHY AND WESTERN SOCIETY — 267
SWAMI VIVEKANANDA IN AMERICA — 267
ON EDUCATION — 268
THE SWAMI VIVEKANANDA IN ENGLAND — 268
ON THE SWISS ALPS — 269
"THE IDEAL OF UNIVERSAL RELIGION" — 270
THE BANQUET FOR RANJIT SINJHI — 271
THE MAJLIS IN CAMBRIDGE — 271
VIVEKANANDA IN THE WEST — 271
BHAKTI — 272
OUR MISSION IN AMERICA — 272
SWAMI VIVEKANANDA AT BELUR [ON EDUCATION] — 273
HINDU WIDOWS — 273

Unpublished — 276

YOUR HIGHNESS — I — 278
YOUR HIGHNESS — II — 279

THE **COMPLETE WORKS** OF SWAMI VIVEKANANDA

VOLUME IX

EPISTLES – FIFTH SERIES

I — SIR

Translated from Bengali

To Balaram Bose:

Glory to Ramakrishna!

GHAZIPUR,
February 6, 1890

RESPECTED SIR,

I have talked with Pavhari Baba. He is a wonderful saint — the embodiment of humility, devotion, and Yoga. Although he is an orthodox Vaishnava, he is not prejudiced against others of different beliefs. He has tremendous love for Mahâprabhu Chaitanya, and he [Pavhari Baba] speaks of Shri Ramakrishna as "an incarnation of God". He loves me very much, and I am going to stay here for some days at his request.

Pavhari Baba can live in Samâdhi for from two to six months at a stretch. He can read Bengali and has kept a photograph of Shri Ramakrishna in his room. I have not yet seen him face to face, since he speaks from behind a door, but I have never heard such a sweet voice. I have many things to say about him but not just at present.

Please try to get a copy of Chaitanya-Bhâgavata for him and send it immediately to the following address: Gagan Chandra Roy, Opium Department, Ghazipur. Please don't forget.

Pavhari Baba is an ideal Vaishnava and a great scholar; but he is reluctant to reveal his learning. His elder brother acts as his attendant, but even he is not allowed to enter his room.

Please send him a copy of Chaitanya-Mangala also, if it is still in print. And remember that if Pavhari Baba accepts your presents, that will be your great fortune. Ordinarily, he does not accept anything from anybody. Nobody knows what he eats or even what he does.

Please don't let it be known that I am here and don't send news of anyone to me. I am busy with an important work.

Your servant,
Narendra

II — SIR

Translated from Bengali

To Balaram Bose:

Glory to Ramakrishna!

GHAZIPUR,
February 11, 1890

RESPECTED SIR,

I have received your book. In Hrishikesh, Kali [Swami Abhedananda] has had a relapse and is again suffering from what seems to be malaria. Once it comes, the fever does not easily leave those who have never had it before. I too suffered the same way when I first had the attack of fever. Kali has never had the fever before. I have not received any letter from Hrishikesh. Where is …?

I am suffering terribly from a backache which began in Allahabad. I had recovered from it some time back, but it has recurred. So I will have to stay here awhile longer because of my back and also because Babaji [Pavhari Baba] has requested it.

What you have written about uncooked bread is true. But a monk dies that way, not like the breaking of a cup and saucer. This time I am not going to be overcome by weakness in any way. And if I die, that will be good for me. It is better to depart from this world very soon.

Your servant,
Narendra

III — SIR

Translated from Bengali

To Balaram Bose:

Salutation to Bhagavan Shri Ramakrishna!

GHAZIPUR,
February 1890

RESPECTED SIR,

I have received an anonymous letter which I have been unable to trace back to the gigantic soul who wrote it. Indeed, one should pay homage to such a man. He who considers a great soul like Pavhari Baba to be no more than water in a hoof print, he who has nothing to learn in this world and who feels it a disgrace to be taught by any other man — truly, such a new incarnation must be visited. I hope that if the government should discover the identity of this person, he will be handled with special care and be placed in the Alipore garden [zoo]. If you happen to know this man, please ask him to bless me, so that even a dog or a jackal may be my Guru — not to speak of a great soul like Pavhari Baba.

I have many things to learn. My master used to say: "As long as I live, so long do I learn". Also please tell this fellow that unfortunately I do not have the time to "cross the seven seas and thirteen rivers" or to go to Sri Lanka in order to sleep after having put oil in the nostrils.

Your servant,
Narendra

P.S. Please have the rose-water brought from Ishan Babu's [Ishan Chandra Mukherjee's] residence if there is delay [in their sending it to the Baranagore Math]. The roses are still not in bloom. The rose-water has just been sent to the residence of Ishan Babu.

IV — BALARAM BABU

Translated from Bengali

To Balaram Bose:

GHAZIPUR,
March 12, 1890

BALARAM BABU,

As soon as you get the railway receipt, please send someone to the railway warehouse at Fairlie Place (Calcutta) to pick up the roses and send them on to Shashi. See that there is no delay in bringing or sending them.

Baburam is going to Allahabad soon. I am going elsewhere.

Narendra

PS. Know it for certain that everything will be spoiled if delayed.

V — TULSIRAM

To Tulsiram Ghosh:

GHAZIPUR,
10 May 1890

DEAR TULSIRAM,

A basket of roses will be sent to you in a few days at Chitpur. Do you please send them up immediately to Shashi [Swami Ramakrishnananda, at the Baranagore Math]. They would not be sent to the care of Balaram Basu, for there would be such nice delays and that would be death to the flowers. I think if sent to Chitpur, to your depot, it would reach you there at the very place; if not, write sharp. Baburam [Swami Premananda] is here, going up in a day or two to Allahabad. I too am going off from this place very soon. I go perhaps to Bareilly and up. What is Balaram Babu [Balaram Bose] doing?

My Pranâms etc. to you all.

Yours affectionately,
Narendra

VI — SHARAT

To Swami Saradananda:

Salutation to Bhagavan Ramakrishna!

CALCUTTA,
32 ASHADHA,
July 15, 1890

MY DEAR SHARAT,

I am sorry to learn that [Vaikunthanath] Sanyal's habits are as yet not Pucca [firm]; and what about Brahmacharya? I don't understand you. If so, the best thing for you both is to come down and live here. The widow of Mohindra Mukherjee is trying head and heart to erect a Math for you, and Surendranath Mitra has left another thousand so that you are very likely soon to get a beautiful place on the river. As for all the hardships up there, I reserve my own opinions.

It was not at all my intention to come down, only the death of Balaram Bose had made me have a peep here and go back. If the mountains be so bad, there is more than enough place for me; only I leave Bengal. If one does not suit, another will. So that is my determination. Everyone here will be so glad at your return here, and from your letter I see it would be downright injurious to you if you didn't come down. So come down at your earliest opportunity. I will leave this place before this letter reaches you; only I won't go to Almora. I have my own plans for the future and they shall be a secret.

As for Sanyal, I do not see how I can benefit him. Of course, you are at liberty to hold your own opinion about the Sanga [holy company] here. That I can find places Sudrishya [having scenic beauty] and Subhiksha [where alms are available] is enough. Sanga is not much, or, I think, not at all necessary for me.

Yours, etc.,
Narendra

VII — MOTHER

To Mrs. G. W. Hale:

MINNEAPOLIS,
21 November 1893

DEAR MOTHER,

I reached Madison safely, went to a hotel, and sent a message to Mr. Updike. He came to see me. He is a Congregational and so, of course, was not very friendly at first; but in the course of an hour or so became very kind to me, and took me over the whole place and the University. I had a fine audience and $100. Immediately after the lecture I took the night train to Minneapolis.

I tried to get the clergymen's ticket, but they could not give me any, not being the headquarters. The thing to be done is to get a permit from every head office of every line in Chicago. Perhaps it is possible for Mr. Hale to get the permits for me. If it is so, I hope he will take the trouble to send them over to me to Minneapolis if they can reach me by the 25th, or to Des Moines if by the 29th. Else I would do it the next time in Chicago. I have taken the money in a draft on the bank, which cost me 40¢.

May you be blessed for ever, my kind friend; you and your whole family have made such a heavenly impression on me as I would carry all my life.

Yours sincerely,
Vivekananda

VIII — MOTHER

To Mrs. G. W. Hale:

MINNEAPOLIS,
24 November 1893.

DEAR MOTHER,

I am still in Minneapolis. I am to lecture this afternoon, and the day after tomorrow go to Des Moines.

The day I came here they had their first snow, and it snowed all through the day and night, and I had great use for the arctics. (A waterproof overshoe.) I went to see the frozen Minnehaha Falls. They are very beautiful. The temperature today is 21° below zero, but I had been out sleighing and enjoyed it immensely. I am not the least afraid of losing the tips of my ears or nose.

The snow scenery here has pleased me more than any other sight in this country.

I saw people skating on a frozen lake yesterday.

I am doing well. Hoping this will find you all the same, I remain yours obediently,

Vivekananda

IX — MOTHER

To Mrs. G. W. Hale:

DETROIT,
14 February 1894.

DEAR MOTHER,

Arrived safely night before last at 1 o'clock a.m. The train was seven hours late, being blocked by snowdrifts on the way. However, I enjoyed the novelty of the sight: several men cutting and clearing the snow and two engines tugging and pulling was a new sight to me.

Here I met Mr. Bagley, the youngest [Paul F. Bagley], waiting for me at the station; and, it being very late in the night, Mrs. Bagley had retired, but the daughters sat up for me.

They are very rich, kind and hospitable. Mrs. Bagley is especially interested in India. The daughters are very good, educated and good-looking. The eldest gave me a luncheon at a club where I met some of the finest ladies and gentlemen of the city. Last evening there was a reception given here in the house. Today I am going to speak for the first time. Mrs. Bagley is a very nice and kind lady. I hope the lectures will please her. With my love and regards for you all, I remain,

Yours sincerely,
Vivekananda

PS — I have received a letter from Slayton in reply to that in which I wrote to him that I cannot stay. He gives me hope. What is your advice? I enclose the letter [from Narasimhacharya] in another envelope.

X — MOTHER

To Mrs. G. W. Hale:

DETROIT,
20 February 1894.

DEAR MOTHER,

My lectures here are over. I have made some very good friends here, amongst them Mr. Palmer, President of the late World's Fair. I am thoroughly disgusted with this Slayton business and am trying hard to break loose. I have lost at least $5,000 by joining this man. Hope you are all well. Mrs. Bagley and her daughters are very kind to me. I hope to do some private lecturing here and then go to Ada and then back to Chicago. It is snowing here this morning. They are very nice people here, and the different clubs took a good deal of interest in me.

It is rather wearisome, these constant receptions and dinners; and their horrible dinners — a hundred dinners concentrated into one — and when in a man's club, why, smoking on between the courses and then beginning afresh. I thought the Chinese alone make a dinner run through half a day with intervals of smoking!!

However, they are very gentlemanly men and, strange to say, an Episcopal clergyman and a Jewish rabbi take great interest in me and eulogize me. Now the man who got up the lectures here got at least a thousand dollars. So in every place. And this is Slayton's duty to do for me. Instead, he, the liar, had told me often that he has agents everywhere and would advertise and do all that for me. And this is what he is doing. His will be done. I am going home. Seeing the liking the American people have for me, I could have, by this time, got a pretty large sum. But Jimmy Mills and Slayton were sent by the Lord to stand in the way. His ways are inscrutable.

However, this is a secret. President Palmer has gone to Chicago to try to get me loose from this liar of a Slayton. Pray that he may succeed. Several judges here have seen my contract, and they say it is a shameful fraud and can be broken any moment; but I am a monk — no self-defence. Therefore, I had better throw up the whole thing and go to India.

My love to Harriets, Mary, Isabelle, Mother Temple, Mr. Matthews, Father Pope and you all.

Yours obediently,
Vivekananda

XI — MOTHER

To Mrs. G. W. Hale:

DETROIT,
February 22, 1894

DEAR MOTHER,

I have got the $200 for the engagements, $175 and $117 by private lectures and $100 as a present from a lady.

This sum will be sent to you tomorrow in cheques by Mrs. Bagley. Today, the banks being closed, we could not do it.

I am going tomorrow to lecture at Ada, Ohio. I do not know whether I will go to Chicago from Ada or not. However, kindly let not Slayton know anything about the rest of the money, as I am going to separate myself from him.

Yours obediently,
Vivekananda

XII — MOTHER

To Mrs. G. W. Hale:

DETROIT,
10 March 1894.

DEAR MOTHER,

Reached Detroit safely yesterday evening. The two younger daughters were waiting for me with a carriage. So everything was all right. I hope the lecture will be a success, as one of the girls said the tickets are selling like hot cakes. Here I found a letter from Mr. Palmer awaiting me with a request that I should come over to his house and be his guest.

Could not go last night. He will come in the course of the day to take me over. As I am going over to Mr. Palmer's, I have not opened the awfully-packed bag. The very idea of repacking seems to me to be hopeless. So I could not shave this morning. However, I hope to shave during the course of the day. I am thinking of going over to Boston and New York just now, as the Michigan cities I can come and take over in summer; but the fashionables of New York and Boston will fly off. Lord will show the way.

Mrs. Bagley and all the family are heartily glad at my return and people are again coming in to see me.

The photographer here has sent me some of the pictures he made. They are positively villainous — Mrs. Bagley does not like them at all. The real fact is that between the two photos my face has become so fat and heavy — what can the poor photographers do?

Kindly send over four copies of photographs. Not yet made any arrangement with Holden. (A lecture agent at Detroit.) Everything promises to be very nice. "Ssenator Ppalmer" is a very nice gentleman and very kind to me. He has got a French chef — Lord bless his stomach! I am trying to starve and the whole world is against me!! He used to give the best dinners in all Washington! Hopeless! I am resigned!

I will write more from Mr. Palmer's house.

If the Himalayas become the inkpot, the ocean ink, if the heavenly eternal Devadaroo becomes the pen, and if the sky itself becomes paper, still I would not be able to write a drop of the debt of gratitude I owe to you and yours. Kindly convey my love to the four full notes and the four half notes of the Hale gamut.

May the blessings of the Lord be upon you and yours ever and ever.

Ever yours in grateful affection,
Vivekananda

XIII — MOTHER

To Mrs. G. W. Hale:

DETROIT,
16 March 1894

DEAR MOTHER,

Since my last, there has been nothing of interest

here. Except that Mr. Palmer is a very hearty, jolly, good old man and very rich. He has been uniformly kind to me. Tomorrow I go back to Mrs. Bagley's because I am afraid she is rather uneasy at my long stay here. I am shrewd enough to know that in every country in general, and America in particular, "she" is the real operator at the nose string.

I am going to lecture here on Monday and in two places near the town on Tuesday and Wednesday. I do not remember the lady you refer me to, and she is in Lynn; what is Lynn, where on the globe its position is — I do not know. I want to go to Boston. What good would it do me by stopping at Lynn? Kindly give me a more particular idea. Nor could I read the name of the lady at whose house you say I met the lady. However, I am in no way very anxious. I am taking life very easy in my natural way. I have no particular wish to go anywhere, Boston or no Boston. I am just in a nice come-what-may mood. Something should turn up, bad or good. I have enough now to pay my passage back and a little sight-seeing to boot. As to my plans of work, I am fully convinced that at the rate it is progressing I will have to come back four or five times to put it in any shape.

As to informing others and doing good that way, I have failed to persuade myself that I have really anything to convey to the world. So I am very happy just now and quite at my ease. With almost nobody in this vast house and a cigar between my lips, I am dreaming just now and philosophising upon that work fever which was upon me. It is all nonsense. I am nothing, the world is nothing, the Lord alone is the only worker. We are simply tools in His hands etc., etc., etc. Have you got the Alaska information? If so, kindly send it to me c/o Mrs. Bagley.

Are you coming to the East this summer? With eternal gratitude and love,

Yours son,
Vivekananda

XIV — MOTHER

To Mrs. G. W. Hale:

DETROIT,
Tuesday, 27 March 1894

DEAR MOTHER,

Herewith I send two cheques of $114 and $75 to be put in the banks for me. I have endorsed them to your care.

I am going to Boston in a day or two. I have got $57 with me. They will go a long way. Something will turn up, as it always does. I do not know where I go from Boston. I have written to Mrs. [Francis W.] Breed but as yet heard nothing from her. His will be done. Not I but Thou — that is always the motto of my life.

With my eternal gratitude, love, and admiration for Mother Church and all the dignitaries,

I remain your son,
Vivekananda

XV — MOTHER

To Mrs. G. W. Hale:

C/O DR. GUERNSEY,
528 FIFTH AVENUE,
NEW YORK,
2 April 1894

DEAR MOTHER,

I am in New York. The gentleman [Dr. Guernsey] whose guest I am is a very nice and learned and well-to-do man. He had an only son whom he lost last July. Has only a daughter now. The old couple have received a great shock, but they are pure and God-loving people and bear it manfully. The lady of the house is very, very kind and good. They are trying to help me as much as they can and they will do a good deal, I have no doubt.

Awaiting further developments. This Thursday

[April 5] they will invite a number of the brainy people of the Union League Club and other places of which the Doctor is a member, and see what comes out of it. Parlour lectures are a great feature in this city, and more can be made by each such lecture than even platform talks in other cities.

It is a very clean city. None of that black smoke tarring everyone in five minutes; and the street in which the Doctor lives is a nice, quiet one.

Hope the sisters are doing well and enjoying their music, both in the opera and the parlour. I am sure I would have appreciated the music at the opera about which Miss Mary wrote to me. I am sure the opera musicians do not show the interior anatomy of their throats and lungs.

Kindly give brother Sam my deep love. I am sure he is bewaring of the vidders. Some of the Baby Bagleys are going to Chicago. They will go to see you, and I am sure you would like them very much.

Nothing more to write. With all respect, love and obedience,

Your son,
Vivekananda.

PS — I have not to ask now for addresses. Mrs. Sherman (Mrs. Bagley's married daughter.) has given me a little book with A., B., C., etc., marks and has written under them all the addresses I need; and I hope to write all the future addresses in the same manner. What an example of self-help I am!!

XVI — MOTHER

To Mrs. G. W. Hale:

[C/O DR. EGBERT GUERNSEY,
528 FIFTH AVENUE],
NEW YORK,
10 April 1894

DEAR MOTHER,

I just now received your letter. I have the greatest regard for the Salvationists; in fact, they and the Oxford Mission gentlemen are the only Christian missionaries for whom I have any regard at all. They live with the people, as the people, and for the people of India. Lord bless them. But I would be very, very sorry of any trick being played by them. I never have heard of any Lord in India, much less in Ceylon. (Now Sri Lanka.) The people of Ceylon and northern India differ more than Americans and Hindus. Nor is there any connection between the Buddhist priest and the Hindu. Our dress, manners, religion, food, language differ entirely from southern India, much less to speak of Ceylon. You know already that I could not speak a word of Narasimha's language!! Although that was only Madras. Well, you have Hindu princesses; why not a Lord, which is not a higher title.

There was a certain Mrs. Smith in Chicago. I met her at Mrs. Stockham's. She has introduced me to the Guernseys. Dr. Guernsey is one of the chief physicians of this city and is a very good old gentleman. They are very fond of me and are very nice people. Next Friday I am going to Boston. I have not been lecturing in New York at all. I will come back and do some lecturing here.

For the last few days I was the guest of Miss Helen Gould — daughter of the rich Gould — at her palatial country residence, an hour's ride from the city. She has one of the most beautiful and large green-houses in the world, full of all sorts of curious plants and flowers. They are Presbyterians, and she is a very religious lady. I had a very nice time there.

I met my friend Mr. Flagg (William Joseph Flagg.) several times. He is flying merrily. There is another Mrs. Smith here who is very rich and pious. She has invited me to dine today.

As for lecturing, I have given up raising money. I cannot degenerate myself any more. When a certain purpose was in view, I could work; with that gone I cannot earn for myself. I have sufficient for going back. I have not tried to earn a penny here, and have refused some presents which friends here wanted to make to me. Especially Flagg — I have refused his money. I had in Detroit tried to refund the money back to the donors, and told them that, there being almost no chance of my succeeding in my enterprise, I had no right to keep their money; but they refused and told me to throw that into the waters if I liked. But I cannot take any more conscientiously. I am very well off, Mother. Everywhere the Lord sends me kind persons and homes; so there is no use of my going into beastly worldliness at all.

The New York people, though not so intellectual as the Bostonians, are, I think, more sincere. The Bostonians know well how to take advantage of everybody. And I am afraid even water cannot slip through their closed fingers!!! Lord bless them!!! I have promised to go and I must go; but, Lord, make me live with the sincere, ignorant and the poor, and not cross the shadow of the hypocrites and tall talkers who, as my Master used to say, are like vultures who soar high and high in their talks, but the heart is really on a piece of carrion on the ground.

I would be the guest of Mrs. Breed for a few days and, after seeing a little of Boston, I would come back to New York.

Hope the sisters are all right and enjoying their concerts immensely. There is not much of music in this city. That is a blessing (?) Went to see Barnum's circus the other day. It is no doubt a grand thing. I have not been as yet downtown. This street is very nice and quiet.

I heard a beautiful piece of music the other day at Barnum's — they call it a Spanish Serenada. Whatever it be, I liked it so much. Unfortunately, Miss Guernsey is not given to much thumping, although she has a good assortment of all the noisy stuffs in the world — and so she could not play it, which I regret ever so much.

Yours obediently,
Vivekananda.

PS — Most probably I will go to Annisquam as Mrs. Bagley's guest. She has got a nice house there this summer. Before that, I will go back to Chicago once more if I can.

XVII — MOTHER

To Mrs. G. W. Hale:

C/O MISS FLORENCE GUERNSEY,
528 FIFTH AVENUE,
NEW YORK,
4 May 1894

DEAR MOTHER,

Herewith I send over $125 in a cheque upon the 5th Avenue Bank to be deposited at your leisure.

I am going to Boston on Sunday, day after tomorrow, and write to you from Boston. With my love to all the family.

I remain yours truly,
Vivekananda.

XVIII — MOTHER

To Mrs. John J. Bagley:

HOTEL BELLEVUE,
EUROPEAN PLAN,
BOSTON,
May 8, 1894

DEAR MOTHER,

I have arrived in Boston again. Last afternoon [I] spoke at Mrs. Julia Ward Howe's club — of course for nothing, but it gives me a prestige. I saw there Mrs. [Ednah Dean] Cheney. Would you not write a letter to her for me? Although I told her I had a card from you, I think a letter is better.

Yours truly,
Vivekananda.

XIX — MOTHER

To Mrs. G. W. Hale:

> HOTEL BELLEVUE, EUROPEAN PLAN,
> BEACON STREET, BOSTON,
> 11 May, 1894

DEAR MOTHER,

I have been since the 7th, lecturing here every afternoon or evening. At Mrs. Fairchild's I met the niece of Mrs. Howe. She was here today to invite me to dinner with her today. I have not seen Mr. Volkinen as yet. Of course, the pay for lecture is here the poorest, and everybody has an axe to grind. I got a long letter full of the prattles of the babies. Your city, i.e. New York, pays far better than Boston, so I am trying to go back there. But here one can get work almost every day.

I think I want some rest. I feel as if I am very much tired, and these constant journeyings to and fro have shaken my nerves a little, but hope to recoup soon. Last few days I have been suffering from cold and slight fever and lecturing for all that; hope to get rid of it in a day or two.

I have got a very nice gown at $30. The colour is not exactly that of the old one, but cardinal, with more of yellow — could not get the exact old colour even in New York.

I have not much to write, for it is the repetition of the old story: talking, talking, talking. I long to fly to Chicago and shut up my mouth and give a long rest to mouth and lungs and mind. If I am not called for in New York, I am coming soon to Chicago.

> Yours obediently,
> Vivekananda.

XX — MOTHER

To Mrs. G. W. Hale:

> HOTEL BELLEVUE EUROPEAN PLAN,
> BEACON STREET, BOSTON,
> 14 May, 1894

DEAR MOTHER,

Your letter was so, so pleasing instead of being long; I enjoyed every bit of it.

I have received a letter from Mrs. Potter Palmer (Social queen of Chicago who made Swami Vivekananda's acquaintance at the Parliament of Religions, in which she had been active. Vide Complete Works, VI.) asking me to write to some of my countrywomen about their society etc. I will see her personally when I come to Chicago; in the meanwhile I will write her all I know. Perhaps you have received $125 sent over from New York. Tomorrow I will send another $100 from here. The Bostonians want to grind their own axes!!

Oh, they are so, so dry — even girls talk dry metaphysics. Here is like our Benares where all is dry, dry metaphysics!! Nobody here understands "my Beloved". Religion to these people is reason, and horribly stony at that. I do not care for anybody who cannot love my "Beloved". Do not tell it to Miss Howe — she may be offended.

The pamphlet I did not send over because I do not like the quotations from the Indian newspapers — especially, they give a haul over coal to somebody. Our people so much dislike the Brâhmo Samâj that they only want an opportunity to show it to them. I dislike it. Any amount of enmity to certain persons cannot efface the good works of a life. And then they were only children in Religion. They never were much of religious men — i.e. they only wanted to talk and reason, and did not struggle to see the Beloved; and until one does that I do not say that he has any religion. He may have books, forms, doctrines, words, reasons, etc., etc., but not religion; for that begins when the soul feels the necessity, the want, the yearning after the "Beloved", and never before. And therefore our society has no right to expect from them anything more than from an ordinary "house-holder".

I hope to come to Chicago before the end of this month. Oh, I am so tired.

> Yours affectionately,
> Vivekananda.

XXI — MOTHER

To Mrs. G. W. Hale:

> 541 DEARBORN AVENUE,
> CHICAGO,
> 9 June 1894

DEAR MOTHER,

We are all doing very well here. Last night the sisters (The daughters of Mrs. Hale: Mary and Harriet.) invited me and Mrs. Norton and Miss Howe and Mr. Frank Howe. We had a grand dinner and softshell crab and many other things, and a very nice time. Miss Howe left this morning.

The sisters and Mother Temple (Mrs. James Matthews, Mr. Hale's sister.>) are taking very good care of me. Just now I am going to see my "oh-my-dear" Gandhi. Narasimha was here yesterday; he wanted to go to Cincinnati where he says he has more chances of success than anywhere else in the world. I gave him the passage, and so I hope I have got the white elephant out of my hands for the time being. How is Father Pope doing now? Hope he has been much benefited by the mudfish business.

I had a very beautiful letter from Miss Guernsey of New York, giving you her regards. I am going downtown to buy a new pair of shoes as well as to get some money, my purse having been made empty by Narasimha.

Nothing more to write. Yes, we went to see the "Charley's Aunt". I nearly killed myself with laughing. Father Pope will enjoy it extremely. I had never seen anything so funny.

> Yours affectionately,
> Vivekananda.

XXII — MOTHER

To Mrs. G. W. Hale:

> NEW YORK,
> 28 June 1894

DEAR MOTHER,

Arrived safely two hours ago. Landsberg was waiting at the station. Came to Dr. Guernsey's house. Nobody was there except a servant. I took a bath and strolled with Landsberg to some restaurant where I had a good meal. Then, I have just now returned to Landsberg's rooms in the Theosophical Society and am writing you this letter.

I haven't been to see my other friends yet. After a good and long rest through the night I hope to see most of them tomorrow. My Love to you all. By the by, somebody stepped on my umbrella on board the train and broke its nose off.

> Your affectionate son,
> Vivekananda.

PS — I have not settled myself. So as to direct letters to me, they can be directed c/o Leon Landsberg, 144 Madison Ave., New York.

XXIII — MOTHER

To Mrs. G. W. Hale:

> C/O LEON LANDSBERG,
> 144 MADISON AVENUE,
> NEW YORK,
> 1 July 1894

DEAR MOTHER,

Hope you are settled down in peace by this time. The babies are doing well in Mudville (Kenosha, Wisconsin) — in their nunnery, I am sure. It is very hot here, but now and then a breeze comes up which cools it down. I am now with Miss [Mary A.] Phillips. Will move off from here on Tuesday to another place.

Here I find a quotation from a speech by Sir Monier Williams, professor of Sanskrit in the Oxford University. It is very strange as coming from one who every day expects to see the whole of India converted to Christianity. "And yet it is a remarkable characteristic of Hinduism that it neither requires nor attempts to make converts. Nor is it at present by any means decreasing in numbers, nor is it being driven out of the field by two such proselytizing religions as Mahomedanism [sic] and Christianity. On the contrary, it is at present rapidly increasing. And far more remarkable than this is that, it is all-receptive, all-embracing and all-comprehensive. It claims to be the one religion of humanity, of human nature, of the entire world. It cares not to oppose the progress of Christianity nor of any other religion. For it has no difficulty in including all other religions within its all-embracing arms and ever-widening fold. And in real fact Hinduism has something to offer which is suited to all minds. Its very strength lies in its infinite adaptability to the infinite diversity of human characters and human tendencies. It has its highly spiritual and abstract side suited to the philosophical higher classes. Its practical and concrete side suited to the man of affairs and the man of the world. Its aesthetic and ceremonial side suited to the man of poetic feeling and imagination. Its quiescent and contemplative side suited to the man of peace and lover of seclusion.

"Indeed, the Hindus were Spinozists 2,000 years before the birth of Spinoza, Darwinians centuries before the birth of Darwin, and evolutionists centuries before the doctrine of evolution had been accepted by the Huxleys of our time, and before any word like evolution existed in any language of the world."

This, as coming from one of the staunchest defenders of Christianity, is wonderful indeed. But he seems to have got the idea quite correct.

Now I am going to send up the orange coat today; as for the books that came to me from Philadelphia, I do not think they are worthy of being sent at all. I do not know what I am going to do next. Patiently wait and resign myself unto His guidance — that is my motto. My love to you all.

Your affectionate son,
Vivekananda.

XXIV — MOTHER

To Mrs. G. W. Hale:

C/O DR. E. GUERNSEY,
CEDAR LAWN,
FISHKILL ON THE HUDSON,
19 July 1894

DEAR MOTHER,

Your kind note reached me here yesterday evening. I am so glad to hear the babies are enjoying. I got the Interior and am very glad to see my friend Mazoomdar's (Pratap Chandra Mazumdar.) book spoken of so highly. Mazoomdar is a great and a good man and has done much for his fellow beings.

It is a lovely summer place, this Cedar Lawn of the Guernseys. Miss Guernsey has gone on a visit to Swampscott. I had also an invitation there, but I thought [it] better to stay here in the calm and silent place full of trees and with the beautiful Hudson flowing by and mountain in the background.

I am very thankful for Miss Howe's suggestion, and I am also thinking of it. Most probably I will go to England very soon. But between you and me, I am a sort of mystic and cannot move without orders, and that has not come yet. Mr. [Charles M.] Higgins, a rich young lawyer and inventor of Brooklyn, is arranging some lectures for me. I have not settled whether I will stop for them or not.

My eternal thanks to you for your kindness. My whole life cannot repay my debt to you. (Original letter: your debt.) You may see from the letter from Madras that there is not a word about Narasimha. What can I do more? I did not get the cheque cashed yet, for there was no necessity. Miss Phillips was very kind to me. She is an old lady, about 50 or more. You need not feel any worry about my being taken care of. The Lord always takes care of His servants; and so long as I am really His servant and not the world's, I am very confident of getting everything that would be good for me. The Guernseys love me very much, and there are many families in New York and Brooklyn who would take the best care of me.

I had a beautiful letter from Mr. Snell, saying that a sudden change for the better has taken place in his fortunes and offering me thrice the money I lent him as a contribution to my work. And he also has beautiful letters from Dharmapala and others from India. But, of course, I politely refused his repayment.

So far so good. I have seen Mr. [Walter Hines] Page, the editor of the Forum here. He was so sorry not to get the article on missionaries. But I have promised to write on other interesting subjects. Hope I will have patience to do so.

I had a letter yesterday from Miss Harriet, (Mrs. Hale's daughter.) from which I learn that they are enjoying Kenosha (A port in southwest Wisconsin, on Lake Michigan.) very much. Lord bless you and yours, Mother Church, for ever and ever. I cannot even express my gratitude to you.

As for me, you need not be troubled in the least. My whole life is that of a vagabond — homeless, roving tramp; any fare, good or bad, in any country, is good enough for me.

Yours ever in love and obedience,
Swami Vivekananda.

XXV — MOTHER

To Mrs. G. W. Hale:

SWAMPSCOTT, MASSACHUSETTS,
23 July 1894

DEAR MOTHER,

I think I have all your questions answered and you are in good humour again.

I am enjoying this place very much; going to Greenacre today or tomorrow and on our way back I intend to go to Annisquam, to Mrs. Bagley's — I have written to her. Mrs. Breed (Mrs. Francis W. Breed of Lynn, Massachusetts.) says, "You are very sensitive".

Now, I fortunately did not cash your check in New York. I wanted to cash it here, when lo! you have not signed your name to it. The Hindu is a dreamer no doubt, but when the Christian dreams he dreams with a vengeance.

Do not be distressed. Somebody gave me plenty of money to move about. I would be taken care of right along. I send herewith the cheque back to you. I had a very beautiful letter from Miss Mary. My love to them.

What is Father Pope doing? Is it very hot in Chicago? I do not care for the heat of this country. It is nothing compared to our India heat. I am doing splendidly. The other day I had the summer cholera; and cramp, etc. came to pay their calls to me. We had several hours nice talk and groans and then they departed.

I am on the whole doing very well. Has the meerschaum pipe reached Chicago? I had nice yachting, nice sea bathing, and am enjoying myself like a duck. Miss Guernsey went home just now. I do not know what more to write.

Lord bless you all.

Affectionately,
Vivekananda.

XXVI — MOTHER

To Mrs. G. W. Hale:

GREENACRE INN,
ELIOT, MAINE,
5 August 1894

DEAR MOTHER,

I have received your letter and am very much ashamed at my bad memory. I unfortunately forgot all about the cheque. Perhaps you have come to know by this time of my being in Greenacre. I had a very nice time here and am enjoying it immensely. In the fall I am going to lecture in Brooklyn, New York. Yesterday I got news that they have completed all the advertising there. I have an invitation today from a friend in New York to go with him to some mountains north of this state of Maine. I do not know whether I will go or not. I am doing pretty well. Between lecturing, teaching, picnicking and other excitements the time is flying rapidly. I hope you are doing very well and that Father Pope is in good trim. It is a very beautiful spot — this Greenacre — and [I] have very nice company from Boston: Dr. Everett Hale, you know, of Boston, and Mrs. Ole Bull, of Cambridge. I do not know whether I will accept the invitation of my friend of New York or not.

So far only this is sure, that I will go to lecture in New York this coming fall. And Boston, of course, is a good field. The people here are mostly from Boston and they all like me very much. Are you having a good time, and Father Pope? Has your house-painting been finished? The Babies, I am sure, are enjoying their Mudville.

I am in no difficulty for money. I have plenty to eat and drink.

With my best love and gratitude to you and Father Pope and the Babies.

Yours affectionately,
Vivekananda.

Excuse this hasty scrawl. The pen is very bad.

The Harrison people sent me two "nasty standing" photos — that is all I have out of them, when they ought to give me 40 minus the 10 or 15 I have got already!!!

XXVII — MOTHER

To Mrs. G. W. Hale:

GREENACRE INN,
ELIOT, MAINE,
8 August 1894

DEAR MOTHER,

I have received the letter you sent over to me coming from India.

I am going to leave this place on Monday next for Plymouth [Massachusetts], where the Free Religious Association is holding its session. They will defray my expenses, of course.

I am all right, enjoying nice health, and the people here are very kind and nice to me. Up to date I had no occasion to cash any cheque as everything is going on smoothly. I have not heard anything from the Babies. Hope they are doing well. You also had nothing to write; however, I feel that you are doing well.

I would have gone over to another place, but Mr. Higginson's invitation ought to be attended to. And Plymouth is the place where the fathers of your country first landed. I want, therefore, to see it.

I am all right. It is useless reiterating my love and gratitude to you and yours — you know it all. May the Lord shower His choicest blessings on you and yours.

This meeting is composed of the best professors of your country and other people, so I must attend it; and then they would pay me. I have not yet determined all my plans, only I am going to lecture in New York this coming fall; every arrangement is complete for that. They have printed advertisements at their own expense for that and made everything ready.

Give my best love to the Babies, to Father Pope, and believe me ever in gratitude and love,

Your Son,
Vivekananda.

P.S. I am very much obliged to the sisters for asking me to tell them if I want anything. I have no want anyway — I have everything I require and more to spare.

"He never gives up His servants."

My thanks and gratitude eternal to the sisters for their kindness in asking about my wants.

XXVIII — MOTHER

To Mrs. G. W. Hale:

C/O MRS. J. J. BAGLEY, ANNISQUAM,
20 August 1894

DEAR MOTHER,

Your letters just now reached me. I had some beautiful letters from India. The letter from Ajit Singh (The Raja of Khetri, a very devoted disciple of the Swami.) shows that the phonograph has not reached yet, and it was dated 8th June. So I do not think it is time yet to get an answer. I am not astonished at my friends' asking Cook & Sons to hunt for me; I have not written for a long time.

I have a letter from Madras which says they will soon send money to Narasimha (Narasimhacharya. Vide the letter dated February 14, 1894.) — in fact, as soon as they get a reply to their letter written to Narasimha. So kindly let Narasimha know it. The photographs have not reached me — except two of Fishkill when I was there last. Landsberg (Leon Landsberg. Vide the letter dated June 28, 1894.) has kindly sent over the letters. From here I will probably go over to Fishkill. The meerschaum was not sent over by me direct, but I left it to the Guernseys. And they are a lazy family in that respect.

I have beautiful letters from the sisters.

By the by, your missionaries try to make me a malcontent before the English government in India, and the Lieutenant Governor of Bengal in a recent speech hinted that the recent revival of Hinduism was against the government. Lord bless the missionary. Everything is fair in love and (religion?).

The word Shri means "of good fortune", "blessed", etc. Paramahamsa is a title for a Sannyâsi who has reached the goal, i.e. realized God. Neither am I blessed nor have I reached the goal; but they are courteous, that is all. I will soon write to my brothers in India. I am so lazy, and I cannot send over the newspaper nonsense day after day.

I want a little quiet, but it is not the will of the Lord, it seems. At Greenacre I had to talk on an average 7 to 8 hours a day — that was rest, if it ever was. But it was of the Lord, and that brings vigour along with it.

I have not much to write, and I do not remember anything of what I said or did all these places over. So I hope to be excused.

I will be here a few days more at least, and therefore I think it would be better to send over my mail here.

I have now almost become dizzy through the perusal of a heavy and big mail, so excuse my hasty scrawl.

Ever affectionately yours,
Swami Vivekananda.

XXIX — MOTHER

To Mrs. G. W. Hale:

ANNISQUAM,
23 August 1894

DEAR MOTHER,

The photographs reached safely yesterday. I cannot tell exactly whether Harrison ought to give me more or not. They had sent only two to me at Fishkill — not the pose I ordered, though.

Narasimha has perhaps got his passage by this time. He will get it soon, whether his family gives him the money or not. I have written to my friends in Madras to look to it, and they write me they will.

I would be very glad if he becomes a Christian or Mohammedan or any religion that suits him; but I am afraid for some time to come none will suit our friend. Only if he becomes a Christian he will have a chance to marry again, even in India — the Christians there permitting it. I am so sorry to learn that it is the "bondage of heathen India" that, after all, was the cause of all this mischief. We learn as we live. So we were all this time ignorantly and blindly blaming our much suffering, persecuted, saintly friend Narasimha, while all the fault was really owing to the "bondage of heathen India"!!!!

But to give the devil his due, this heathen India has been supplying him with money to go on a spree again and again. And this time too "heathen India" will [take] or already has taken our "enlightened" and persecuted friend from out of his present scrape, and not "Christian America"!! Mrs. Smith's plan is not bad after all — to turn Narasimha into a missionary of Christ. But unfortunately for the world, many and many a time the flag of Christ has been entrusted to such hands. But I would beg to add that he will then be only a missionary of Smithian American Christianity, not Christ's. Arrant humbug! That thing to preach Lord Jesus!!! Is He in want of men to uphold His banner? Pooh! the very idea is revolting. Do good to India indeed! Thank your charity and call back your dog — as the tramp said. Keep such good workers for America. The Hindus will have a quarantine against all such [outcasting] to protect their society. I heartily advise Narasimha to become a Christian — I beg your pardon, a convert to Americanism — because I am sure such a jewel is unsaleable in poor India. He is welcome to anything that will fetch a price. I know the gentleman whom you name perfectly well, and you may give him any information about me you like. I do not care for sending scraps and getting a boom for me. And these friends from India bother me enough for newspaper nonsense. They are very devoted, faithful and holy friends. I have not much of these scraps now. After a long search I found a bit in a Boston Transcript. I send it over to you. This public life is such a botheration. I am nearly daft.

Where to fly? In India I have become horribly public — crowds will follow me and take my life out. I got an Indian letter from Landsberg. Every ounce of fame can only be bought at the cost of a pound of peace and holiness. I never thought of that before. I have become entirely disgusted with this blazoning. I am disgusted with myself. Lord will show me the way to peace and purity. Why, Mother, I confess to you: no man can live in an atmosphere of public life, even in religion, without the devil of competition now and then thrusting his head into the serenity of his heart. Those who are trained to preach a doctrine never feel it, for they never knew religion. But those that are after God, and not after the world, feel at once that every bit of name and fame is at the cost of their purity. It is so much gone from that ideal of perfect unselfishness, perfect disregard of gain or name or fame. Lord help me. Pray for me, Mother. I am very much disgusted with myself. Oh, why the world be so that one cannot do anything without putting himself to the front; why cannot one act hidden and unseen and unnoticed? The world has not gone one step beyond idolatry yet. They cannot act from ideas, they cannot be led by ideas. But they want the person, the man. And any man that wants to do something must pay the penalty — no hope. This nonsense of the world. Shiva, Shiva, Shiva.

By the by, I have got such a beautiful edition of Thomas à Kempis. How I love that old monk. He caught a wonderful glimpse of the "behind the veil" — few ever got such. My, that is religion. No humbug of the world. No shilly-shallying, tall talk, conjecture — I presume, I believe, I think. How I would like to go out of this piece of painted humbug they call the beautiful world with Thomas à Kempis — beyond, beyond, which can only be felt, never expressed.

That is religion. Mother, there is God. There all the saints, prophets and incarnations meet. Beyond the Babel of Bibles and Vedas, creeds and crafts, dupes and doctrines — where is all light, all love, where the miasma of this earth can never reach. Ah! who will take me thither? Do you sympathize with me, Mother? My soul is groaning now under the hundred sorts of bondage I am placing on it. Whose India? Who cares? Everything is His. What are we? Is He dead? Is He sleeping? He, without whose command a leaf does not fall, a heart does not beat, who is nearer to me than my own self. It is bosh and nonsense — to do good or do bad or do fuzz. We do nothing. We are not. The world is not. He is, He is. Only He is. None else is. He is.

Om, the one without a second. He in me, I in Him. I am like a bit of glass in an ocean of light. I am not, I am not. He is, He is, He is.

Om, the one without a second.

Yours ever affectionately,
Vivekananda.

XXX — MOTHER

To Mrs. G. W. Hale:

ANNISQUAM,
[Postmarked: August 28, 1894]

DEAR MOTHER,

I have been for three days at Magnolia. Magnolia is one of the most fashionable and beautiful seaside resorts of this part. I think the scenery is better than that of Annisquam. The rocks there are very beautiful, and the forests run down to the very edge of the water. There is a very beautiful pine forest. A lady of Chicago and her daughter, Mrs. Smith and Mrs. Sawyer, were the friends that invited me up there. They had also arranged a lecture for me, out of which I got $43. I met a good many Boston people — Mrs. Smith Junior, who said she knows Harriet, and Mrs. Smith the elder, [who] knows you well.

In Boston the other day I met a Unitarian clergyman who said he lives next to you in Chicago. I have unfortunately forgotten his name. Mrs. Smith is a very nice lady and treated me with all courtesy. Mrs. Bagley is kind as ever, and I will have to remain here a few days more, I am afraid. Prof. Wright and I are having a good time. Prof. Bradley of Evanston has gone home. If you ever meet him at Evanston, give him my best love and regards. He is really a spiritual man.

I do not find anything more to write.

Some unknown friend has sent me from New York a fountain pen. So I am writing with it to test it. It is working very smoothly and nicely as you can judge from the writing. Perhaps Narasimha's difficulties have been settled by this time, and "heathen India" has helped him out yet, I hope.

What is Father Pope doing? What the Babies are doing and where are they? What news of our Sam? Hope he is prospering. Kindly give him my best love. Where is Mother Temple now?

Well, after all, I could fill up two pages. Yes, there was a Miss Barn (?) who said she met me at your house. She is a young lady of Chicago.

Magnolia is a good bathing place and I had two baths in the sea. A large concourse of men and women go to bathe there every day — the most part men. And strange, women do not give up their coat of mail even while bathing. That is how these mailclad she-warriors of America have got the superiority over men.

Our Sanskrit poets lavish all the power of expression they have upon the soft body of women — the Sanskrit word for women is "Komala", the soft body; but the mailclad ones of this country are "armadillas", I think. You cannot imagine how ludicrous it appears to a foreigner who never saw it before. Shiva, Shiva.

Now Narasimha's Mrs. Smith does not torture you anymore with letters, I hope. Did I tell you I met your friend Mrs. H. O. Quarry at Swampscott? — she can swamp a house for all that, not to speak of a cott — and that I met there the woman that pulls by the nose Mr. Pullman? And I also heard there the best American singer, (Miss Emma Thursby.) they said — she sang beautifully; she sang "Bye Baby Bye". I am having a very, very good time all the time, Lord be praised.

I have written to India not to bother me with constant letters. Why, when I am travelling in India nobody writes to me. Why should they spend all their superfluous energy in scrawling letters to me in America? My whole life is to be that of a wanderer — here or there or anywhere. I am in no hurry. I had a foolish plan in my head unworthy of a Sannyasin. I have given it up now and mean to take life easy. No indecent hurry. Don't you see, Mother Church? You must always remember, Mother Church, that I cannot settle down even at the North Pole, that wander about I must — that is my vow, my religion. So India or North Pole or South Pole — don't care where. Last two years I have been travelling among races whose language even I cannot speak. "I have neither father nor mother nor brothers nor sisters nor friends nor foes, nor home nor country — a traveller in the way of eternity, asking no other help, seeking no other help but God."

Yours ever affectionately,
Vivekananda.

XXXI — MOTHER

To Mrs. G. W. Hale:

> [GLOUCESTER, MASSACHUSETTS]
> 4 September 1894

DEAR MOTHER,

The bundle was the report of the meeting. Hope you will succeed in publishing some in the Chicago papers.

Here is a letter from Dewanji to you which will explain his sending a pamphlet to Mr. Hale The rugs are coming. When they come, take them in, even paying the duty if any. I will pay it to you afterwards. I have plenty of money, more than $150 in pocket. Will get more tonight. Here are some newspaper clippings, and an Indian Mirror I will send later on. Some have been sent to Mr. Barrows; don't hope he will give them publicity. Now for your Mrs. Bartlett.

I am in haste. [Will] write more with the clippings. Write to me always, kind Mother — I become very anxious when I do not hear from you. Write, whether I reply sharp or not.

> Yours ever affectionately,
> Vivekananda.

XXXII — MOTHER

To Mrs. G. W. Hale:

> ANNISQUAM,
> 5 September 1894

DEAR MOTHER,

The news of the arrival of the phonograph from Khetri has not come yet. But I am not anxious, because I just now got another letter from India wherein there is no mention of the photographs I sent, showing that parcels reach later than letters.

Herewith I send you an autograph letter of H.H. the Maharaja of Mysore, the chief Hindu king in India. You may see on the map [that] his territory occupies a very large portion of southern India.

I am very glad that he is slowly being gained over to my side. If he wills, he can set all my plans to work in five days. He has an income of $150 million dollars; think of that.

May Jagadamba [the Mother of the Universe] turn his mind towards the good work. He says he quite appreciates my good words — they were about my plans for educating the poor. Hope he will soon show it in material shape.

My love to all. Why the babies do not prattle?

> Your son,
> Vivekananda.

XXXIII — MOTHER

To Mrs. G. W. Hale:

> HOTEL BELLEVUE, EUROPEAN PLAN,
> BEACON STREET, BOSTON,
> 12 September 1894

DEAR MOTHER,

I hope you will immediately send me over the little scrap from the Indian Mirror about my Detroit lectures which I sent you.

> Yours,
> Vivekananda.

XXXIV — MOTHER

To Mrs. G. W. Hale:

> HOTEL BELLEVUE,
> BEACON STREET, BOSTON,
> 13 September 1894

DEAR MOTHER,

Your very kind note came just now. I was suffering for the last few days from cold and fever. I am all right now. I am glad all the papers reached you safe.

The newspaper clippings are with Mrs. Bagley; only a copy has been sent over to you. By the by, Mrs. Bagley becomes jealous if I send away everything to you. That is between you and me. The Indian Mirror is with Prof. Wright, and he will send it over to you. There is yet no news of the phonograph. Wait one week more and then we will enquire. If you see a letter with the Khetri stamp, then surely the news is coming. I do not smoke one third as much as I used to when Father Pope's eternal box was ready and open day and night. Haridasbhai is to be addressed as Shri only. On the envelope, Dewan Bahadoor ought to be written, as that is a title. Perhaps the note from the Maharaja of Mysore has reached you by this time.

I will remain a few days yet in Boston and the vicinity. The bank book is in the bank. We did not take it out, but the cheque book is with me. I am going to write out my thoughts on religion; in that, no missionaries have any place. I am going to lecture in New York in autumn, but I like teaching small circles better, and there will be enough of that in Boston.

The rugs I wanted to be sent from India; and they will come from Punjab, where the best rugs are made.

I had a beautiful letter from Sister Mary. (Mary Hale.)

Narasimha must have got money or passage by this time, and his people have taken care to send him Thomas Cook's passage from place to place. I think he is gone now.

I do not think the Lord will allow his servant to be inflated with vanity at the appreciation of his countrymen. I am glad that they appreciate me — not for my sake, but that I am firmly persuaded that a man is never improved by abuse but by praise, and so with nations. Think how much of abuse has been quite unnecessarily hurled at the head of my devoted, poor country, and for what? They never injured the Christians or their religion or their preachers. They have always been friendly to all. So you see, Mother, every good word a foreign nation says to them has such an amount of power for good in India. The American appreciation of my humble work here has really done a good deal of benefit to them. Send a good word, a good thought — at least to the down-trodden, vilified, poor millions of India instead of abusing them day and night. That is what I beg of every nation. Help them if you can; if you cannot, at least cease from abusing them.

I did not see any impropriety in the bathing places at the seashore, but only vanity in some: in those that went into water with their corsets on, that was all.

I have not got any copy of the Inter-Ocean yet. (A leading Chicago newspaper.)

With my love to Father Pope, babies, and to you, I remain

Your obedient son,
Vivekananda.

XXXV — MOTHER

To Mrs. G. W. Hale:

HOTEL BELLEVUE,
BEACON S,
TREET , BOSTON,
19 September 1894

DEAR MOTHER,

The huge packet received. It was a few pamphlets sent over to me from my monastery in Calcutta. No news at all about the phonograph. I think it is high time we make them inquire into it.

The two volumes of Todd's [Tod's] history of Rajasthan have been presented to me by Mrs. Potter Palmer. I have asked her to send it over to your care. The babies will like reading it very much, and after they finish I will send it over with my Sanskrit books to Calcutta.

I did not ask you to send me the typewritten news clippings at all, but a little slip I sent over some time ago from the Indian Mirror. Perhaps it did not reach you at all. You need not send the typewritten thing at all.

I do not require any clothes here; there are plenty of them. I am taking good care of my cuffs and collars, etc.

I have more clothes than are necessary. Very soon I will have to disburse myself of half of them at least.

I will write to you before I go to India. I am not flying off without giving you due intimation.

Yours,
Vivekananda.

P.S. — My love to Babies and Father Pope.

XXXVI — MOTHER

To Mrs. G. W. Hale:

HOTEL BELLEVUE,
BEACON STREET, BOSTON,
24 September 1894

DEAR MOTHER,

I have not heard from you a long while. I am still in Boston and will be a few days more.

I am afraid the phonograph has not reached India at all, or something is the matter with it. Kindly ask Mr. — to inquire. The receipt is with you on which they will enquire.

Ever affectionately yours,
Vivekananda.

XXXVII — MOTHER

To Mrs. G. W. Hale:

HOTEL BELLEVUE,
BEACON STREET, BOSTON,
27 September 1894

DEAR MOTHER,

The bundles all came safely. One was newspapers from India. The other was the short sketch of my Master published by Mr. Mazumdar long ago. In the latter bundle there are two sextos or pamphlets. One, my Master's sketch; the other, a short extract to show how what Mr. [Keshab] Chandra Sen and [Pratap Chandra] Mazumdar preached as their "New Dispensation" was stolen from my Master's life. The latter therefore you need not distribute, but I hope you will distribute my Master's life to many good people.

I beg you to send some to Mrs. Guernsey, Fishkill on the Hudson, N.Y.; Mrs. Arthur Smith and Mrs. [Miss Mary A.] Phillips, 19 West 38th Street, New York (both); to Mrs. Bagley, Annisquam, Mass.; and Prof. J. Wright, Professor of Greek, Harvard, Mass.

The newspapers — you may do whatever you like, and I hope you will send any newspaper scrap you get about me to India.

Yours etc.,
Vivekananda.

XXXVIII — MOTHER

To Mrs. G. W. Hale:

C/O MRS. OLE BULL,
168 BRATTLE STREET,
CAMBRIDGE, MASS.
5 October 1894

DEAR MOTHER,

I have not heard from you for long. Have you received the huge packages I sent over to you? Have you heard anything about the phonograph from the express office?

I will be with Mrs. Ole Bull a few days, and then I go to New York to Mrs. Guernsey's.

Yours ever affectionately,
Vivekananda.

XXXIX — MOTHER

To Mrs. G. W. Hale:

C/O MRS. OLE BULL,
RIVERVIEW, 168 BRATTLE STREET,
CAMBRIDGE, MASS.,
[Postmarked: Oct. 10, 1894, 4:30 a.m.]

DEAR MOTHER,

Received two letters from you and a large number from India but none from Khetri.

I am sorry the sisters have got bad colds and more sorry for your getting worried over it. Nothing can make a Christian worry. I hope Narasimha will be a good boy this time forth. Sister Mary is coming to Boston — good. I am going off from here tomorrow to Baltimore. I had enough to pay all my expenses here; and since I am living with Mrs. Bull, there is no expense. She is a rich and highly cultured lady. She has given me $500 for my work or anything I like. As I am not going west very soon, I will have a bank account here in Boston. From Philadelphia I go to Washington, and then I will run between New York and Boston. So I do not think I will be able to see you, except perhaps Sister Mary. I want so very much that Mary will see Mrs. Bull and others of my friends here. I have the fat of the land as usual, and my dinner is cooking very well both here and in India. Do not make it public, Mother — that is between you and me and the babies — and do not worry yourself about anything. All things come to him that waits. I am going to send the greater part of the money I have got to India and then money will come faster. I have always found that the faster I spend, the faster it comes. Nature abhors a vacuum. I am in very good spirits, only you must not stop keeping me informed about yourself, Babies and Father Pope from time to time.

Perhaps you remember the two letters that came from Mysore — I want one of those envelopes with the Mysore King's seal on the outside to be sent to Miss Phillips, 19 West 38th Street, New York.

I cannot go to New York now nor to Chicago, although I had a number of invitations and offers from both the places. I must see now the capital and the other cities. I am in His Hands. If Miss Mary be in Boston, sometime I may hope to see her.

I am glad that Narasimha was never fast — hope he will never be.

From India they always write me to come, come, come. They do not know the secret. I am acting more from here than I will ever do from there.

Kindly send my letters to this address and they will reach me safe wherever I be. This will be one of my homes when I am in Boston.

Lord bless you all, dear Mother.

Yours ever affectionately,
Vivekananda.

XL — MRS. BULL

To Mrs. Ole Bull:

1123 SAINT PAUL STREET,
BALTIMORE,
17 October 1894.

DEAR MRS. BULL,

I could not find time earlier to write you — I was so incessantly knocking about. We had a nice meeting last Sunday at Baltimore and [are] going to have one more next Sunday. Of course, they do not financially help me a bit; but as I promised to help them and like the idea, I speak for them.

In the letters you sent over from India was an address sent over to me from Calcutta by my fellow citizens for my work here and a number of newspaper cuttings. I will send them on to you later.

Yesterday I went to see Washington and met Mrs. Colville and Miss Young, who were very kind to me.

I am going to speak at Washington again and then will go over to Philadelphia and from there to New York.

Your affectionate Son,
Vivekananda.

XLI — MISS THURSBY

To Miss Emma Thursby:

[WASHINGTON, D.C.,
26 October 1894]

DEAR MISS THURSBY,

I received your kind note and the introductory letters. I will make it a point to see the ladies and hope to be benefitted much by it.

I had a beautiful letter from Mr. Flagg. I am soon coming to N.Y. where I hope to see you.

With my deepest love and gratitude,

I remain yours faithfully,
Vivekananda.

XLII — MOTHER

To Mrs. G. W. Hale:

[WASHINGTON, D.C.,
October 27, 1894]

DEAR MOTHER,

I received your very kind note and all the India letters just now. I will make it a point to see Mrs. Whitland [?]. I have been very kindly treated by Mrs. [Enoch] Totten.

Will you kindly order 100 photographs from Harrison, and send them over to India to Ramdayal Chakravarty, c/o Swami Ramakrishnananda, Varahanagar Math, Alambazar, Calcutta? I will pay for it when I come to Chicago.

I have nothing especial to write — except I had good treatment everywhere. How I long to give up this life of weariness and blazoning day and night.

I will go from here to New York and will come back to see you in Chicago before I start for England.

Yours etc.,
Vivekananda.

XLIII — MOTHER

To Mrs. G. W. Hale:

BALTIMORE, [MARYLAND],
3 November 1894

DEAR MOTHER,

I do not know what to say about this phonograph business. It takes six months to go to India!! and the company cannot get an inquiry in another six months!!! American express, indeed!! Well — however, they are bound to make good my money. Mother, do not lose the receipt of the express company.

I am going to New York as soon as possible.

Yours affectionately,
Vivekananda.

XXXIV — MOTHER

To Mrs. G. W. Hale:

NEW YORK,
18 November 1894

DEAR MOTHER,

I have been very late this time in writing you as Sister Mary has already written to you, no doubt, about me.

The clothes have all reached safe, only I will send over some of the summer and other clothes as it will be impossible to carry the burden all along with me.

The certainty about going to Europe this December has gone; so I am uncertain when I go.

Sister Mary has improved a great deal from what I saw her last. She lives with a number of fox-hunting squires and is quite happy. I hope she will marry one of those fellows with long pockets. I am going again to see her tomorrow at Mrs. Spalding's — I was there last afternoon. I will be in N.Y. this month; then I go to Boston and perhaps will be there all through December. When I was sick in

Boston last spring, I went over to Chicago, and not to Detroit as Mrs. Bagley expected. So this time I am going to Detroit first and then to Chicago, if possible. Else I altogether give up the plan of going to the West soon.

There is more chance of working my plans out in the East than in the West, as it now appears.

I have got news of the phonograph — it has reached safe, and the Râjâ wrote to me a very nice letter on that. I have a lot of addresses and other nonsense from India. I have written home to them not to send any more newspapers. My love to the babies at home and I am going to visit the baby abroad.

Mrs. Guernsey has been at death's door. She is now recovering slowly. I have not seen her yet. She is not strong enough to see anybody. Hope she will soon be strong.

My love to Father Pope and everyone.

Your ever affectionate son,
Vivekananda.

XLV — MOTHER

To Mrs. G. W. Hale:

C/O MRS. OLE BULL,
168 BRATTLE STREET,
CAMBRIDGE, MASS.,
6 December 1894

DEAR MOTHER,

I have not heard long from you. What is the matter with you? I am here in Cambridge and will be here for three weeks to come and will have to lecture and hold classes. Here is a Chicago lady, Mrs. [Milward] Adams, who lectures on tone building etc.

Today we had a lecture from Lady Henry Somerset on Woman Suffrage. Miss Willard of Chicago was here and Julia Ward Howe.

Col. Higginson, Dr. [J. Estlin] Carpenter of Eng. and many other friends were present. Altogether it was a grand affair. I have received a letter from India informing me that the phonograph was duly received.

I have sent part of my money to India and intend sending nearly the whole of it very soon. Only, I will keep enough for the passage back. Saw Mother Temple several times in New York. She was kind as usual. So was Mrs. Spalding.

Sister Mary wrote me a letter from Brookline [Massachusetts]. I am sure she would have enjoyed Lady Somerset's lecture so much. I wrote her about it, but I have not heard from her yet.

I will go to see her the first day I get some time. I am very busy. Hope the sisters at home are enjoying themselves. I will try to run into Chicago for a few days if I can.

Please write me all about the holy family as soon as you get time.

Mrs. Guernsey was very ill and still so weak that she cannot get out of her room.

Miss Helen Bagley was seized with diphtheria in New York and suffered a good deal. She has recovered, however, and the Bagleys have gone home to Detroit.

With my Love to you all, I remain,

Ever yours affectionately,
Vivekananda.

P.S. — Kindly send my India mail c/o Mrs. Sara Ole Bull, 168 Brattle Street, Cambridge, Mass.

XLVI — MOTHER

To Mrs. G. W. Hale:

[CAMBRIDGE, MASS.,
21 December 1894]

DEAR MOTHER,

I am glad that Haridas Viharidas (The Dewan of Junagadh.) has sent the rugs. I am afraid they will take a long time to reach here. The Raja (Maharaja Ajit Singh, the Raja of Khetri.) was very much pleased with the phonograph, as he writes, and has heard my voice several times. Hope he will bring it into life.

I have not seen Sister Mary yet, but hope to see her this week as I am going away to New York next Tuesday. Cannot come by any means to Chicago now, for I expect to go to Washington from New York and hope to be pretty busy in New York.

If I can snatch up a few days between the lecture in Brooklyn on the 30th and the next series in New York, I will fly to Chicago for a few days. If I had time just now, it would have been better for me, for the half — fare ticket will expire after this month.

I have been kept very busy here this month so could not go to Boston even for a day. Now I have time and hope to see Sister Mary.

How are the babies at home? Mrs. M. Adams of Chicago, who lectures on voice building and walking etc., has been lecturing here all this time. She is a very great lady in every respect and so intelligent. She knows all of you and likes the "Hale girls" very much. Sister Isabel[le] knows her especially, I think.

Do not you see, Mother — I am determined to work my project out. I must see the light. India can cheer alone — but no money. In the East and South I am getting slowly friends who will help me in my work, I am sure, as they have done already. They all like me more and more.

I have made friends of Lady Somerset and Miss Willard, you will be glad to know. So you see, Mother, you are the only attraction in Chicago; and so long I am in this country, wherever you live is my home. As soon as I have time I will run in to see you and the sisters. But I have no other hopes in the West; nor will you advise me to destroy the only hope I have of success in these parts of the country by giving it up and going to Chicago to be idle as the day is long.

Mrs. Bull and a few other ladies here who are helping me on are not only sincere and love me but they have the power to do as leaders of society. Would that you had millions.

With my love to you all,

Your ever affectionate Son,
Vivekananda.

XLVII — MISS THURSBY

To Miss Emma Thursby:

CHICAGO,
541 DEARBORN AVENUE,
17 January 1895

DEAR MISS THURSBY,

I am very sorry to learn about the passing on of Mr. Thorp. Mrs. Bull must have felt it deeply. Still he has passed on after a good and useful life. All is for the best.

I have been lecturing every day to a class in Mrs. Adams's rooms at the Auditorium. Today I also lecture there and in the Evening to a class of Miss Josephine Locke's at the Plaza Hotel.

Have you seen Mrs. Peake in New York? She is lecturing to a class at Mrs. Guernsey's.

Miss Locke is as kind as usual. She is enamoured of Mrs. Peake as are many of Miss Locke's friends, you will be glad to learn.

Mrs. Peake has made a very favourable impression on Chicago. So she does wherever she goes.

Mrs. Adams invited me to an organ concert in the Auditorium. She is so good and kind to me. Lord bless her.

I have not seen Mr. Young, nor, I am afraid, [will] I have time to see [him,] as I start for New York on Friday next.

I will hear him once in New York.

I was so busy here these two weeks.

I have got a new scarlet coat but can get no orange here.

Ever with blessings,

Your brother,
Vivekananda.

XLVIII — ADHYAPAKJI

To Professor John H. Wright:

54 W. 33 STREET,
NEW YORK,
1 February 1895

DEAR ADHYAPAKJI,

You must be immersed in your work now; however, taking advantage of your kindness to me, I want to bother you a little.

What was the original Greek idea of the soul, both philosophical and popular? What books can I consult (Translations, of course) to get it?

So with the Egyptians and Babylonians and Jews?

Will you kindly name me the books? I am sure you are perfectly well and so are Mrs. Wright and the children.

Ever gratefully and fraternally,

Yours,
Vivekananda.

XLIX — MOTHER

To Mrs. G. W. Hale:

54 W. 33., NEW YORK,
18 March [February] 1895

DEAR MOTHER,

I am sure you are all right by this time. The babies write from time to time and so I get your news regularly. Miss Mary is in a lecturing mood now — good for her. Hope she will not let her energies fritter away now — a penny saved is a penny gained. Sister Isabel[le] has sent me the French Books and the Calcutta pamphlets have arrived, but the big Sanskrit books ought to come. I want them badly. Make them payable here, if possible, or I will send you the postage.

I am doing very well. Only some of these big dinners kept me late, and I returned home at 2 o'clock in the morning several days. Tonight I am going to one of these. This will be the last of its kind. So much keeping up the night is not good for me. Every day from 11 to 1 o'clock I have classes in my rooms and I talk [to] them till they [grow] tired. The Brooklyn course ended yesterday. Another lecture I have there next Monday.

Bean soup and rice or barley is now my general diet. I am faring well. Financially I am making the ends meet and nothing more because I do not charge anything for the classes I have in my rooms. And the public lectures have to go through so many hands.

I have a good many lectures planned ahead in New York, which I hope to deliver by and by. Sister Isabel wrote to me a beautiful letter and she does so much for me. My eternal gratitude to her.

Baby has stopped writing; I do not know why.

Kindly tell Baby to send me a little Sanskrit book which came from India. I forgot to bring it over. I want to translate some passages from it.

Mr. [Charles M.] Higgins is full of joy. It was he who planned all this for me, and he is so glad that everything succeeded so well.

Mrs. Guernsey is going to give up this house and going to some other house. Miss [Florence] Guernsey wants to marry but her father and mother do not like it at all. I am very sorry for her, poor "Sister Jenny" — and so many men are after her. Here is a very rich railway gentleman called Mr. [Austin] Corbin; his only daughter, Miss [Anna] Corbin, is very much interested in me. And though she is one of the leaders of the 400, she is very intellectual and spiritual too, in a way. Their house is always chock full of swells and foreign aristocracy. Princes and Barons and whatnot from all over the world. Some of these foreigners are very bright. I am sorry your home-manufactured aristocracy is not very interesting. Behind her parlor she has a long arbour with all sorts of palms and seats and electric light. There I will have a little class next week of a score of long-pockets. The Fun is not bad. "This world is a great humbug after all", Mother. "God alone is real; everything else is a dream only." Mother Temple says she does not like to be bossed by you and that is why she does not come to Chicago. She is very happy nearby. Between swells and Delmonico and Waldorf dinners, my health was going to be injured. So I quickly turned a thorough vegetarian to avoid all invitations. The rich are really the salt of this world — they are neither food nor drink. Goodbye for the present.

Your ever affectionate Son,
Vivekananda.

L — MOTHER

To Mrs. G. W. Hale:

54 W. 33RD ST., NEW YORK,
11 March 1895

DEAR MOTHER,

Many thanks for your kind letter. I will be only too glad to have an orange coat, provided it be light as summer is approaching.

I do not remember whether the Cook's letters of credit I have are limited as to their time or not. It is high time we look into them. If they are limited, don't you think it is better to put them in some bank? I have about a thousand dollars in the Boston bank and a few hundred in the New York — they all go to India by this week or next. So it is better that I look into the Cook's letters, and it will be foolish to get into trouble by having them past the date.

There are a few more Sanskrit books which have not been sent — one pretty thick and broad, the other two very thin. Kindly send them as soon as you can.

Mrs. [Milward] Adams, Mrs. [Ole] Bull, and Miss Emma Thursby are gone to Chicago today.

With eternal love to the babies and to you and Father Pope.

I remain ever your affectionate Son,
Vivekananda.

LI — MOTHER

To Mrs. G. W. Hale:

[54 W. 33RD ST., NEW YORK],
14 March 1895

DEAR MOTHER,

The last letter you sent over is a notice from the Chicago post office of a parcel received by them. I think it is some books sent to me from India. The rugs cannot come through the post office (?) I do not know what to do. I send you therefore back this notice, and if they deliver it to you, all right — else I hope you will ask them to send it over to New York and kindly give them my address.

Yours obediently,
Vivekananda.

LII — MOTHER

To Mrs. G. W. Hale:

[NEW YORK,
April 25, 1895]

DEAR MOTHER,

I was away a long time in the country. Came back day before yesterday.

I think the summer coat is in Chicago. If so, will you kindly send it over c/o Miss Phillips, 19 W. 38 Str., New York? It is getting hot here every day.

I will remain in New York till the end of May, at least.

Hoping you are all in perfect health. I remain,

Yours truly,
Vivekananda.

LIII — MOTHER

To Mrs. G. W. Hale:

> 54 W. 33.,
> NEW YORK,
> [April 26, 1895]

DEAR MOTHER,

Perhaps you did not receive my letter asking you to send the Calcutta pamphlets about the Paramahamsa Ramakrishna. Kindly send them to me at 54 W. 33, and also the pamphlets about the Calcutta meeting if you have any. Also the summer coat to the care of Miss Phillips, 19 W. 38.

As I do not see any probability of my going soon to Chicago, I am thinking of drawing all my money from the Chicago bank to New York. Will you kindly ascertain the exact total amount I have in Chicago so that I may draw it out at once and deposit it in some New York bank?

Kindly do these and I will bother you no more. I have written to India long ago about the rugs. I do not know whether Dewanji is alive or dead. I have no information.

I am all right and will be more than a month yet in New York. After that I am going to the Thousand Islands — wherever that place may be — for a little summer quiet and rest. Mrs. Bagley has been down here to see me and attended several of my classes.

The classes are going on with a boom; almost every day I have one, and they are packed full. But no "money" — except they maintain themselves. I charge no fees, except as the members contribute to the rent etc. voluntarily.

It is mostly probable that I will go away this summer.

With my love to all,

> Ever gratefully yours,
> Vivekananda.

LIV — MOTHER

To Mrs. G. W. Hale:

> 54 W. 33 NEW YORK,
> The 1st of May 1895

DEAR MOTHER,

Many, many thanks for sending the coat. Now I am well equipped for summer. I am so sorry the rugs could not come before I leave this country. They will come if Dewanji is alive.

I have been out of town a few days and have now come back all right — healthy as ever.

Lord bless you ever and ever for your untiring kindness to me.

> Ever your grateful Son,
> Vivekananda.

P.S. The History of Rajasthan I present you, and the satchel to the babies.

LV — FRIEND

To Mr. Francis H. Leggett:

> 54 W. 33RD ST.,
> NEW YORK,
> The 4th of May 1895

DEAR FRIEND,

Many thanks for your kind present. The cigars are indeed delicious — and a hundred times so, as coming from you.

With everlasting love and regards,

> I remain yours truly,
> Vivekananda.

LVI — MOTHER

To Mrs. G. W. Hale:

54 W. 33,
NEW YORK,
16th May '95

DEAR MOTHER,

Your kind note duly reached. The books have arrived safe and more are coming. The Sanskrit books pay no duty, being classics. I expect a big package from Khetri. The big packet was from the Raja of Khetri, sending me an address from a meeting held of Rajput nobility at Mount Abu, for my work in this country.

I do not know whether I will be able to come over to Chicago or not. I am trying to get a free pass; in case I succeed I will come, else not. Financially this winter's work was no success at all — I could barely keep myself up — but spiritually very great. I am going to the Thousand Islands for the summer to visit a friend and some of my pupils will be there.

I have got plenty of books now to read from India, and I will be quite engaged this summer.

The Khetri package will not arrive soon, so kindly make arrangements that it will be received during your absence if you go away. [There] will have to be paid a heavy duty for [it,] I am afraid.

Mrs. [Florence] Adams brought me the love from the [Hale] Sisters on her way to Europe. She started this morning. A large package of books also I expect soon. The original Upanishads — there is no duty on them.

I have had some trouble with my stomach; hope it will be over in a few days.

With love to all,

I am ever your affectionate Son,
Vivekananda.

LVII — MOTHER

To Mrs. Ole Bull:

NEW YORK,
The 28th May '95

DEAR MOTHER,

Your last kind letter to hand. This week will be the last of my classes. I am going next Tuesday with Mr. Leggett to Maine. He has a fine lake and a forest there. I will be two or three weeks there.[6]* Thence I go to the Thousand Islands. Also I have an invitation to speak at a parliament of religions at Toronto, Canada, on July 18th. I will go there from Thousand Islands and return back.

So far everything is going on well with me.

Ever your grateful son,

I am ever your affectionate Son,
Vivekananda.

P.S. My regards and love to your daughter and pray for her speedy recovery.

LVIII — SIR

To Dr. Paul Carus:

19 W. 38TH ST.,
NEW YORK,
June [May] 28, '95.

DR. PAUL CARUS, LA SALLE, ILL.

DEAR SIR,

I am just now in receipt of your letter and will be very happy to join the religions Congress at Toronto. Only, as you are well aware of, the financial means of a "Bhikshu" (A Hindu or Buddhist monk.) are very limited. I will be only too glad to do anything in my power to help you and wait further particulars and directions.

Hoping to hear from you soon and thanking you very much for your great sympathy with Buddhistic India.

I remain ever fraternally your,
Vivekananda.

LIX — MOTHER

Mrs. Ole Bull:

4th June '95

DEAR MOTHER,

Today I leave New York at 5 p.m. by steamer with Mr. Leggett.

The classes were closed on Saturday last [June 1] and so far the work has been very successful, no small part of which is due to you.

Ever praying for you and yours,

I am ever your faithful Son,
Vivekananda.

P.S. I will acquaint you with my whereabouts as soon as I know it myself.

LX — DOCTOR

To Dr. Paul Carus:

C/O MISS DUTCHER,
THOUSAND ISLAND PARK,
N.Y.,
[June 1895]

DEAR DOCTOR,

I am in this place now and had to change some of my plans on account of the Toronto Congress.

I am therefore not quite sure whether I will be able to come to Oak Island Conference. It is very possible, however, that I will be able to do so.

I also hope Mr. [Charles Carroll] Bonney will come. He is a noble, noble soul — one who sincerely wishes the fellowship of all humanity.

Is it not true, Dr., that Mr. Bonney, as I have every reason to think, originated the plan of the parliament of religions?

I will certainly try my best to come.

Thanking you very much for your kindness, I remain

Ever yours in the Lord of Compassion,
Vivekananda.

P.S. Will you kindly inform me what lines of thought you want me to take.

LXI — MOTHER

To Mrs. G. W. Hale:

C/O MISS DUTCHER'S,
THOUSAND ISLAND PARK,
N.Y.,
2nd July 1895

DEAR MOTHER,

You did not write to me a single line for a long time. Neither did Sister Mary write about the duty paid on the rugs [from the Dewan of Junagadh]. I am afraid the rugs are small.

Here is another consignment from Raja Ajit Singh [the Maharaja of Khetri] consisting of carpets, shawls, etc., etc., for which the bill of lading you sent me the other day. This consignment has no duty to pay because it was all prepaid in India, and the bill of lading says so expressly. I will send you the bill of lading and the receipt for the duty. Kindly take one more trouble for me and get it out of the express company. And keep it with you till I come. The goods have arrived in New York and I had a notice of that. They are on their way to Chicago.

In two or three days I will send the bill of lading and the receipt for duty paid, to you. I foolishly asked Miss Phillips, as soon as I got the Company's (Original letter: Companies'.) notice, to get them out before I got the bill of lading. Now the bill of lading shows that it is bound for Chicago. So I am bound to give you this trouble. I am so sorry. Again with my usual business instincts — I forgot to note down the name of the express company. So I have written to New York for the letters of the Company. As soon as that comes I will send over to you.

I am going to Europe by the end of August or a little later.

I will come to see you by the end of August.
Lord bless you and yours for ever and ever.

Your ever affectionate Son,
Vivekananda.

LXII — MOTHER

To Mrs. G. W. Hale:

THOUSAND ISLAND PARK, N.Y.,
C/O MISS DUTCHER,
July 3, 1895

DEAR MOTHER,

Herewith I send you the bill of landing and the inventory of the goods sent from India. The duty, as you will find, has been prepaid, so there is no botheration on that score. The goods have reached Hull. [6]* They will be here by the middle of this month. And if you see a letter with the Morris American Express Co. name on the envelope, tear it open. You need not forward it to me, for that will be the notice of arrival to Chicago. I am sure Dewanji's carpets were too small, but why do you not write to me about the duty if you had to pay it? I insist upon paying it myself. The Raja's things seem to come very quick. I am so glad too I will have something to present to Mrs. Bagley, Mrs. Bull, etc.

[Enclosed in the above letter was the following note.]

541 DEARBORNAVE.
CHICAGO.
TO THE MORRIS EXPRESS CO.—

DEAR SIR,

Please permit Mrs. G. W. Hale of 541 Dearborn Ave., Chicago, to act for me about the goods sent to me from India and receive the same.

I have the honor to be, sir, your most obedient servant,

Swami Vivekananda.

LXIV — MOTHER

To Mrs. G. W. Hale:

THOUSAND ISLAND PARK,
C/O MISS DUTCHER,
N. Y.,
27th July '95

DEAR MOTHER,

I will be ever so much obliged if you kindly look into the "bead" affair. (Rudrâksha beads sent from India. Vide letter dated January 17, 1895 in pay it to you when I come.

I start from here next week. I will be in Detroit a day or two on my way. I will be in by the third or fourth of August.

With Everlasting love, your Son,
Vivekananda.

[Enclosed in the above letter was the following note.]

27th July '95
TO THE STATES EXPRESS COMPANY
FOREIGN DEPARTMENT.

DEAR SIR,

Herewith I authorize Mrs. George W. Hale to take delivery of the "beads" that have been expressed to me from India. Hoping they will be regularly delivered to her, I remain yours obediently,

Swami Vivekananda.

LXV — MOTHER

To Mrs. G. W. Hale:

C/O MISS DUTCHER,
THOUSAND ISLAND PARK,
30th August [July] '95

DEAR MOTHER,

I was starting for Chicago, Thursday next [August 1], but your letter stopped me. The letter and the package have safely arrived.

Write to me or wire if you want me to come to Chicago. I will then start for Chicago next week, i.e. on Tuesday next [August 6]. I thought Sister Mary was at home. When are the other babies coming? My going to Europe is not yet settled finally. The babies have not written me a line — not one of them.

Oh, Mother, my heart is so, so sad. The letters bring the news of the death of Dewanji. Haridas Viharidas has left the body. He was as a father to me. Poor man, he was the last 5 years seeking the retirement from business life, and at last he got it but could not enjoy it long. I pray that he may never come back again to this dirty hole they call the Earth. Neither may he be born in heaven or any other horrid place. May he never again wear a body — good or bad, thick or thin. What a humbug and illusion this world is, Mother, what a mockery this life. I pray constantly that all mankind will come to know the reality, i.e. God, and this "Shop" here be closed for ever.

My heart is too full to write more. Write to me or wire if you like.

Your ever obedient Son,
Vivekananda.

P.S. We will think of the coming package [from the Maharaja of Khetri] in Chicago. How long will you be in Chicago? If it is only a week or so, I need not come. I will meet you in New York. If more than that, I come to see you.

LXVI — MOTHER

To Mrs. G. W. Hale:

C/O MISS DUTCHER,
THOUSAND ISLAND PARK,
N. Y.,
[July 31, 1895]

DEAR MOTHER,

I am afraid I can not come to see you and neither will you advise me. I am going with a friend (Mr. Francis Leggett.) to Europe, at his expense. We go first to Paris and from there to London. My friend will go to Italy and I to London. I will, however, come back to New York in September. So I am not going away for good.

I start on the 17th. So you see, it is impossible to come and go that way for 3 or 4 days.

(The goods mentioned in Swami Vivekananda's letter dated [6]July 2, 1895.)

The package from India ought to have reached by this time. If they come, kindly take the delivery and send it back to New York to Miss Mary Phillips, 19 W. 38. If the package does not come to Chicago before you go away, then kindly send the bill of lading etc. to Miss Mary Phillips, 19. W. 38. The babies [the Hale daughters] did not write me a line, nor did they intimate where they are. I absolutely do not know anything about them. As they do not want it, it seems I ought not to disturb them with my letters. But you kindly convey them my love and eternal, undying blessings. So to you, Mother and Father Pope. I will pen a longer epistle in a few days. We will see each other next spring in Chicago, Mother, if we all live.

Ever gratefully your Son,
Vivekananda.

LXVII — FRIEND

To Mr. Francis Leggett:

[THOUSAND ISLAND PARK, U.S.A.,
August 1895]

DEAR FRIEND,

I received your note duly.

Very kind of you and noble to ask me to have my own time to London. Many thanks for that. But I am in no hurry for London and, moreover, I want to see you married in Paris and then I go over to London.

I will be ready, Father Leggett, at hand and in time — never fear.

Yours affectionately ever,
Vivekananda.

LXVIII — MRS. G. W. HALE

To Mrs. G. W. Hale:

THE WESTERN UNION TELEGRAPH COMPANY.,
RECEIVED AT: PLAZA HOTEL DRUG STORE,,
NORTH AVE. & CLARK STREET.,
THOUSAND ISLAND, N.Y., 2, '95,

[August 2, 1895]

8 jw ws 11 paid 1.33 p.m.

MRS. G. W. HALE,

541 DEARBORN AVE.

WHY ANY CHARGES DUTY PREPAID (This evidently again refers to the goods sent by the Maharaja of Khetri. Vide the letter addressed to Mrs. G. W. Hale dated [6]July 2, 1895.) YOU HAVE DOCUMENTS WRITE FULL PARTICULARS.

Vivekananda.

LXIX — CHRISTINA

To Sister Christine:

19 WEST 38TH STREET,
9th August '95

DEAR CHRISTINA,

You must be enjoying the beautiful weather very much. Here, it is extremely hot but it does not worry me much. I had a pleasant journey from Thousand Islands to New York; and though the Engine was derailed, I did not know anything of it, being asleep all the time. Miss Waldo went out of the train at Albany. I did not see her off as I was asleep. I have not heard anything from her yet. Hope to hear soon. Dr. [L. L. Wight] and Miss [Ruth] Ellis must have gone home by this time.

We gave them a telepathic message but Miss Ellis has not got it sure, else she would write.

I am making preparations for my departure.

I came in time for one of the meetings here and had another one last evening — going to have one more this evening and almost every evening till I go over.

What is Mrs. Funkey [Mary Caroline Funke] doing, and Miss [Mary Elizabeth] Dutcher? Do you go to meditate on the mountain as usual? Did you hear from Kripananda?

Write to me as soon as you can — I am so anxious to hear from you.

Ever yours with blessings and love,
Vivekananda.

P.S. My love and blessings to Mrs. Funkey and Miss Dutcher.

LXX — MOTHER

To Mrs. Ole Bull:

19 WEST 38TH STREET,
NEW YORK,
9th August '95

DEAR MOTHER,

Your note duly received. I saw also Miss Thursby yesterday. After the hard work at the Thousand Islands, I am taking a few days quiet and preparation for my departure. So I cannot come to Greenacre. I am with Miss Phillips and will be till the 17th, on which day I depart for Europe. I have seen Mr. Leggett. You remember Mrs. Sturges, the widow in black in my classes. She is going to marry Mr. Leggett in Paris. They will be married the 1st week we arrive, and then they go on a tour through Europe, and I, to England. I hope to return in a few weeks — back to New York.

Kindly give to Miss Hamlin [Elizabeth L. Hamlen], to Miss [Sarah] Farmer, Dr. [L. L. Wight] and Miss Howe, and all our friends my greetings, love and good-bye.

Ever sincerely your Son,
Vivekananda.

LXXI — SISTER CHRISTINE

To Sister Christine:

[The following telegram was sent on Swami Vivekananda's behalf.]

POSTAL TELEGRAPH-CABLE COMPANY,
RECEIVED AT MAIN OFFICE, COR.,
GRISWOLD,
LAFAYETTE AVE., DETROIT, MICH.,
43. NY. FC. W...10 PAID. 12:45 PM,
NEW YORK, N.Y.,
[August 17, 1895]

MISS CHRISTINA GREENSTIDEL,

418 ALFRED ST., DETROIT, MICH.

SWAMM [SWAMI] LEAVING SENDS YOU AND MRS. FUNKE LOVE AND BLESSING.

Kripananda.

LXXII — ISABELLE MCKINDLEY

To Miss Isabelle McKindley:

80 OAKLEY STREET,
CHELSEA, S.W.,
LONDON,
24th October '95

We meet and part. This is the law and ever ever be. I sadly ask O gentle ones

Do you remember me?

I haven't had any news from Chicago, nor did I write as I did not want to bother you — also I did not know where to.

Accompanying is a newspaper notice of a lecture I delivered in London. It is not bad. The London audiences are very learned and critical, and the English nature is far from being effusive. I have some friends here — made some more — so I am going on.

My bed is in the foaming deep
What care I, friend, the dew!

It is a queer life, mine — always travelling, no rest. Rest will be my death — such is the force of habit. Little success here, little there — and a good deal of bumping. Saw Paris a good [deal]. Miss Josephine M'cLeod [MacLeod], a New York friend, showed it all over to me for a month. Even there, the kind American girl! Here in England they know us more. Those that do not like the Hindus, they hate them; those that like, they worship them.

It is slow work here, but sure. Not frothy, not superficial. English women as a rule are not as highly educated as the American women, nor are so beautiful. They are quite submissive wives or hidden-away daughters or church-going mothers — the embodiments of crystallized conventionality. I am going to have some classes at the above address.

Sometimes — and generally when I score a success — I feel a despondence; I feel as if everything is vain — as if this life has no meaning, as if it is a waking dream. Love, friendship, religion, virtue, kindness — everything, a momentary state of mind. I seem to long to go; in spite of myself I say, how far — O how far! Yet the body-and-mind will have to work its Karma out. I hope it will not be bad.

How are you all going on? Where is Mother Church? Is she interviewing the ghosts of the Thotmeses and Rameses in the Pyramids — or calmly going her round of duties at home?

Yet the life seems to grow deep and at the same time lose its hold on itself.

Not disgust, nor joy for life, but a sort of indifference — things will take their course; who can resist — only stand by and look on. Well, I will not talk about myself so much. Egregious egotist! I always was that, you know. How about you all? Great fun this life, isn't it? Don't go to the extremes. A calm, restful, settled married life is good for the majority of mankind. Mr. [Edward T.] Sturdy, the friend with whom I am living now, was in India several times. He mixed with our monks and is very ascetic in his habits, but he is married at last and has settled down. And [he] has got a beautiful little baby. Their life is very nice. The wife, of course, doesn't much care about metaphysics or Sanskrit, but her whole life is in her husband — and husband's soul is in Sanskrit metaphysics! Yet it is a good combination of theory and practice, I think. Write me all about yourselves if you have time and inclination, and give Mother Church my eternal gratitude.

My movements are so, so uncertain. Yet I will be a month more in London.

With never-ending gratitude and love,
Vivekananda.

LXXIII — CHRISTINA

To Sister Christine:

228 W. 39TH STREET,
[NEW YORK],
8th Dec. '95

DEAR CHRISTINA,

I am once more on American Soil and have taken lodgings at 228 W. 39, where I begin work from Monday next. Sometime after Christmas I intend to make a tour through Detroit and Chicago.

I do not care for public lecturings at all — and do not think I shall have any more public lectures charging admission. If you will see Mrs. Phelps and others of our friends and arrange some classes (strictly on nonpayment basis), it will facilitate things a good deal.

Write at your earliest opportunity and give Mrs. Phunkey [Funke] and all our friends my deepest love and gratitude.

Yours ever in the Lord,
Vivekananda.

P.S. Kripananda is over full of praise of you and Mrs. Funkey [Funke] and sends his loving regards for you.

LXXIV — CHRISTINA

To Sister Christine:

228 W. 39TH STREET,
[NEW YORK,
Dec. 10, 1895

DEAR CHRISTINA,

Perhaps by this time you have received my first letter. I received yours just now.

I had a splendid success in England and have left a nucleus there to work till my arrival next summer. You will be astonished to learn that some of my strongest friends are big "guns" of the Church of England.

This Christmas I am going away a week, from 24th Decem., to the country with Mr. and Mrs. Leggett — after that I resume my work. In the meanwhile the classes have begun.

I have written to you my intention of taking a quick turn through Detroit and Chicago in the meanwhile and [then] return back.

Give Mrs. Phelps my love and kindly arrange the classes [in Detroit] with her. The best thing is to arrange for a public lecture where I give out my general plan of work. The Unitarian church is available; and if the lecture is free, there will be a big crowd. The collection most possibly will cover the expenses. Then out of this we will get the materials of a big class and then hurry them through, leaving Mrs. Phelps and you and Mrs. Funkey [Funke] to work on with them.

This plan is entirely feasible and if Mrs. Phelps and Mrs. Bagley desire it, they can work it out very quickly.

Ever yours with love and blessings,
Vivekananda.

LXXV — CHRISTINA

To Sister Christine:

> 228 W. 39TH STREET,
> NEW YORK,
> 12 December 1895

DEAR CHRISTINA,

I am going away out of town from the 24th of this month and will come back on the 2nd of January. From the 24th — the 2nd I will not be here. I will settle the dates for Detroit and Chicago after hearing from you and from Chicago.

[Paragraph excised from the original letter.]

My love to Mrs. Phunkey [Funke] [excised] and all other friends.

> Yours ever in the Lord,
> Vivekananda.

LXXVI — YOUR HIGHNESS

To the Maharaja of Limdi:

> Cathiawad, Bombay,
> CHICAGO,
> 14th Dec. '95

YOUR HIGHNESS,

The gentleman whom I have the pleasure of introducing to you was the chairman of the Parliament of Religions held in Chicago.

He is a holy and noble gentleman. We owe him a deep debt of gratitude; and as he is going to make a tour through India, I hope your Highness will extend him the same hospitality as he has to us.

> Yours with blessings,
> Vivekananda.

LXXVII — SIR

To the Dewan of Mysore, Madras (His Excellency Seshahari Iyer, K. C. S. I.):

> CHICAGO,
> the 14th Dec. '95

DEAR SIR,

The gentleman I have the pleasure of introducing to you was the chairman of the Chicago Parliament of religions.

All India owes him a deep debt of gratitude. He is now on a tour through our country, and I am sure you will help him in seeing your part of the country and oblige.

> Yours with blessings,
> Vivekananda.

LXXVIII — CHRISTINA

To Sister Christine:

> 228 W. 39TH STREET,
> NEW YORK,
> December 24, 1895

DEAR CHRISTINA,

Merry Christmas and happy New Year to you. I am going today to the country. I return in 10 days.

About the tour through Detroit — I will fix it later on. I am afraid if I go just now, everything here will fall to pieces.

I will come anyway, but I am afraid it will be later than I expected.

My love to Mrs. Phelps, Mrs. Phunkey [Funke] and all our friends and Christmas greetings.

> Ever yours in the Lord,
> Vivekananda.

P.S. Kripananda sends his greetings too.

LXXIX — MRS. OLE BULL

To Mrs. Ole Bull:

>228 W. 39,
>NEW YORK,
>24 December 1895

Merry Christmas and happy New Year to you, dear Mrs. Bull. And may peace and health rest on you and yours for ever. I am going out of town today and will be back in ten days.

My love to all.

>Yours affectionately,
>Vivekananda.

LXXX — SIR

To the Editor of Light of the East:

>1896.

DEAR SIR,

Many thanks for your kindly sending me several copies of the Light of the East. I wish the paper all success.

As you have asked for my suggestion [that] I can make towards improving the paper — I must frankly state that in my life-long experience in the work, I have always found "Occultism" injurious and weakening to humanity. What we want is strength. We Indians, more than any other race, want strong and vigorous thought. We have enough of the superfine in all concerns. For centuries we have been stuffed with the mysterious; the result is that our intellectual and spiritual digestion is almost hopelessly impaired, and the race has been dragged down to the depths of hopeless imbecility — never before or since experienced by any other civilised community. There must be freshness and vigour of thought behind to make a virile race. More than enough to strengthen the whole world exists in the Upanishads. The Advaita is the eternal mine of strength. But it requires to be applied. It must first be cleared of the incrustation of scholasticism, and then in all its simplicity, beauty and sublimity be taught over the length and breadth of the land, as applied even to the minutest detail of daily life. "This is a very large order"; but we must work towards it, nevertheless, as if it would be accomplished to-morrow. Of one thing I am sure — that whoever wants to help his fellow beings through genuine love and unselfishness will work wonders.

>Yours truly,
>Vivekananda.

LXXXI — MRS. BULL

To Mrs. Ole Bull:

>228 W. 39TH STREET,
>NEW YORK,
>The 3rd Jan. '96

DEAR MRS. BULL,

I have had a letter from Mr. Trine asking me to have some classes at the Procopeia in February. I do not see my way to go to Boston in February, however I may like it. I have given up for the present my plan of going to Detroit and Chicago in February. Later on I will try. Miss [Josephine] Locke will see to my having classes in Chicago and I have some friends in Detroit I may go to Baltimore for a few days in the meanwhile. I enjoyed my visit with the Leggetts exceedingly. It has braced me for further work. I am very well both physically and mentally.

Wishing you a happy New Year,

>I remain yours affectionately,
>Vivekananda.

LXXXII — MRS. FUNKEY

To Mrs. Charles (Mary) Funke:

>228 W. 39,
>NEW YORK,
>The 6th Jan. 1896.

DEAR MRS. FUNKEY [FUNKE],

Many, many thanks for the sweet flowers. It recalls to me the beautiful times we had at the Thousand Islands and presages many such summer gatherings.

The work here had begun in right earnest, and we will advance it farther this year than in the last.

I am therefore uncertain as to the exact date of my coming to Detroit. I will come, however, very soon.

Yours ever in the Lord,
Vivekananda.

LXXXIII — MRS. BULL

To Mrs. Ole Bull:

228 W. 39TH STREET,
NEW YORK,
10 January 1896

DEAR MRS. BULL,

I have received your letter and also another from the Secretary of the Harvard Metaphysical Club.

I will be only too glad to come to Boston for the Harvard lecture especially — but these are the difficulties in the way: First, the work here will fall to pieces; secondly, I have begun to write in right earnest. I want to finish some text books to be the basis of work when I am gone. I want to hurry through four little text books before I go.

Of course it is impossible to come this month as the notices of the four Sunday lectures are out. In the first week of February I have again a lecture at Brooklyn at Dr. Janes's. My idea now is to make a tour to Boston, Detroit, and Chicago in March and then come back to New York a week or so and then start for England. In March I will be able to stay a few weeks at each of these places. Of course it is true that [as] yet I have no competent persons here to carry on the work like Sturdy in England, nor any sincere friend to stand by me except you.

I will do anything you want me to, and if you think it is good for me to come to Boston in February, I am ready.

Ever yours with gratitude, love, and blessings,
Vivekananda.

P.S. I have not much faith in that Procopeia business, (The Procopeia Club) except as a nucleus to work from.

My love to Miss Hamlin and all the other friends there.

LXXXIV — CHRISTINA

To Sister Christine:

24th Jan. '95 ['96]

DEAR CHRISTINA,

I have not heard from you [for] long. Hope everything is going on well with you and Mrs. Phunkey [Funke].

Did you receive my poem? I had a letter from Mrs. Phelps today. I am coming to Detroit next March early, as I will have to finish my February course in New York. The public lectures will be printed as they are delivered right along. The class lectures will very soon be collected and edited in little volumes.

May the Lord bless you ever and ever.

Yours ever with love and blessings,
Vivekananda.

LXXXV — MRS. BULL

To Mrs. Ole Bull:

228 W. 39,
NEW YORK,
The 6th of Feb. '96

DEAR MRS. BULL,

I received your last duly, but owing to many things I have given up the idea of taking rest next month. I go to Detroit the first week of March and then, towards the middle or last week, come to Boston. I have not much faith in working such things as the Procopeia [Club] etc.— because these mixed-up conglomerations of all isms and ities — mostly fads — disturb the steadiness of the mind, and life becomes a mass of frivolities. I am very glad, however, to get an opportunity to talk to the graduates of Harvard. This does not mean that I am not coming to Procopeia. I will come but it will be only for your sake. There is one if, however — and that is if I am physically able. My health has nearly broken down. I have not slept even one night soundly in New York since I came; and this year there is incessant work, both with the pen and the mouth. The accumulated work and worry of years is on me now, I am afraid. Then a big struggle awaits me in England. I wish to go to the bottom of the sea and have a good, long sleep.

To Detroit I must go, dead or alive, as I have disappointed them several times last year. There were big money offers from near Chicago. I have rejected them as I do not any longer believe in paid lectures and their utility in any country. If after Detroit I feel the body able to drag itself on to Boston, I will come, else I will remain in Detroit or some other quiet place and rest to recuperate for the coming work in England. So far I have tried to work conscientiously — let the fruits belong to the Lord. If they were good they will sprout up sooner or later; if bad, the sooner they die the better. I am quite satisfied with my task in life. I have been much more active than a Sannyasin ought to be. Now I will disappear from society altogether. The touch of the world is degenerating me, I am sure, so it is time to be off. Work has no more value beyond purifying the heart. My heart is pure enough; why shall I bother my head about doing good to others? "If you have known the Atman as the one, only existence and nothing else exists, desiring what? — for whose desire you trouble yourself?" This universe is a dream, pure and simple. Why bother myself about a dream? The very atmosphere of the world is poison to the Yogi, but I am waking up. My old iron heart is coming back — all attachments of relatives, friends, disciples are vanishing fast. "Neither through wealth nor through progeny, but by giving up everything as chaff is that immortality attained" — the Vedas. I am so tired of talking too; I want to close my lips and sit in silence for years. All talk is nonsense.

Yours faithfully,
Vivekananda.

LXXXVI — MISS THURSBY

To Miss Emma Thursby:

228 W. 39TH STREET,
NEW YORK,
February 26th, 1896

DEAR MISS THURSBY,

Will you oblige me by giving Mr. Goodwin any particulars you can with reference to the business arrangements made for my 6 lectures with Miss Corbin. He will see her, with the idea of obtaining payment.

Thanking you in anticipation, and with best regards,

Very truly yours,
Vivekananda.

LXXXVII — FRIEND

To Shri Giridharidas Mangaldas Viharidas Desai:

228 W. 39TH STREET,
NEW YORK

DEAR FRIEND,

Excuse my delay in replying to your beautiful note.

Your uncle was a great soul, and his whole life was given to doing good to his country. Hope you will all follow in his footsteps.

I am coming to India this winter, and cannot express my sorrow that I will not see Haribhai once more.

He was a strong, noble friend, and India has lost a good deal in losing him.

I am going to England very soon where I intend to pass the summer, and in winter next I come to India.

Recommend me to your uncles and friends.

Ever always the well-wisher of your family,
Vivekananda.

PS: My England address is: C/o E. T. Sturdy, Esq., High View, Caversham, Reading, England.

LXXXVIII — CHRISTINA

To Sister Christine:

C/O THE PROCOPEIA,
45 ST., BOTOLPH STREET,
BOSTON, MASS.,
22nd March '96

DEAR CHRISTINA,

Herewith [words excised] to countersign it and put it [words excised]. I am afraid I have made a mistake in writing Miss to your name. In that case you will have to sign also as Miss etc.

I am enjoying Boston very much, especially the old friends here.

They are all kind. Reply promptly. Write fully later on.

With everlasting love and blessings,

Yours etc.,
Vivekananda.

LXXXIX — MRS. FUNKEY

To Mrs. Charles (Mary) Funke:

C/O THE PROCOPEIA,
45 ST., BOTOLPH STREET,
BOSTON, MASS.,
22nd March '96

DEAR MRS. FUNKEY [FUNKE],

I had no time to write a line even, I was so busy. I am enjoying Boston immensely, only hard work. The meeting with old friends is very pleasing, no doubt. The so-called class swelled up to 500 people last night and, am afraid, will go on increasing. Everything going on splendidly. Mr. Goodwin as nice as ever. We are all friends here. I go next week to Chicago.

Hope everything is going on well with you there. Kindly give my love to Mrs. Phelps, Mr. Phelps and all the rest of my friends.

With all love and blessings,

Yours,
Vivekananda.

XC — CHRISTINA

To Sister Christine:

1628 INDIANA AVE.,
CHICAGO, ILL.,
[April 6, 1896]

DEAR CHRISTINA,

[Line excised.] reply as soon as possible.

I am going forward to New York on Thursday [April 9] and [will] start for England on the 15th of April.

Goodby and love to you all — to Mrs. Funkey [Funke], to Mrs. Phelps and all the rest of our friends.

In this life we meet and part again and again; but the mind is omnipresent and can be, hear, and feel anywhere.

Yours with love and blessings,
Vivekananda.

P.S. Give Kripananda and Miss [Martha] Hamilton my love and blessings when you meet them next.

[Written in the margin:] I will go to New York next Friday [April 10].

XCI — CHRISTINA

To Sister Christine:

> HIGH VIEW, CAVERSHAM,
> READING, LONDON,
> 26th April '96

DEAR CHRISTINA,

How are things going on with you? I am all safe and sound here in England. Going to begin work from May fourth. How is Mrs. Funkey [Funke]?

Give them all my Love. Write me all about yourself and Mrs. Funkey when you have time. Address me at 63 St., George's Road, S.W. London.

Where is Krip. [Swami Kripananda]? What is he doing now? Has he been able to get up any classes yet? Has his temper gone down?

Give them all my love — and [to] Miss Hamilton and to all my friends and to the Rabbi [Grossman of Detroit].

> Yours ever with love and blessings,
> Vivekananda.

XCII — MRS. BULL

To Mrs. Ole Bull:

> 63 ST GEORGE'S ROAD,
> LONDON. S.W.,
> May 8, 1896

DEAR MRS. BULL,

Your last letter to Sturdy at hand. They, I am sorry to say, leave us nowhere. I could not make anything out of them.

What are we to do? Is the book going to be published or not? Prof. [William] James's introduction (Preface to Swami Vivekananda's Râja-Yoga.) is of no use in England. So why wait so long for that; and what use are those long explanations about him?

Our hands are tied down. Why do you not write something plain and decisive? Life is short and time is flying. I am so sorry you are losing sight of that. Your letters are full of explanations [and] directions, but not one word about what is to be done!!! So much red tape about printing a little book!! Empires are managed with less manipulation than that, I am sure!! So kindly write at your earliest something precise about the book and whether it is going to be printed or not, and pray make the writing a little legible.

Poor Sturdy is out of his wits as to what to do; he has gone through the Mss. long ago.

Joking apart, I am very sorry you are not coming over this year. We are in Lady Isabel's house. (The house was rented from Lady Isabel Margesson.) Miss [Henrietta] Müller has taken some rooms in it too. Goodwin is here with us. We have not yet made any big stir here. The classes have begun; they are not yet what we expected. We [have] had only two yet.

We will work on steadily the next 4 or 5 months. Sturdy is as patient and persevering and hopeful as ever.

It is cool enough here yet to have a fire in the grate.

Give my love to Mrs. Adams, Miss Thursby and all other friends. My love to Mr. Fox and blessings.

> Yours with love and blessings,
> Vivekananda.

XCIII — SIR

To Mr. Francis Leggett:

(Swami Vivekananda enclosed the following document in a [6]July 6, 1896 letter written to Francis Leggett.)

> 63 ST. GEORGE'S ROAD,
> LONDON, S.W.,
> 6th July 1896

TO FRANCIS LEGGETT, ESQ.

DEAR SIR,

Herewith I constitute you as my attorney and representative in regards to all publication pamphlets etc., written or dictated by me, their copyright, sale, etc., in the U.S. of America.

Yours affectionately,
Vivekananda.

XCIV — MRS. BULL

To Mrs. Ole Bull:

63 ST. GEORGE'S ROAD,
LONDON, S.W.,
6th July 1896

DEAR MRS. BULL,

I have sent to Mr. Leggett by last mail the power of attorney, and, as you desired, this is to notify you of the fact and absolve you from the responsibilities of the power of attorney which I gave you in America last year.

Yours affectionately,
Vivekananda.

Saradananda and Goodwin have arrived, I am sure, by this time. I have a nice letter from Dr. Jain [Dr. Lewis G. Janes]. I am going to Switzerland for a vacation in a few days. I mean to stay there a month or more. I will return to London in the next fall. I do not know when I go back to India.

Things are growing nicely here.

With love to all.

XCV — MOTHER

To Mrs. G. W. Hale:

July 7, 1896

DEAR MOTHER,

[On the] 18th of this month I start for Switzerland for a holiday. I will come back to London again to work in the Autumn. The work in England bids fair to be much better and deeper than in the U.S. And here in London is the heart of India also. Where are you now? I am passing through Geneva on my way to the Hills. I will be there a day or two.

If you be somewhere near, I will make it a point to come to see you. Did you hear Annie Besant? How did you like her? What about your plans of going to India next winter? What about the innocents (Mary and Harriet Hale and Isabelle and Harriet McKindley.) at home? I haven't had any news of them. My love to Father Pope, Mother Temple (Mrs. James Matthews, Mr. Hale's sister.) and yourself. Kindly answer as I will be only a few days here.

Ever yours with love and gratitude,
Vivekananda.

XCVI — SIR

A letter to the editor, which appeared in the July 11, 1896 issue of the Light.

63, ST. GEORGE'S-ROAD, S.W.

SIR,

Allow me to put a few words in your estimable journal as comments on an article in your paper dated July 4th. I must thank you without reserve for the kind and friendly spirit manifested throughout the article towards me and the philosophy I preach; but, as there is a fear of misconstruction in one part of it — especially by my Spiritualistic friends — I want to clear my position. The truth of correspondence between the living and the dead is, I believe, in every religion, and nowhere more than in the Vedantic sects of India, where the fact of mutual help between the departed and the living has been made the basis of the law of inheritance. I would be very sorry if I be mistaken as antagonistic to any sect or form of religion, so far as they are sincere. Nor do I hold that any system can ever be judged by the frauds and failures that would naturally gather round every method under the present circumstances. But, all the same, I cannot but believe that every thoughtful person would agree with me when I affirm that people should be warned of their dangers, with love and sympathy. The lecture alluded to could but accidentally touch the subject of Spiritualism; but I take this opportunity of conveying my deep admiration for the Spiritualist community for the positive good they have done already, and are doing still: (1) the preaching of a universal sympathy; (2) the still greater work of helping the human race out of doctrines which inculcate fear and not love. Ever ready to co-operate with, and at the service of, all who are striving to bring the light of the spirit,

I remain yours sincerely,
Vive Kananda.

XCVII — MRS. BULL

To Mrs. Ole Bull:

63 ST. GEORGE'S ROAD,
18th July '96

DEAR MRS. BULL,

I received your last note duly — and you already know my gratitude and love for you and that I perfectly agree with most of your ideas and work.

I did not understand, however, one point. You speak of Sturdy and myself being members. Members of what? I, as you well know, can not become a member of any society.

I am very glad to learn that you have been favourably impressed by Saradananda. There is one big mistake you are labouring under. What do you mean of [my] writing to my workers more confidentially and not to you? I seldom write to anyone — I have no time to write. I have no workers. Everyone is independent to work as one likes. I do not bother my head about these little things at all. I can give ideas — that is all; let people work them out any way they like, and Godspeed to all.

"He who works unattached to persons and giving up the fruits of work is a genuine worker" — Gitâ.

Yours Ever with love and gratitude,
Vivekananda.

XCVIII — BLESSED AND BELOVED

To Sister Christine:

[POSTMARKED: SAAS-FEE],
SWITZERLAND.
5th August 1896

BLESSED AND BELOVED,

Surrounded on all sides by eternal snow peaks, sitting on the grass in a beautiful wood, my thoughts go to those I love — so I write.

I am in Switzerland — constantly on the move — getting a much needed rest. It is a miniature Himalayas, and has the same effect of raising the mind up to the Self and driving away all earthly feelings and ties. I am intensely enjoying it. I feel so, so uplifted. I cannot write, but I wish you will have the same for ever — when your feet do not want, as it were, to touch the material earth — when the soul finds itself floating, as it were, in an ocean of spirituality.

Prof. Max Müller has written in the Nineteenth Century an article on my Master. Read it if you can — August number.

I hope you are enjoying this beautiful summer and are perfectly rested after hard work.

My love to all. Blessings to all.

Yours ever with love and blessings,
Vivekananda.

P.S. A few Alpine flowers growing almost in the midst of eternal snow I send you, praying that you may attain spiritual hardihood amidst all snows and ice of this life.

XCIX — CHRISTINA

To Sister Christine:

> AIRLIE LODGE, RIDGEWAY GARDENS,
> WIMBLEDON, ENGLAND,
> October 6, 1896

DEAR CHRISTINA,

I am sure you got my letter from Switzerland.

I am now in London, back after having travelled through Germany and Holland.

How are things going with you? Had you a nice summer? How are you physically and spiritually? How is Mrs. Fhunkey [Funke] and all the other friends? Have you any news of Baby?[6]* Where is Kr [Kripananda] and what is he doing now?

I have another Sannyasin over here with me now, who will work here whilst I am away to India, where I go this winter.

I will write to you in extenso later; tonight it is so late and I am so weary.

With all love and blessings,

> Yours,
> Vivekananda.

C — NOBLE

To Sister Nivedita:

> 14, GREYCOAT GARDENS,
> WESTMINSTER,
> October 29, 1896

DEAR MISS [MARGARET] NOBLE,

I will be at yours on Friday next, at 4 p.m.

I did not know of any arrangements made to meet anybody Friday last, hence my absence.

> Yours,
> Vivekananda.

CI — MISS NOBLE

To Sister Nivedita:

> 14, GREYCOAT GARDENS,
> WESTMINSTER, S.W.,
> 5 December 1896

DEAR MISS NOBLE,

Many thanks for sending the kind present from Mr. Beatty. I have written to him acknowledging his beautiful gift.

As for you, my dear, noble, kind friend, I only would say this — we Indians lack in many things, but there is none on earth to beat us in gratefulness. I remain,

> Ever yours gratefully,
> Vivekananda.

CII — CHRISTINA

To Sister Christine:

> ON BOARD PRINZ REGENT LUITPOLD,
> 3rd January 1897.

DEAR CHRISTINA,

By two p.m. today I reach Port Said. Asia once more. I have not heard from you [for] long. Hope everything is going on well with you. How are Mrs. Funke, Mrs. Phelps, and all other friends?

My love to all.

> Write when you feel like it,
> Vivekananda.

CIII — MADRAS COMITTEE

To the Madras Committee:

[After Swami Vivekananda Colombo on Friday, January 15, 1897, the Madras Committee, which was planning a reception for the Swami, sent the following

message: "Motherland rejoices to welcome you back". In reply, Swami Vivekananda sent a wire.]

[Postmarked: January 15, 1897]

MY LOVE AND GRATITUDE TO MY COUNTRYMEN.

CIV — GENTLEMEN

To the Hindu Students of Trichinapally:

[February 16, 1897]

GENTLEMEN,

I have received your address with great pleasure and sincerely thank you for the kind expressions contained therein.

I much regret, however, that time effectually prevents my paying even a short visit to Trichinopoly at present. In the autumn, however, I propose making a lecture tour throughout India, and you may rely upon it that I shall then not fail to include Trichinopoly in the programme.

Again thanking you, and with my blessings to all.

Sincerely yours,
Vivekananda.

CV — CHRISTINA

To Sister Christine:

DARJEELING,,
[RETURN ADDRESS: ALAMBAZAR MATH, CALCUTTA],
16th March 1897.

DEAR CHRISTINA,

Many, many thanks for the photograph and the poem. I never saw anything half as beautiful. The work I had to do to reach Calcutta from Ceylon was so immense that I could not earlier acknowledge your precious gift. The work has broken me down completely, and I have got "diabetes", an incurable disease, which must carry me off — at least in a few years.

I am now writing to you from Darjeeling, the nearest hill station to Calcutta, with a climate as cool as London. It has revived me a bit. If I live, I will come to America next year or so.

How are things going on with you all? How are Mrs. Funkey [Funke] and Mrs. Phelps?

Are you laying by a few dollars whenever you can? That is very important.

I am in a hurry for the mail. You will be glad to know that the Indian people have, as it were, risen in a mass to honour me. I am the idol of the day. Mr. Goodwin is going to publish in book form all the addresses given to me and the speeches in reply. The demonstrations all over have been simply unique.

Yours with all love,
Vivekananda.

CVI — MRS. BULL

To Mrs. Ole Bull:

ALAMBAZAR MATH,
CALCUTTA,
[DARJEELING],
26th March 1897

DEAR MRS. BULL,

The demonstrations and national jubilations over me are over — at least I had to cut them short, as my health broke completely down. The result of this steady work in the West and the tremendous work of a month in India upon the Bengalee constitution is "diabetes". It is a hereditary foe and is destined to carry me off, at best, in a few years' time. Eating only meat and drinking no water seems to be the only way to prolong life — and, above all, perfect rest for the brain. I am giving my brain the needed rest in Darjeeling, from where I am writing you now.

I am so glad to hear about Saradananda's success. Give him my best love and do not allow him [to] do too much work. The Bengalee body is not the same as the American.

Mr. Chatterjy (Mohini) came to see me in Calcutta, and he was very friendly. I gave him your message. He is quite willing to work with me. Nothing more to write, only I am bent upon seeing my monastery started; and as soon as that is done, I come to America once more.

By the by, I will send to you a young lady from England — one Gertrude Orchard. She has been a governess, but she has talent in art etc., and I wished her to try her chance in America. I will give her a letter to you and Mrs. [Florence] Adams.

With my love to Mrs. Adams, Miss Thursby, Miss Farmer (the noble sister) and all the rest of our friends.

With eternal love and gratitude,

Yours affectionately,
Vivekananda.

CVII — RAM RAM

Translated from Bengali

To Pandit Ram Ram Samjami:

DARJEELING,
[April] 1897

DEAR RAM RAM,

I received your first letter in Calcutta. I was busy there, and so it seems that I forgot to reply. You have deplored this in your letter, but that is not right. I do not forget anyone — especially those who have received grace from "Him".

While I was in England, I received your Avadhuta-Gîtâ. It is beautifully printed. You mentioned Karma-Yoga — I do not have that book with me. It was printed in Madras. If there are any copies at the Math, I shall ask them to send one to you.

I have been very sick, so right now I am staying at Darjeeling. As soon as I feel better, I shall return to Calcutta...

Please accept my special love. I pray for your welfare always.

Yours etc.,
Vivekananda.

CVIII — MISS NOBLE

To Sister Nivedita:

DARJEELING,
3rd April 1897.

DEAR MISS NOBLE,

I have just found a bit of important work for you to do on behalf of the downtrodden masses of India.

The gentleman I take the liberty of introducing to you is in England on behalf of the Tiyas, a plebeian caste in the native State of Malabar.

You will realize from this gentleman what an amount of tyranny there is over these poor people, simply because of their caste.

The Indian Government has refused to interfere on grounds of non-interference in the internal administration of a native State. The only hope of these people is the English Parliament. Do kindly everything in your power to help this matter [in] being brought before the British Public.

Ever yours in the truth,
Vivekananda.

CIX — LALAJEE

To Lala Badri Sah of Almora

DARJEELING,
7th April '97.

DEAR LALAJEE,

Just received your kind invitation through telegram. Perhaps you have already heard that I have been attacked by "Diabetes", a fell disease.

That unsettled all our plans, and I had to run up to Darjeeling, it being very cool and very good for the disease.

I have felt much better since, and the doctors therefore do not want me to move about, as that brings about a relapse. If my present state of health continues for a month or two, I think I will be in a condition to come down to the plains and come to Almora to see you all. I am very sorry that I have caused you a good deal of trouble, but you see it could not be helped — the body was not under my control.

With all love to yourself and other friends in Almora.

Yours affectionately,
Vivekananda.

CX — BADRI SAH

To Lala Badri Sah:

DEVALDHAR BAGICHA,
Thursday, [June 1897]

DEAR BADRI SAH,

I have been very sorry to learn that you are not well. It would please me very much if you would come down here for a few days, at any rate, with us; and I am sure it would do you good.

Yours with blessings,
Vivekananda.

CXI — MOTHER

To Mrs. Francis Leggett:

ALMORA,
20 June '97

DEAR MOTHER,

Herewith I take the liberty to introduce to you Miss Tremayne of London, a particular friend of mine going over to the States.

Any help given to her would greatly oblige.

Yours in the Lord,
Vivekananda.

CXII — MRS. BULL

To Mrs. Ole Bull:

ALMORA,
20 June '97

DEAR MRS. BULL,

Herewith I take the liberty of introducing Miss Tremayne of London.

I like nothing so much as being serviceable to young and energetic persons — and any help given to her in America will greatly oblige.

Yours in the Lord,
Vivekananda.

CXIII — FRIEND

To Mr. Sokanathan, Colombo:

ALMORA,
30th June 1897.

MY DEAR FRIEND,

The bearer of this note, Swami Shivananda, is [being] sent to Ceylon, as promised by me during my sojourn. He is quite fit for the work entrusted to his care, of course, with your kind help.

I hope you will introduce him to other Ceylon friends.

Yours ever in the Lord,
Vivekananda.

CXIV — SHIVANANDA

Translated from Bengali

To Swami Shivananda:

ALMORA,
The 9th July 1897

DEAR SHIVANANDA, (This address was written in English)

I haven't received any word of your arrival yet. I heard that Alasinga has gone there with his relations by way of Jaipur. We stayed at the Binsar Dak Bungalow [rest-house] for two or three days, and then I left for Shyamdhura. At this, Miss [Henrietta] Müller got infuriated and left for Almora. Terribly upset, Miss Müller accused Shivananda of telling her first that I shall live with a friend as his guest and of renting later such a big house for the season at 80 rupees without consulting her. Very cross with everybody, she has been reproving one and all but has cooled down a little when I said I would pay half of the rent...

Shashi himself [Swami Ramakrishnananda] should handle the entire amount of 100 rupees which the Raja of Ramnad is donating (every month); he should send a detailed account of the monthly income and expenditure to the Math — otherwise there won't be any check. Advise him to spend as little as necessary on Thakur's worship, for the money is [primarily] "for propagation of Truth".

The phrase "for propagation of Truth" was written in English.)

In case Gupta [Swami Sadananda] has lost his mental balance, ask him to come to Almora — but only when the boy selected for Shashi reaches there. I received a letter from R. A. [Rajam Aiyer?]. The money he sent has reached the Math. I have received two volumes of Ramanuja's commentary. Advise him to send me the third. Ask G. G. [Narasimhachari] to send me similar commentaries by Madhva and others, if he can.

A public meeting will have to be organized at Madras to present an address of welcome to the Raja [Ajit Singh] of Khetri and to Pratap Singh of Jodhpur for their boldness in visiting England as well as for representing their principalities in India in the Jubilee celebration. This has to be done on their return to India, but for that you have to endeavour from now on. Please go to Colombo and arrange a similar public meeting there.

Give my love to Kidi [Singaravelu Mudaliar] and Doctor [Nanjunda Rao]; ask Kidi why he hasn't written to me. What is wrong with him? Has he lost his devotion? Bear this in mind that you should not assume a teacher's place in the beginning. Do all your work with humility; otherwise everything will crumble to pieces. Please see that there is no opposition, criticism or obstacles to Shashi's work in Madras, for everybody should obey him — whoever may be in charge of a particular centre. If Shashi goes to Ceylon, he will have to obey your authority, etc. Make sure that every centre sends a weekly report to the Math. I have not seen a single one from Shashi yet. "O Rama! How hard it is to turn a donkey into a horse, even by beating!"

Above all "obedience" and "esprit de corps".[1] The work cannot succeed unless there is perfect obedience to the authority of the Order and sacrifice of individual views for the sake of the Order. Trinair gunatvam âpannair badhyante mattadantinah — "Blades of grass woven into a rope can restrain even mad elephants".

With love to Sashi and Gupta,
Vivekananda.

CXV — CHRISTINA

To Sister Christine:

KHETRI,
13th December 1897.

MY DEAR CHRISTINA,

How funny all these dreams and evil prognostications of yours! You don't want to send me evil influ-

---
1. Swami Vivekananda wrote this sentence in English. The French Phrase *esprit de corps* means "the spirit of loyalty".

ences by thinking that way of me! I will be only too glad to lose 50 lbs. of my weight. A little rest puffs me up, and I am the same bloated monk as ever.

I am all right except [for] a bad cold the last few days, owing to exposure and travel in the desert. I thank you for the letter though. I am pleased with it enormously, as it shows the mind.

Give Mrs. Funkey [Funke], Baby [Stella Campbell], and all the rest my love, and, as you know, yourself —

Yours ever in the Lord,
Vivekananda.

PS — I will write a better note when this cold has left.

CXVI — SISTER CHRISTINE

To Sister Christine:

JODHPUR, RAJPUTANA,
4th January 1898.

Love and greetings etc. to thee, dear Christina, and a happy New Year. May it find you younger in heart, stronger in body, and purer in spirit.

I am still travelling in season and out of season. Lecturing some, working a good deal.

Have you seen Mr. [Edward T.] Sturdy of England, who, I learn, has been to Detroit? Did you like him?

I am quite well and strong. Hope to meet you this blessed year again in America.

I am going to Calcutta in a few days, where I intend to be the rest of this cold weather. Next summer, I start for England or America most probably.

Yours ever in the Lord,
Vivekananda.

CXVII — MISS NOBLE

To Sister Nivedita:

CALCUTTA,
30th January 1898

MY DEAR MISS NOBLE,

This is to introduce Prof. M. Gupta, who has been already introduced to you on board the boat that brought you over to shore.

He has very kindly consented to devote an hour or more every day to teach you Bengali. I need not state that he is a genuine, good and great soul.

Yours ever in the Lord,
Vivekananda.

P.S. I am afraid you felt badly today.

CXVIII — CHRISTINA

To Sister Christine:

THE MATH, BELOOR, HOWRAH DIST.,
BENGAL, INDIA,
11th March 1898.

MY DEAR CHRISTINA,

I simply wonder what has become of you. It is an age [that] I did not hear from you, and I expected so much after Sturdy's visit to Detroit. How did you like the man? What about Baby and the Devendorfs? How is Mrs. Funkey [Funke]? What are you going to do this summer? Take rest, dear Christina; I am sure you require it badly.

Mrs. Bull of Boston and Miss MacLeod of New York are now in India. We have changed our Math from the old, nasty house to a house on the banks of the Ganges. This is much more healthy and beautiful. We have also got a good piece of land very near on the same side where Mrs. Bull and Miss MacLeod are putting up now. It is wonderful how they accommodate themselves to our Indian life of privation and hardship! My, these Yanks can do anything! After the luxuries of Boston and New York, to be quite content and happy in this wretched little house!! We intend to travel a bit together in Kashmir, and then I come to America with them and am sure to get a hearty welcome from my friends. What do you think? Is it welcome news to you? Of course, I cannot undergo the same amount of work as before; that, dear Christina, I am sorry, I will no more be able to do. I will do a little work and [take] a good deal of rest. No more getting crowds and making noise, but quiet, silent, personal work will be all I intend to do.

This time I will quietly come and quietly go away, seeing only my old friends, and no noise.

Write soon, as I am so anxious.

Yours ever in the Lord,
Vivekananda.

"There are two sorts of persons — one sort has the heart of water, the other of stone. The one easily takes an impression, and as easily throws it off; the other seldom takes an impression, but once it takes, it is there for ever. Nay, the more they struggle to cast it off, the more it cuts deep into the stone soul." — R. K. [Ramakrishna] Paramahamsa

CXIX — MARGARET

To Sister Nivedita:

MATH, BELUR,
HOWRAH, BENGAL,
16th March 1898.

MY DEAR MARGARET,

It is needless to let you know, you have fulfilled all my expectations in your last lecture.

It appears to me that the platform is the great field where you will be of great help to me, apart from your educational plans. I am glad to learn that Miss [Henrietta] Müller is going to have a place on the river. Are you also going to Darjeeling? So you will all the better work after a trip up there! Next season I am planning a series of lectures for you all over India.

Ever yours with all love and blessings,
[Stamp with Swamiji's portrait]
The Calcutta boy

CXX — DHIRA MATA

To Mrs. Ole Bull:

DARJEELING,
The 4th April '98

MY DEAR DHIRA MATA,

I am afraid you are getting roasted down there in the heat of Calcutta. Here it is nice and cool and rather chill when it rains, which it does almost every day. Yesterday the view of the snows was simply superb, and it is the most picturesque city in the world; there is such a mass of colour everywhere, especially in the dress of the Lepchas and Bhutias and the Paharees. Had it not been for the awful, corrugated iron roofs everywhere, it would have been twenty times more picturesque.

My health was not bad in Calcutta; here it is the same — only, the sugar has entirely disappeared, the specific gravity being only 13. I slept very well last night too; but the morning ride up, or climb, of a few miles is proving too much for my adipose tissues. The flannel clothes only made me worse, so I have given them up and have gone to my summer dress and am all right.

I have sent you Sturdy's letter already — poor fellow — I do not know what to do for him. He is really "living in a desert of his own making" — you see, one thing is not good for every one. Marriage has indeed proved a hell for Sturdy. And he can not come, although "he is skirting the coast of India". Lord help the poor boy. May He cut all his bonds and make him free soon. Aye, it is good that he is feeling the bondage — and not "hugging and kissing its spokes of agony".

I gave a little lecture to the Hindus here yesterday, and I told them all their defects purposely and with their permission. I hope it will make them howl.

Miss Müller has taken a bungalow here and she is

coming on Wednesday. I do not know whether Miss Noble is coming with her. She [Miss Noble] had better be your guest in Kashmir as according to our plan.

Have you got that place yet or changed [places]? I am going to Kashmir anyway, as I have promised.

I will be here only a few days and then I come to Calcutta, to be there only a week — and [then] I start for the N.W. Of course this is not the time to see anything in the N.W.P.; (North-West Provinces, now Uttar Pradesh.) everything is burning there. Yet that heat is much healthier than that of Bengal.

Yours ever in the Lord,
Vivekananda.

CXXI — JAGMOHAN

To Munshi Jagmohanlal:

BALLEN VILLE,
DARJEELING,
15 April 1898

MY DEAR JAGMOHAN,

If you can find out all the letters that I addressed to H.H. on my way to — and stay in — Japan, Europe and America, please do send them carefully packed, under registered cover, to my address in the Math, as early as possible.

With blessing to you, I remain,

Yours truly,
Vivekananda.

CXXII — MISS MACLEOD

To Miss Josephine MacLeod:

DARJEELING,
19th April '98

MY DEAR MISS MACLEOD,

Miss Müller is very glad to learn that you intend inviting Miss Noble to join our party to Kashmir.

It has her hearty approval. On her way back, Miss Müller will start something for her in Calcutta. She need not come to Darjeeling at all.

Hope you are enjoying the baking quite a bit. I start this week most probably.

Yours ever in the Lord,
Vivekananda.

CXXIII — SIR

To the Officer in Charge of Telegrams, Srinagar:

April 19, 1898.

SIR,

Please allow Miss M'cLeod [MacLeod] or her agent to receive any telegrams that you have received for me and receipt the same.

Yours truly,
Vivekananda.

CXXIV — MISS MACLEOD / MRS. BULL

To Miss Josephine MacLeod or Mrs. Ole Bull:

SESHNAG,
CHANDANBARI, KASHMIR,
[EN ROUTE FROM SRINAGAR TO AMARNATH],
[End of July 1898]

I send back the old Dandi (A simple palanquin.) as it is difficult to carry it through. I have got another like Margaret's. Please send it back to the Tahsildar of Vernag, Khand Chand, Esq., whom you already know. We are all right. Margot has discovered some new flowers and is happy. There is not much ice so the road is good.

Yours affectionately,
Vivekananda.

P.S. Keep this Dandi till I come and pay the coolies (2) 4 Rs., 2 annas each.

CXXV — MR. J. J. GOODWIN'S MOTHER

To Mr. J. J. Goodwin's mother:

[On receiving news of the untimely death of Josiah J. Goodwin, Swami Vivekananda sent the following paragraph along with the poem "Requiescat in Pace" (This poem has been previously published in Complete Works, IV.) to the newspapers as well as to Goodwin's mother.]

ALMORA,
June 1898

With infinite sorrow I learn the sad news of Mr. Goodwin's departure from this life, the more so as it was terribly sudden and therefore prevented all possibilities of my being at his side at the time of death. The debt of gratitude I owe him can never be repaid, and those who think they have been helped by any thought of mine ought to know that almost every word of it was published through the untiring and most unselfish exertions of Mr. Goodwin. In him I have lost a friend true as steel, a disciple of never — failing devotion, a worker who knew not what tiring was, and the world is less rich by one of those few who are born, as it were, to live only for others.

[UNSIGNED]

CXXVI — YOUR HIGHNESS

To Maharaja Ajit Singh, the Raja of Khetri:

SRINAGAR,
10 August 1898

YOUR HIGHNESS,

I have long not heard any news of you. How are things going on with you both bodily and mentally?

I have been to see Shri Amarnathji. It was a very enjoyable trip and the Darshana was glorious.

I will be here about a month more, then I return to the plains. Kindly ask Jagmohan to write to the Dewan Saheb of Kishangarh to get for me the copies of Nimbârka Bhâshya which he promised.

With all love,

Yours,
Vivekananda.

CXXVII — CHRISTINA

To Sister Christine:

THE MATH, BELOOR, HOWRAH DIST.,
25th October, 1898.

MY DEAR CHRISTINA,

How are you? I am very anxious about your health. I have long not had any letter from you.

My health again failed badly. I had, therefore, to leave Kashmir in haste and come to Calcutta. The doctors say I ought not go tramping again this winter. That is such a disappointment, you know. However, I am coming to the U. S. this summer. Mrs. Bull and Miss MacLeod enjoyed this year's trip to Kashmir immensely, and now they are having a glimpse of the old monuments and buildings of Delhi, Agra, Jeypore [Jaipur], etc.

Do write a nice, long letter if you have time, and do not work yourself to death. Duty is duty, no doubt; but we have our duties, not only to our mother etc., but to others also. Sometimes one duty asks for physical sacrifice, whilst the other insists on great care for our health. Of course, we follow the stronger motive, and [I] do not know which will prove stronger in your case. Anyhow, take great care of your body, now that your sisters have come to your help.

How do you manage the family? — the expenses etc? Write me all you like to write. Give me a long chat, will you? Do!

I am getting better every day — and then the long months before I can start for the U.S. Never mind, "Mother" knows what is best for us. She will show the way. I am now in Bhakti. As I am growing old, Bhakti is taking the place of Jnâna. Did you get the new Awakened India? How do you like it?

Ever yours in the Lord,
Vivekananda.

CXXVIII — YOUR HIGHNESS

Maharaja Ajit Singh, the Raja of Khetri:

MATH BELUR,
22 November 1898

YOUR HIGHNESS,

Many thanks for your kind note and the Nimbarka Bhashya — reached through Jaga Mohan Lalji.

I approach your Highness today on a most important business of mine, knowing well that I have not the least shame in opening my mind to you, and that I consider you as my only friend in this life. If the following appeals to you, good; if not, pardon my foolishness as a friend should.

As you know already, I have been ailing since my return. In Calcutta your Highness assured me of your friendship and help for me personally and [advised me] not to be worried about this incurable malady. This disease has been caused by nervous excitement; and no amount of change can do me good, unless the worry and anxiety and excitement are taken off me.

After trying these two years a different climate, I am getting worse every day and now almost at death's door. I appeal to your Highness's work, generosity and friendship. I have one great sin rankling always in my breast, and that is [in order] to do a service to the world, I have sadly neglected my mother. Again, since my second brother has gone away, she has become awfully worn-out with grief. Now my last desire is to make Sevâ [give service] and serve my mother, for some years at least. I want to live with my mother and get my younger brother married to prevent extinction of the family. This will certainly smoothen my last days as well as those of my mother. She lives now in a hovel. I want to build a little, decent home for her and make some provision for the youngest, as there is very little hope of his being a good earning man. Is it too much for a royal descendent of Ramchandra to do for one he loves and calls his friend? I do not know whom else to appeal to. The money I got from Europe was for the "work", and every penny almost has been given over to that work. Nor can I beg of others for help for my own self. About my own family affairs — I have exposed myself to your Highness, and none else shall know of it. I am tired, heartsick and dying. Do, I pray, this last great work of kindness to me, befitting your great and generous nature and [as] a crest to the numerous kindnesses you have shown me. And as your Highness will make my last days smooth and easy, may He whom I have tried to serve all my life ever shower His choicest blessings on you and yours.

Ever yours in the Lord,
Vivekananda.

P.S. This is strictly private. Will you please drop a wire to me whether you will do it or not?

CXXIX — YOUR HIGHNESS

To Maharaja Ajit Singh, the Raja of Khetri:

MATH BELOOR,
HOWRAH DISTRICT,
1 December 1898

YOUR HIGHNESS,

Your telegram has pleased me beyond description, and it is worthy of your noble self. I herewith give you the details of what I want.

The lowest possible estimate of building a little home in Calcutta is at least ten thousand rupees. With that it is barely possible to buy or build a house in some out-of-the-way quarter of the town — a little house fit for four or five persons to live in.

As for the expenses of living, the 100 Rs. a month your generosity is supplying my mother is enough for her. If another 100 Rs. a month be added to it for my lifetime for my expenses — which unfortunately this illness has increased, and which, I hope, will not be for long a source of trouble to you, as I expect only to live a few years at best — I will be perfectly happy. One thing more will I beg of you — if possible, the 100 Rs. a month for my mother be made permanent, so that even after my death it may regularly reach her. Or even if your Highness ever gets reasons to stop your love and kindness for me, my poor old mother may be provided [for], remembering the love you once had for a poor Sâdhu.

This is all. Do this little work amongst the many other noble deeds you have done, knowing well whatever else can be proved or not, the power of Karma is self-evident to all. The blessings of this good Karma shall always follow you and yours. As for me, what shall I say — whatever I am in the world has been almost all through your help. You made it possible for me to get rid of a terrible anxiety and face the world and do some work. It may be that you are destined by the Lord to be the instrument again of helping yet grander work, by taking this load off my mind once more.

But whether you do this or not, "once loved is always loved". Let all my love and blessings and prayers follow you and yours, day and night, for what I owe you already; and may the Mother, whose play is this universe and in whose hands we are mere instruments, always protect you from all evil.

Ever yours in the Lord,
Vivekananda.

CXXX — MARGOT

To Sister Nivedita:

3 p.m. Sunday,
[Early 1899]

MY DEAR MARGOT,

I am sorry I cannot come to see Dr. Mahoney — I am ill. I have not yet broken my fast.

Have you stopped teaching my little cousin?

Yours with love,
Vivekananda.

CXXXI — NIVEDITA

To Sister Nivedita:

[Early 1899?]

MY DEAR NIVEDITA,

The address of my cousin is 127 Manicktala Street. The husband's name is Durga Prasanna Bose. The wife's name is most probably not known to the people you will meet in the male department. Therefore it is the custom to ask for the wife of so-and-so.

Manicktala Street is that which runs east and west, south of the tank garden.

Yours with love,
Vivekananda.

CXXXII — CHRISTINA

To Sister Christine:

THE MATH, BELUR,
DIST. HOWRAH, BENGAL, INDIA,
|26th January 1899.

MY DEAR CHRISTINA,

Excuse this long delay in replying to your very beautiful note. The fact is, I was once more in the vale of death. The old diabetes has now disappeared. In its place has come what some doctors call asthma, others dyspepsia, owing to nervous prostration. However, it is a most worrying disease, giving one the sensation of suffocation — sometimes for days. I am best only in Calcutta; so I am here for rest and quiet and low diet. If I get well by March, I am going to start for Europe. Mrs. Bull and others are gone; sorry I could not accompany them owing to this disease.

I have carefully weighed your plans for coming over. I will be ever so glad to see you, you know it well; but, my dear, the Indian summer will not suit you, and if you start now it will be midsummer when you reach India. Then, you must not hope of making any living here. It is impossible for me to make a living most times in my own country. Then all the surroundings are so, so wretched and different from what you see around you, e.g. you will find me going about in loin-cloth — will that shock you? Three-fourths of the population only wearing a strip of white cloth about their loins — can you bear that?

I must stop here; I am so weak. If I do not get well by March, I will write you to come, for I wish it ever so much to see you once before I pass away.

Do not be the least anxious, dear. Things must be as "Mother" wishes. Ours is only to obey and work

Ever yours in the Lord,
Vivekananda.

PS. Mrs. Bull will reach Cambridge, Mass., soon. You may write to her there on the particulars.

PPS. I have again lost your address. Please give the correct one in your next.

CXXXIII — RAJA

To Swami Brahmananda:

THE MATH, BELUR,
Friday [March (?) 1899]

MY DEAR RAJA,

Please pay 100 Rs. to Sister Nivedita immediately for plague work and credit it to a separate plague account.

Ever yours in the Lord,
Vivekananda.

CXXXIV — S

To Swami Swarupananda, editor of Prabuddha Bharata, Mayavati:

[March 1899]

MY DEAR S[WARUPANANDA],

I have no objection whether Mrs. Sevier's name goes on top or mine or anybody else's; the prospectus ought to go in the name of the Seviers, mustering my name also if necessary. I send you a [6]few lines for your consideration in the prospectus. The rest are all right.

I will soon send the draft deed.

Vivekananda.

CXXXV — MARGOT

To Sister Nivedita:

THE MATH, BELUR,
March 2nd, 1899

MY DEAR MARGOT,

Will you look into your trunks for a Sanskrit book of mine, which was, you know, in your keeping in Kashmir. I do not find it in our library here.

I have been thinking of your friend Miss [Sarala] Ghosal's coming to see the Math on Sunday. The difficulty is here. The ebb tide will be on till 5 p.m. In that case our big boat can go down easily to bring the party up; and going back, if the party starts long before 5 p.m., say 4 p.m., will be all right. To come up will take at least two hours from Baghbazar. If the party starts from Baghbazar — say at 12 a.m. — and reaches the Math at 2 p.m. for lunch and then starts back by 4 p.m., it will be nice.

If you cannot start as early as that, I will advise you to send the carriage to wait at Baranagore on the other side so that our boat can ferry the party over any time they like. The boat journey in that case will only be on coming.

With all love and blessings,
Vivekananda.

CXXXVI — SIR

To Ishwar Chandra Ghosh:

> MATH, BELUR,
> HOWRAH DIST.,
> 6th March '99

MY DEAR SIR,

Many thanks for your kind invitation. I am so sorry that so many days' delay should occur in reply to your note.

I was very ill at the time, and the gentleman on whom the duty fell of replying could not do it, it seems. I got notice of it just now.

I am not yet sufficiently recovered to take advantage of your kindness. This winter I had made it a point of visiting your part of the country. But my Karma will have otherwise. I will have to wait to give myself the pleasure of visiting the seat of civilisation of ancient Bengal.

With my thanks again for all your kindness, I remain,

> Yours in the Lord,
> Vivekananda.

CXXXVII — MARGOT

To Sister Nivedita:

> THE MATH, BELUR,
> March 2nd, 1899

MY DEAR MARGOT,

I could not come today. I am so, so sorry. The body would not allow — neither can I come to the Boses'. I have written to them.

I have an engagement tomorrow.

Possibly I may see you in the evening.

> With all love and blessings,
> Vivekananda.

CXXXVIII — CHRISTINA

To Sister Christine:

> THE MATH, BELUR,
> DIST. HOWRAH, BENGAL, INDIA,
> 10th May 1899.

MY DEAR CHRISTINA,

I am getting better again. In my mind the whole of my complaint is bad assimilation of food and nervous exhaustion. The first, I am taking care of; the second will completely pass off when I meet you again. The great joy of meeting old, old friends, you know! Cheer up! There is no cause for anxiety. Do not believe a single desponding line I write now, because I am at times not myself. I get so nervous.

I start this summer for Europe anyway, as you say in America. With all love and blessings,

> Yours ever in the Lord,
> Vivekananda.

CXXXIX — MISS MACLEOD

To Miss Josephine MacLeod:

[When Swami Vivekananda sailed from Calcutta, he dispatched the following cablegram.]

> [CALCUTTA,
> June 21, 1899]

STARTED. WIRE STURDY.

CXL — CHRISTINA

To Sister Christine:

> SUEZ,
> 14th July 1899.

MY DEAR CHRISTINA,

You see this time I am really out, and hope to reach London in two weeks. I am sure to come to

America this year and earnestly hope will have the opportunity of seeing you. I am so materialistic yet, you know! Want to see my friends in the gross body.

I had a beautiful letter from Baby [Stella Campbell] before I left. I am soon going to pen a reply to your care, as directed. I could not write her earlier.

I was so, so bad in health in India. My heart went wrong all the way — what with mountain climbing, bathing in glacier water and nervous prostration! I used to get terrible fits [of asthma] — the last lasting about seven days and nights. All the time I was suffocating and had to stand up.

This trip has almost made a new man of me. I feel much better and, if this continues, hope to be quite strong before I reach America. How are you? What are you doing? Write everything about yourself, c/o E. T. Sturdy Esq., 25 Holland Villas Road, London, W.

With everlasting love and blessings,

Yours ever in the Lord,
Vivekananda.

days are long enough for all the chatter I will assail you with.

We go to Wimbledon for a day or two, and then I come back to London and find lodgings for myself and make plans.

Come to the Dock if that is possible and discreet. Yes, it is discreet, as there is a lady in the party and others will come to meet her. Only, Christina, don't if you feel the least tired or unwell. I hope you are enjoying London immensely.

The Orientals do not like any effusion of feeling. They are trained to hide all expression.

Is Mrs. Funkey [Mary Caroline Funke] with you? If so, give her my best love.

I am much, much better just now. I am really quite another man this time. I was nearly dead in Calcutta when I started, but this voyage has improved me immensely.

Hoping soon to see you,

Ever yours in the Lord,
Vivekananda.

CXLI — CHRISTINA

To Sister Christine:

MARSEILLES,
23rd July 1899.

MY DEAR CHRISTINA,

Your very, very welcome wire just came. By next Sunday we arrive in London, Albert Dock. We are a party of four: myself, another Sannyasin, a Calcutta boy going to study in America, and Miss [Margaret] Noble. Miss Noble is a young lady from Wimbledon, near London, who has been working in India on the education of girls.

Our stay in England will not be long, I am afraid, as this is neither the season nor am I in fit condition to work much. Anyhow, we will be in London a few weeks — at least myself — then go to the U.S. We will talk over all this and infinite things besides when we meet. I do not think even English summer

CXLII — SISTER CHRISTINE

To Sister Christine:

TELEGRAM

TO:

CHRISTINA GRINNSTIDEL
[GREENSTIDEL],
23 CROWIIURST RD., ANGELL RD.,
BRIATON, LDN.

30 July 1899

GOLCONDA DUE DOCKS 6 AM MONDAY. (Vide Swami Vivekananda's letter dated)

CXLIII — MOTHER

To Mrs. Ole Bull:

> THE LYMES, WOODSIDE,
> WIMBLEDON, ENGLAND,
> 6 August 1899

MY DEAR MOTHER,

Your letter directed to Sturdy at hand. I am very thankful for your kind words. As for me, I don't know what I am to do next or anything to do at all. On board the steamer I was all right, but since landing [I am] feeling quite bad again. As to mental worry, there has been enough of late. The aunt whom you saw had a deep-laid plan to cheat me, and she and her people contrived to sell me a house for 6,000 Rs., or £400, and I bought [it] for my mother in good faith. Then they would not give me possession, hoping that I would not go to court for the shame of taking forcible possession as a Sannyasin.

I do not think I have spent even one rupee from what you and others gave me for the work. Cap. Sevier gave me 8,000 Rs. with the express desire of helping my mother. This money, it seems, has [also] gone to the dogs. Beyond this, nothing has been spent on my family or even on my own personal expenses — my food etc. being paid for by the Khetri Raja, and more than half of that went to the Math every month. Only, if Brahmananda spends some in the lawsuit [against the aunt], as I must not be robbed that way — if he does, I will make it good anyway, if I live to do it.

The money which I got in Europe and America by lecturing alone, I spent just as I like; but every cent I got for the work has been accounted for and is in the Math, and the whole thing ought to be clear as daylight if Brahmananda never cheated me. I don't believe he will ever cheat me. I got a letter at Aden from Saradananda that they were preparing an account. I have not received any yet.

I have no plans yet, nor care to make any. Neither do I wish to work. Let the Mother find other workers. I have my burden enough already.

> Ever your devoted son,
> Vivekananda.

CXLIV — ISABEL

To Miss Isabelle McKindley:

> RIDGELY MANOR,
> STONE RIDGE, N.Y.,
> 31st August '99

MY DEAR ISABEL,

Many thanks for your kind note. I will be so, so glad to see you. Miss M'cLeod [MacLeod] is going to write you to stop a day and a night here on your way to the West.

My love to the holy family in Chicago, and hope surely to be able to come West and have great fun.

So you are in Greenacre at last. Is this the first year you have been there? How do you like the place? [You have] seen Miss Farmer, of course. Kindly convey her my kindest regards and to all the rest of my friends there.

> Ever yours affectionately,
> Vivekananda.

CXLV — CHRISTINA

To Sister Christine:

> RIDGELY MANOR,
> 20th September 1899.

DEAR CHRISTINA,

I am much better, thank you. Hitherto, excepting three days, there has not been any wet weather to speak of here. Miss [Margaret] Noble came yesterday, and we are having a jolly good time. I am very, very sorry to say I am growing fat again. That is bad. I will eat less and grow thin once more.

You are again at work — so do I find — only with a little variation of the old occupation. Better rest than mere idling. Do you like my new poem? (Vide letter.) Miss Noble thinks it is nice. But that is her way with everything I do. So you also say. I will now send my writings to missionary papers to get a fierce criticism.

With all love to you and Mrs. Funkey [Funke],

Ever yours affectionately,
Vivekananda.

CXLVI — MOTHER CHURCH

To Mrs. G. W. Hale:

RIDGELY MANOR,
5 October 1899

MY DEAR MOTHER CHURCH,

Many, many thanks for your kind words.

I am so glad you are working on as ever. I am glad because the wave of optimism has not caught you yet. It is all very well to say everything is right, but that is apt to degenerate into a sort of laissez-faire. I believe with you that the world is evil — made more hideous with a few dashes of good.

All our works have only this value, that they awaken some to the reality of this horror — and [those] flee for refuge to some place beyond, which is called God, or Christ, or Brahma, or Buddha, etc. Names do not make much difference.

Again, we must always remember ours is only to work — we never attain results. How can we? Good can never be done without doing evil. We cannot breathe a breath without killing thousands of poor little animals. National prosperity is another name for death and degradation to millions of other races. So is individual prosperity the beggaring of many. The world is evil — and will ever remain so. It is its nature, and cannot be changed — "Which one of you by taking thought…" etc. (Matthew 6.27.)

Such is truth. The wisdom is therefore in renunciation, that is, to make the Lord our all in all. Be a true Christian, Mother — like Christ, renounce everything and let the heart and soul and body belong to Him and Him alone. All this nonsense which people have built round Christ's name is not His teaching. He taught to renounce. He never says the earth is an enjoyable place. And your time has come to get rid of all vanities — even the love of children and husband — and think of the Lord and Him alone.

Ever your Son,
Vivekananda.

CXLVII — MOTHER

To Mrs. G. W. Hale:

[RIDGELY MANOR],
NEW YORK, N.Y.,
23 October 1899

MY DEAR MOTHER,

I was taking a few days' complete rest and so am late in replying to your very kind note. Accept my congratulations on the anniversary of your marriage. I pray many, many such returns may come to you.

I am sure my previous letter was coloured by the state of my body, as indeed is the whole of existence to us. Yet, Mother, there is more pain than pleasure in life. If not, why do I remember you and your children almost every day of my life, and not many others? Happiness is liked so much because it is so rare, is it not? Fifty percent of our life is mere lethargy, ennui; of the rest, forty percent is pain, only ten happiness — and this for the exceptionally fortunate. We are oft-times mixing up this state of ennui with pleasure. It is rather a negative state, whilst both pleasure and pain are nearer positive, though not positive.

Pleasure and pain are both feeling, not willing. They are only processes which convey to the mind excitements or motives of action. The real positive action is the willing, or impulse to work, of the mind — begun when the sensation has been taken in (pleasure and pain); thus the real is neither pleasure nor pain. It has no connection with either. Quite different from either. The barking of the dog awakens his master to guard against a thief or receive his dearest friend. It does not follow, therefore, that the dog and his master are of the same nature or have any degree of kinship. The feelings of pleasure or pain similarly awaken the soul to activity, without any kinship at all.

The soul is beyond pain, beyond pleasure, sufficient in its own nature. And no hell can punish it, nor any heaven can bless it. So far philosophy.

I am coming soon to Chicago, and hope to say "Lord bless you" to you and your children. All love as usual to my Christian relatives, scientific or quacks.

Vivekananda.

CXLVIII — CHRISTINA

To Sister Christine:

C/O F. H. LEGGETT, ESQ.,
RIDGELY MANOR,
STONE RIDGE, ULSTER CO., N.Y.,
25th October 1899.

DEAR CHRISTINA,

What is the matter with you? Write me a line to tell me how you are and what you are doing now.

I am tired of this place, and will come down to New York for a few days soon. I start thence for Chicago and, if you like, will stop at Detroit on my way to How-do-you-do. I am much better, indeed quite a different man, though not completely cured — for that, time is necessary.

Yours,
Vivekananda.

CXLIX — CHRISTINA

To Sister Christine:

RIDGELY MANOR,
30th October 1899.

MY DEAR CHRISTINA,

Did you not get my last letter? I am very anxious to know how you are. Write a line to tell me you are in very good health.

I am afraid the previous one was misdirected, so I send this c/o Mrs. Funkey [Funke].

Do write soon. I am thinking of Battle Creek food. Baby insists on that. Do you think it will do me any good? Write soon.

Ever yours in the Lord,
Vivekananda.

PS — Where is this Battle Creek? Is it near Detroit? I am seriously thinking of giving it a trial. I am not bad, but unfit for any exertion, even for a walk. This sort of life is no good to live. I [will] try Battle Creek, and if that fails, get out quick.

Write me about Battle Creek.

CL — CHRISTINA

To Sister Christine:

RIDGELY MANOR,
4th November 1899.

MY DEAR CHRISTINA,

The letter was all right in reaching. It was only my nervousness. I am sure you will understand and excuse this. I eagerly expect t o see you in Cambridge. I am going to New York next week. Thence I go for a few days to Washington and then to Cambridge. Do come. And mind you, I must learn German. I am determined to be a French and German scholar. French, I think, I can manage with the help of a dictionary. If I can do that much German in a month, I will be so glad.

It naturally takes time for a letter to reach from here. We have one delivery and one posting a day.

With all love,

Ever yours in the Lord,
Vivekananda.

My eternal love and blessings to Mrs. Funkey [Funke].

CLI — CHRISTINA

To Sister Christine:

21 WEST 34TH STREET,
NEW YORK,
10th November 1899.

MY DEAR CHRISTINA,

I received your letter just now. I am now in New York. Dr. [Egbert] Guernsey analysed my urine yesterday, and there was no sugar or albumen in it. So my kidneys are all right, at least at present. The heart is only nervous, requires calming! — some cheerful company and good, loving friends and quiet. The only difficulty is the dyspepsia, and that is the evil. For instance, I am all right in the morning and can walk miles, but in the evening it is impossible to walk after a meal — the gas — that depends entirely up on food, does it not? I ought to try the Battle Creek food. If I come to Detroit, there will be quiet and Battle Creek food for me.

But if you come to Cambridge with all the instructions of the Battle Creek food, I will have it prepared there; or, between you and me, we will cook it. I am a good hand at that. You don't know a thing about cooking. Well, you may help in cleaning the plates etc. I always get money when I need it badly. "Mother" always sees to that. So, no danger on that head. I am not in the least danger of life, the Doctors agree — only if this dyspepsia goes away. And that is "food", "food", "food", and no worry. Oh, what a worry I have had! Say we go somewhere else and make a little party and keep house ourselves. In Cambridge, Mrs. Bull has a quiet separate place — her studio house. You can have rooms there. I wish you to know Mrs. Bull. She is a saint, a real saint, if ever there was one. Wait for my next letter. I will write today again, or tomorrow after seeing Mrs. Bull.

Ever yours in the Lord,
Vivekananda.

CLII — CHRISTINA

To Sister Christine:

C/O DR. E. GUERNSEY,
180 WEST 59TH STREET,
NEW YORK,
12th November 1899.

CHRISTINA,

Mrs. Bull has gone to Boston without seeing me. I am with the Guernseys. All today laid up with colds.

Oh, these nasty colds. The doctor here declares my case as entirely one of nervous exhaustion. Even the dyspepsia is entirely nervous.

I will be a few days yet here, and then I don't know where I go. I have a great mind to try health food. As for you, write unreservedly where you [would] like me to be. If you think it best for me to come to Detroit, write or wire on receipt of this. I will come immediately. Only difficulty is now the dyspepsia.

With love to Mrs. Funkey [Funke],

Ever yours with blessings,
Vivekananda.

P.S. If Cambridge is best, say that immediately.

CLIII — MRS. BULL

To Mrs. Ole Bull:

180 W. 59,
C/O E. GUERNSEY, M.D.,
12 November 1899

DEAR MRS. BULL,

I am laid up with a bad cold. The clothes are not ready — they will be next week. I don't know what my next step will be. Dr. Guernsey is very kind. Several Doctors have examined me and none could detect any organic disease.

Even the kidney complications for the present have disappeared.

Well, the whole thing is then dyspepsia. I want ever so much to try Battle Creek food. There is a restaurant which cooks only Battle Creek food. Do you think it should be best for me to try it just now? If so, I go to Detroit. In that case, send me my terracotta, thick cashmere coat.

Ever yours in the Lord,
Vivekananda.

Had three treatments already from Helmer. Going to take some next week. None can do anything for this "wind". That is why dieting should be tried at any cost.

CLIV — CHRISTINA

To Sister Christine:

21 WEST 34TH STREET,
NEW YORK,
21st November 1899.

MY DEAR CHRISTINA,

Circumstances have so fallen that I have to start for California tomorrow. It is for my physical benefit too; as the doctor says, I had better be off where the severe winter of the North cannot reach.

Well, thus my plans are made and marred. Anyway — come over to Cambridge when you feel like it. Mrs. Bull will only be too happy to do anything for you she can.

I hope to stop in Detroit on my way back. The Lord's will — as we say.

Ever yours in the Lord,
Vivekananda.

CLV — DHIRA MATA

To Mrs. Ole Bull:

CHICAGO,
30 November 1899

MY DEAR DHIRA MATA,

I am going to leave this place tonight. They have given me a new trunk — a big one. The Maspero book is with me, only the second volume. The first volume must be in Boston. Kindly send it c/o Joe [Miss Josephine MacLeod].

They have been very kind. Madame [Emma] Calvé, came to see me day before yesterday. She is a great woman.

I have nothing to write here except that Margo [Sister Nivedita] is doing very well, except some people were complaining last night that she frightened them with her assertion that Swami can not make mistakes!!!

Hope things are going on with you very well. This is in haste. I write in length from California.

Ever your son,
Vivekananda.

My love to Mrs. [Olea] Vaughn. (Mrs. Ole Bull's daughter.)

CLVI — MOTHER

To Mrs. G. W. Hale:

THE CALIFORNIA LIMITED,
SANTA FE ROUTE,
1 December 1899

MY DEAR MOTHER,

Excuse this scrawl as the train is dancing.

I passed a good night and hope to have a good time all through. With all love for the sisters and Mr. [Clarence] Woolley (Husband of Mrs. Hale's daughter Harriet.) and Bud and Father Pope.

With love,
Vivekananda.

CLVII — MARGOT

To Sister Nivedita:

THE CALIFORNIA LIMITED,
SANTA FE ROUTE,
December 2nd, 1899

MY DEAR MARGOT,

Two nights are passed — today the third will come. If it proves as pleasant and somnolent as the last two, I [shall] rejoice.

The scenery today I am passing through is much like the neighborhood of Delhi, the beginning of a big desert, bleak hills, scanty, thorny shrubs, very little water. The little streams are frozen, but during the middle of the day it is hot. Must be [illegible] I presume, in summer.

I send this to the care of Mrs. Adams, (Probably Mrs. Milward Adams.) as I don't know your address. The Chicago work will not give you much, I am sure, except in education in the methods here, which I am sure will work out soon.

With all love and blessings,
Vivekananda.

CLVIII — MOTHER

To Mrs. G. W. Hale:

LOS ANGELES,
6 December 1899

MY DEAR MOTHER,

A few lines to say my safe arrival and am going to resume my usual work of lecturing here.

I am much better than I was in Chicago and hope soon to become well again.

I cannot tell you how I enjoyed once more the little visit with my American Mother and Sisters.

Harriet has scored a triumph really. I am charmed with Mr. Woolley — only hope Mary will be equally fortunate. It gives me a new lease of life to see people happy. May they all be happy.

Ever with love, your son,
Vivekananda.

CLIX — CHRISTINA

To Sister Christine:

921 WEST 21ST STREET,
LOS ANGELES,
9th December 1899.

MY DEAR CHRISTINA,

After all, it is good for me, and good for those I love, that I should come here. Here at last in California! One of our poets says: "Where is Benares, where is Kashmir, where Khorasan, where Gujarat! O Tulsi! thus, man's past Karma drags him on". And I am here. After all it is best, isn't it? Are you going to Boston? I am afraid you are not. I have not unsettled any of your plans, have I? — unnecessary expenses? Well, if any, I will make it up. Only the trouble is yours. I am ashamed of my eccentricities. Well, how are you? What are you doing? How are things going with you? Sleep if you can; it is better to sleep than get awakened. I pray that all good may come to thee — all peace, all strength to do and suffer. I have a great deal of strength to do, but very little to suffer.

I am so selfish again, always thinking of my own sufferings and paying no heed to others. Pray for me; send strong thoughts that I may have strength to suffer. I know you will. Now, I mean to remain a few weeks in this city. After that, "Mother" knows. I am physically much better now than I have been for months. The weakness of the heart is nearly gone. The dyspepsia is also much better, and [there is] very little. I can walk miles now without feeling it in the heart. If this continues, I expect to have a new lease on life. I am so, so sorry of asking you to come to Boston and flying away. If you are there, I hope you will enjoy the place and the meetings. If you have given it up — well, did you take leave and not go to Boston? My! what a bungle! Well, I ask a thousand pardons, if such is the case. Things must look brighter anyway, sooner or later. What of these little, few days of life!

How is Mrs. Funke? Loads of love for her. How long a leave [do] you get at Christmas? When does it begin? If you feel inclined and willing, write me a long note, will you? But don't tell my friends my whereabouts. I want to be off from the world for a time, if I can. Will you kindly send Mr. Freer's address to Mrs. Bull? She needs it. I had a lecture here last night. The hall was not crowded, as there was very little ad[vertisement], but a fairly good — sized audience though. I hope they were pleased. If I feel better, I am going to have classes in this city soon. I am on the business path this time, you know. Want a few dollars quick, if I can.

Ever yours in the Lord,
Vivekananda.

CLX — BRAHMANANDA

To Swami Brahmananda:

[Swami Vivekananda sent the following cablegram to his brother-monk.]

[Postmarked: December 13, 1899]

PERFECTLY CURED. BLESS ALL.
VIVEKANANDA.

CLXI — CHRISTINA

To Sister Christine:
921 WEST 21ST STREET,
LOS ANGELES,
27th December 1899.

DEAR CHRISTINA,

So you are awake and can't go to sleep any more. Good! Keep awake, wide awake. It was good I came here. For, in the first place, I am cured. What do you think of this — able to walk, and every day walk three miles after a heavy dinner! Good! Isn't it?

I am making money fast — twenty-five dollars a day now. Soon I will work more and get fifty dollars a day. In San Francisco I hope to do still better — where I go in two or three weeks. Good again — better, say I — as I am going to keep the money all to myself and not squander it any more. And then I will buy a little place in the Himalayas — a whole hill — about say, six thousand feet high with a grand view of the eternal snows. There must be springs and a tiny lake. Cedars — the Himalayan cedar forests — and flowers, flowers everywhere. I will have a little cottage; in the middle, my vegetable gardens, which I will work myself — and — and — and — my books — and see the face of man only once in a great while. And the world may go to ruin round about my ears, I would not care. I will have done with all my work — secular or spiritual — and retire. My! how restless I have been all my life! Born nomad. I don't know; this is the present vision. The future is to come yet. Curious —all my dreams about my own happiness are, as it were, bound to come to nothing; but about others' well-being — they as a rule prove true.

I am so glad you are happy and peaceful under Mrs. Bull's hospitable roof. She is a great, great woman — one whom to see is a pilgrimage.

No snow here — exactly like northern India in winter. Some days, even warmer — cool in the morning and evening, in the middle of the day, warm, in the sun, hot. The roses are about us, gardens everywhere, and the beautiful palms. But I like the snow: crisp, crackling under the feet, white, white, white — all round white!

I don't think I have anything with the kidneys or the heart. The whole thing was about indigestion and it is now nearly cured. A month more, and I will be strong like a lion and hardy like a mule. The poor English are getting it hot from the Boers. Mourning in every home in England and still the war goes on. Such is human folly. How long will it take for man to become civilized! Will wars ever cease? Mother knows! The New Year is sure to bring about a great change. Pray some good may come to India. I send you all joy, all love, all success for the New Year and many, many more to come.

So you did well, you think, by coming to Mrs. Bull. I am glad. I wanted you to know Mrs. Bull thoroughly. Remain there as long as you can. It will do you good, I am sure. Take heart and be of cheer, for next year is sure to bring many joys and a hundred blessings.

Yours truly,
Vivekananda.

CLXII — MARGO

To Sister Nivedita

LOS ANGELES,
[Early February 1900]

DEAR MARGO [MARGOT],

You have the Gopâla. Add the Sâvitri story to that. I send you four more herewith. They ought to make a nice volume. Work on them a bit, will you. If you get a publisher in Chicago, all right; if not, Mr. Leggett promised to publish them sometime ago.

Yours,
Vivekananda.

P.S. The preliminary parts should be struck off.

CLXIII — JOE

To Miss Josephine MacLeod:

1231 PINE STREET,
SAN FRANCISCO,
March 2nd 1900

DEAR JOE,

Your note enclosing two from France and three from India just received. I have had general good news and am happy.

Financially, I have got $300 in Los Angeles. About Mrs. Bowler, she has about a hundred odd dollars in cash. Mrs. Hendrick and she have not paid up as yet. That money — $300 in all — is with her. She will send it to me whenever I write.

Rev. Benjamin Fay Mills, a very popular Unitarian preacher in Oakland, invited me from here and paid the fare to San Francisco. I have spoken twice in Oakland to 1500 people each time. Last time I got from collection $30. I am going to have classes at 50 cents admission each.

San Francisco had one lecture the other night [February 23] at 50¢ each. It paid its expenses. This Monday [Sunday?] I am going to speak free — after that a class.

I went to see Mrs. Hurst [Hearst]. She was not at home. I left a card — so with Prof. Le Conte

Mary [Hale] writes that you wrote her of my coming any day to the East. I don't know. Here I have a large following —ready — made by my books. Will get some money, not much. St. Francis [Francis Leggett] may put the money in the bank for me — but can that be done without my signature? And I am here? It is good if it can be done. Did you see any possibility of my books being sold for good to any publisher?

The French invitation is all right. But it seems impossible to write any decent paper on the subject we chose. Because if I have to lecture and make money, very little time will be left for anything else. Again, I can not find any books (Sanskrit) here. So let me try to make a little money if I can and go to France all the same, but send them no paper. No scholarly work can be done in this haphazard and hurried fashion. It means time and study.

Shall I write to Mr. [Gerald] Nobel an acknowledgement and thanks? Write to me fully on these subjects if you can before you leave [for Europe]. My health is going on the same way. The gas is there more or less and this city is all climbing up[hill] that tires me much.

With all love,

Yours affectionately,
Vivekananda.

P.S. Did anybody else respond to Mrs. Leggett's call?

CLXIV — CHRISTINA

To Sister Christine:

1719 TURK STREET,
SAN FRANCISCO, CALIFORNIA,
12th March 1900.

DEAR CHRISTINA,

Just now received a letter from you through New York. I, the other day, wrote you one c/o Mrs. Funke, as I was not sure which of your addresses in my notebook was the correct one! Mental telepathy or foolishness — what is it?

By this time you must have got mine. There is nothing particular about me, except things are going on at the same rate — very little money — making, a good deal of work, and moving about. I leave here in April and come to Chicago for a few days, then to Detroit and then, through New York, go to England. I hope you are all right. I am very calm and peaceful mentally, and hope to remain so for the rest of my life.

How are Mrs. Funkey [Funke] and the rest of our friends?

With all love,
Vivekananda.

CLXV — SISTER CHRISTINE

To Sister Christine:

1719 TURK STREET,
SAN FRANCISCO,
[April 9, 1900.]

Hello! What's the matter with you — gone to sleep? Have not had any news of you for a long time.

I am getting better every day, and one of these days — say in a few weeks — I am coming straight to say how-d'you-do. Well, I will be here two weeks more, then to a place called Stockton — thence to the East. I may stop a few days in Chicago. I may not.

Beginning of May, I come [for] sure to Detroit. I will, of course, write to you. How is life going on with you — grinding, as usual? Any improvements? Write a chatty letter if you feel like. I am dying to get news.

Ever yours in the Truth,
Vivekananda.

CLXVI — MARGOT

To Sister Nivedita:

C/O DR. LOGAN,
770 OAK STREET,
SAN FRANCISCO, CALIFORNIA,
17th May [1900].

DEAR MARGOT,

I am sorry, I cannot come to Chicago yet for a few days. The doctor (Dr. Logan) says I must not undertake a journey till completely strong. He is bent on making me strong. My stomach is very, very good and nerves fine. I am getting on. A few days more and I will be all right. I received your letter with the enclosed.

If you leave for New York soon, take my mail with you. I am coming to New York direct. If you leave New York before I leave, put my mail in a cover and deposit with Turiyananda, and tell him to keep it for me and not to open it on any account, nor any one of my Indian letters. Turiyananda will take charge. Also see that my clothes and books are at the Vedanta Society's rooms in New York.

I will write you more soon — an introduction to Mrs. Huntington. This affair should be private.

With love and blessings,
Vivekananda.

P.S. As I have got to stop at Chicago for my ticket, will you ask anybody to take me in for a day or two, if Mrs. Hale is gone East by that time?

CLXVII — MARGOT

To Sister Nivedita:

770 OAK STREET,
SAN FRANCISCO, CALIFORNIA,
18th May 1900.

DEAR MARGOT,

Enclosed find the letter of introduction to Mrs. Huntington. She can, if she likes, make your school a fact with one stroke of her pen. May Mother make her do it!

I am afraid I will have to go direct to New York, as by that time the Hales will be off. I cannot start for two weeks at least yet. Give the Hales my love.

With love and blessings,

Yours,
Vivekananda.

P.S. I received your letter, including Yum's [Miss Josephine MacLeod's].

CLXVIII — MOTHER

To Mrs. Ole Bull (in London):

SAN FRANCISCO,
18 May 1900

MY DEAR MOTHER,

Many thanks for Joe's [Miss Josephine MacLeod's] and your letters. I have again a bad relapse — and [am] struggling out of it. This time I am perfectly certain that with me all diseases are nervous. I want rest for two, three years — and not the least bit of work between. I will take rest with the Seviers in the Himalayas.

Mrs. [James Henry] Sevier gave me 6,000 Rs. for family — this was distributed between my cousin, aunt, etc. The 5,000 Rs. for buying the house was borrowed from the Math funds. Do not stop the remittance you send to my cousin, whatever Saradananda may say to the contrary. Of course I do not know what he says.

I have long given up the idea of a little house on the Ganges, as I have not the money.

But I have got some in Calcutta and some with the Leggetts, and if you give a thousand more, that will be a fund for my own personal expenses (as you know I never took Math money) as well as for my mother. Kindly write to Saradananda to give up the little house plan. I am not going to write any more for weeks yet — till I completely recover. I hope to get over [it] in a few weeks from now — it was a terrible relapse. I am with a Doctor friend [Dr. Milburn H. Logan], and he is taking every care of me.

Tell Joe that going amongst different people with a message also does not belong to the Sannyasin; for a Sannyasin, [there] is quiet and retirement, scarcely seeing the face of man.

I am now ripe for that, physically at least. If I don't go into retirement, nature will force me to it. Many thanks that temporal things have been so well arranged by you.

With all love to Joe and yourself —

Your Son,
Vivekananda.

CLXIX — CHRISTINA

To Sister Christine:

C/O DR. LOGAN,
770 OAK STREET,
SAN FRANCISCO, CALIFORNIA,
19th May 1900.

DEAR CHRISTINA,

How are you? When is your vacation to commence? I am still in California. Hope to start for the East in two or three weeks more.

Write me all about yourself and how things are going on. How is Mrs. Funkey [Funke]? And the other friends?

Yours as ever,
Vivekananda.

CLXX — ABHEDANANDA

To Swami Abhedananda:

> 770 OAK STREET,
> SAN FRANCISCO, CAL.,
> C/O DR. LOGAN, M.D.,
> [May 19, 1900?]

MY DEAR ABHEDANANDA,

I am very, very glad to hear about the new home of the Vedanta Society. As things stand, I will have to come to New York direct from here — without stoppage — but it will be two or three weeks yet, I am afraid. Things are coming up so fast that I can not but change my plans and stop a few more days.

I am trying my best to get one of you for a flying visit to this Coast — it is a great country for Vedanta.

Get all my books and clothes etc., in your home. I am coming soon. My love to Mrs. Crane. Is she still living on beef-steak and hot water? Miss [Sarah Ellen] Waldo and Mrs. Coulston write about the publication of a new edition of Karma-Yoga. I have written to Miss Waldo all about it. The money in hand from the sale of books ought to be spent, of course.

Do you see my books and clothes all safe there? They were with Mrs. Bull in Boston.

> With all love,
> Vivekananda.

CLXXI — CHRISTINA

To Sister Christine:

> VEDANTA SOCIETY,
> 102 EAST 58TH STREET,
> NEW YORK,
> 9th June 1900.

DEAR CHRISTINA,

I could not write more, as the last few weeks of my stay in California was one more relapse and great suffering. However, I got one great benefit out of it inasmuch as I came to know I have really no disease, except worry and fear. My kidneys are as sound as any other healthy man's. All the symptoms of Bright's disease etc., are only brought on by nerves.

I wrote you one, however, from 770 Oak Street, San Francisco, to which I did not get any reply. Of course, I was bedridden then and my address book was not in the place I was in. There was a mistake in number. I cannot believe you did not reply willingly.

As you see, now I am in New York, and will be here a few days. I have an invitation from Mrs. Walton of Cleveland, Ohio. I have accepted it. She writes me you are also invited and have accepted her invitation. Well, we will meet in Cleveland then. I am sure to see you before I go to Europe — either there or anywhere you wish. If you don't think it would be possible for you to come to Ohio, I will come to any other place you want me to come to say goodbye.

When is your school going to close? Write me all about your plans — do!

Miss Noble wants me very much to go to Cleveland. I would be very, very glad to get a few weeks' seclusion and rest before I start with friends who do not disturb me at all. I know I will find rest and peace that way, and you can help me any amount in that. In Cleveland, of course, there will be a few friends always and much talkee-talkee as a matter of course. So if you think I will have real peace and rest elsewhere, just write all about it.

My reply to the Cleveland lady depends on your letter.

How I wish I were in Detroit or elsewhere just now, among friends who I know are good and true always. This is weakness; but when the physical vitality is lowered and the nerves all unstrung, I feel so, so much to depend upon somebody. You will be glad to learn I made a little money in the West. So I will be quite able to pay my expenses.

Write soon.

> Yours affectionately,
> Vivekananda.

CLXXII — CHRISTINA

To Sister Christine:

> VEDANTA SOCIETY,
> 102 EAST 58TH STREET,
> NEW YORK,
> 13th June 1900.

DEAR CHRISTINA,

There is no cause for any anxiety. As I wrote, I am healthier than ever; moreover, all the past fear of kidney troubles has passed away. "Worry" is the only disease I have, and I am conquering it fast.

I will be here a week or two, and then I come to Detroit. If things so happen that I cannot come, I will sure send for you. Anyway, I am not going to leave this country before seeing you. Sure, sure — I must see you first, and then go to Europe.

Things are looking cheerful once more, and good luck, like ill, also comes in bunches. So I am sure it will be smooth sailing every way now, for some time at least.

With love to Mrs. Funkey [Funke],

> Ever yours in the Truth,
> Vivekananda.

CLXXIII — CHRISTINA

To Sister Christine:

> VEDANTA SOCIETY,
> 102 EAST 58TH STREET,
> NEW YORK,
> 15th June 1900.

MY DEAR CHRISTINA,

I am getting better every day, only this New York is a bad place for sleep. Again, I am working some, though not hard, to get the old friends together and put the thing in shape.

Now, you know, I will in a week or so finish this work and then be ready for a real quiet of a week or two or more.

Detroit, alas! will be no better than New York. With so many old friends! How can you avoid friends whom you really love?

I will have perfect freedom at yours — sure — but how can I avoid seeing friends and the eternal visiting and paying visits and much talkee-talkee? Do you know any other place within eight or ten hours (I want to avoid night rides) of riding from New York where I can be quiet and free from the people? (Lord bless them.) I am dead tired seeing people just now. Just think of that and everything else; if, after all, you think Detroit is the best place for me, I am ready to come.

> Yours truly,
> Vivekananda.

PS — I am also thinking of a quiet place.

CLXXIV — CHRISTINA

To Sister Christine:

> VEDANTA SOCIETY,
> 102 EAST 58TH STREET,
> NEW YORK,
> 27th June 1900.

DEAR CHRISTINA,

This is my plan just now. I will have to remain in New York a few days yet to see my books through. I am going to publish another edition of Karma-Yoga and the London lectures in a book form. Miss Waldo is editing them, and Mr. Leggett will publish.

Then, I think, if I am to remain in this country a few weeks more, it is better that you get a rest and change. Newport is a celebrated seaside place — four hours from New York. I am invited there. I will go there this week and, as promised, I [will] find quiet and retirement and freedom. I will try to find a place for you and wire you as soon as found.

I am sure in Detroit you cannot have rest. A little change of place and quiet from time to time is a great factor in renewing one's vigour.

Well, if you think that you would have better rest and quiet in Detroit, drop a line and I come. It is only seventeen hours from New York to Detroit, and I am quite strong to undertake it. I am free to go already; only I really want you to take a good, long rest for some weeks at least.

Don't be afraid of expenses. Mother has amply provided that and will provide, so long I am unselfish.

Think [over] all the pros and cons, and write at your earliest convenience.

I am going to Newport anyway, just to see what it looks like. I will write you all about [it] as soon as I am there.

Ever yours in the Lord,
Vivekananda.

CLXXV — MRS. HANSBROUGH

To Mrs. Alice (Shanti) Hansbrough:

THE VEDANTA SOCIETY,
102 EAST 58TH STREET, NEW YORK, N.Y.,
[End of June 1900]

DEAR MRS. HANSBROUGH,

I have not written you a line since you left San Francisco. I am well and things are going on well with me.

I am in New York once more, where they have got now a home for the Society and their headquarters. I and the other Swamis also live there.

A San Francisco lady [Miss Minnie C. Boock] now here owns a plot of land near Mt. Hamilton, 12 miles east of Lick observatory — 160 acres in area. She is going to make us a present of it. It would be nice for a summer gathering for us in California. If friends like to go there now, I will send them the written authority. Will you write to Mrs. Aspinall and Miss Bell etc., about it? I am rather desirous it should be occupied this summer as soon as possible. There is only a log cabin on the land; for the rest they must have tents.

I am sorry I can not spare a Swami yet.

With all love to you and Mrs. [Carrie Mead] Wyckoff and the baby of the family.

Ever yours in the Truth,
Vivekananda.

P.S. Tell Helen [the youngest Mead sister] — I thank her for her kind invitation, but [am] so sorry [I] can not accept it now. After all, you three sisters have become a part of my mind forever. What about the club?

CLXXVI — SISTER CHRISTINE

To Sister Christine:

[On July 3, 1900, before departing for Detroit with Swami Turiyananda and Miss Minnie Boock, Swami Vivekananda dispatched a telegram.]

[POSTMARKED: NEW YORK,
July 3, 1900]

STARTED REACH TOMORROW WEDNESDAY 2 P.M. COME STATION WABASH.

Swami Vivekananda.

CLXXVII — MRS. HANSBROUGH

To Mrs. Alice (Shanti) Hansbrough:

102 E. 58TH STREET,
NEW YORK,
3rd July 1900.

MY DEAR MRS. HANSBROUGH,

This is to introduce Swami Turiyananda. The lady who gave the piece of land for Vedanta work belongs to Los Angeles. She has taken Turiyananda with her. He is a great spiritual teacher — but has no experience in platform work.

The best thing would be to help him to start a centre for quiet and rest and meditation in the land near San Jose.

With all love to the holy Trinity.

Ever yours in the Lord,
Vivekananda.

CLXXVIII — ABHEDANANDA

To Swami Abhedananda:

102 E. 58TH STREET,
NEW YORK,
24 July 1900.

DEAR ABHEDANANDA,

I would have gladly remained here, but sastây kisti mât. Got a fine berth — one room all to myself — on a fine vessel. As soon as August comes it will be a terrible Bhida [crowd] as the companies are reducing prices.

Things are going quite all right. Mr. Johnson has returned to their house, and all the rooms are full except two. You write to Mrs. Crane whether you want to get them or not.

You need not feel the least anxiety about the N.Y. work; it will go as a marriage bull next season. Give my love to Mrs. [Mary B.] Coulston and explain to her the circumstances.

With all love,
Vivekananda.

CLXXIX — CHRISTINA

To Sister Christine:

À BORD DU PAQUEBOT LA CHAMPAGNE,
Friday morning, 9 a.m.,
3rd August 1900.

DEAR CHRISTINA,

It is foggy this morning. We are in the channel — expect to reach [Le Havre] at 12 a.m. [noon]. It has been a very bad voyage — rolling and raining and dark nearly all the time. Terrible rolling all through. Only last night I had good sleep. On other occasions the rolling makes me sleep well, but this time I don't know what was the matter; the mind was so whirling. Anyway, I am well and soon to reach land.

Hope to reach Paris this evening.

I send this to Detroit, expecting you there.

With all love and blessings,
Vivekananda.

CLXXX — MRS. LEGGETT

To Mrs. Francis Leggett:

[Swami Vivekananda sent the following telegram on Friday, August 3, 1900, when the S.S. Champagne (which he had boarded in New York on July 26) docked at Le Havre, France.]

[Postmarked: Friday, August 3, 1900]

ARRIVE A HUIT HRES STLAZARE — VIVEKANANDA

[Translation: "I arrive at eight o'clock (p.m.) St. Lazare — Vivekananda".]

CLXXXI — CHRISTINE

To Sister Christine:

6, PLACE DES ETATS-UNIS,
14th August 1900

DEAR CHRISTINE,

Your letter from New York reached just now. You must have got mine from France, directed to 528 Congress.

Well — it was a dreary, funeral-like time. Just think what it is to a morbid man like me!

I am going to the Exposition, etc., trying to pass time. Had a lecture here. Père Haycinth [Hyacinthe], the celebrated clergy — man here, seems to like me much. Well, well what? Nothing. Only, you are so good, and I am a morbid fool — that is all about it. But "Mother" — She knows best. I have served Her through weal or woe. Thy will be done. Well, I have news of my lost brother [Mahendranath Datta]. He is a great traveller, that is good. So you see, the cloud is lifting slowly. My love to your mother and sister and to Mrs. Funkey [Funke].

With love,
Vivekananda.

CLXXXII — NIVEDITA

To Sister Nivedita:

6, PLACE DES ETATS UNIS,
PARIS,
23rd August 1900.

DEAR NIVEDITA,

The manuscript accounts of the Math just reached. It is delightful reading. I am so pleased with it.

I am going to print a thousand or more to be distributed in England, America and India. I will only add a begging paragraph in the end.

What do you think the cost will be?

With love to you and Mrs. Bull,
Vivekananda.

CLXXXIII — CHRISTINE

To Sister Christine:

6, PLACE DES ETATS-UNIS, PARIS,
23rd August 1900

DEAR CHRISTINE,

What is the matter with you? Are you ill? Unhappy? What makes you silent? I had only one little note from you in all this time.

I am getting a bit nervous about you — not much. Otherwise I am enjoying this city. Did Mrs. A. P. Huntington write you?

I am well — keeping well as far as it is possible with me.

With love,
Vivekananda.

CLXXXIV — CHRISTINA

To Sister Christine:

6 PLACE DES ETATS UNIS,
PARIS,
15th September 1900.

DEAR CHRISTINA,

Your letter was very reassuring. I am so glad this summer did you good. So you did not get enamoured of New York City.

Well, I am getting enamoured of Paris. I now am living with a M. Jules Bois, a French savant, who has been a student and admirer of my works.

He talks very little English; in consequence, I have to trot out my jargon French and am succeeding well, he says. I can now understand if he will talk slowly.

Day after tomorrow I go to Bretagne [Brittany] where our American friends are enjoying the sea breeze — and the massage.

I go with M. Bois for a short visit; après cet [after that] I don't know where I go. I am getting quite Frenchy, connaissezvous [do you know]? I am also studying grammaire and hard at work. [Sentence torn off] In a few months I hope to be Frenchy, but by that time I will forget it by staying in England.

I am strong, well and content — no morbidity.

Au revoir,
Vivekananda.

CLXXXV — MOTHER

To Mrs. Ole Bull,
66, RUE AMPERE,
22nd October 1900

DEAR MOTHER,

I am sorry to learn you are not well. Hope you will soon be better. Things seem to turn out better for me.

Mr. Maxim of the gun fame is very much interested in me, and he wants to put in his book on China and the Chinese something about my work in America. I have not any documents with me; if you have, kindly give them to him. He will come to see you and talk it over with you. Canon Hawes [Reverend Hugh Reginald Haweis] also keeps track of my work in England. So much about that. It may be that Mother will now work up my original plan of international work. In that case, you will find your work of the Conference has not been in vain.

It seems that after this fall in my health, physical and mental, it is going to open out that way — larger and more international work. Mother knows best.

My whole life has been divided into successive depressions and rises — and so, I believe, is the life of everyone. I am glad, rather than not, these falls come. I understand it all; still, I suffer and grumble and rage!! Perhaps that is a part of the cause of the next upheaval.

I think you will be in America by the time we return; if not, I will see you in London again. Anyhow, adieu for the present. We start day after tomorrow for Egypt etc. And all blessings ever be on you and yours is, as always, my prayer.

Your son,
Vivekananda.

PS: To Margot [Sister Nivedita] my love, and I am sure she will succeed.

CLXXXVI — ALBERTA

To Miss Alberta Sturges:
[Swami Vivekananda sent the following postcard.]

[CONSTANTINOPLE,
November 1, 1900]

DEAR ALBERTA,

How are you? I am having a grand Turkish time.

Yours,
Vivekananda.

CLXXXVII — CHRISTINA

To Sister Christine:
[On a postcard, picturing the old decayed fortress walls of Istanbul, Swami Vivekananda wrote the following note.]

[Postmarked: November 1, 1900]

DEAR CHRISTINA,

I am having a good time here. So I hope you also are having in Detroit —

Yours truly,
Vivekananda.

CLXXXVIII — MARGO

To Sister Nivedita:
[On a picture postcard showing dervishes and local fish merchants, Swami Vivekananda wrote the following note.]

[Postmarked: Constantinople,
November 1, 1900]

Dear Margo [Margot], the blessings of the howling dervishes go with you — Yours in the Lord,

Vivekananda.

P.S. All love to Mrs. Bull.

CLXXXIX — SISTER CHRISTINE

To Sister Christine:

[On a postcard, showing the temple of Hepaistos, popularly called Thesion, Swami Vivekananda wrote.]

[POSTMARKED: ATHENS,
November 11, 1900]

Great fun. I write without the possibility of being written to, as I am changing place all the time. How do you do?

Vivekananda.

CXC — YOUR HIGHNESS

To Maharaja Ajit Singh, the Raja of Khetri:

THE MATH,
BELOOR,
HOWRAH DIST.,
[December 1900]

YOUR HIGHNESS,

Very glad to learn that you and the Coomar [the Royal Prince] are enjoying good health. As for me, my heart has become very weak. Change, I do not think, will do me any good, as for the last 14 years I do not remember to have stopped at one place for three months at a stretch. On the other hand, if by some chance I can live for months in one place, I hope it will do me good. I do not mind this, however; I feel that my work in this life is done. Through good and evil, pain and pleasure, my life —boat has been dragged on. The one great lesson I was taught is that life is misery, nothing but misery. Mother knows what is best. Each one of us is in the hands of Karma — it works out itself, and no nay. There is only one element in life which is worth having at any cost — and it is love. Love immense and infinite, broad as the sky and deep as the ocean. This is the one great gain in life. Blessed is he who gets it.

Ever yours in the Lord,
Vivekananda.

CXCI — MOTHER

To Mrs. Ole Bull (in London):

DACCA,
20 March 1901.

MY DEAR MOTHER,

At last I am in Eastern Bengal. This is the first time I am here, and never before knew Bengal was so beautiful. You ought to have seen the rivers here — regular rolling oceans of fresh water, and everything so green — continual production. The villages are the cleanest and prettiest in all India.

Joe [Miss Josephine MacLeod] is perhaps by this time in Japan. I received a long and beautiful letter from Margot. Tell Margot that there has been of late a regular fall of fortune on the Kashmir Raja; things are all changing to his benefit. Mr. Mookherjey is now Governor of Kashmir. Saradananda had a bad fever. He is well now, but weak. He possibly goes to Darjeeling for a change. Mrs. [M. N.] Banerjey, who is at Calcutta, is very anxious to take him to the hills. Mohin [Mahendranath Datta], my brother, is in India, in Karachi near Bombay, and he corresponds with Saradananda. He writes to say he is going to Burma, China, etc. The traders who lure him have shops in all those places. I am not at all anxious about him. He is a very selfish man.

I have no news from Detroit. I received one letter from Christina nine months ago, but I did not reply. Perhaps that may have vexed her.

I am peaceful and calm — and am finding every day the old begging and trudging life is the best for me after all.

Mrs. Sevier I left at Belur. She is the guest of Mrs. Banerjey, who has rented Nilambar Mookherjey's house on the river (the old Math). She goes very soon to Europe.

Things are going on, as is in the nature of things. To me has come resignation.

With all love,

Ever your Son,
Vivekananda.

PS — All blessings on Margot's work. Mother is leading, I am sure.

CXCII — SIR

To Ramesh Chandra Dutta:

THE MATH, P.O. BELUR,
DIST. HOWRAH, BENGAL,
4 April 1901.[7]*

DEAR SIR,

I am so very glad to learn from a person of your authority of the good work Sister Nivedita is doing in England. I join in earnest prayer with the hopes you entertain of her future services to India by her pen.

I have not the least desire that she should leave her present field of utility and come over to India.

I am under a deep debt of gratitude to you, Sir, for your befriending my child, and hope you will never cease to advise her as to the length of her stay in England and the line of work she ought to undertake.

Her book on Kâli has been very popular in India. The debt our Motherland already owes you is immense, and we are anxiously awaiting the new book of yours.

May all blessings ever attend you and yours is the constant prayer of —

Yours humbly,
Vivekananda.

CXCIII — MARGOT

To Sister Nivedita:

THE MATH, BELUR,
HOWRAH DISTRICT, BENGAL,
4 April 1901.

DEAR MARGOT,

A letter came just now from Mr. R. Dutt [Ramesh Dutta] praising you and your work in England very much and asking me to wish you to stop longer in England.

It requires no imagination to learn that I am overjoyed at all the news about you Mr. Dutt so kindly sends.

Of course, you stay as long as you think you are working well. Yum [Miss Josephine MacLeod] had some talk about you with Mother [Holy Mother, Sarada Devi], and she desired you to come over. Of course, it was only her love and anxiety to see you — that was all; but poor Yum has been much too serious for once, and hence all these letters. However, I am glad it should happen, as I learnt so much about your work from Mr. Dutt, who can't be accused of a relative's blind love.

I have written to Mrs. Bull already about this matter. I am now at last in Dacca and had some lectures here. I depart for Chandranath tomorrow, near Chittagong, the farthest eastern extremity of Bengal. My Mother, aunt, cousin, another cousin's widow, and nine boys are with me. They all send you love.

I had just now a few lines from Mrs. Bull, also a letter from Mr. Sturdy. As it would be almost impossible for me to write for some days now, I ask you to thank Mrs. Bull for me for her letter, and tell her kindly that I have just now a long letter from Miss [Christina] Greenstidel of Detroit. She mentions a beautiful letter from Mrs. Bull. Sturdy writes about the publication of any further edition of Raja-Yoga by Longmans. I leave that consideration with Mrs. Bull. She may talk over the matter with Sturdy and do what she thinks proper.

Please give Sturdy my best love, and tell him I am on the march and will take time to reply to his letter; in the meanwhile the business will be looked after by Mrs. Bull.

With everlasting love and blessings,
Vivekananda.

CXCIV — CHRISTINE

To Sister Christine:

THE MATH, BELUR,
HOWRAH DIST., BENGAL,
[April 4, 1901]

DEAR CHRISTINE,

The subsequent proceedings have been so much interesting; and the interest has been growing so rapidly of late, that one could scarcely utter a word.

I am glad to learn of Mrs. [Ole] Bull's sweet letter to you; she is an angel. You are peaceful and happy — good. I am growing towards it too.

I am en route to Chandranath on pilgrimage.

I have been anxiously awaiting a letter from you, and it seemed it would never come.

I am sure to be happy — can't help thinking so. After so much struggle, the result must come. Things take their own course; it is I who am to brighten up, I find. And I am trying my best. And you can help me by writing nice letters now and then; will you?

Margot [Sister Nivedita] is doing splendid work in England with Mrs. Bull's backing. Things are going on nicely.

I am sleeping better and the general health is not bad.

With everlasting love and blessings,
Vivekananda.

P.S. Please enquire of Miss [Sarah Ellen] Waldo about the publication of Karma and Jnâna Yogas and write.

CXCV — INTRODUCTION

Letter of Introduction:

GAUHATI,
April 17, 1901

I have great pleasure in certifying the great amiability and helpfulness of the brothers Shivakanta and Lakshmikanta, Pandas of Shri Kamakhya Peetham.

They are men who help most and are satisfied with the least.

I can unhesitatingly recommend them to the Hindu public visiting this most holy shrine.

Swami Vivekananda.

CXCVI — CHRISTINE

To Sister Christine:

THE MATH, BELUR,
HOWRAH DIST., BENGAL,
13th May 1901.

DEAR CHRISTINE,

I arrived in the Math yesterday. This morning came your short note. You must have got my letters by this time, and [I] hope this will give you a taste of how sometimes silence is gold.

I have beautiful letters from everywhere this morning and am quite happy. I paid a long visit of two months to Assam and different parts of eastern Bengal. For combined mountain and water scenery, this part of the country is unrivalled.

Either I am to go to Europe this summer, and thence to the U.S., or you come over to India — things are all getting ready to that end. Mother knows Her ways. For one thing, I am calm, very calm, and hope to keep a hold on this state for a long time; and you are my best help to keep this poise, are you not? I will write more in my next; just now these few lines — and a hundred pardons I beg for their scantiness. Yet silence tells more sometimes than all the speech in the world.

With all love and blessings,

Ever yours in the Lord,
Vivekananda.

CXCVII — MOTHER

To Mrs. Ole Bull:

THE MATH, BELUR,
13 May 1901

DEAR MOTHER,

I reached Calcutta yesterday. This morning arrived your letter containing three cheques for my cousin. They shall reach her regularly.

I have not had any letter from Joe [Miss Josephine MacLeod] from Japan, but several I find awaiting me from on board steamer. She also sends me a newspaper cutting to be sent to Professor Geddes. I enclose it in this letter and expect you to direct it to Prof. Geddes.

Saradananda has been three weeks in Darjeeling, where he has improved greatly. I wish he will remain some time longer there. Mr. Bannerjy is the kindest of hosts.

Mrs. Sevier is in London at 2, Maisemore Mansions, Canfield Gardens, London, N.W.

You are right: my experiences are bringing about calmness — great calmness.

Mrs. Patterson and children are off to Europe. General [C. B. Patterson] is alone and very desirous that I would call. I will the next time I go to town.

My cousin and mother and the rest send love, and my eternal love you know always.

Ever your son,
Vivekananda.

P.S. All love and blessings for Margot [Sister Nivedita].

CXCVIII — MRS. HANSBROUGH

To Mrs. Alice (Shanti) Hansbrough:

THE MATH,
HOWRAH DIST.,
BENGAL, INDIA,
3rd June 1901

DEAR MRS. HANSBROUGH,

The contribution of six pounds and three shillings to the Math by the Los Angeles club has duly reached. Swami Brahmananda will write to you a separate acknowledgement. But as I happen to be here just now and have not had long any direct communication with you, I feel like having a chat with you as of yore, even though it be through the post. Now how are you and the Baby and the holy Trinity and the oldest who brings up the rear?

How are all our Los Angeles friends? Poor Mrs. [Emeline F.] Bowler, I hear, has passed away. She was an angel. Where is Miss Strickney? Please tender her my sincerest love, gratitude and prayers when you meet her next.

How are all the San Francisco friends? How is our Madam (Mrs. Benjamin Aspinall.) — the noble, the unselfish? What is she doing now? Quietly gone back to her Home of Truth work?

Are you pleased with Turiyananda and his work? Is the [Shanti] Ashrama progressing?

With everlasting love and blessings,

Ever yours in the Lord,
Vivekananda.

CXCIX — FRIEND

To Mr. Okakura Kakuzo:

THE MATH, BELUR,
HOWRAH DIS.,
BENGAL, INDIA,
18th June 1901

DEAR FRIEND,

Allow me to call you a friend. We must have been such in some past birth. Your cheque for 300 rupees duly reached and many thanks for the same.

I am just thinking of going to Japan, but with one thing or another and my precarious health, I cannot expedite matters as I wish.

Japan to me is a dream — so beautiful that it haunts one all his life.

With all love and blessings,
Vivekananda.

Kakudzo [Kakuzo] Okakura Esq.,
Tokyo, Japan.

CC — CHRISTINA

To Sister Christine:

THE MATH, BELUR,
DIST. HOWRAH, BENGAL, INDIA,
[End of June 1901]

DEAR CHRISTINA,

Your very welcome letter just reached. A few days ago a precious little bit of poem also reached. I wish it ever so much you were the writer thereof. Anyhow, most of us feel, though unable to express; and then, "There are thoughts that lie too deep for tears". Regularity in anything is not in my line of life, but that need not make you irregular. I pray you to drop a few lines every now and then. Of course, when I am not in this body, I am sure the news will reach you, and then you will have to stop writing.

Miss MacLeod wishes me to join her in Japan, but I am not sure. Most probably I am not going, especially as I expect both her and Mrs. Ole Bull in India, in November. Two whole months consumed in coming and going; only one month's stay in Japan — that does not pay, I am afraid.

Say, I am getting enormously fat about the middle — alas!

Mrs. [Charlotte] Sevier, who is now in England, returns in a few months to India. She has invited Mrs. Bull etc. to be her guests in the Himalayas. I wish they could be there during summer.

I have manfully borne the terrific heat of my country in the plains, and now I am facing the deluging rains of my country. Do you know how I am taking rest? I have got a few goats and sheep and cows and dogs and cranes! And I am taking care of them the whole day! It is not trying to be happy; what for? Why should one not be unhappy as well — both being nonsense? — but just to kill time.

Do you correspond with Mrs. Bull or Nivedita?

Don't worry, don't be anxious; for me the "Mother" is my protection and refuge; and everything must come round soon, better than my fondest dreams can paint.

With all love,
Vivekananda.

CCI — CHRISTINE

To Sister Christine:

THE MATH, BELUR,
DIST. HOWRAH, BENGAL,
6th August 1901.

Letters are sometimes, dear Christina, like mercy — good to the one that sends and the other that receives.

I am so happy that you are calm and resigned as ever. You are ever that. "Mother knows", indeed; only I know that "Mother" not only knows, but does — and is going to do something very fine for me in the near future. What do you think will be very good for me on earth? Silver? Gold? Pooh! I have got something infinitely better; but a little gold will not be amiss to keep my jewel in proper surroundings, and it is coming, don't you think so?

I am a man who frets much, but waits all the same; and the apple comes to my mouth by itself. So, it is coming, coming, coming.

Now, how are you? Growing ever thinner, thinner, thinner, eh? Do have a very good appetite and good sleep in anticipation of the coming good time — to be in trim for welcoming its advent.

How did the heat feel this year? We read all sorts of horrible stories about American heat waves. You have beaten the world's records, even in heat —

that's Yankee push, surely.

Well, you are right as about taste: I renounce the yellow of gold and the white of silver, but stick to amber always — that is to my taste.

Amber and corals I always hated; but of late I am awakening to their beauty. One learns as he lives, is it not?

I am going to Darjeeling tomorrow for a few days and will write to you from there. Now gute Nacht [good night] and au revoir [good-bye] for the present.

Ever yours truly,
Vivekananda.

CCII — CHRISTINE

To Sister Christine:

THE MATH, BELUR,
DIST. HOWRAH, BENGAL,
27th August 1901.

DEAR CHRISTINE,

I am expecting a long, long letter from you; and, like all expectations of mine, [it] will not be realized, I fear.

Well, I need not bother you with the usual string of questions: How are you? What are you doing all this summer? etc. I am sure the Mother will [do] so much as to keep you in good health at least.

Now, Christina, for many reasons this letter happens to be short, very. It is written with the special purpose that as soon as you get this, send me your latest photograph.

Did you write to Miss [Sarah Ellen] Waldo about the publication of the books? I get no news and, what is more important, no money (that is between you and me) from the sale.

Did you have any news of Margot [Sister Nivedita], of Mrs. [Ole] Bull etc.? And are you happy? I sometimes feel I am, other times it is clouded. Well, it is all the body, after all — material. Goodbye.

Yours with love and blessings,
Vivekananda.

PS — Do send the photo as soon as possible.

CCIII — CHRISTINE

To Sister Christine:

THE MATH, BELUR,
DIST. HOWRAH, BENGAL,
2nd September 1901.

MY DEAR CHRISTINE,

I have been looking at one of your old photos — the only one you sent four or five years ago; and then I remember how changed and reduced you looked last summer; and it came to me that you must be awfully thin now, as it seems very hard for you to get rid of anxieties. This is simply foolish. Things will, of course, take their shape. We only make ourselves miserable by moping. It is very hard to manipulate one's philosophy to contribute to one's daily need. So it is with you, as with me. But it is easiest to take the teacher's chair and read a lecture. And that has been my life's business!! Indeed, that is the reason why there are more disciples up to the mark than teachers. The upshot of all this is that you must create a huge appetite, then gorge, then sleep and grow fat, fat, fat. Plump is the English word, is it not?

As for me, I am very happy. Of course, Bengal brings the asthma now and then, but it is getting tame, and the terrible things — Bright's disease and diabetes — have disappeared altogether. Life in any dry climate will stop the asthma completely, I am sure. I get reduced, of course, during a fit, but then it takes me no time to lay on a few layers of fat. I have a lot of cows, goats, a few sheep, dogs, geese, ducks, one tame gazelle, and very soon I am going to have some milk buffaloes. These are not your American bison, but huge things — hairless, half-aquatic in habits, and [that] give an enormous quantity of very rich milk.

Within the last few months, I got two fits [of asthma] by going to two of the dampest hill stations in Bengal — Shillong and Darjeeling. I am not going to try the Bengalee mountains any more.

Mrs. Bull and Nivedita are in Norway. I don't know when they [will] come over to India. Miss MacLeod is in Japan. I have not heard from her [for] a long while. They all are expected here in November, and will have a "hot time in this old town" etc. I pray you can come, and the Mother will open the door for it. I cannot but say my prayers mostly have been heard, up to date.

Well now, Christina, send me one of your latest photos next mail, will you? I want to see how much of fat you have accumulated in one year.

Anyhow, I will have to go to America with Mrs. Bull, I am sure. [Excision] By the by, excusez-moi, our Calcutta is never so hot as your Detroit or New York, with its added advantage — we are not required by our society to wear many things. The old Greeks used to think that wearing too many clothes and [feeling] shame to show any part of the body a peculiarity of barbarians! So the Hindus think, down to the present day. We are the most scantily clothed people in the whole world. Bless the Lord! How one would live otherwise in our climate!

3rd September —

I left the letter unfinished last night. The foreign English mail starts day after tomorrow. So begin again. The moon is not up yet, but there is a sunless glow upon the river. Our mighty Ganges (She is indeed mighty now, during the rains) is splashing against the walls of the house. Numerous tiny boats are flitting up and down in the dark; they have come to fish for our shads, which come up the river this season.

How I wish you were here to taste our shads — one of the most delicate fish in the world. It is raining outside — pouring. But the moment this downpour ceases, I rain through every pore — it is so hot yet. My whole body is covered by big patches of prickly heat. Thank goodness there are no ladies about! If I had to cover myself in this state of things, I surely would go crazy.

I have also my theme, but I am not despondent. I am sure very soon to pan it out into a beautiful ecstasy [excision]. I am half crazy by nature; then my overtaxed nerves make me outrageous now and then. As a result I don't find anybody who would patiently bear with me! I am trying my best to make myself gentle as a lamb. I hope I shall succeed in some birth. You are so gentle. Sometimes I did frighten you very much, did I not, Christina? I wish I were as gentle as you are. Mother knows which is best.

I would not take any supper tonight, as I ate rather heartily of the aforesaid shad! Then I have to think, think, think on my theme; and some subjects I think best in bed because the whole is made clear to me in dream. Therefore, I am going to bed, and gute Nacht, bon soir,[9]* etc., etc. No, no, it is now about 10 a.m. in Detroit. Therefore, a very happy day to you. May all good realities reach you today while I am expecting dreams.

Ever yours with love and blessings,
Vivekananda.

CCIV — CHRISTINE

To Sister Christine:

THE MATH, BELUR,
DIST. HOWRAH, BENGAL,
25th September 1901.

DEAR CHRISTINE,

I could not write you last mail, excusez [excuse]. But I have been expecting one from you for a long time. Hope one will come this mail.

I am just thinking of going over to Japan, as Miss [Josephine] MacLeod is so insistent. Perhaps something will be done; who knows?

From Japan, of course, a peep into America seems inevitable.

Not much news of Mrs. [Ole] Bull or Margot [Sister Nivedita]. Margot is rested, well, and strong. She will come to India some day, perhaps. I am soon expecting Mrs. [Charlotte] Sevier though. Her work is needing her. Her beautiful home in the Himalayan forests is a temptation, especially now when a huge tiger is roaming in her compound and killed a horse, a buffalo, and her pair of mastiffs in broad daylight; a number of bears [are] playing havoc with her vegetable garden; and lots of porcupines [are] doing mischief everywhere!!! She went out of the way to buy land in a forest — she and her husband liked it so much.

There is not much to write this week. Words only tire one, except one which is inexhaustible, infinite.

So, goodbye till next week.

Ever with love and blessings,
Vivekananda.

PS — Just now comes a telegram from Miss MacLeod and a letter also. She is so insistent that I am thinking of going over to Japan. In that case, we cross over to America this winter, and thence to England.

CCV — CHRISTINA

To Sister Christine:

THE MATH, BELUR,
DIST. HOWRAH, BENGAL,
8th October 1901.

DEAR CHRISTINA,

Yours of September 9 came to hand yesterday. I congratulate you on your successful visit to the Huron Lake; a few more of them (according to your letter) will force you to sympathize with our condition — oh, the gasping and the melting and the puffing and all the rest of them!

However, nothing in the world like a plump, ripe fruit.

I had to give up my trip to Japan: firstly, because I am not in a working trim yet; secondly, [I] don't much care to make such a long voyage (one month) alone; thirdly, what am I to talk to them, I wonder.

Our heat too has been fierce and is continuing unusually long this year. I am blacker than a Negro by this time.

The California work is progressing famously.

They want one or two men more. I would send, if I could, but I have not any more spare men. Poor Turiyananda is suffering from malaria yet, and is awfully overworked.

Do you know whether they published my Jnana-Yoga or not? I got a copy of a second edition of Karma-Yoga only.

I am bobbing up and down in the current of life. Today it is rather down, so I finish the letter here.

Yours with all love and blessings,
Vivekananda.

CCVI — CHRISTINA

To Sister Christine:

THE MATH, BELUR,
DIST. HOWRAH, BENGAL,
14th October 1901.

MY DEAR CHRISTINA,

Just now came a letter from Mrs. Bull, but none from you, as I expected one this mail.

Mrs. Bull writes, "I wrote Christina recently to ask her if she were to be free in case the opportunity opened for her to go to the East. I send you her reply".

I went through several times your letter to Mrs. Bull. It surely was horrible; and you have been all this time hiding the real state of affairs from me and posing great cheerfulness!!

You will be a precious fool to lose the opportunity if such comes and is offered by Mrs. Bull. You will only have to take a year's leave. The rest will all be arranged by Mrs. Bull, including, I am sure, all your anxiety for those you will have to leave behind in Detroit.

You have been good, too good to be human, and you are so, still. But it is no use making oneself unnecessarily miserable. "Mother's will", surely, if the chance comes; and it has got to come, I know.

I would not write you about my health; for after

all this hide and seek, even though it was for my good, I think you have not much of a right to know the truth about my health.

But to some things you have eternal rights, and amongst others, to my eternal love and blessings,

Vivekananda.

CCVII — MARGO

To Sister Nivedita:

THE MATH,
P.O. BELUR, HOWRAH,
12th November 1901.

MY DEAR MARGO [MARGOT],

Since the Durgâ Pujâ I have been very ill, and so could not reply to your letter earlier.

We had a grand Puja here of Durga, lasting nearly four days; but, alas, I was down with fever all the time.

We had a grand image, and a huge Puja it was. Then we had the Lakshmi Puja following close, and then night before yesterday, we had the Kali Puja. It is always after midnight — this Puja. I am better now, and we will find a house for you as soon as you come.

I am so glad you are accompanying Mrs. [Ole] Bull. She requires all care; and she always thinks of herself the last. Joe [Miss Josephine MacLeod] is coming to India shortly — at Christmas time with some Japanese friends. I am expected to meet her in Madras.

I am going off to the N.W.P. [North-Western Provinces] etc. soon, as Bengal is malarious — now that the rains are over.

Mrs. Bull has been a mother to us all, and any time and service spent for her is as nothing to what she has been doing for us all. Remain with her as long as she wants you — the work can wait well; "Mother" sees to her work. We needn't be anxious.

By the by, Miss [Henrietta] Müller is here in Calcutta. She wrote a letter to Akhandananda, with whom she has been in regular correspondence — care of the Math. So I sent some flowers and fruits and a letter of welcome to her hotel. I have not had a reply yet.

Mrs. [Charlotte] Sevier, I expect, has already started. Swarupananda had his heart weakened by the constant uphill and downhill. He is here and improving.

Things are going on well with us, slowly but surely. The boys of late have been very active, and it is work only that tells and nothing else.

Yours with all love and blessings,
Vivekananda.

CCVIII — CHRISTINA

To Sister Christine

THE MATH, P.O. BELUR, HOWRAH,
12th November 1901.

DEAR CHRISTINA,

The morning's mail brought me a photograph from Detroit. I thank the sender very much for promptness. Well, I liked it much. But the old one is the profile view; this, the front. Then again, the phenomenal fat seems to be only imaginary on somebody's part. In a way, I am more used to the old one, and, as such, I cannot slight an old friend. So let me say both are good. The one is an evolution of the other — for the better. I expected a line but it has not arrived yet; [it] may tomorrow. We have a proverb here: "One river is equal to forty miles". There is only a river between Calcutta and our Math, and yet such a round — about way for the mail. Sometimes it comes dribbling for days.

Mrs. [Ole] Bull and Nivedita must have started for the U.S. by this time. Nivedita is sure to see you in Detroit. Mrs. Bull is anxious to induce you to join her Indian party via Japan. If you can take leave for some months, do come. Mother will arrange anyhow; I need not trouble myself.

Mrs. Sevier has started already, it seems — alone.

We had grand Pujas (worships) here in our Math this year. The biggest of our Pujas is the Mother worship, lasting nearly four days and nights. We brought a clay image of Mother with ten hands, standing with one foot on a lion, the other on a demon. Her two daughters — the Goddess of Wealth and the Goddess of Learning and Music — on either side on lotuses; beneath, her two sons — the God of War and that of Wisdom.

Thousands of people were entertained, but I could not see the Puja, alas! I was down with high fever all the time. Day before yesterday, however, came the Puja of Kali. We had an image, too, and sacrificed a goat and burned a lot of fireworks. This night every Hindu home is illuminated, and the boys go crazy over fireworks. There are, of course, several cases of severe burns in the hospitals. We had less fireworks but more Puja, recitation of Mantras, offering of flowers, food and songs. It lasted only one night.

I am expected to leave Calcutta and Bengal in a few days, as this country becomes very malarious this month, after the rains. It is pleasant and cool now, and the north Himalayan wind is blowing.

We have fenced in a lot of our grounds to protect our vegetables from our cows and goats and sheep. The other day one of my [a portion excised] …but the mother was either so wicked or [a portion excised] …that she would not look at her young. I tried to keep them alive on cow's milk, but the poor things died in the night! Two of my ducks are sitting on their eggs. As this is their first time, and the male does not help them a bit, I am trying my best to keep up their strength by good feeding. We cannot keep chickens here — they are forbidden to us.

With all love,
Vivekananda.

CCIX — CHRISTINE

To Sister Christine:

THE MATH, P.O. BELUR, HOWRAH,
25th November 1901.

DEAR CHRISTINE,

It seems your bottle of nerve tonic did not do you much good, your assurances to the contrary. It must have been a curious error. I must have been down with fever or asthma or something else at that time. Still a thousand, thousand pardons. This was my first, and it will be my last, offence. Your letter that went to Miss [Josephine] MacLeod has not come back yet. Perhaps Miss MacLeod is bringing the letter with her, as she is coming over to India from Japan herself, accompanied by her Japanese converts (male, of course, as she is a lady missionary).

Well, well, I so wish things would so arrange themselves that I could see you once more. Mother knows. By the by, my right eye is failing me badly. I see very little with that one. It will be hard for me for some time either to read or write; and as it is getting worse every day, my people are urging me to go to Calcutta and consult a doctor. I will go soon, as soon as I recover from a bad cold I have on.

I am so glad you were so taken by Abhedananda; only I thought one Hindu was good for a lifetime.

Poor Miss Joe [Miss Josephine MacLeod] — so she remains ignorant as to the real cause of my not going over to Japan! You need not be the least anxious — there is no harm done; and if there were, Joe and especially Mrs. [Ole] Bull make it their life's duty to befriend those I love.

I will try your tonic when it arrives; and the gift, I pray, will even be followed by the giver, for surely a [words excised] …is more stimulating and healing than dead drugs.

With all love,
Vivekananda.

CCX — CHRISTINE

To Sister Christine:

THE MATH, P.O. BELUR, HOWRAH,
27th November 1901.

DEAR CHRISTINE,

It is almost sure, I did not write any letter to you that week in which [I] made that infamous blunder. As I wrote you two letters a few days previously, it is not at all probable that I wrote you another. Then Miss [Josephine] MacLeod [would have] sent the letter back. I must have written only one letter that week to Miss MacLeod, giving her my reasons for not going to Japan; and somehow it so happened that the hand wrote the most familiar name on the envelope. So you need not expect any letter of yours back from Japan, as there was none; and if there were, you shall have it.

I am just under another spell of catarrh and asthma. Yesterday a cyclone blew over the place, and several trees and a bit of the roof are damaged. It is gloomy yet and cold. You know it is almost impossible to write with the asthma on. So au revoir [good-bye].

Vivekananda.

CCXI — CHRISTINE

To Sister Christine:

THE MATH, P.O. BELUR, HOWRAH,
12th December 1901.

DEAR CHRISTINE,

Well, then, you wanted to know all about my state of health, and you insist. You shall have it.

You know, the last three years I have been getting albuminuria now and then. It is not constant, nor is it yet of any organic character. The kidneys are structurally all right. Only they throw out albumen now and then.

This is worse than throwing out sugar in diabetes. Albumen poisons the blood, attacks the heart and does all sorts of mischief. Catching cold always increases it. This time it has caused a small blood vessel in the right eye to burst, so that I scarcely see with that eye.

Then the circulation has become very rapid. The doctors have put me to bed; and I am forbidden to eat meat, to walk or even stand up, to read and write.

Already there is some benefit in this lying-down process, as I sleep a lot and have a good appetite and am digesting my meals. Curious, is it not, that inactivity should bring on sleep and appetite? There is no cause to be anxious at all.

Mrs. [Charlotte] Sevier arrived in Calcutta three days ago; and by the last advice from Nivedita, Mrs. Bull and she will start on the 13th December, if they can secure berths, or on the 30th December at least. I pray Mrs. Bull has already invited you and that you have got your year's leave and are coming over, and that you will get this letter in India redirected. If Mother does not fulfil this prayer, sure She will take me across the water soon, and [line excised] …The doctor says if I keep to my bed for three months, I will get completely cured.

Now, don't worry. If good days are not coming, we will make them, that is all. Hang it! I must have good days now and, that too, very soon. You know, I always keep my word. Mother must do it, or I throw Her overboard. I am not so submissive as you are.

Our old-school physicians pour in tons of iron and other metals — including gold, silver, pearls, etc. — down our throats. I should be a man of iron by this time; perhaps yours will be the last touch to make my body one of steel.

This is our best season for eating turtles, but they are all black. The green [ones] can only be found in America. Alas! I am prevented from the taste of meat.

Now, noble heart, take courage. Don't mope: you have buffeted [too] many a storm in life, old war horse, to be like a silly boarding-school girl. Things must go all right. I am not going to die or to be ill just now; I am determined to be healthy. You know my grit.

Miss [Josephine] MacLeod sent you your letter. What was it about? Was there anything queer? I am glad she had it. She writes beautifully about you. She has already started, and we will have a jolly good company this winter here in Calcutta.

Mrs. [Ole] Bull, Miss MacLeod, Mrs. Sevier and Nivedita and I will be overjoyed if somebody else will be thrown into the bargain. I can't get any more value, eh? I must stop. Am going to look after my geese and ducks just for five minutes, breaking the doctor's command to lie down all the time. One of the geese is a silly, fearful bird, always despondent and anxious. She likes to be all alone by herself and is miserable — very much like another goose I know in another place.

> Here my story ends
> And spinach top bends.
> Why is spinach withering?
> Because the goat is browsing.
> Why is the goat browsing?
> Because no grass is growing.
> Why no grass is growing?
> The gardener is not watering.
> Why there is no watering?
> The Master is not commanding.
> Why is he not commanding?
> An ant has bitten the Master!

This is a nursery rhyme told after a story, and it is true of us all. It is only an ant bite, after all — the trouble here; is it not?

Ever yours,
Vivekananda.

CCXII — CHRISTINE

To Sister Christine:

THE MATH, BELUR,
DIST. HOWRAH, BENGAL, INDIA,
18th December 1901.

DEAR CHRISTINE,

I am much better, and the rest is doing me good. I have found out that lying in bed all the time gives me as much sleep as wanted and good digestion too. Albumen and sugar vanish immediately [when] I begin taking rest.

Mrs. Bull and Nivedita start for India from Marseilles today, and unless they change their plan, [they] must be in India before this reaches you — two weeks before.

Herewith I send you four hundred and eighty dollars by cheque drawn on Thomas Cook & Son, Broadway, New York. They have no branch office in Detroit. On receipt of this, you write to Thomas Cook & Son, Broadway, New York, that you have got a cheque from India — mentioning the amount and number — drawn by Thomas Cook & Son on the firm of Thomas Cook & Son, and want to be advised as to how to cash it. Don't send the cheque ahead. (Excuse all these details. I feel you are a baby in business, though I am worse.) This is to pay your "passage to India"[6]* if you think fit to accept Mrs. Sevier's invitation. If you get leave and come, I am sure you will find somebody who is coming to England, at least. Then from there, again, somebody who is coming to Egypt. You come with them as far as Italy, thence direct on a boat to India.

Second-class passage across the Atlantic is all right, but the second class from Italy to Bombay is rather bad. There are always a few rough men and fast women. There is money enough for travelling first class all through, if you so like.

The Mother will see to it, even as [She did when] this money came. Drop me a line as soon as you engage your passage —better a week ahead; otherwise I don't see how the letter can reach me. The vessel to India you get from London; and possibly a letter may reach me with the name of the vessel, etc. In any case, however, you wire me as soon as you land and get into a good hotel. You will find many persons to receive you — and me too, most probably.

In case, however, things take another turn and you cannot come, no matter. Do with the money just as it pleases you.

It is very probable that after Miss [Josephine] MacLeod and Mrs. [Ole] Bull have been through India, they are going home via Japan; and, of course, I am going with them. In that case I will be in California next fall.

It will be a nice trip, and would it not be a fine tour round the world if you get leave and come?

Do just as the Mother opens the way for you, and do not worry.

Yours with all love and blessings,
Vivekananda.

CCXIII — SISTER CHRISTINE

To Sister Christine:

THE MATH, BELUR,
DIST. HOWRAH, BENGAL, INDIA,
25th December 1901.

A Merry Christmas and Happy New Year is the usual congratulation. Alas! The stars brought you a tremendous blow. (Sister Christine's mother had passed away.) Blessed be the name of the Lord. After all, it is only "Thy will be done" — our only refuge. I will not insult you by offering you consolation — you know it all already. Only this line to remind you of one who is in entire sympathy with you and who knows that all your plans must be good in joy or sorrow, as you are dedicated to the eternal Mother. Well, the Mother phenomenal has merged in the Mother absolute, eternal. Thy will be done.

By this time you must have made a decision, or, rather, the "Mother" has shown you the way, surely. I rest content.

The soldier of the Queen has gone abroad to fight for Her cause, leaving all he loves to Her care. The soldier is to look to his duty. The Queen of the Universe knows the rest.

With all love as usual,
Vivekananda.

CCXXIV — CHRISTINE

To Sister Christine:

THE MATH, BELUR, DIST. HOWRAH,
27th May 1902.

MY DEAR CHRISTINE,

I am sorry I could not visit the mountains this time. My health, though not improved as much as I [had] wished, is not bad. The liver has been benefited — [that] is a great gain. The rains will commence very soon in the hills. So it is useless for me to take all the trouble of that terrible route.

I am so happy to learn the mountains are doing you good. Eat a lot, sleep as much as you can, and get plump. Stuff yourself till you get plump or you burst.

So the place did not suit Mr. Okakura [Kakuzo] — why? There must have been something to annoy him very much that he left the place so abruptly. Did he not like the scenery? Was it not sublime enough for him? Or the Japanese do not like sublimity at all? They only like beauty.

One of the boys writes that the little boy is getting disobedient etc. Mrs. Sevier wants me to take him down. So I do. I have asked Sadananda and another monk (whom I want for work here) to go to Almora and wait for the monsoon, and when it breaks, to come down.

If you feel you are becoming the least burdensome to Mrs. Sevier, write me immediately. It would be a sin to put further pressure on her — she does so much for me. However, she likes you very much and writes that you look be-au-ti-ful in saris.

I have just now two kids and three lambs added to the family. There was one more kid, but he got himself drowned in the yellow fish tank. How is Margot? Is she still there, or gone away with Mr. Okakura? How is she pulling on with the boys?

What do you do the whole day? How do you pass the day? Write me all details, and frequently; but do not expect long letters from me often.

Give my love to Mrs. Sevier, to Margot and the rest, and you may take a few spoonfuls, if you like,

With only this,
Vivekananda.

PS — Have an eye on the little chap. The boys are already jealous of him. They did spoil another boy that way before.

CCXXV — CHRISTINE

To Sister Christine:

> THE MATH, BELUR, DIST. HOWRAH,
> 14th June 1902.

MY DEAR CHRISTINE,

Your letters had to wait a few days, as I was out of town in a village. Well, many thanks for all the information I got. Mr. Okakura [Kakuzo] has been to the Math, but I was away. He will be in Calcutta a few weeks more and then goes to Bombay. He intends taking a house near the city to learn intimately the customs of Bengalees. I am so glad to learn Margo's [Sister Nivedita's] intention to stop at Mayavati longer. She really requires good rest, and she had none in Europe, I am sure of that. If she were amenable to my advice as of old, I would take away every book and every scrap of paper from her, make her walk some, eat a lot and sleep a lot more. As to talking, I would have the merriest conversation all the while.

I have a beautiful letter from Mrs. Sevier, and [am] so happy to learn that she loves you more and more. But plumpness is the criterion, mon amie [my friend], for a' [all] that.

So there was a great flutter in our dovecote owing to my letters, but things must have assumed their old form by this time. The boy, my nephew, is going to be sometime yet in the Ashrama; make him talk English with a good accent — do. No foreign language can be learnt properly unless you talk in it from childhood.

Mr. Bose is still there, I hope; and you must have liked him immensely. He is a man, a brick. Tender him my best regards, will you?

Have you any water in the lakes now? Do you get the snows clearer? It has been raining all through this summer here. We had very few burning days, only a number of stuffy ones. Our rains also have nearly set in. In a week the deluge will commence in earnest.

As for me, I am much stronger than before; and when seven miles of jolting in a bullock-cart and railway travel of thirty-four miles did not bring back the dropsy to the feet, I am sure it is not going to return.

But anyway, it is the Math that suits me best just now.

With all love,
Vivekananda.

CCXXVI — CHRISTINE

To Sister Christine:

> THE MATH, BELUR, DIST. HOWRAH,
> 15th June 1902.

DEAR CHRISTINE,

Just now received your note. I am quite easy in my mind so long [as] you live with Mrs. [Charlotte] Sevier at Mayavati. You know, anxiety is one thing I must avoid to recover. I will be very anxious if you are in Calcutta, at Baghbazar. I am slowly recovering. Stay with Mrs. Sevier as long as you can. Don't come down with Margot [Sister Nivedita].

With love,
Vivekananda.

CCXXVII — CHRISTINE

To Sister Christine:

> THE MATH, BELUR, DIST. HOWRAH,
> 21st June 1902.

MY DEAR CHRISTINE,

You have not the least cause to be anxious. I am getting on anyhow and am quite strong. As to diet, I find I have to restrict myself and not follow the prescription of my doctor to eat anything I like. The pills continue, however. Will you ask the boys if they can get "Amalaki" [Emblic myrobalan] fruits in the place now? We cannot get them in the plains now. They are rather sour and puckery eaten raw; but make marmalade of whole [ones] — delicious. Then they are the best things for fermentation I ever get.

No anxiety on the score of Marie Louise's arrival in Calcutta. She has not yet made any noise.

Things go on the same. I am trying to go to Monghyr — a place near Calcutta and said to be very salubrious.

We will think of your coming to Baghbazar after Nivedita has fairly started; till then keep quiet and lay on food.

With all love to yourself, the boys and Mother [Mrs. Charlotte Sevier],

> Vivekananda.

PS — I am laying on adipose tissues fast — especially about the abdominal regions: "It is fearful to see!"

LECTURES AND DISCOURSES

THE WOMEN OF INDIA

New Discoveries, Vol. 2, pp. 411-26.

The following lecture was delivered at Cambridge, December 17, 1894, and recorded by Miss Frances Willard's stenographer.

Swami Vivekananda faced bigotry in America on several issues of Indian culture — one was the Indian woman. Naturally he sought to correct Western misconceptions. When he lectured in his own country, however, there was no greater advocate for improving the life of Indian women than the Swami.

In speaking about the women of India, ladies and gentlemen, I feel that I am going to talk about my mothers and sisters in India to the women of another race, many of whom have been like mothers and sisters to me. But though, unfortunately, within very recent times there have been mouths only to curse the women of our country, I have found that there are some who bless them too. I have found such noble souls in this nation as Mrs. [Ole] Bull and Miss [Sarah] Farmer and Miss [Frances] Willard, and that wonderful representative of the highest aristocracy of the world, whose life reminds me of that man of India, six hundred years before the birth of Christ, who gave up his throne to mix with the people. Lady Henry Somerset has been a revelation to me. I become bold when I find such noble souls who will not curse, whose mouths are full of blessing for me, my country, our men and women, and whose hands and hearts are ever ready to do service to humanity.

I first intend to take a glimpse into times past of Indian history, and we will find something unique. All of you are aware, perhaps, that you Americans and we Hindus and this lady from Iceland [Mrs. Sigrid Magnusson] are the descendants of one common ancestry known as Aryans. Above all, we find three ideas wherever the Aryans go: the village community, the rights of women and a joyful religion[1].

The first [idea] is the system of village communities — as we have just heard from Mrs. Bull concerning the North. Each man was his own [lord?] and owned the land. All these political institutions of the world we now see, are the developments of those village systems. As the Aryans went over to different countries and settled, certain circumstances developed this institution, others that.

The next idea of the Aryans is the freedom of women. It is in the Aryan literature that we find women in ancient times taking the same share as men, and in no other literature of the world.

Going back to our Vedas — they are the oldest literature the world possesses and are composed by your and my common ancestors (they were not written in India — perhaps on the coast of the Baltic, perhaps in Central Asia — we do not know).

Their oldest portion is composed of hymns, and these hymns are to the gods whom the Aryans worshipped. I may be pardoned for using the word gods; the literal translation is "the bright ones". These hymns are dedicated to Fire, to the Sun, to Varuna and other deities. The titles run: "such-and-such a sage composed this verse, dedicated to such-and-such a deity".

In the tenth chapter comes a peculiar hymn — for the sage is a woman — and it is dedicated to the one God who is at the background of all these gods. All the previous hymns are spoken in the third person, as if someone were addressing the deities. But this hymn takes a departure: God [as the Devi] is speaking for herself. The pronoun used is "I". "I am the Empress of the Universe, the Fulfiller of all prayers." (Vide "Devi Sukta", Rig-Veda 10.125)

This is the first glimpse of women's work in the Vedas. As we go on, we find them taking a greater share — even officiating as priests. There is not one passage throughout the whole mass of literature of the Vedas which can be construed even indirectly as signifying that woman could never be a priest. In fact, there are many examples of women officiating as priests.

Then we come to the last portion of these Vedas — which is really the religion of India — the

---

1. Since Swami Vivekananda's time there has been more research on the spread of the Aryan culture.

concentrated wisdom of which has not been surpassed even in this century. There, too, we find women preeminent. A large portion of these books are words which have proceeded from the mouths of women. It is there — recorded with their names and teachings.

There is that beautiful story of the great sage Yâjnavalkya, the one who visited the kingdom of the great king Janaka. And there in that assembly of the learned, people came to ask him questions. One man asked him, "How am I to perform this sacrifice?" Another asked him, "How am I to perform the other sacrifice?" And after he had answered them, there arose a woman who said, "These are childish questions. Now, have a care: I take these two arrows, my two questions. Answer them if you can, and we will then call you a sage. The first is: What is the soul? The second is: What is God?" (Brihadâranyaka Upanishad 3.8.1.-12.)

Thus arose in India the great questions about the soul and God, and these came from the mouth of a woman. The sage had to pass an examination before her, and he passed well.

Coming to the next stratum of literature, our epics, we find that education has not degenerated. Especially in the caste of princes this ideal was most wonderfully held.

In the Vedas we find this idea of marrying — the girls chose for themselves; so the boys. In the next stratum they are married by their parents, except in one caste.

Even here I would ask you to look at another side. Whatever may be said of the Hindus, they are one of the most learned races the world has ever produced. The Hindu is the metaphysician; he applies everything to his intellect. Everything has to be settled by astrological calculation.

The idea was that the stars govern the fate of every man and woman. Even today when a child is born, a horoscope is cast. That determines the character of the child. One child is born of a divine nature, another of a human, others of lower character.

The difficulty was: If a child who was of a monster-character was united with a child of a god-character, would they not have a tendency to degenerate each other?

The next difficulty was: Our laws did not allow marriage within the same clans. Not only may one not marry within his own family — or even one of his cousins — but one must not marry into the clan of his father or even of his mother.

A third difficulty was: If there had been leprosy or phthisis or any such incurable disease within six generations of either bride or bridegroom, then there must not be a marriage.

Now taking [into account] these three difficulties, the Brahmin says: "If I leave it to the choice of the boy or girl to marry, the boy or girl will be fascinated with a beautiful face. And then very likely all these circumstances will bring ruin to the family". This is the primary idea that governs our marriage laws, as you will find. Whether right or wrong, there is this philosophy at the background. Prevention is better than cure.

That misery exists in this world is because we give birth to misery. So the whole question is how to prevent the birth of miserable children. How far the rights of a society should extend over the individual is an open question. But the Hindus say that the choice of marriage should not be left in the hands of the boy or girl.

I do not mean to say that this is the best thing to do. Nor do I see that leaving it in their hands is at all a perfect solution. I have not found a solution yet in my own mind; nor do I see that any country has one.

We come next to another picture. I told you that there was another peculiar form of marriage (generally among the royalty) where the father of the girl invited different princes and noblemen and they had an assembly. The young lady, the daughter of the king, was borne on a sort of chair before each one of the princes in turn. And the herald would repeat: "This is Prince So-and-so, and these are his qualifications". The young girl would either wait or say, "Move on". And before the next prince, the crier would also give a description, and the girl would say, "Move on". (All this would be arranged beforehand;

she already had the liking for somebody before this.) Then at last she would ask one of the servants to throw the garland over the head of the man, and it would be thrown to show he was accepted. (The last of these marriages was the cause of the Mohammedan invasion of India.) (Vide prince, who became the Queen of Delhi.) These marriages were specially reserved for the prince caste.

The oldest Sanskrit poem in existence, the Râmâyana, has embodied the loftiest Hindu ideal of a woman in the character of Sitâ. We have not time to go through her life of infinite patience and goodness. We worship her as God incarnate, and she is named before her husband, Râma. We say not "Mr. and Mrs.", but "Mrs. and Mr." and so on, with all the gods and goddesses, naming the woman first.

There is another peculiar conception of the Hindu. Those who have been studying with me are aware that the central conception of Hindu philosophy is of the Absolute; that is the background of the universe. This Absolute Being, of whom we can predicate nothing, has Its powers spoken of as She — that is, the real personal God in India is She. This Shakti of the Brahman is always in the feminine gender.

Rama is considered the type of the Absolute, and Sita that of Power. We have no time to go over all the life of Sita, but I will quote a passage from her life that is very much suited to the ladies of this country.

The picture opens when she was in the forest with her husband, whither they were banished. There was a female sage whom they both went to see. Her fasts and devotions had emaciated her body.

Sita approached this sage and bowed down before her. The sage placed her hand on the head of Sita and said: "It is a great blessing to possess a beautiful body; you have that. It is a greater blessing to have a noble husband; you have that. It is the greatest blessing to be perfectly obedient to such a husband; you are that. You must be happy".

Sita replied, "Mother, I am glad that God has given me a beautiful body and that I have so devoted a husband. But as to the third blessing, I do not know whether I obey him or he obeys me. One thing alone I remember, that when he took me by the hand before the sacrificial fire — whether it was a reflection of the fire or whether God himself made it appear to me — I found that I was his and he was mine. And since then, I have found that I am the complement of his life, and he of mine".

Portions of this poem have been translated into the English language. Sita is the ideal of a woman in India and worshipped as God incarnate.

We come now to Manu the great lawgiver. Now, in this book there is an elaborate description of how a child should be educated. We must remember that it was compulsory with the Aryans that a child be educated, whatever his caste. After describing how a child should be educated, Manu adds: "Along the same lines, the daughters are to be educated — exactly as the boys"[1].

I have often heard that there are other passages where women are condemned. I admit that in our sacred books there are many passages which condemn women as offering temptation; you can see that for yourselves. But there are also passages that glorify women as the power of God. And there are other passages which state that in that house where one drop of a woman's tear falls, the gods are never pleased and the house goes to ruin. Drinking wine, killing a woman and killing a Brahmin are the highest crimes in the Hindu religion. I admit there are condemnatory sentences [in some of our books]; but here I claim the superiority of these Hindu books, for in the books of other races there is only condemnation and no good word for a woman.

Next, I will come to our old dramas. Whatever the books say, the dramas are the perfect representation of society as it then existed. In these, which were written from four hundred years before Christ onward, we find even universities full of both boys and girls. We would not [now] find Hindu women, as they have since become cut off from higher education[2]. But [at that time], they were everywhere

---

1. The text of this sentence is not found in the extant Manu Samhitâ. Vide Mahânirvâna Tantra 8.47.

2. Since Swami Vivekananda's time, higher education among women in India has spread rapidly.

pretty much the same as they are in this country — going out to the gardens and parks to take promenades.

There is another point which I bring before you and where the Hindu woman is still superior to all other women in the world — her rights. The right to possess property is as absolute for women in India as for men — and has been for thousands and thousands of years.

If you have any lawyer friend and can take up commentaries on the Hindu law, you will find it all for yourselves. A girl may bring a million dollars to her husband, but every dollar of that is hers. Nobody has any right to touch one dollar of that. If the husband dies without issue, the whole property of the husband goes to her, even if his father or mother is living. And that has been the law from the past to the present time. That is something which the Hindu woman has had beyond that of the women of other countries.

The older books — or even newer books — do not prohibit the Hindu widows from being married; it is a mistake to think so. They give them their choice, and that is given to both men and women. The idea in our religion is that marriage is for the weak, and I don't see any reason to give up that idea today. They who find themselves complete — what is the use of their marrying? And those that marry — they are given one chance. When that chance is over, both men and women are looked down upon if they marry again; but it is not that they are prohibited. It is nowhere said that a widow is not to marry. The widow and widower who do not marry are considered more spiritual.

Men, of course, break through this law and go and marry; whereas women — they being of a higher spiritual nature — keep to the law. For instance, our books say that eating meat is bad and sinful, but you may still eat such-and-such a meat — mutton, for instance. I have seen thousands of men who eat mutton, and never in my life have I seen a woman of higher caste who eats meat of any kind. This shows that their nature is to keep the law — keeping more towards religion. But do not judge too harshly of Hindu men. You must try to look at the Hindu law from my position too, for I am a Hindu man.

This non-marriage of widows gradually grew into a custom. And whenever in India a custom becomes rigid, it is almost impossible to break through it — just as in your country, you will find how hard it is to break through a five-day custom of fashion. In the lower castes, except two, the widows remarry.

There is a passage in our later law books [which states] that a woman shall not read the Vedas. But they are prohibited to even a weak Brahmin. If a Brahmin boy is not strong-minded, the law is applied to him also. But that does not show that education is prohibited to them, for the Vedas are not all that the Hindus have. Every other book women can read. All the mass of Sanskrit literature, that whole ocean of literature — science, drama, poetry — is all for them. They can go there and read everything, except the [Vedic] scriptures[1].

In later days the idea was that woman was not intended to be a priest; so what is the use of her studying the Vedas? In that, the Hindus are not so far behind other nations. When women give up the world and join our Order, they are no longer considered either men or women. They have no sex. The whole question of high or low caste, man or woman, dies out entirely.

Whatever I know of religion I learned from my master, and he learned it of a woman.

Coming back to the Rajput woman, I will try to bring to you a story from some of our old books — how during the Mohammedan conquest, one of these women was the cause of what led to the conquest of India.

A Rajput prince of Kanauj — a very ancient city — had a daughter [Samjukta]. She had heard of the military fame of Prithvi Raj [King of Ajmere and Delhi] and all his glory, and she was in love with him.

Now her father wanted to hold a Râjasuya sacrifice, so he invited all the kings in the country. And in that sacrifice, they all had to render menial ser-

---

1. Today Indian women are no longer barred from reading any scriptures — Vedic or non-Vedic.

vice to him because he was superior over all; and with that sacrifice he declared there would be a choice by his daughter.

But the daughter was already in love with Prithvi Raj. He was very mighty and was not going to acknowledge loyalty to the king, her father, so he refused the invitation. Then the king made a golden statue of Prithvi Raj and put it near the door. He said that that was the duty he had given him to perform — that of a porter.

The upshot of the whole affair was that Prithvi Raj, like a true knight, came and took the lady behind him on his horse, and they both fled.

When the news came to her father, he gave chase with his army, and there was a great battle in which the majority of both armies was killed. And [thus the Rajputs were so weakened that] the Mohammedan empire in India began.

When the Mohammedan empire was being established in northern India, the Queen of Chitore [Râni Padmini] was famed for her beauty. And the report of her beauty reached the sultan, and he wrote a letter for the queen to be sent to his harem. The result was a terrible war between the King of Chitore and the sultan. The Mohammedans invaded Chitore. And when the Rajputs found they could not defend themselves any more, the men all took sword in hand and killed and were killed, and the women perished in the flames.

After the men had all perished, the conqueror entered the city. There in the street was rising a horrible flame. He saw circles of women going around it, led by the queen herself. When he approached near and asked the queen to refrain from jumping into the flames, she said, "This is how the Rajput woman treats you", and threw herself into the fire.

It is said that 74,500 women perished in the flames that day to save their honour from the hands of the Mohammedans. Even today when we write a letter, after sealing it we write "74½" upon it, meaning that if one dares to open this letter, that sin of killing 74,500 women will be upon his head.

I will tell you the story of another beautiful Rajput girl[2]. There is a peculiar custom in our country called "protection". Women can send small bracelets of silken thread to men. And if a girl sends one of these to a man, that man becomes her brother.

During the reign of the last of the Mogul emperors — the cruel man who destroyed that most brilliant empire of India — he similarly heard of the beauty of a Rajput chieftain's daughter. Orders were sent that she should be brought to the Mogul harem.

Then a messenger came from the emperor to her with his picture, and he showed it to her. In derision she stamped upon it with her feet and said, "Thus the Rajput girl treats your Mogul emperor". As a result, the imperial army was marched into Rajputana.

In despair the chieftain's daughter thought of a device. She took a number of these bracelets and sent them to the Rajput princes with a message: "Come and help us". All the Rajputs assembled, and so the imperial forces had to go back again.

I will tell you a peculiar proverb in Rajputana. There is a caste in India called the shop class, the traders. They are very intelligent — some of them — but the Hindus think they are rather sharp. But it is a peculiar fact that the women of that caste are not as intelligent as the men. On the other hand, the Rajput man is not half as intelligent as the Rajput woman.

The common proverb in Rajputana is: "The intelligent woman begets the dull son, and the dull woman begets the sharp son". The fact is, whenever any state or kingdom in Rajputana has been managed by a woman, it has been managed wonderfully well.

We come to another class of women. This mild Hindu race produces fighting women from time to time. Some of you may have heard of the woman [Lakshmi Bai, Queen of Jhansi] who, during the Mutiny of 1857, fought against the English soldiers and held her own ground for two years — leading

---

2. Chârumati, or Rupamati, daughter of Vikram Singh, King of Kishangarh, in Rajasthan. Charumati is the heroine of Râjasimha, a Bengali historical novel written by Bankim Chandra Chatterjee.

modern armies, managing batteries and always charging at the head of her army. This queen was a Brahmin girl.

A man whom I know lost three of his sons in that war. When he talks of them he is calm, but when he talks of this woman his voice becomes animated. He used to say that she was a goddess — she was not a human being. This old veteran thinks he never saw better generalship.

The story of Chand Bibi, or Chand Sultana [1546 - 1599], is well known in India. She was the Queen of Golconda, where the diamond mines were. For months she defended herself. At last, a breach was made in the walls. When the imperial army tried to rush in there, she was in full armour, and she forced the troops to go back[1].

In still later times, perhaps you will be astonished to know that a great English general had once to face a Hindu girl of sixteen.

Women in statesmanship, managing territories, governing countries, even making war, have proved themselves equal to men — if not superior. In India I have no doubt of that. Whenever they have had the opportunity, they have proved that they have as much ability as men, with this advantage — that they seldom degenerate. They keep to the moral standard, which is innate in their nature. And thus as governors and rulers of their state, they prove — at least in India — far superior to men. John Stuart Mill mentions this fact.

Even at the present day, we see women in India managing vast estates with great ability. There were two ladies where I was born who were the proprietors of large estates and patronesses of learning and art and who managed these estates with their own brains and looked to every detail of the business.

Each nation, beyond a general humanity, develops a certain peculiarity of character — so in religion, so in politics, so in the physical body, so in mental habitude, so in men and women, so in character. One nation develops one peculiarity of character, another takes another peculiarity. Within the last few years the world has begun to recognize this.

The very peculiarity of Hindu women, which they have developed and which is the idea of their life, is that of the mother. If you enter a Hindu's home, you will not find the wife to be the same equal companion of the husband as you find her here. But when you find the mother, she is the very pillar of the Hindu home. The wife must wait to become the mother, and then she will be everything.

If one becomes a monk, his father will have to salute him first because he has become a monk and is therefore superior to him. But to his mother he — monk or no monk — will have to go down on his knees and prostrate himself before her. He will then put a little cup of water before her feet, she will dip her toe in it, and he will have to drink of it. A Hindu son gladly does this a thousand times over again![2]

Where the Vedas teach morality, the first words are, "Let the mother be your God" (Taittiriya Upanishad 1.11.) — and that she is. When we talk of woman in India, our idea of woman is mother. The value of women consists in their being mothers of the human race. That is the idea of the Hindu.

I have seen my old master taking little girls by the hands, placing them in a chair and actually worshipping them — placing flowers at their feet and prostrating himself before these little children — because they represented the mother God.

The mother is the God in our family. The idea is that the only real love that we see in the world, the most unselfish love, is in the mother — always suffering, always loving. And what love can represent the love of God more than the love which we see in the mother? Thus the mother is the incarnation of God on earth to the Hindu.

"That boy alone can understand God who has been first taught by his mother." I have heard wild stories about the illiteracy of our women. Till I was a boy of ten, I was taught by my mother. I saw my

---

1. The soldiers were so impressed with Chand Bibi's military prowess and courage that they referred to her as Chand Sultana, which means "Chand — the Empress".

2. This custom is a gesture meant to acknowledge the mother not only as the first teacher and preceptor in one's life, but also as an embodiment of the all-loving God.

grandmother living and my great-grandmother living, and I assure you that there never was in my line a female ancestor who could not read or write, or who had to put "her mark" on a paper. If there was a woman who could not read or write, my birth would have been impossible. Caste laws make it imperative.

So these are wild stories which I sometimes hear — such as the statement that in the Middle Ages reading and writing were taken away from Hindu women. I refer you to Sir William Hunter's History of the English People, where he cited Indian women who could calculate a solar eclipse.

I have been told that either too much worship of the mother makes the mother selfish or too much love of the children for the mother makes them selfish. But I do not believe that. The love which my mother gave to me has made me what I am, and I owe a debt to her that I can never repay.

Why should the Hindu mother be worshipped? Our philosophers try to find a reason and they come to this definition: We call ourselves the Aryan race. What is an Aryan? He is a man whose birth is through religion. This is a peculiar subject, perhaps, in this country; but the idea is that a man must be born through religion, through prayers. If you take up our law books you will find chapters devoted to this — the prenatal influence of a mother on the child.

I know that before I was born, my mother would fast and pray and do hundreds of things which I could not even do for five minutes. She did that for two years. I believe that whatever religious culture I have, I owe to that. It was consciously that my mother brought me into the world to be what I am. Whatever good impulse I have was given to me by my mother — and consciously, not unconsciously.

"A child materially born is not an Aryan; the child born in spirituality is an Aryan." For all this trouble — because she has to make herself so pure and holy in order to have pure children — she has a peculiar claim on the Hindu child. And the rest [of her traits] is the same with all other nations: she is so unselfish. But the mother has to suffer most in our families.

The mother has to eat last. I have been asked many times in your country why the [Hindu] husband does not sit with his wife to eat — if the idea is, perhaps, that the husband thinks she is too low a being. This explanation is not at all right. You know, a hog's hair is thought to be very unclean. A Hindu cannot brush his teeth with the brushes made of it, so he uses the fibre of plants. Some traveller saw one Hindu brushing his teeth with that and then wrote that "a Hindu gets up early in the morning and gets a plant and chews it and swallows it!" Similarly, some have seen the husband and wife not eating together and have made their own explanation. There are so many explainers in this world, and so few observers — as if the world is dying for their explanations! That is why I sometimes think the invention of printing was not an unmixed blessing. The real fact is: just as in your country many things must not be done by ladies before men, so in our country the fact is that it is very indecorous to munch and munch before men. If a lady is eating, she may eat before her brothers. But if the husband comes in, she stops immediately and the husband walks out quickly. We have no tables to sit at, and whenever a man is hungry he comes in and takes his meal and goes out. Do not believe that a Hindu husband does not allow his wife to sit at the table with him. He has no table at all.

The first part of the food — when it is ready — belongs to the guests and the poor, the second to the lower animals, the third to the children, the fourth to the husband, and last comes the mother. How many times I have seen my mother going to take her first meal when it was two o'clock. We took ours at ten and she at two because she had so many things to attend to. [For example], someone knocks at the door and says, "Guest", and there is no food except what was for my mother. She would give that to him willingly and then wait for her own. That was her life and she liked it. And that is why we worship mothers as gods.

I wish you would like less to be merely petted and patronized and more to be worshipped! [You], a member of the human race! — the poor Hindu does not understand that [inclination of yours]. But when you say, "We are mothers and we command", he bows down. This is the side then that the Hindus have developed.

Going back to our theories — people in the West came about one hundred years ago to the point that they must tolerate other religions. But we know now that toleration is not sufficient toward another religion; we must accept it. Thus it is not a question of subtraction, it is a question of addition. The truth is the result of all these different sides added together. Each of all these religions represents one side, the fullness being the addition of all these. And so in every science, it is addition that is the law.

Now the Hindu has developed this side. But will this side be enough? Let the Hindu woman who is the mother become the worthy wife also, but do not try to destroy the mother. That is the best thing you can do. Thus you get a better view of the universe instead of going about all over the world, rushing into different nations and criticizing them and saying, "The horrid wretches — all fit to be barbecued for eternity!"

If we take our stand on this position — that each nation under the Lord's will is developing one part of human nature — no nation is a failure. So far they have done well, now they must do better! [Applause]

Instead of calling the Hindus "heathens", "wretches", "slaves", go to India and say, "So far your work is wonderful, but that is not all. You have much more to do. God bless you that you have developed this side of woman as a mother. Now help the other side — the wife of men".

And similarly, I think (I tell it with the best spirit) that you had better add to your national character a little more of the mother side of the Hindu nature! This was the first verse that I was taught in my life, the first day I went to school: "He indeed is a learned man who looks upon all women as his mother, who looks upon every man's property as so much dust, and looks upon every being as his own soul".

There is the other idea of the woman working with the man. It is not that the Hindus had not those ideals, but they could not develop them.

It is alone in the Sanskrit language that we find four words meaning husband and wife together. It is only in our marriage that they [both] promise, "What has been my heart now may be thine". It is there that we see that the husband is made to look at the Pole-star, touching the hand of his wife and saying, "As the Pole-star is fixed in the heavens, so may I be fixed in my affection to thee". And the wife does the same.

Even a woman who is vile enough to go into the streets can sue her husband and have a maintenance. We find the germs of these ideas in all our books throughout our nation, but we were not able to develop that side of the character.

We must go far beyond sentiment when we want to judge. We know it is not emotion alone that governs the world, but there is something behind emotion. Economic causes, surrounding circumstances and other considerations enter into the development of nations. (It is not in my present plan to go into the causes that develop woman as wife.)

So in this world, as each nation is placed under peculiar circumstances and is developing its own type, the day is coming when all these different types will be mixed up — when that vile sort of patriotism which means "rob everybody and give to me" will vanish. Then there will be no more one-sided development in the whole world, and each one of these [nations] will see that they had done right.

Let us now go to work and mix the nations up together and let the new nation come.

Will you let me tell you my conviction? Much of the civilization that comprises the world today has come from that one peculiar race of mankind — the Aryans[1].

[Aryan] civilization has been of three types: the Roman, the Greek, the Hindu. The Roman type is the type of organization, conquest, steadiness — but lacking in emotional nature, appreciation of beauty

---

1. It may be noted here that today many historians and anthropologists would describe the Aryans as a linguistic group rather than a race. — Publisher.

and the higher emotions. Its defect is cruelty. The Greek is essentially enthusiastic for the beautiful, but frivolous and has a tendency to become immoral. The Hindu type is essentially metaphysical and religious, but lacking in all the elements of organization and work.

The Roman type is now represented by the Anglo-Saxon; the Greek type more by the French than by any other nation; and the old Hindus do not die! Each type has its advantage in this new land of promise. They have the Roman's organization, the power of the Greek's wonderful love for the beautiful, and the Hindu's backbone of religion and love of God. Mix these up together and bring in the new civilization.

And let me tell you, this should be done by women. There are some of our books which say that the next incarnation, and the last (we believe in ten), is to come in the form of a woman.

We see resources in the world yet remaining because all the forces that are in the world have not come into use. The hand was acting all this time while other parts of the body were remaining silent. Let the other parts of the body be awakened and perhaps in harmonious action all the misery will be cured. Perhaps, in this new land, with this new blood in your veins, you may bring in that new civilization — and, perhaps, through American women.

As to that ever blessed land which gave me this body, I look back with great veneration and bless the merciful being who permitted me to take birth in that holiest spot on earth. When the whole world is trying to trace its ancestry from men distinguished in arms or wealth, the Hindus alone are proud to trace their descent from saints.

That wonderful vessel which has been carrying for ages men and women across this ocean of life may have sprung small leaks here and there. And of that, too, the Lord alone knows how much is owing to themselves and how much to those who look down with contempt upon the Hindus.

But if such leaks there are, I, the meanest of her children, think it my duty to stop her from sinking even if I have to do it with my life. And if I find that all my struggles are in vain, still, as the Lord is my witness, I will tell them with my heartfelt benediction: "My brethren, you have done well — nay, better than any other race could have done under the same circumstances. You have given me all that I have. Grant me the privilege of being at your side to the last and let us all sink together".

THE FIRST STEP TOWARDS JNANA

A Jnâna-Yoga class delivered in New York, Wednesday, December 11, 1895, and recorded by Swami Kripananda.

The word Jnâna means knowledge. It is derived from the root Jnâ — to know — the same word from which your English word to know is derived. Jnana-Yoga is Yoga by means of knowledge. What is the object of the Jnana-Yoga? Freedom. Freedom from what? Freedom from our imperfections, freedom from the misery of life. Why are we miserable? We are miserable because we are bound. What is the bondage? The bondage is of nature. Who is it that binds us? We, ourselves.

The whole universe is bound by the law of causation. There cannot be anything, any fact — either in the internal or in the external world — that is uncaused; and every cause must produce an effect.

Now this bondage in which we are is a fact. It need not be proved that we are in bondage. For instance: I would be very glad to get out of this room through this wall, but I cannot; I would be very glad if I never became sick, but I cannot prevent it; I would be very glad not to die, but I have to; I would be very glad to do millions of things that I cannot do. The will is there, but we do not succeed in accomplishing the desire. When we have any desire and not the means of fulfilling it, we get that peculiar reaction called misery. Who is the cause of desire? I, myself. Therefore, I myself am the cause of all the miseries I am in.

Misery begins with the birth of the child. Weak and helpless, he enters the world. The first sign of life is weeping. Now, how could we be the cause of misery when we find it at the very beginning? We have caused it in the past. [Here Swami Vivekananda entered into a fairly long discussion of "the very interesting theory called Reincarnation". He continued:]

To understand reincarnation, we have first to know that in this universe something can never be produced out of nothing. If there is such a thing as a human soul, it cannot be produced out of nothing. If something can be produced out of nothing, then something would disappear into nothing also. If we are produced out of nothing, then we will also go back into nothing. That which has a beginning must have an end. Therefore, as souls we could not have had any beginning. We have been existing all the time.

Then again, if we did not exist previously, there is no explanation of our present existence. The child is born with a bundle of causes. How many things we see in a child which can never be explained until we grant that the child has had past experience — for instance, fear of death and a great number of innate tendencies. Who taught the baby to drink milk and to do so in a peculiar fashion? Where did it acquire this knowledge? We know that there cannot be any knowledge without experience, for to say that knowledge is intuitive in the child, or instinctive, is what the logicians would call a "petitio principii".

It would be the same [logic] as when a man asks me why light comes through a glass, and I answer him, "Because it is transparent". That would be really no answer at all because I am simply translating his word into a bigger one. The word "transparent" means "that through which light comes" — and that was the question. The question was why light comes through the glass, and I answered him, "Because it comes through the glass".

In the same way, the question was why these tendencies are in the child. Why should it have fear of death if it never saw death? If this is the first time it was ever born, how did it know to suck the mother's milk? If the answer is "Oh, it was instinct", that is simply returning the question. If a man stands up and says, "I do not know", he is in a better position than the man who says, "It is instinct" and all such nonsense.

There is no such thing as instinct; there is no such thing as nature separate from habit. Habit is one's second nature, and habit is one's first nature too. All that is in your nature is the result of habit, and habit is the result of experience. There cannot be any knowledge but from experience.

So this baby must have had some experience too. This fact is granted even by modern materialistic science. It proves beyond doubt that the baby brings with it a fund of experience. It does not enter into this world with a "tabula rasa" — a blank mind upon which nothing is written — as some of the old philosophers believed, but ready equipped with a bundle of knowledge. So far so good.

But while modern science grants that this bundle of knowledge which the child brings with it was acquired through experience, it asserts, at the same time, that it is not its own — but its father's and its grandfather's and its great-grandfather's. Knowledge comes, they say, through hereditary transmission.

Now this is one step in advance of that old theory of "instinct", that is fit only for babies and idiots. This "instinct" theory is a mere pun upon words and has no meaning whatsoever. A man with the least thinking power and the least insight into the logical precision of words would never dare to explain innate tendencies by "instinct", a term which is equivalent to saying that something came out of nothing. But the modern theory of transmission through experience — though, no doubt, a step in advance of the old one — is not sufficient at all. Why not? We can understand a physical transmission, but a mental transmission is impossible to understand.

What causes me — who am a soul — to be born with a father who has transmitted certain qualities? What makes me come back? The father, having certain qualities, may be one binding cause. Taking for granted that I am a distinct soul that was existing before and wants to reincarnate — what makes my soul go into the body of a particular man? For the explanation to be sufficient, we have to assume a hereditary transmission of energies and such a thing as my own previous experience. This is what is called Karma, or, in English, the Law of Causation, the law of fitness.

For instance, if my previous actions have all been towards drunkenness, I will naturally gravitate towards persons who are transmitting a drunkard's character. I can only take advantage of the organism produced by those parents who have been transmitting a certain peculiar influence for which I am fit by my previous actions. Thus we see that it is true that a certain hereditary experience is transmitted from father to son, and so on. At the same time, it is my past experience that joins me to the particular cause of hereditary transmission.

A simply hereditary transmission theory will only touch the physical man and would be perfectly insufficient for the internal soul of man. Even when looking upon the matter from the purest materialistic standpoint — viz. that there is no such thing as a soul in man, and man is nothing but a bundle of atoms acted upon by certain physical forces and works like an automaton — even taking that for granted, the mere transmission theory would be quite insufficient.

The greatest difficulties regarding the simple hypothesis of mere physical transmission will be here: If there be no such thing as a soul in man, if he be nothing more than a bundle of atoms acted upon by certain forces, then, in the case of transmission, the soul of the father would decrease in ratio to the number of his children; and the man who has five, six or eight children must, in the end, become an idiot. India and China — where men breed like rats — would then be full of idiots. But, on the contrary, we find that the least amount of lunacy is in India and China.

The question is, What do we mean by the word transmission? It is a big word, but, like so many other impossible and nonsensical terms of the same kind, it has come into use without people understanding it. If I were to ask you what transmission is, you would find that you have no real conception of its meaning because there is no idea attached to it.

Let us look a little closer into the matter. Say, for instance, here is a father. A child is born to him. We see that the same qualities [which the father possesses] have entered into his child. Very good. Now how did the qualities of the father come to be in the child? Nobody knows. So this gap the modern physicists want to fill with the big word transmission. And what does this transmission mean? Nobody knows.

How can mental qualities of experience be condensed and made to live in one single cell of protoplasm? There is no difference between the protoplasm of a bird and that of a human brain. All we can say with regard to physical transmission is that it consists of the two or three protoplasmic cells cut from the father's body. That is all. But what nonsense to assume that ages and ages of past human experience got compressed into a few protoplasmic cells! It is too tremendous a pill they ask you to swallow with this little word transmission.

In olden times the churches had prestige, but today science has got it. And just as in olden times people never inquired for themselves — never studied the Bible, and so the priests had a very good opportunity to teach whatever they liked — so even now the majority of people do not study for themselves and, at the same time, have a tremendous awe and fear before anything called scientific. You ought to remember that there is a worse popery coming than ever existed in the church — the so-called scientific popery, which has become so successful that it dictates to us with more authority than religious popery.

These popes of modern science are great popes indeed, but sometimes they ask us to believe more wonderful things than any priest or any religion ever did. And one of those wonderful things is that transmission theory, which I could never understand. If I ask, "What do you mean by transmission?" they only make it a little easier by saying, "It is hereditary transmission". And if I tell them, "That is rather Greek to me", they make it still easier by saying, "It is the adherence of paternal qualities in the protoplasmic cells". In that way it becomes easier and easier, until my mind becomes muddled and disgusted with the whole thing.

Now one thing we see: we produce thought. I am talking to you this evening and it is producing thought in your brain. By this act of transmission we understand that my thoughts are being transmitted into your brain and your mind, and producing other thoughts. This is an everyday fact.

It is always rational to take the side of things which you can understand — to take the side of fact. Transmission of thought is

perfectly understandable. Therefore we are able to take up the [concept of] transmission of thought, and not of hereditary impressions of protoplasmic cells alone. We need not brush aside the theory, but the main stress must be laid upon the transmission of thought.

Now a father does not transmit thought. It is thought alone that transmits thought. The child that is born existed previously as thought. We all existed eternally as thought and will go on existing as thought.

What we think, that our body becomes. Everything is manufactured by thought, and thus we are the manufacturers of our own lives. We alone are responsible for whatever we do. It is foolish to cry out: "Why am I unhappy?" I made my own unhappiness. It is not the fault of the Lord at all.

Someone takes advantage of the light of the sun to break into your house and rob you. And then when he is caught by the policeman, he may cry: "Oh sun, why did you make me steal?" It was not the sun's fault at all, because there are thousands of other people who did much good to their fellow beings under the light of the same sun. The sun did not tell this man to go about stealing and robbing.

Each one of us reaps what we ourselves have sown. These miseries under which we suffer, these bondages under which we struggle, have been caused by ourselves, and none else in the universe is to blame. God is the least to blame for it.

"Why did God create this evil world?" He did not create this evil world at all. We have made it evil, and we have to make it good. "Why did God create me so miserable?" He did not. He gave me the same powers as [He did] to every being. I brought myself to this pass.

Is God to blame for what I myself have done? His mercy is always the same. His sun shines on the wicked and the good alike. His air, His water, His earth give the same chances to the wicked and the good. God is always the same eternal, merciful Father. The only thing for us to do is to bear the results of our own acts.

We learn that, in the first place, we have been existing eternally; in the second place that we are the makers of our own lives. There is no such thing as fate. Our lives are the result of our previous actions, our Karma. And it naturally follows that having been ourselves the makers of our Karma, we must also be able to unmake it.

The whole gist of Jnana-Yoga is to show humanity the method of undoing this Karma. A caterpillar spins a little cocoon around itself out of the substance of its own body and at last finds itself imprisoned. It may cry and weep and howl there; nobody will come to its rescue until it becomes wise and then comes out, a beautiful butterfly. So with these our bondages. We are going around and around ourselves through countless ages. And now we feel miserable and cry and lament over our bondage. But crying and weeping will be of no avail. We must set ourselves to cutting these bondages.

The main cause of all bondage is ignorance. Man is not wicked by his own nature — not at all. His nature is pure, perfectly holy. Each man is divine. Each man that you see is a God by his very nature. This nature is covered by ignorance, and it is ignorance that binds us down. Ignorance is the cause of all misery. Ignorance is the cause of all wickedness; and knowledge will make the world good. Knowledge will remove all misery. Knowledge will make us free. This is the idea of Jnana-Yoga: knowledge will make us free! What knowledge? Chemistry? Physics? Astronomy? Geology? They help us a little, just a little. But the chief knowledge is that of your own nature. "Know thyself." You must know what you are, what your real nature is. You must become conscious of that infinite nature within. Then your bondages will burst.

Studying the external alone, man begins to feel himself to be nothing. These vast powers of nature, these tremendous changes occurring — whole communities wiped off the face of the earth in a twinkling of time, one volcanic eruption shattering to pieces whole continents — perceiving and studying these things, man begins to feel himself weak. Therefore, it is not the study of external nature that makes [one] strong. But there is the internal nature of man—a million times more powerful than any volcanic eruption or any law of nature — which conquers nature, triumphs over all its laws. And that alone teaches man what he is.

"Knowledge is power", says the proverb, does it not? It is through knowledge that power comes. Man has got to know. Here is a man of infinite power and strength. He himself is by his own nature potent and omniscient. And this he must know. And the more he becomes conscious of his own Self, the more he manifests this power, and his bonds break and at last he becomes free.

How to know ourselves? the question remains now. There are various ways to know this Self, but in Jnana-Yoga it takes the help of nothing but sheer intellectual reasoning. Reason alone, intellect alone, rising to spiritual perception, shows what we are.

There is no question of believing. Disbelieve everything — that is the idea of the Jnani. Believe nothing and disbelieve everything — that is the first step. Dare to be a rationalist. Dare to follow reason wherever it leads you.

We hear everyday people saying all around us: "I dare to reason". It is, however, a very difficult thing to do. I would go two hundred miles to look at the face of the man who dares to reason and to follow reason. Nothing is easier to say, and nothing is more difficult to do. We are bound to follow superstitions all the time — old, hoary superstitions, either national or belonging to humanity in general — superstitions belonging to family, to friends, to country, to fashion, to books, to sex and to what-not.

Talk of reason! Very few people reason, indeed. You hear a man say, "Oh, I don't like to believe in anything; I don't like to grope through darkness. I must reason". And so he reasons. But when reason smashes to pieces things that he hugs unto his breast, he says, "No more! This reasoning is all right until it breaks my ideals. Stop there!" That man would never be a Jnani. That man will carry his bondage all his life and his lives to come. Again and again he will come under the power of death. Such men are not made for Jnana. There are other methods for them — such as bhakti-yoga, Karma-Yoga, or Râja-Yoga — but not Jnana-Yoga.

I want to prepare you by saying that this method can be followed only by the boldest. Do not think that the man who believes in no church or belongs to no sect, or the man who boasts of his unbelief, is a rationalist. Not at all. In modern times it is rather bravado to do anything like that.

To be a rationalist requires more than unbelief. You must be able not only to reason, but also to follow the dictates of your reason. If reason tells you that this body is an illusion, are you ready to give it up? Reason tells you that heat and cold are mere illusions of your senses; are you ready to brave these things? If reason tells you that nothing that the senses convey to your mind is true, are you ready to deny your sense perception? If you dare, you are a rationalist.

It is very hard to believe in reason and follow truth. This whole world is full either of the superstitious or of half-hearted hypocrites. I would rather side with superstition and ignorance than stand with these half-hearted hypocrites. They are no good. They stand on both sides of the river.

Take anything up, fix your ideal and follow it out boldly unto death. That is the way to salvation. Half-heartedness never led to anything. Be superstitious, be a fanatic if you please, but be something. Be something, show that you have something; but be not like these shilly-shallyers with truth — these jacks-of-all-trades who just want to get a sort of nervous titillation, a dose of opium, until this desire after the sensational becomes a habit.

The world is getting too full of such people. Contrary to the apostles who, according to Christ, were the salt of the earth, these fellows are the ashes, the dirt of the earth. So let us first clear the ground and understand what is meant by following reason, and then we will try to understand what the obstructions are to our following reason.

The first obstruction to our following reason is our unwillingness to go to truth. We want truth to come to us. In all my travels, most people told me: "Oh, that is not a comfortable religion you talk about. Give us a comfortable religion!"

I do not understand what they mean by this "comfortable religion". I was never taught any comfortable religion in my life. I want truth for my religion. Whether it be comfortable or not, I do not care. Why should truth be comfortable always? Truth many times hits hard — as we all know by our experience. Gradually, after a long intercourse with such persons, I came to find out what they meant by their stereotypical phrase. These people have got into a rut, and they do not dare to get out of it. Truth must apologize to them.

I once met a lady who was very fond of her children and her money and her everything. When I began to preach to her that the only way to God is by giving up everything, she stopped coming the next day. One day she came and told me that the reason for her staying away was because the religion I preached was very uncomfortable. "What sort of religion would be comfortable to you?" I asked in order to test her. She said: "I want to see God in my children, in my money, in my diamonds".

"Very good, madam", I replied. "You have now got all these things. And you will have to see these things millions of years yet. Then you will be bumped somewhere and come to reason. Until that time comes, you will never come to God. In the meantime, go on seeing God in your children and in your money and your diamonds and your dances."

It is difficult, almost impossible, for such people to give up sense enjoyment. It has grown upon them from birth to birth. If you ask a pig to give up his sty and to go into your most beautiful parlour, why it will be death to the pig. "Let go, I must live there", says the pig.

[Here Swami Vivekananda explained the story of the fishwife: "Once a fishwife was a guest in the house of a gardener who raised flowers. She came there with her empty basket, after selling fish in the market, and was asked to sleep in a room where flowers were kept. But, because of the fragrance of the flowers, she couldn't get to sleep for a long time. Her hostess saw her condition and said, 'Hello! Why are you tossing from side to side so restlessly?' The fishwife said: 'I don't know, friend. Perhaps the smell of the flowers has been disturbing my sleep. Can you give me my fish-basket? Perhaps that will put me to sleep'."]

So with us. The majority of mankind delights in this fish smell — this world, this enjoyment of the senses, this money and wealth and chattel and wife and children. All this nonsense of the world — this fishy smell — has grown upon us. We can hear nothing beyond it, can see nothing beyond it; nothing goes beyond it. This is the whole universe.

All this talk about heaven and God and soul means nothing to an ordinary man. He has heaven already here. He has no other idea beyond this world. When you tell him of something higher, he says, "That is not a comfortable religion. Give us something comfortable". That is to say that religion is nothing but what he is doing.

If he is a thief and you tell him that stealing is the highest thing we can do, he will say, "That is a comfortable religion". If he is cheating, you have to tell him that what he is doing is all right; then he will accept your teaching as a "comfortable religion". The whole trouble is that people never want to get out of their ruts — never want to get rid of the old fish-basket and smell, in order to live. If they say, "I want the truth", that simply means that they want the fish-basket.

When have you reached knowledge? When you are equipped with those four disciplines [i.e. the four qualifications for attainment discussed in Vedantic literature: discrimination between the real and the unreal, renunciation, the six treasures of virtue beginning with tranquillity, and longing for liberation]. You must give up all desire of enjoyment, either in this life or the next. All enjoyments of this life are vain. Let them come and go as they will.

What you have earned by your past actions none can take away from you. If you have deserved wealth, you can bury yourself in the forest and it will come to you. If you have deserved good food and clothing, you may go to the north pole and they will be brought to you. The polar bear will bring them. If you have not deserved them, you may conquer the world and will die of starvation. So, why do you bother about these things? And, after all, what is the use of them?

As children we all think that the world is made so very nice, and that masses of pleasures are simply waiting for our going out to them. That is every schoolboy's dream. And when he goes out into the world, the everyday world, very soon his dreams vanish. So with nations. When they see how every city is built upon ruins — every forest stands upon a city — then they become convinced of the vanity of this world.

All the power of knowledge and wealth once made has passed away — all the sciences of the ancients, lost, lost forever. Nobody knows how. That teaches us a grand lesson. Vanity of vanities; all is vanity and vexation of the spirit. If we have seen all this, then we become disgusted with this world and all it offers us. This is called Vairâgya, non-attachment, and is the first step towards knowledge.

The natural desire of man is to go towards the senses. Turning away from the senses takes him back to God. So the first lesson we have to learn is to turn away from the vanities of the world.

How long will you go on sinking and diving down and going up for five minutes, to again sink down, again come up and sink, and so on — tossed up and down? How long will you be whirled on this wheel of Karma — up and down, up and down? How many thousands of times have you been kings and rulers? How many times have you been surrounded by wealth and plunged into poverty? How many thousands of times have you been possessed of the greatest powers? But again you had to become men, rolling down on this mad rush of Karma's waters. This tremendous wheel of Karma stops neither for the widow's tears nor the orphan's cry.

How long will you go on? How long? Will you be like that old man who had spent all his life in prison and, when let out, begged to be brought back into his dark and filthy dungeon cell? This is the case with us all! We cling with all our might to this low, dark, filthy cell called this world — to this hideous, chimerical existence where we are kicked about like a football by every wind that blows.

We are slaves in the hands of nature — slaves to a bit of bread, slaves to praise, slaves to blame, slaves to wife, to husband, to child, slaves to everything. Why, I go about all over the world — beg, steal, rob, do anything — to make happy a boy who is, perhaps, hump-backed or ugly-looking. I will do every wicked thing to make him happy. Why? Because I am his father. And, at the same time, there are millions and millions of boys in this world dying of starvation — boys beautiful in body and in mind. But they are nothing to me. Let them all die. I am apt to kill them all to save this one rascal to whom I have given birth. This is what you call love. Not I. Not I. This is brutality.

There are millions of women — beautiful in body and mind, good, gentle, virtuous — dying of starvation this minute. I do not care for them at all. But that Jennie who is mine — who beats me three times a day, and scolds me the whole day — for that Jennie I am going to beg, borrow, cheat and steal so that she will have a nice gown.

Do you call that love? Not I. This is mere desire, animal desire — nothing more. Turn away from these things. Is there no end to these hideous dreams? Put a stop to them.

When the mind comes to that state of disgust with all the vanities of life, it is called turning away from nature. This is the first step. All desires must be given up — even the desire of getting heaven.

What are these heavens anyhow? Places where to sing psalms all the time. What for? To live there and have a nice healthy body with phosphorescent light or something of this kind coming out of every part, with a halo around the head, and with wings and the power to penetrate the wall?

If there be powers, they must pass away sooner or later. If there is a heaven — as there may be many heavens with various grades of enjoyment — there cannot be a body that lives forever. Death will overtake us, even there.

Every conjunction must have a disjunction. No body, finer or coarser, can be manufactured without particles of matter coming together. Whenever two particles come together, they are held by a certain attraction; and there will come a time when those particles will separate. This is the eternal law. So, wherever there is a body — either grosser or finer, either in heaven or on earth — death will overcome it.

Therefore, all desires of enjoyment in this life, or in a life to come, should be given up. People have a natural desire to enjoy; and when they do not find their selfish enjoyments in this life, they think that after death they will have a lot of enjoyment somewhere else. If these enjoyments do not take us towards knowledge in this life, in this world, how can they bring us knowledge in another life?

Which is the goal of man? Enjoyment or knowledge? Certainly not enjoyment. Man is not born to have pleasure or to suffer pain. Knowledge is the goal. Knowledge is the only pleasure we can have.

All the sense pleasures belong to the brute. And the more the pleasure in knowledge comes, these sense pleasures fall down. The more animal a man is, the more he enjoys the pleasures of the senses. No man can eat with the same gusto as a famished dog. No man was ever born who could feel the same pleasure in eating as an ordinary bull. See how their whole soul is in that eating. Why, your millionaires would give millions for that enjoyment in eating — but they cannot have it.

This universe is like a perfectly balanced ocean. You cannot raise a wave in one place without making a hollow in another one. The sum total of energy in the universe is the same throughout. You spend it in some place, you lose it in another. The brute has got it, but he spent it on his senses; and each of his senses is a hundred times stronger than that of man.

How the dog smells at a distance! How he traces a footstep! We cannot do that. So, in the savage man. His senses are less keen than the animal's, but keener than the civilized man's.

The lower classes in every country intensely enjoy everything physical. Their senses are stronger than those of the cultured. But as you go higher and higher in the scale, you see the power of thought increasing and the powers of the senses decreasing, in the same ratio.

Take a [brute], cut him [as it were] to pieces, and in five days he is all right. But if I scratch you, it is ten to one you will suffer for weeks or months. That energy of life which he displays — you have it too. But with you, it is used in making up your brain, in the manufacture of thought. So with all enjoyments and all pleasures. Either enjoy the pleasure of the senses — live like the brute and become a brute — or renounce these things and become free.

The great civilizations — what have they died of? They went for pleasure. And they went further down and down until, under the mercy of God, savages came to exterminate them, lest we would see human brutes growling about. Savages killed off those nations that became brutalized through sense enjoyment, lest Darwin's missing link would be found.

True civilization does not mean congregating in cities and living a foolish life, but going Godward, controlling the senses, and thus becoming the ruler in this house of the Self.

Think of the slavery in which we are [bound]. Every beautiful form I see, every sound of praise I hear, immediately attracts me; every word of blame I hear immediately repels me. Every fool has an influence over my mind. Every little movement in the world makes an impression upon me. Is this a life worth living?

So when you have realized the misery of this physical existence — when you have become convinced that such a life is not worth living — you have made the first step towards Jnana.

BHAKTI-YOGA

New Discoveries, Vol. 3, pp. 543-54.

A bhakti-yoga class delivered in New York, Monday morning, January 20, 1896, and recorded by Mr. Josiah J. Goodwin.

We finished in our last [class the subject] about Pratikas. One idea more of the preparatory Bhakti, and then we will go on to the Parâ, the Supreme. This idea is what is called Nishthâ, devotion to one idea.

We know that all these ideas of worship are right and all good, and we have seen that the worship of God, and God alone, is Bhakti. The worship of any other being will not be Bhakti, but God can be worshipped in various forms and through various ideas. And we have seen that all these ideas are right and good, but the difficulty is here: If we just stop with this last conclusion, we find that in the end we have frittered away our energies and done nothing.

It is a great tendency among liberal people to become a jack-of-all-trades and master of none — to nibble a little here and there and, in the long run, find they have nothing. In this country it many times grows into a sort of disease — to hear various things and do nothing.

Here is the advice of one of our old Bhaktas: "Take the honey from all flowers, mix with all with respect, say yea, yea to all, but give not up your seat". This giving not up your own seat is what is called Nishtha. It is not that one should hate, or even criticize, the ideals of other people; he knows they are all right. But, at the same time, he must stick to his own ideal very strictly.

There is a story of Hanumân, who was a great worshipper of Râma. Just as the Christians worship Christ as the incarnation of God, so the Hindus worship many incarnations of God. According to them, God came nine times in India and will come once more. When he came as Rama, this Hanuman was his great worshipper. Hanuman lived very long and was a great Yogi.

During his lifetime, Rama came again as Krishna; and Hanuman, being a great Yogi, knew that the same God had come back again as Krishna. He came and served Krishna, but he said to him, "I want to see that Rama form of yours". Krishna said, "Is not this form enough? I am this Krishna; I am this Rama. All these forms are mine". Hanuman said, "I know that, but the Rama form is for me. The Lord of Jânaki (Janaki is a name of Sitâ.) and the Lord of Shri (Shri is a name of Laksmi.) are the same. They are both the incarnations of the Supreme Self. Yet the lotus-eyed Rama is my all in all". This is Nishtha — knowing that all these different forms of worship are right, yet sticking to one and rejecting the others. We must not worship the others at all; we must not hate or criticize them, but respect them.

The elephant has two teeth coming out from his mouth. These are only for show; he cannot eat with them. But the teeth that are inside are those with which he chews his food. So mix with all, say yea, yea to all, but join none. Stick to your own ideal of worship. When you worship, worship that ideal of God which is your own Ishta, your own Chosen Ideal. If you do not, you will have nothing. Nothing will grow.

When a plant is growing, it is necessary that it should be hedged round lest any animal should eat it up. But when it has become strong and a huge gigantic tree, do not care for any hedges — it is perfect in itself. So when just the seed of spirituality is growing, to fritter away the energies on all sorts of religious ideas — a little of this and a little of that: a little of Christianity, a little of Buddhism, and, in reality, of nothing — destroys the soul.

This [acceptance] has its good side; and in the end we will come to it. Only do not put the cart before the horse.

In the first place, we are bound to become sectarians. But this should be the ideal of sectarianism — not to avoid anyone. Each of us must have a sect, and that sect is our own Ishta — our own chosen way. However, that should not make us want to kill other people — only to hold onto our own way. It is sacred and it should not be told to our own brothers, because my choice is sacred, and his [also] is sacred. So keep that choice as your own. That should be the [attitude of] worship of everyone. When you pray to your own Ideal, your own Ishta, that is the only God you shall have. God exists in various phases, no doubt, but for the time being, your own Ishta is the only phase for you.

Then, after a long course of training in this Ishta — when this plant of spirituality has grown and the soul has become strong and you begin to realize that your Ishta is everywhere — [then] naturally all these bondages will fall down. When the fruit becomes ripe, it falls of its own weight. If you pluck an unripe fruit it is bitter, sour. So we will have to grow in this thought.

Simply hearing lectures and all this nonsense — making the Battle of Waterloo in the brain, simply unadjusted [undigested?] ideas — is no good. Devotion to one idea — those that have this will become spiritual, will see the light. You see everyone complaining: "I try this" and "I try that", and if you cross-question them as to what they try, they will say that they have heard a few lectures in one place and another, a handful of talks in one corner and another. And for three hours, or a few days, they worshipped and thought they had done enough. That is the way of fools, not the way to perfection — not the way to attain spirituality.

Take up one idea, your Ishta, and let the whole soul be devoted to it. Practise this from day to day until you see the result, until the soul grows. And if it is sincere and good, that very idea will spread till it covers the whole universe. Let it spread by itself; it will all come from the inside out. Then you will say that your Ishta is everywhere and that He is in everything.

Of course, at the same time, we must always remember that we must recognize the Ishtas of others and respect them — the other ideas of God — or else worship will degenerate into fanaticism. There is an old story of a man who was a worshipper of Shiva. There are sects in our country who worship God as Shiva, and others who worship Him as Vishnu. This man was a great worshipper of Shiva, and to that he added a tremendous hatred for all worshippers of Vishnu and would not hear the name of Vishnu pronounced. There are a great number of worshippers of Vishnu in India, and he could not avoid hearing the name. So he bored two holes in his ears and tied two little bells onto them. Whenever a man mentioned the name of Vishnu, he moved his head and rang the bells, and that prevented his hearing the name.

But Shiva told him in a dream, "What a fool you are! I am Vishnu, and I am Shiva; they are not different—only in name. There are not two Gods". But this man said, "I don't care. I will have nothing to do with this Vishnu business".

He had a little statue of Shiva and made it very nice, built an altar for it. One day he bought some beautiful incense and went home to light some of the incense for his God. While the fumes [smoke] of his incense were rising in the air, he found that the image was divided into two: one half remained Shiva, and the other half was Vishnu. Then the man jumped up and put his finger under the nostril of Vishnu so that not a particle of the smell could get there.

Then Shiva became disgusted, and the man became [was turned into] a demon. He is [known as] the father of all fanatics, the "bell-eared" demon. He is respected by the boys of India, and they worship him. It is a very peculiar kind of worship. They make a clay image and worship him with all sorts of horrible smelling flowers. There are some flowers in the forests of India which have a most pestilential smell. They worship him with these and then take big sticks and beat the image. He [the "bell-eared" demon] is the father of all fanatics who hate all other gods except their own.

This is the only danger in this Nishthâ Bhakti — becoming this fanatical demon. The world gets full of them. It is very easy to hate. The generality of mankind gets so weak that in order to love one, they must hate another; they must take the energy out of one point in order to put it into another. A man loves one woman and then loves another; and to love the other, he has to hate the first. So with women. This characteristic is in every part of our nature, and so in our religion. The ordinary, undeveloped weak brain of mankind cannot love one without hating another. This very [characteristic] becomes fanaticism in religion. Loving their own ideal is synonymous with hating every other idea.

This should be avoided and, at the same time, the other danger should be avoided. We must not fritter away all our energies, [otherwise] religion becomes a nothing with us — just hearing lectures. These are the two dangers. The danger with the liberals is that they are too expansive and have no intensity. You see that in these days religion has become very expansive, very broad. But the ideas are so broad that there is no depth in them. Religion has become to many merely a means of doing a little charity work, just to amuse them after a hard day's labour — they get five minutes religion to amuse them. This is the danger with the liberal thought. On the other hand, the sectarians have the depth, the intensity, but that intensity is so narrow. They are very deep, but with no breadth to it. Not only that, but it draws out hatred to everyone else.

Now, if we can avoid both these dangers and become as broad as the uttermost liberals and as deep as the bluest fanatic, then we will solve the problem. Our idea is how that can be done. It is by this theory of Nishtha — knowing that all these ideals that we see are [good] and true, that all these are so many parts of the same God and, at the same time, thinking that we are not strong enough to worship Him in all these forms, and therefore must stick to one ideal and make that ideal our life. When you have succeeded in doing that, all the rest will come. Here ends the first part of Bhakti: the formal, the ceremonial and the preparatory.

You must remember that the first lesson in this Bhakti was on the disciple. Who is the disciple? What are the necessary qualifications for a disciple? You read in the scriptures: "Where the speaker is wonderful, so is the listener. When the teacher is wonderful, so is the taught. Then alone will this spirituality come".

Mankind generally thinks that everything is to be expected from the teacher. Very few people understand that they are not fit to be taught. In the disciple first this is necessary: that he must want — he must really want spirituality.

We want everything but spirituality. What is meant by want? Just as we want food. Luxuries are not wants, but necessaries are wants. Religion is a necessary thing to very few; and to the vast mass of mankind it is a luxury. There are a hundred things in life without which they can live, until they come to the shop and see a new and artistic something and they want to buy it. Ninety-nine and nine-tenths per cent of mankind comes to religion in this way. It is one of the many luxuries they have in life. There is no harm in this. Let them have all they want; but they are entirely mistaken if they think they can fool God. He cannot be fooled. They will only fool themselves and sink down lower and lower until they become like brutes. Those therefore will become spiritual who want [spirituality] — who feel the necessity of religion, just as they feel the necessity of clothes, the necessity of work, the necessity of air to breathe.

A necessary thing is that without which we cannot live; and a luxury is that which is simply the gratification of a momentary desire.

The second qualification in the disciple is that he must be pure; and the other is that he must be persevering — he must work. Hearing is only one part; and the other part is doing.

The second necessity in Bhakti was the teacher. The teacher must be properly qualified. The main idea in that lecture was that the teacher must have the seed of spirituality. The teacher is not a talker, but the transmitter of spiritual force which he has received from his teacher, and he from others, and so on, in an unbroken current. He must be able to transmit that spiritual current.

When the teacher and the taught are both ready, then the first step in bhakti-yoga comes. The first part of bhakti-yoga is what is called the preparatory [stage], wherein you work through forms.

The next lecture was on the Name — how in all scriptures and in all religions Name has been exalted and how that Name does us good. The Bhakti-Yogi must always think that the Name itself is God — nothing different from God. The Name and God are one.

Next, it was taught how, for the Bhakti-Yogi, humility and reverence are necessary. The Bhakti-Yogi must hold himself as a dead man. A dead man never takes an insult, never retaliates; he is dead to everyone. The Bhakti-Yogi must reverence all good people, all saintly people, for the glory of the Lord shines always through His children.

The next lesson was on the Pratikas. In that it was taught that Bhakti is only when you worship God. Worshipping anyone else is not Bhakti. But we can worship anything we like if we think it is God. If we do not think it is God, that worship is not Bhakti. If you think it is God, it is all right.

There was a certain Yogi who used to practise meditation in a lonely part of the forest, on the banks of a river. There was a poor cowherd, a very ignorant man, who used to tend his herd in that forest. Every day he used to see this same Yogi meditating by the hour, practising austerities, living alone and studying. Somehow the cowherd got curious as to what he did. So he came to the Yogi and said, "Sir, can you teach me the way to God?" This Yogi was a very learned, great man, and he replied, "How will you understand God — you common cowherd? Blockhead, go home and tend your cows and don't bother your head with such things".

The poor fellow went away, but somehow a real want had come to him. So he could not rest, and he came again to the Yogi and said, "Sir, won't you teach me something about God?"

Again he was repulsed: "Oh, you blockhead, what can you understand of God? Go home". But the cowherd could not sleep; he could not eat. He must know something about God.

So he came again; and the Yogi, in order to quiet the man, as he was so insisting, said, "I'll teach you about God".

The man asked, "Sir, what sort of being is God? What is His form? How does He look?"

The Yogi said, "God is just like the big bull in your herd. That is just God. God has become that big bull".

The man believed him and went back to his herd. Day and night he took that bull for God and began to worship it. He brought the greenest grass for that bull, rested close to it and gave it light, sat near it and followed it. Thus days and months and years passed. His whole soul was there [in the bull].

One day he heard a voice, as it were, coming out of the bull. "The bull speaks!" [the cowherd thought.]"

"My son, my son."

"Why, the bull is speaking! No, the bull cannot speak."

Again he went away, and sat near meditating in great misery of his heart. He did not know anything. Again he heard the voice coming out of the bull: "My child, my child".

He went near. "No, the bull cannot speak." Then he went back again and sat despondent.

Again the voice came, and that time he found it out. It was from his own heart. He found that God was in him. Then he learned the wonderful truth of the Teacher of all teachers: "I am with thee always". And the poor cowherd learned the whole mystery.

Then he goes back to the Yogi, and when he is at some distance the Yogi sees him. The Yogi has been the most learned man in the country, practising austerity for years — meditating, studying. And this cowherd, an ignorant blockhead, never studied a book nor learned his letters. But he comes — his whole body, as it were, transfigured, his face changed, the light of heaven shining round his face. The Yogi got up. "What is this change? Where did you get this?""

"Sir, you gave me that."

"How? I told you that in joke."

"But I took it seriously. And I got everything I wanted out of that bull, for is He not everywhere?"

So that bull was the Pratika. And that man worshipped the bull as his Pratika — as God — and he got everything out of it. So that intense love — that desire — brings out everything. Everything is in ourselves, and the external world and the external worship are the forms, the suggestions that call it out. When they become strong, the Lord within awakens.

The external teacher is but the suggestion. When faith in the external teacher is strong, then the Teacher of all teachers within speaks; eternal wisdom speaks in the heart of that man. He need not go any more to any books or any men or any higher beings; he need not run after supernatural or preternatural beings for instruction. The Lord Himself becomes his instructor. He gets all he wants from himself. [There is] no more need to go to any temple or church. His own body has become the greatest temple in the world, and in that temple lives the Lord of Creation. In every country great saints have been born, wonderful lives have been [lived] — coming out of the sheer power of love.

So all these external forms of Bhakti — this repetition of the Name, worship of Pratika, this Nishtha, this Ishta — are but the preparations until that eternal power wakes up. Then alone comes spirituality — when one goes beyond these laws and bounds. Then all laws fall down, all forms vanish, temples and churches crumble into dust and die away. It is good to be born in a church, but it is the worst possible fate to die in a church. It is good to be born in a sect, and the worst possible thing to die in a sect with sectarian ideas.

What sect can hold a child of the Lord? What laws bind him? What forms shall he follow? What man shall he worship? He worships the Lord Himself. He Himself teaches him. He lives in the temple of all temples, the Soul of man.

So this is the goal towards which we are going — the supreme Bhakti — and all that leads up to this is but preparation. But it is necessary. It prepares the infinite Soul to come out of this bondage of books and sects and forms; these [ultimately] fly away and leave but the Soul of man. These are superstitions of an infinite amount of time. This "my father's religion", "my country's religion", or "my book", or my this and that, are but the superstition of ages; they vanish. Just as when one is pricked with a thorn he takes another thorn to get the first out and then throws both of them away, so this superstition is in us.

In many countries — even into the soft brains of little babies — are put the most horrible and diabolical nonsense, as sect ideas. Parents think they are doing good to the child, but they are merely murdering it to satisfy Mrs. Grundy. What selfishness! There is nothing that men out of fear of themselves or out of fear of society will not do. Men will kill their own children, mothers will starve their own families, brothers will hate brothers to satisfy forms — because Mrs. So-and-so will be pleased and satisfied.

We see that the vast mass of mankind is born in some church or temple of [some religious] form and never comes out of it. Why? Have these forms helped the growth of spirituality? If through these forms we step onto the highest platform of love, where forms vanish and all these sectarian ideas go away, how is it that the vast majority of men are always grovelling in some form or another? They are all atheists; they do not want any religion.

If a man comes to this country without any friend or without knowing anyone — supposing he is a blackguard in his own country — the first thing he will do in this country will be to join a church. Will that fellow ever have religion?

Do you mean to say that those women who go to churches to show their dresses will ever have religion or will come out of forms? They will go back and back. And when they die, they will become like animals.

Do you mean to say that those men who go to church to look at the beautiful faces of women will ever have religion? Those who have certain social religions — because society requires that they shall belong to Mr. So-and-so's church or because that was their father's church — will they ever have religion? They understand certain broad views, but they must keep a certain social position — and will keep it through eternity.

What you want, you get. The Lord fulfils all desires. If you want to keep a certain position in society you will do so; if you want the church, you will get that and not Him. If you want to play the fool all your life with all these churches and foolish organizations, you will have them and have to live in them all your lives. "Those that want the departed, go to the departed and get ghosts; but those that love Him, all come to Him." So those that love Him alone will come to Him, and those that love others will go to wherever they love.

That drill business in the temples and churches — kneeling down at a certain time, standing at ease, and all that drill nonsense, all mechanical, with the mind thinking of something else — all this has nothing to do with real religion.

There was a great prophet in India, Guru Nânak, born [some] four hundred years ago. Some of you have heard of the Sikhs — the fighting people. Guru Nanak was [the founder and also] a follower of the Sikh religion.

One day he went to the Mohammedans' mosque. These Mohammedans are feared in their own country, just as in a Christian country no one dare say anything against their religion…So Guru Nanak went in and there was a big mosque, and the Mohammedans were standing in prayer. They stand in lines: they kneel down, stand up, and repeat certain words at the same times, and one fellow leads. So Guru Nanak went there. And when the mullah was saying "In the name of the most merciful and kind God, Teacher of all teachers", Guru Nanak began to smile. He says, "Look at that hypocrite". The mullah got into a passion. "Why do you smile?"

"Because you are not praying, my friend. That is why I am smiling."

"Not praying?"

"Certainly not. There is no prayer in you."

The mullah was very angry, and he went and laid a complaint before a magistrate and said, "This heathen rascal dares to come to our mosque and smiles at us when we are praying. The only punishment is instant death. Kill him".

Guru Nanak was brought before the magistrate and asked why he smiled.

"Because he was not praying."

"What was he doing?" the magistrate asked.

"I will tell you what he was doing if you will bring him before me."

The magistrate ordered the mullah to be brought. And when he came, the magistrate said, "Here is the mullah. [Now] explain why you laughed when he was praying".

Guru Nanak said, "Give the mullah a piece of the Koran [to swear on]. [In the mosque] when he was saying 'Allah, Allah', he was thinking of some chicken he had left at home".

The poor mullah was confounded. He was a little more sincere than the others, and he confessed he was thinking of the chicken, and so they let the Sikh go. "And", said the magistrate [to the mullah], "don't go to the mosque again. It is better not to go at all than to commit blasphemy there and hypocrisy. Do not go when you do not feel like praying. Do not be like a hypocrite, and do not think of the chicken and say the name of the Most Merciful and Blissful God".

A certain Mohammedan was praying in a garden. They are very regular in their prayers. When the time comes, wherever they are, they just begin, fall down on the ground and get up and fall down, and so on. One of them was in a garden when the call for prayer came, so he knelt there prostrate on the ground to pray. A girl was waiting in the garden for her lover, and she saw him on the other side. And in her hurry to reach him, she did not see the man prostrate and walked over him. He was a fanatical Mohammedan — just what you call here a Presbyterian, the same breed. Both believe in barbecuing eternally. So you can just imagine the anger of this Mohammedan when his body was walked over — he wanted to kill the girl. The girl was a smart one, and she said, "Stop that nonsense. You are a fool and a hypocrite".

"What! I am a hypocrite?"

"Yes, I am going to meet my earthly lover, and I did not see you there. But you are going to meet your heavenly lover and should not know that a girl was passing over your body."

THE MUNDAKA UPANISHAD

New Discoveries, Vol. 3, pp. 557-68.

A Jnâna-Yoga class delivered in New York, January 29, 1896, and recorded by Mr. Josiah J. Goodwin.

In the last Jnana-Yoga (Vide Complete Works, II.) lecture, we read one of the Upanishads; we will read another [the Mundaka Upanishad]. Brahmâ was the first of the Devas, the Lord of this cycle and its protector. He gave this knowledge of Brahman, which is the essence of all knowledge, to his son Atharvan. The latter handed it over to his son Angiras, he to his son, Bharadvâja, and so on.

There was a man called Shaunaka, a very rich man, who went to this Angiras as a learner. He approached the teacher and asked him a question. "Tell me, sir, what is that which, being known, everything else is known?"

One [knowledge] is supreme and the other is inferior. The Rig-Veda is the name of one of the different parts of the Vedas. Shikshâ is the name of another part. All different sciences are inferior. What is the supreme science? That is the only science, the supreme science, by which we reach the Unchangeable One. But that cannot be seen, cannot be sensed, cannot be specified. Without colour, without eyes, without ears, without nose, without feet — the Eternal, the Omnipresent, the "Omnipenetrating", the Absolute — He from whom everything comes. The sages see Him, and that is the supreme knowledge.

Just as the Urnanâbhi, a species of spider, creates a thread out of his own body and takes it back, just as the plants grow by their own nature, and all these things are yet separate and apparently different (the heart is, as it were, different from the other parts of a man's body; the plants are different from the earth; the thread is different from the spider — yet they [the earth, the spider and so on] were the causes, and in them these things act), so from this Unchangeable One has come this universe.

First, out of Brahman comes the knowledge of desire and from that comes the manifestation of Creator, or the Golden Womb. From that comes intelligence, from that, matter and all these different worlds.

This is the truth — that for those who want to come to salvation or attain to other enjoyments, various ways are told in the Vedas.

Then it [the Mundaka Upanishad] goes on to say how they will reach these blessings. When they die they will go through the sun's rays to places which are very beautiful, where after death they will go to heaven and live for some time, but from there they will again fall.

Here are two words — Ishtam and Purtam. Sacrificial and other rituals are called Ishtam, and Purtam is making roads, building hospitals and so on. "Fools are they who think that rituals and doing good work are high and that there is nothing higher." They get what they desire and go to heaven, but every enjoyment and every sorrow must have an end. And so that ends, and they fall back and back and become men again, or still lower. Those that give up the world and learn to control the senses live in a forest. Through the rays of the sun they reach that immortality where lives He who is the Absolute.

Thus the sage, examining all desires of good or evil works, throws away all duties and wants to know that, getting which there is no more return, no more change. And to know that, he goes to the Guru, the teacher, with fuel in his hand.

There is a myth in our country about going to the Guru with fuel in one's hands as a sign of helping him in making sacrifices, as he will not take presents.

Who is a teacher? He who knows the secrets of the scriptures, he whose soul has gone unto Brahman, who does not care for works or going to heaven or all these things.

Unto such a disciple, who has controlled his mind, has become peaceful and calm, has given up all this tremendous wave that rises in the mind by desire ("I will do this and that" and all those desires which are at best only disturbing, such as name and fame, which impel mankind to do all sorts of things) — to that disciple in whom all these vexatious desires have been calmed down, the teacher teaches the way which is the science of Brahman, by which he can know that One who never changes and who is the Truth.

Then comes what he [Angiras] taught:

This is the truth, O gentle one, as from a mass of burning flame myriads of sparks come out of the same nature as the fire, even so from this Unchangeable One all these forms, all these ideas, all this creation, come out; and unto Him it [the creation] goes back.

But the Eternal One is everlasting, formless, without beginning, inside and outside of every being — beyond all life, beyond all mind, the Pure One, beyond even the unchangeable, beyond everything. From Him is born the vital principle. From Him comes the mind. From Him come all organs of the senses. From Him are air, light, water and this earth which holds all beings. These heavens are, as it were, His head; His eyes, the sun and moon. The cardinal points are, as it were, His ears. The eternal knowledge of the Vedas is, as it were, His manifested speech. His life is the air. His heart is this universe; His feet, this world. He is the Eternal Self of every being.

From Him have come the different Vedas. From Him have come the gods of the Sâdhyas. The latter are superior men, much higher than ordinary men and very much like the gods.

From Him are all men. From Him are all animals. From Him is all life; from Him, all the forces in the mind; from Him all truth, all chastity. The seven organs are all from Him. The seven objects of perception are from him; the seven actions of perception are from Him. From Him are the seven worlds in which the life currents flow. From Him are all these seas and oceans. From Him are all rivers that roll into the sea; from Him are all plants and all liquids.

He is the inside. He is the inner Soul of every being. This great Purusha, this great One — He is this universe, He is the work, He is the sacrifice. He is Brahman, and He is the trinity. He who knows Him frees his own soul from the bond of ignorance and becomes free.

He is the bright one. He is inside every human soul. From Him are all name and form; all the animals and men are from Him. He is the one Supreme. He who knows Him becomes free.

How to know Him? Take this bow, which is the Upanishad, the knowledge of the Vedanta; place upon that bow the sharpened rod [arrow] of worship; stretch that bow by what? — by making the mind of the same form as He, by knowing that you are He. Thus strike at it; strike at that Brahman with this rod. This One is the bow. This human mind is the rod [arrow]. Brahman is the object which we want to hit. This object is to be hit by concentrating the mind. And just when the rod has hit [its mark], the rod penetrates into the object and becomes one with it — a unity. Even so, this soul, the rod, is to be thrown upon the object so that it will become one with It — in Whom are the heavens, this earth and the skies, in Whom are the mind and all that lives.

In the Upanishads there are certain passages which are called the great words, which are always quoted and referred to.

In Him, that One — in Him alone, the Atman — exist all other worlds. What is the use of all other talk? Know Him alone. This is the bridge over this life to reach universality.

He [Angiras] goes on to show a practical way. So far it is very figurative.

Just as all the spokes of a wheel meet at the axle, even so in this body is that place from which all the arteries flow and at which they all meet. There, meditate upon the Om that is in the heart. May thou succeed. May the gentle one with success attain the goal. May you go beyond all darkness to Him who is omniscient, the All-Knowing. His glory is in heaven, on earth and everywhere.

He who has become the mind, the Prâna, He who is the leader in the body, He who is established in the food, the energy of life. By supreme knowledge the sages see Him whose nature is bliss, who shines as immortality.(Mundaka Upanishad 2.2.8.) (This is another of the sentences very much quoted.)

There are two words: one is Jnâna, the other Vijnâna. Jnana may be translated as science — this means intellectual [knowledge] only — and Vijnana as realization. God cannot be perceived by intellectual knowledge. He who has realized [the Self] by that supreme knowledge — what will become of that man?

All the knots of the heart will be cut asunder. All darkness will vanish forever when you have seen the Truth.

How can you doubt? How foolish and childish you will think these fights and quarrels of different sciences and different philosophies and all this. You will smile at them. All doubts will vanish, and all work will go away. All work will vanish.

Beyond, the golden sheath is there — without any impurity, without parts [indivisible] — He, the Brahman. His is the brightness, the Light of all light — the knowers of the Atman realize Him as such. And when you have done that, the sun cannot illumine, nor the moon, nor the stars. A flash of lightning cannot illumine the place; it is mental — away, deep in the mind. He shining, everything else shines; when He shines within, the whole man shines. This universe shines through His light.

Take such passages [for memorizing] later on, when studying the Upanishads.

The difference between the Hindu mind and the European mind is that whereas in the West truths are arrived at by examining the particular, the Hindu takes the opposite course. There is no [such] metaphysical sublimity as in the Upanishads.

It [the Mundaka Upanishad] leads you on, beyond the senses — infinitely more sublime than the suns and stars. First Angiras tried to describe God by sense sublimities — that His feet are the earth, His head the heavens. But that did not express what he wanted to say. It was in a sense sublime. He first gave that idea to the student and then slowly took him beyond, until he gave him the highest idea — the negative — too high to describe.

He is immortal, He is before us, He is behind us, He is on the right side, He is on the left, He is above, He is beneath.

Upon the same tree there are two birds with most beautiful wings, and the two birds always go together — always live together. Of these, one is eating the fruits of the tree; the other, without eating, is looking on. So in this body are the two birds always going together. Both have the same form and beautiful wings. One is the human soul, eating the fruits; the other is God Himself, of the same nature. He is also in this body, the Soul of our soul. He eats neither good nor evil fruits, but stands and looks on.

But the lower bird knows that he is weak and small and humble, and tells all sorts of lies. He says he is a woman, or he is a man or a boy. He says he will do good or do bad; he will go to heaven and will do a hundred sorts of things. In delirium he talks and works, and the central idea of his delirium is that he is weak.

Thus he gets all the misery because he thinks he is nobody. He is a created little being. He is a slave to somebody; he is governed by some god or gods, and so is unhappy.

But when he becomes joined with God, when he becomes a Yogi, he sees that the other bird, the Lord, is his own glory. "Why, it was my own glory whom I called God, and this little "I", this misery, was all hallucination; it never existed. I was never a woman, never a man, never any one of these things." Then he gives up all his sorrow.

When this Golden One, who is to be seen, is seen — the Creator, the Lord, the Purusha, the God of this universe — then the sage has washed off all stains of good and bad deeds. (Good deeds are as much stains as bad deeds.) Then he attains to total sameness with the Pure One. The sage knows that He who is the Soul of all souls — this Atman — shines through all.

He is the man, the woman, the cow, the dog — in all animals, in the sin and in the sinner. He is the Sannyâsin, He is in the ruler, He is everywhere.

Knowing this the sage speaks not. (He gives up criticizing anyone, scolding anyone, thinking evil of anyone.) His desires have gone into the Atman. This is the sign of the greatest knowers of Brahman — that they see nothing else but Him.

He is playing through all these things. Various forms — from the highest gods to the lowest worms — are all He. The ideas want to be illustrated.

First of all the writer showed us the idea that if we want to get to heaven and all these places, we will get there. That is to say, in the language of the Vedas, whatever one desires that he sees.

As I have told you in previous lectures, the Atman neither comes nor goes. It has neither birth nor death. You are all omnipresent, you are the Atman. You are at this moment in heaven and in the darkest places too. You are everywhere. Where are you not? Therefore how can you go anywhere? These comings and goings are all fictions — the Atman can never come nor go.

These visions change. When the mind is in a particular condition it sees a certain vision, dreams a certain dream. So in this condition, we are all seeing this world and man and animals and all these things. But in this very place, this condition will change. And the very thing we are seeing as earth, we shall see as heaven, or we may see it as the opposite place or as any place we like.

All this depends on our desires. But this dream cannot be permanent, just as we know that any dream in the night must break. Not one of these dreams will be permanent. We dream that which we think we will do. So these people who are always thinking in this life of going to heaven and meeting their friends, will have that as soon as their dream of this life is ended. And they will be compelled by their desires of this life to see these other dreams. And those who are superstitious and are frightened into all such ideas as hell will dream that they are in the hot place. Those whose ideas in this life are brutal — when they die, will become pigs and hogs and all these things. With each one, what he desires he finds.

This book starts by telling us that those who know nothing better than a little road-making or hospital-building and such good works will have a good dream when they die. They will dream that they are in a place where they will have god-bodies and can eat anything they like, jump about, go through walls and so on, and sometimes come down and startle someone.

In our mythology there are the Devas, who live in heaven, and the Devakas, who are very much the same but a little more wicked. The Devas are like your angels, only some of them from time to time become wicked and find that the daughters of men are good. Our deities are celebrated for this sort of thing. What can you expect of them? They are here — simply hospital-makers — and have no more knowledge than other men. They do some good work with the result that they become Devas. They do their good work for fame or name or some reward and get this reward, dreaming that they are in heaven and doing all these things.

Then there are demons who have done evil in this life. But our books say that these dreams will not last very long, and then they will either come back and take the old dream again as human beings, or still worse. Therefore, according to these books, it behooves every sensible, right-thinking man, once and for all, to brush aside all such foolish ideas as heavens and hells.

Two things exist in the world — dream and reality. What we call life is a succession of dreams — dream within dream. One dream is called heaven, another earth, another hell, and so on. One dream is called the human body, another the animal body, and so on — all are dreams. The reality is what is called Brahman, that Being who is Existence, Knowledge, Bliss.

He is the Guru — the sage who wants to get rid of all these dreams, to stand aside and know his own nature — who wants to go beyond this self-hypnotism.

When we desire, we are hypnotizing ourselves. Just as I desire "I will go to heaven", that hypnotizes me, and I begin to find I am in heaven directly I die, and will see angels and all sorts of things. I have seen about fifty people who have come from death's door, and they all have told me stories about being in heaven. These are the mythologies of our country, and it shows that it is all hypnotism.

Where Western people make a great mistake is here. So far as you have these ideas of heaven and hell, we agree with you. But you say this earth is real. That cannot be. If this is real, heavens and hells are real, because the proof of each of these is the same. If one is a hypnotic condition, the whole of it must be so.

Vedantists say that not only are heavens hypnotic, but so is this life and everything here. Some people want to go from one hypnotic condition to another, and these are what we call the fools of the world — the Samsârins, the travellers who go from dream to dream, from one hypnotic trance to another. For fifty years they are under the idea that they are men and women.

What nonsense is [this —] a man or a woman in the soul? It is terrible hypnotism. How can the soul have any sex? It is self-hypnotism. You have hypnotized yourself and think you are men and women. If we are fools, we will again hypnotize ourselves and want to go to heaven, and hear all this trash of gods and goddesses and all sorts of humbug, and will kneel down and pray, and have god-bodies by the millions to worship on thrones. At the end, we have to hypnotize ourselves again.

We are all in the same boat here, and all who are in the same boat see each other. Stand aside — free, beyond dream and hypnotism. Some fools have hypnotized themselves that they have bodies and wives and all these things. I also am a fool and have hypnotized myself that I have senses and all these things. So we are all in the same boat and see each other. Millions of people may be here whom we do not see, touch or feel. Just as in hypnotism there may be three books before you, but you are hypnotized and are told that one of them does not exist. And you may live for a year in that condition and never see it. Suppose thirty men are under the same hypnotic influence and are told that this book does not exist. Those who are in this condition will all fail to see the book. Men, women, animals are all hypnotized, and all see this dream because they are all in the same boat.

The Vedanta philosophy says that this whole

universe — mental, physical, moral — is hypnotic. Who is the cause of this hypnotism? You yourself are to blame. This weeping and wailing and knocking your heads into corners [against brick walls, as it were] will not do you the least good.

However, knocking everything [that is hypnotic] on the head [leads to] what is called non-attachment; and clinging to more and more hypnotism is attachment. That is why in all religions you will find they wanted to give up the world, although many of them do not understand it. These fellows used to starve themselves in a forest and see the devil coming to them.

You have heard those wonderful stories of India — of how those magicians can make a man see a rope rise from the ground to the skies. I have not seen any of them. One of the Mogul emperors, Jahangir, mentions it. He says, "Allah, what do these devils do? They take a rope or a chain, and the chain is thrown up and up until it becomes firm — as if it were stuck to something. Then they let a cat go up the chain — then a dog, then a wolf, then a tiger, then a lion. All walk up the chain and vanish. Sometimes they will send men up the chain. Two men will go up and begin to fight, and then both of them vanish. And after a while you hear a noise of fighting — and [then] a head, a hand, and a foot fall. And, mind you, there are two or three thousand people present. The fellow showing it has only a loincloth on". They say this is hypnotism — throwing a net over the audience.

That is what they call their science. It exists within a certain limit. But if you go beyond this limit or come within it, you do not see it. The man who is playing does not see anything. So if you stand near him, you do not see anything. Such is the hypnotism here.

So we have first to get beyond the circle (Jnana) or stand within the circle of the hypnotism (Bhakti) with God, the great Player who is playing all these things — the whole universe He projects.

Chapter after chapter comes and goes. This is called Mâyâ, the power which creates all these tremendous things. He who is the ruler of this Maya, is God; and he who is ruled by Maya [is the soul]. Just as in the case of that chain — so the man who was standing in the centre had the power and was not deluded, but all that audience was governed by Maya. So that portion of Atman which rules Maya is called God, and the little bits of the Atman deluded by it are called souls — you and I.

The Bhakta says, Crawl nearer and nearer to the hypnotist, and when you get to the centre you do not see anything. You get clear of it.

The Jnâni does not care to undergo all this trouble — it is a dangerous way. Unless a man becomes a lunatic, when he finds himself covered with mud, will he take more mud to wash himself? So why increase the hypnotism? Get out of the circle; cut it off and be free. When you are free you will be able to play, even without being caught yourself. Now you are caught, then you will catch — that will be all the difference.

Therefore in the first part of this book, we are told that we must give up all this idea of heaven and of birth and death and so on. It is all nonsense; no man was ever born or ever died. They are all in hypnotism. So is eternal life and all this nonsense. Heaven is hypnotism and so is earth.

It is not as materialists say: that heaven is a superstition and God is a superstition, but he himself is not a superstition. If one is superstition — if one link is nonexistent — the whole chain is nonexistent. The existence of the whole chain depends on the existence of one link — and that of one link, on the whole.

If there is no heaven, there is no earth; and if there is no God, there is no man. You are under this hypnotism; and as long as you are under it, you will have to see God and nature and the soul. And when you are beyond this hypnotism, God will vanish[8]* — so will nature, and so will the soul.

Therefore, first of all, we will have to give up all these ideas of God and heaven and enjoying the fruits of these; and all that going to heaven will be one more dream.

Next, after showing these things, the book goes on to tell us how to get out of this hypnotism. And the one idea that is brought out through all these ideas is to be one with that Universal Being. The thing manifested — the Universal Being — is not anything of these; these are all nonsense — Maya. (The Swami has been discussing the two aspects of Maya. On the previous page, ([9]a few paragraphs earlier) he described Maya as the power of Brahman; here he is referring to Maya as the world-appearance.) But that upon which all these things are being played — the background upon which all this picture is written — [is we ourselves]; we are one with Him [that Universal Being]. You know you are one with Him, only you must realize it.

He gave us two words: one is intellectual knowledge, and the other is realization. That is to say, intellectual assent is within this realization, and realization is beyond it. Therefore intellectual assent is not sufficient.

Every man can say this theory is right, but that is not realization; he must realize it. We can all say we understand that this is hypnotism, but that is not realization. That will be when the hypnotism will break — even for a moment. It will come in a flash; it must come. If you struggle it will come.

When it does vanish, all idea of body will go along with it — that you have sex or body — just as a lamp blows out. Then what will become of you? If some part of your Karma remains, this world will come back again — but not with the same force. You have known that it is what it is; you will know no more bondage. So long as you have eyes you will have to see; or ears [you will have to] hear — but not with the same force.

I had read all sorts of things about the mirage, but had never seen it before until about four years ago when I was travelling in western India. Of course, as a Sannyasin I was travelling on foot, making my slow marches. So it took me about a month to travel through that country. Every day I saw such beautiful lakes and the shadows of trees on the shores of those lakes, and the whole thing was quivering in the breeze — and birds flying, and animals. Every day I saw this and thought what a beautiful country it was. But when I reached some village, I found it was all sand. I said, How is it?

One day I was very thirsty and thought I would drink a little water at the lake. But when I approached, it disappeared, and with a flash [the thought] came into my mind: "This is the mirage about which I read all my life". But the strange thing is that I was travelling for a month and could never recognize that it was a mirage — and in one moment it vanished. I was very glad to know this was the mirage about which I had read all my life.

Next morning I saw the lake again, and along with it came the idea: "That is the mirage". All that month I had been seeing the mirage and could not distinguish between reality and mirage. But in that one moment I caught the idea.

From that time, when I see a mirage, I will say, "That is a mirage", and never feel it. Such will it be with this world when the whole thing will vanish once; and after that, if you have to live out your past work, you will not be deceived.

Take a carriage with two wheels. Suppose I cut one of the wheels from the axle. The other wheel will run for some time by its past momentum and will then fall. The body is one wheel, and the soul another; and they are joined by the axle of delusion. Knowledge is the axe which will cut the axle, and the soul will stop immediately — will give up all these vain dreams.

But upon the body is that past momentum, and it will run a little, doing this and that, and then it will fall down. But only good momentum will be left, and that body can only do good. This is to warn you not to mistake a rascal for a free man. It will be impossible for that [free] man to do evil. So you must not be cheated.

When you become free the whole hypnotism has vanished and you know the distinction between the reality and the mirage. [The mirage] will no more be a bondage. The most terrible things will not be able to daunt you. A mountain [could] fall upon you, but you will not care. You will know it for a mirage.

HISTORY OF THE ARYAN RACE

A Jnâna-Yoga class delivered in London, England, on Thursday morning, May 7, 1896, and recorded by Mr. Josiah J. Goodwin.

I have told you how I would divide the subject into four Yogas, but, as the bearing of all these various Yogas is the same — the goal they want to arrive at is the same — I had better begin with the philosophical portion: the Jnana-Yoga. Jnâna means knowledge, and, before going into the principles of the Vedanta philosophy, I think it is necessary to sketch in a few words the origin and the beginning and the development — the historical portion of that system. Most of you are now familiar with the words Arya and Aryan, and many things have been written on these words.

About a century ago there was an English judge in Bengal, Sir William Jones. In India, you know, there are Mohammedans and Hindus. The Hindus were the original people, and the Mohammedans came and conquered them and ruled over them for seven hundred years. There have been many other conquests in India; and whenever there is a new conquest, the criminal laws of the country are changed. The criminal law is always the law of the conquering nation, but the civil law remains the same. So when the English conquered India, they changed the criminal law; but the civil law remained. The judges, however, were Englishmen and did not know the language of the country in which the civil laws were written, and so they had to take the help of interpreters, lawyers of India, and so on. And when any question about Indian law arose, these scholars would be referred to.

One of these judges, Sir William Jones, was a very ripe scholar, and he wanted to go to the fountain-head himself, to take up the language himself and study it, instead of relying upon these interpreters who, for instance, might be bribed to give any verdict. So he began to study the law of the Gentoos, as the Hindus were called. Gentoo is probably a form of the word gentile, used by the Portuguese and Spaniards — or "heathen", as you call it now. When the judge began to translate some of the books into English, he found that it was very hard to translate them correctly into English at first hand. What was his surprise when he found that if he translated them first into Latin, and next into English, it was much easier. Then he found in translating that a large number of Sanskrit words were almost the same as in Latin. It was he who introduced the study of Sanskrit to the Europeans. Then as the Germans were rising in scholarship — as well as the French — they took up the language and began to study it.

With their tremendous power of analysis, the Germans found that there was a similarity between Sanskrit and all the European languages. Among the ancient languages, Greek was the nearest to it in resemblance. Later, it was found that there was a language called Lithuanian, spoken somewhere on the shores of the Baltic — an independent kingdom at that time and unconnected with Russia. The language of the Lithuanians is strikingly similar to Sanskrit. Some of the Lithuanian sentences are less changed from Sanskrit forms than the northern Indian languages. Thus it was found that there is an intimate connection between all the various languages spoken in Europe and the two Asiatic languages — Persian and Sanskrit. Many theories are built upon it as to how this connection came. Theories were built up every day, and every day smashed. There is no knowing where it is going to stop.

Then came the theory that there was one race in ancient times who called themselves Aryans. They found in Sanskrit literature that there was a people who spoke Sanskrit and called themselves Aryans, and this is mentioned also in Persian literature. Thus they founded the theory that there was in ancient times a nation [of people] who called themselves Aryans and who spoke Sanskrit and lived in Central Asia. This nation, they said, broke into several branches and migrated to Europe and Persia; and wherever they went, they took their own languages. German, Greek and French are but remnants of an old tongue, and Sanskrit is the most highly developed of these languages.

These are theories and have not been proved yet; they are mere conjectures and guesses. Many difficulties come in the way — for instance, how the Indians are dark and the Europeans are fair. Even within the same nations speaking these languages — in England itself — there are many with yellow hair and many with black. Thus there are many questions which have not yet been settled.

But this is certain, that all the nations of Europe except the Basques, the Hungarians, the Tartars and the [Finns?] (Vide Complete Works, VIII.) — excepting these, all the Europeans, all the northern Indians and the Persians speak branches of the same language. Vast masses of literature are existing in all these Aryan tongues: in Greek, in Latin, in modern European languages — German, English, French — in ancient Persian, in modern Persian and in Sanskrit.

But in the first place, Sanskrit literature alone is a very big mass. Although, perhaps, three-fourths of it has been destroyed and lost through successive invasions, yet, I think, the sum total of the amount of literature in Sanskrit would outbalance any three or four European languages taken together, in number of books. No one knows how many books are there yet and where they are, because it is the most ancient of all these Aryan languages. And that branch of the Aryan race which spoke the Sanskrit language was the first to become civilized and the first to begin to write books and literature. So they went on for thousands of years. How many thousands of years they wrote no one knows. There are various guesses — from 3000 B.C. to 8000 B.C. — but all of these dates are more or less uncertain.

Each man in writing about these ancient books and dates is first of all prejudiced by his earlier education, then by his religion, then by his nationality. If a Mohammedan writes about the Hindus, anything that does not glorify his own religion he very scrupulously pushes to one side. So with the Christians — you can see that with your own writers. In the last ten years your literature has become more respectable. So long as they [the Christians] had full play, they wrote in English and were safe from Hindu criticism. But, within the last twenty years, the Hindus have begun writing in English, so they are more careful. And you will find that the tone has quite changed within the last ten or twenty years.

Another curiosity about the Sanskrit literature is that it, like any other language, has undergone many changes. Taking all the literature in these various Aryan languages — the Greek or the Latin or all these others — we find that all the European branches were of very recent date. The Greek came much later — a mere child in comparison with the Egyptian or the Babylonian.

The Egyptians and the Babylonians, of course, are not Aryans. They are separate races, and their civilizations antedate all the European civilization. But with the exception of the ancient Egyptians, they were almost coeval [with the Aryans]; in some accounts, they were even earlier. Yet in Egyptian literature, there are certain things to be accounted for — the introduction of the Indian lotus on old temples, the lotus Gangetic. It is well known that this only grows in India. Then there are the references to the land of Punt. Although very great attempts have been made to fix that land of Punt on the Arabs, it is very uncertain. And then there are the references to the monkeys and sandalwood of southern India — only to be found there.

The Jews were of a much later date than the Greek Aryans. Only one branch of the Semitic race of Babylon and this nondescript, unknowable race — the Egyptians — were much older than the Aryans, except the Hindus.

So this Sanskrit has undergone very much change as a matter of course, having been spoken and written through thousands of years. It necessarily follows that in other Aryan languages, as in Greek and Roman, the literature must be of much later date than Sanskrit. Not only so, but there is this peculiarity, that of all regular books that we have in the world, the oldest are in Sanskrit — and that is the mass of literature called the Vedas. There are very ancient pieces in the Babylonian or Egyptian literature, but they cannot be called literature or books, but just a few notes, a short letter, a few words, and so on. But as finished, cultured literature, the Vedas are the oldest.

These Vedas were written in the peculiar archaic Sanskrit, and for a long time — even today — it is thought by many European antiquarians that these Vedas were not written, but were handed down by father to son, learned by rote, and thus preserved. Within the last few years, opinion is veering round, and they are beginning to think that they must have been written in most ancient times.

Of course they have to make theories in this way. Theory after theory will have to be built up and destroyed until we reach truth. This is quite natural. But when the subject is Indian or Egyptian, the Christian philosophers rush in to make theories; while if the subject is nearer home, they think twice first. That is why they fail so much and have to keep on making fresh theories every five years. But this much is true, that this mass of literature, whether written or not, was conveyed and, not only that, but is at the present day conveyed by word of mouth. This is thought to be holy.

You find in every nation when a new idea, a new form, a new discovery or invention comes in, the old things are not brushed aside all at once, but are relegated to the religion of holiness. The ancient Hindus used to write on palm leaves and birch bark; and when paper was invented they did not throw aside all the palm leaves, but used to consider writing on palm leaves and birch bark holy. So with the Jews — they used to write only on parchment, and parchment is now used for writing in their temples. So you find when new customs come in, the old ones become holy. So this form of transmitting the literature of the Vedas from teacher to disciple by word of mouth, although antiquated and almost useless now, has become holy. The student may refresh his memory by books, but has to learn by word of mouth of a teacher. A great many modifications will always gather round such a fact to make its holiness more rational, but this is the law.

These Vedas are a vast mass of literature by themselves. That is to say, in those ancient times, in every country, religion was the first ideal to spring out of the heart of man, and all the secular knowledge that men got was made over to religion.

Secondly, people who deal with religion and in later times came to be called priests — being the first thinkers of every nation — not only thought about religious subjects, but secular matters also; and, as such, all knowledge was confined to them. These masses of knowledge — both secular and religious — will always be gathered together and made into a vast mass of literature.

In much later times, this is the case. For instance, in studying the Bible of the Jews, we find the same thing. The Talmud contained a vast mass of information on all subjects and so did the Pentateuch. In the same way, the Vedas give information on various subjects. They have come together and form one book. And in later times, when other subjects were separated from religion — when astronomy and astrology were taken out of religion — these subjects, being connected with the Vedas and being ancient, were considered very holy.

Almost the largest portion of the Vedas has been lost. The priests who carried it down to posterity were divided into so many families; and, accordingly, the Vedas were divided into so many parts. Each part was allotted to a family. The rituals, the ceremonies, the customs, the worship of that family were to be obtained from that [respective] portion of the Vedas. They preserved it and performed all the ceremonies according to that. In course of time, [some of] these families became extinct; and with them, their portion of the Vedas was lost, if these old accounts be true.

Some of you know that the Vedas are divided into four parts. One is called the Rig-Veda, another Yajur-Veda, another Sâma-Veda, and the fourth Atharva-Veda. Each one of these, again, was divided into many branches. For instance, the Sama-Veda had one thousand branches, of which only about five or six remain; the rest are all lost. So with the others. The Rig-Veda had 108, of which only one remains; and the rest are all lost.

Then [there were] these various invasions. India has been the one country to which every nation that has become strong wants to go and conquer

— it being reputed to be very rich. The wealth of the people had become a fable, even in the most ancient history. [Many foreign invaders] rushed to become wealthy in India and conquered the country. Every one of these invasions destroyed one or more of these families, burned many libraries and houses. And when that was so, much literature was lost. It is only within the last few years that ideas have begun to spring up about the retention of these various religions and books. Before that, mankind had to suffer all this pillaging and breaking down. Most stupendous creations of art were lost forever. Wonderful buildings — where, from a few bits of remnants now in India, it can be imagined how wonderful they were — are completely gone...

[The fanatical belief of many of these invaders into India is] that those who do not belong to their sect have no right to live. They will go to a place where the fire will never be quenched when they die; in this life they are only fit to be made into slaves or murdered; and that they have only the right to live as slaves to "the true believers", but never as free men. So in this way, when these waves burst upon India, everything was submerged. Books and literature and civilization went down.

But there is a vitality in that race which is unique in the history of humanity, and perhaps that vitality comes from non-resistance. Non-resistance is the greatest strength. In meekness and mildness lies the greatest strength. In suffering is greater strength than in doing. In resisting one's own passions is far higher strength than in hurting others. And that has been the watchword of the race through all its difficulties, its misfortunes and its prosperity. It is the only nation that never went beyond its frontiers to cut the throats of its neighbours. It is a glorious thing. It makes me rather patriotic to think I am born a Hindu, a descendant of the only race that never went out to hurt anyone, and whose only action upon humanity has been giving and enlightening and purifying and teaching, but never robbing.

Three-quarters of the wealth of the world has come out of India, and does even now. The commerce of India has been the turning point, the pivot, of the history of the world. Whatever nation got it became powerful and civilized. The Greeks got it and became the mighty Greeks; the Romans got it and became the mighty Romans. Even in the days of the Phoenicians it was so. After the fall of Rome, the Genoese and the Venetians got it. And then the Arabs rose and created a wall between Venice and India; and in the struggle to find a new way there, America was discovered. That is how America was discovered; and the original people of America were called Indians, or "Injuns", for that reason. Even the Dutch got it — and the barbarians — and the English and they became the most powerful nation on earth. And the next nation that gets it will immediately be the most powerful.

Think of all this mass of energy that our nation displays — where does it get it? In India, they are the producers and you are the enjoyers, no doubt. They produced this — the patient, toiling millions of Hindus under the whip and slavery of everyone. Even the missionaries, who stand up to curse the millions of India, have been fattened upon the work of these millions, and they do not know how it has been done. Upon their blood the history of the world has been turning since we know history, and will have to turn for thousands of years more. What is the benefit? It gives that nation strength. They are, as it were, an example. They must suffer and stand up through all, fighting for the truths of religion — as a signpost, a beacon — to tell unto mankind that it is much higher not to resist, much higher to suffer, that if life be the goal, as even their conquerors will admit, we are the only race that can be called immortal, that can never be killed. (Vide Complete Works, IV)

Where are the Greeks today — they whose armies marched over the whole world? Gone, thousands of years — nobody knows where. Vanished, as soon as the barbarians of the north came and attacked them. Where are the mighty Romans, whose cohorts came and trampled the face of the earth? Where are they today? Gone — vanished like the morning dew, and left behind in the march.

But here are the Hindus — three hundred million strong. And think of the fertility of the race! They can increase more than the whole world can kill them. This is the vitality of the race. Although not belonging very much to our subject, I wanted to bring these things before you.

Generally the uneducated minds, the vulgar minds of every nation, like the vulgar mobs in every big city, cannot grasp, cannot see, cannot understand, any fine movement. The causes, the real movements in this world of ours, are very fine; it is only the effects that are gross and muscular. The mind is the real cause of this body, the fine movements behind. The body is the gross, the external. But everyone sees the body; very few see the mind. So with everything; the masses, the brutal, ignorant masses of every race, see a triumphant procession, stampeding horses, arms and cannonades, and these they understand. But those fine, gentle workings that are going on behind — it is only the philosopher, the highly cultivated man or woman, that can understand.

To return to our Vedanta, I have said that the Sanskrit in which the Vedas were written is not the same Sanskrit in which books were written about a thousand years later than the Vedas — the books that you read in your translations of poets and other classical writers of India. The Sanskrit of the Vedas was very simple, archaic in its composition, and possibly it was a spoken language. But the Sanskrit that we have now was never a spoken language, at least for the last three thousand years. Curiously enough, the vast mass of literature was written in a language which was dead, covering a period of three thousand years. Dramas and novels were written in this dead language. And all the time it was not spoken in the homes; it was only the language of the learned.

Even in the time of Buddha, which was about 560 years before the Christian era, we find that Sanskrit had ceased to be a spoken language. Some of his disciples wanted to teach in Sanskrit, but the master studiously refused. He wanted to teach in the language [of the people], because he said he was the prophet of the people. And that is how it has come about that the Buddhistic literature is in Pali, which was the vernacular of that time.

This vast mass of literature — the Vedas — we find in three groups. The first group is the Samhitâs, a collection of hymns. The second group is called the Brâhmanas, or the [group dealing with different kinds of] sacrifice. The word Brahmana [by usage] means [what is achieved by means of] the sacrifice. And the other group is called the Upanishads (sittings, lectures, philosophic books). Again, the first two parts together — the hymns and the rituals — are called the Karmakânda, the work portion; and the second, or philosophic portion (the Upanishads), is called the Jnânakânda, the knowledge portion. This is the same word as your English word knowledge and the Greek word gnos — just as you have the word in agnostic, and so on.

The first portion is a collection of hymns in praise of certain gods, as Agni, fire; Mitra, the sun; and so forth. They are praised and oblations are offered to them. I have said these hymns are to the gods. I have used the word gods until I make you familiar with the Sanskrit word Deva, because the word gods is very misleading. These Devas mean the "bright ones", and gods in India are less persons than positions. For instance, Indra and Agni are not names of particular persons, but particular posts in this universe. There is the post of President, the presiding post over certain elements, the presiding post over certain worlds, and so forth. According to these theologians, you and I — most of us — probably have been some of these gods several times. It is only temporarily that a soul can fill one of these positions. And after his time is over, he gives way; another soul is raised from this world by good works and takes that position — he becomes [for example] Agni. In reading Sanskrit philosophy or theology, people always get bothered by the changing of these gods. But this is the theory — that they are names of positions, that all souls will have to fill them again and again; and these gods, when the soul has attained to that position, can help mankind. So gifts and praise are offered to them. How this idea came to the Aryans we do not know, but in the earliest portion of the Rig-Veda we find this idea perfected and completed.

Behind and beyond all these Devas and men and

animals and worlds is the Ruler of this universe, Ishvara — somewhat similar to what in the New Testament is called God the Creator, Preserver, the Ruler of this universe. These Devas are not to be confused with Ishvara at all, but in the English language you have the same word for both. You use the word God in the singular and the plural. But the gods are the bright ones — the Devas — and God is Ishvara. This we find even in the oldest portions of the Vedas.

Another peculiarity is that this Ishvara, this God, is manifesting Himself in all these various forms of bright ones. This idea — that the same God manifests Himself in various forms — is a very rudimentary idea of the Vedas, even in the oldest portions. There was a time when a sort of monotheistic idea entered the Vedas, but it was very quickly rejected. As we go on, perhaps you will agree with me that it was very good that it was rejected.

So we find in these oldest portions of the Samhitas that there were these various Devas — [being praised as] the manifestations of someone very much higher than they [had left] behind, so that sometimes each one of them was taken up and adjectives piled on it and at last it was said, "You are the God of the universe". Then such passages as this occurred: "I am God, worshipped as the fire", and so forth. "It is the One; sages call Him variously." "He is that one existence; the sages call Him by various names." This I ask you to remember, because this is the turning point, the key-note of all thought that India has produced — "He is that One Being; sages call Him variously." All Hindu philosophy — either theistic or atheistic or monotheistic, dualistic or nondualistic — has that as the core, the centre. And by thousands of years of culture in the race, it is impossible for the Hindu race to go [away from] that idea.

That germ became a big tree; and that is why there was never a religious persecution in India, at least by the Hindus. That explains their liberality and welcome to any religion from any part of the world which came to settle there. That is how, even at the present day, Indian Rajas go and perform Mohammedan ceremonies and enter Mohammedan mosques, although [some] Mohammedans took the first opportunity to kill a number of "the heathens".

"He is the One Being; sages call Him variously."

There have been two theories advanced in modern times with regard to the growth of religions. The one is the tribal theory; the other is the spirit theory. The tribal theory is that humanity in its savage state remains divided into many small tribes. Each tribe has a god of its own — or sometimes the same god divided into many forms, as the god of this city came to that city, and so on; Jehovah of this city and of such-and-such mountain [came to such-and-such city or mountain]. When the tribes came together, one of them became strong.

Take the case of the Jews. They were divided into so many tribes, and each tribe had a god called either Baal or Moloch which in your Old Testament is translated as "the Lord". There was the Moloch of this state and that state, of this mountain and that mountain, and there was the Moloch of the chest, who used to live in a chest. This latter tribe became strong and conquered the surrounding tribes and became triumphant. So that Moloch was proclaimed the greatest of all Molochs. "Thou art the Java [?] of the Molochs. Thou art the ruler of all the Baals and Molochs." Yet the chest remained. So this idea was obtained from tribal gods.

There is the other theory of Spiritualism — that religion begins with the worship of ancestors. Ancestor worship was among the Egyptians, among the Babylonians, among many other races — the Hindus, the Christians. There is not one form of religion among which there has not been this ancestor worship in some form or other.

Before that they thought that this body had a double inside it and that when this body dies the double gets out and lives so long as this body exists. The double becomes very hungry or thirsty, wants food or drink, and wants to enjoy the good things of this world. So he [the double] comes to get food; and if he does not get it, he will injure even his own children. So long as the body is preserved the double will live. Naturally the first attempt, as we see, was to preserve the body, mummify the body, so that the body will live forever.

So with the Babylonians was this sort of spirit worship. Later on as the nations advanced, the cruel forms died out and better forms remained. Some place was given to that which is called heaven, and they placed food here so that it might reach the double there. Even now the pious Hindus must, one day a year at least, place food for their ancestors. And the day they leave off [this habit] will be a sorry day for the ancestors. So you also find this ancestor worship to be one cause of religion. There are in modern times philosophers who advance the theory that this has been the root of all religions. There are others who advance the theory that the root of all religions was the tribal assimilation of gods into one.

Among the Jews of the Old Testament you do not find any mention of soul. It is only in the Talmud that it is found. They got it from the Alexandrians, and the Alexandrians from the Hindus — just as the Talmud had [developed] later on the idea of transmigration of the soul. But the old Jews had grand ideas of God. The God of the Jews developed into the Great God — the Omnipotent, Omniscient, All-Merciful — and all this came to them from the Hindus, but not through the idea of the soul. So Spiritualism could not have played any part in that, because how could the man who did not believe in any soul after death have anything to do with Spiritualism?

On the other hand, in the oldest portion of the Vedas, there is very little of Spiritualism, if anything at all. These Devas [of the Vedas] were not [related to Spiritualism] — although later on they became so; and this idea of Someone behind them, of whom they were manifestations, is in the oldest parts.

Another idea is that when the body dies, the soul [which] is immortal remains beatified. The very oldest Aryan literature — whether German or Greek — has this idea of soul. The idea of soul has come from the Hindus.

Two people have given all the religion to the world — the Hindus and the Jews. But it is only with the Hindus that the idea of soul comes at first, and that was shared by the Aryan races.

The peculiarity you find is that the Semitic races and the Egyptians try to preserve the dead bodies, while the Aryans try to destroy them. The Greeks, the Germans, the Romans — your ancestors before they became Christians — used to burn the dead. It was only when Charlemagne made you Christians with the sword — and when you refused, [he] cut off a few hundred heads, and the rest jumped into the water — that burying came here. You see at once the metaphysical significance of burning the dead. The burying of the dead (Preserving the dead by the burying of the body.) can only remain when there is no idea of the soul, and the body is all. At best there came the idea later on that this very body will have another lease of life, after so many years — mummies will come out and begin to walk the streets again.

But with the Aryans the idea was from the first that the soul is not the body, but would live on. There are some old hymns in the Rig-Veda: when the bodies are burnt they say, "Take him gently, purify him, give him a bright body, take him to the land where the fathers live — wherethere is no more sorrow and where thereis joy forever". (Rig-Veda 10.16.4.)

It is curious that though in modern times many hideous and cruel forms of religion crept into India, there is one peculiar idea that divides the Aryan from all other races of the world: that their religion, in the Hindu form, accepted this Indra as one [with the Ultimate Reality]. Three-quarters of the mythology of the Vedas is the same as that of the Greeks; only the old gods became saints in the new religion. But they were originally the gods of the Samhitas.

One other peculiarity we remark — that it is a cheerful, joyful, at times almost hilarious religion; there is not a bit of pessimism in it. The earth is beautiful, the heavens are beautiful, life is immortal. Even after death they get a still more beautiful body, which has none of the imperfections of this body, and they go to live with the gods and enjoy heaven forever.

On the other hand, with the Semitic races, the very first inception of religion was one of horror. A man crouched in his little house for fear. All round his house were those doubles. The family ancestors of the Jews were there, ready to pounce upon anybody and tear him to pieces if bloody sacrifices were not given to them. Even when you find that this [double] idea coagulated into one — "Thou art the Elohim of the Jews, Thou art the Elo[him] of the [Babylonians?]" — even then the idea of sacrifice remained.

The idea of sacrifice in India was not with this first portion. But in the next portion we find the same idea in India too, in the Brahmanas. The idea of sacrifice was originally simply giving food [to the gods], but gradually it was raised and raised until it became a sacrifice to God. Philosophy came in to mystify it still more and to spin webs of logic round it. Bloody sacrifices came into vogue. Somewhere we read that three hundred bullocks have been roasted, or the gods are smelling the sacrifices and becoming very glad. Then all sorts of mystical notions got about — how the sacrifice was to be made in the form of a tri-angle or a square, a triangle within a square, a pentagon, and all sorts of figures. But the great benefit was the evolution of geometry. When they had to make all these figures — and it was laid down strictly how many bricks should be used, and how they should be laid, and how big they should be — naturally geometry came [into being]. The Egyptians evolved geometry [by] their [irrigation] — [they] made canals to take the Nile water inside their fields — and the Hindus, by their altars.

Now there is another particular difference between the idea of sacrifice in India and [that] of the Jews. The real meaning of sacrifice is worship, a form of worship by oblations. At first it was simply giving food to the bright ones, or the higher beings. They had gross food just as we have. Later on philosophy stepped in and the idea came that they, being higher beings, could not eat the same food as we do. Their bodies are made of finer particles. Our bodies cannot pass through a wall; theirs find no resistance in gross material. As such, they cannot be expected to eat in the same gross way as we do.

[Some parts of the transcription of the remaining portion of this lecture, recorded by Mr. J. J. Goodwin, were found in a severely damaged condition. Hence we have reproduced below only the legible fragments as they appeared in the original.]

…"O Indra, I offer you this oblation. O Agni, I offer you this oblation." The answer is that these words have a mystical power in Sanskrit. And when a man, in a certain state of mind, pronounces these words, he sets in motion a set of psychological causes, and these causes produce a certain effect. That is the evolution of thought.

To make it clearer, suppose a man was childless and wanted a son. He worshipped Indra, and if he got a son he said Indra gave him the son. Later on they said Indra did not exist. Who, then, gave him the son? The whole thing is a matter of cause and effect.……

They said it was not giving the gods food, but simply laying my sins upon the head of another victim. "My sins go upon the goat's head, and, if the goat be killed, my sins are forgiven." That idea of sacrifice of the Jews never entered India, and perhaps that has saved us many a pang, many a trouble.

Human nature is selfish, and the vast majority of men and women weak; and to teach vicarious sacrifice makes us more and more weak. Every child is taught that he is nothing until the poor fellow becomes hypnotized into nothing. He goes in search of somebody to cling onto, and never thinks of clinging to himself…(Vide Complete Works, VIII for similar ideas.)

NOTES OF LECTURES AND CLASSES

Swami Vivekananda delivered scores of lectures and classes during his relatively short ministry. Unfortunately the Swami was not always accompanied by a professional stenographer who could keep pace with the exceptional speed of his extempore deliveries. However, a few students managed to take notes of some lectures and classes, which are today the only available records of works that would otherwise have been lost to the world.

The original quotation marks of the note-takers have been reproduced. — Publisher

THE RELIGION OF INDIA

New Discoveries, Vol. 2, pp. 145-49, 155-56.

These notes of daily morning classes delivered at Greenacre, Maine, in the summer of 1894 and recorded by Miss Emma Thursby were discovered among Miss Emma Thursby's papers at the New-York Historical Society. They have been lightly edited in order to conform to the style of the Complete Works.

Notes taken miscellaneously from discourses given by Swami Vivekananda under the "Pine" at Greenacre in July and August 1894.

The name of Swami's master was Ramakrishna Paramahamsa. The signification of Vivekananda is conscious bliss.

Meditation is a sort of prayer and prayer is meditation. The highest meditation is to think of nothing. If you can remain one moment without thought, great power will come. The whole secret of knowledge is concentration. Soul best develops itself by loving God with all the heart. Soul is the thinking principle in man, of which mind is a function. Soul is only the conduit from Spirit to mind.

All souls are playing, some consciously, some unconsciously. Religion is learning to play consciously.

The Guru is your own higher Self.

Seek the highest, always the highest, for in the highest is eternal bliss. If I am to hunt, I will hunt the rhinoceros. If I am to rob, I will rob the treasury of the king. Seek the highest.

[Some of the following passages are the Swami's free translations from Indian scriptures, including the Avadhuta-Gîtâ of Dattâtreya.]

If you know you are bound [you are bound]; if you know you are free, you are free. My mind was never bound by yearnings of this world; for like the eternal blue sky, I am the essence of Knowledge, of Existence and of Bliss. Why weepest thou, Brother? Neither death nor disease for thee. Why weepest thou, Brother? Neither misery nor misfortune for thee. Why weepest thou, Brother? Neither change nor death was predicated of thee. Thou Art Existence Absolute.

I know what God is; I cannot speak [of] Him to you. I know not [what] God is; how can I speak [of] Him to you? But seest not thou, my brother, that thou wert He, thou wert He? Why go seeking God here and there? Seek not, and that is God. Be your own Self — One that cannot be confessed or described, One that can be perceived in our heart of hearts. One beyond all compare, beyond limit, unchangeable like the blue sky. Oh! learn the All Holy One. Seek for nothing else.

Where changes of nature cannot reach, thought beyond all thought, unchangeable, immovable, whom all books declare, all sages worship, O Holy One! Seek for nothing else.

Beyond compare, Infinite Oneness — no comparison is possible. Water above, water beneath, water on the right, water on the left. No wave on that water, no ripple. All silence, all eternal bliss. Such will come to thy heart. Seek for nothing else. Thou art our father, our mother, our dear friend. Thou bearest the burden of this world. Help us to bear the burden of our lives. Thou art our friend, our lover, our husband. Thou art ourselves. Four sorts of people worship Me. Some want the delights of the physical world. Some want money, some want religion. Some worship Me because they love Me.

Real love is love for love's sake. I do not ask health or money or life or salvation. Send me to a thousand hells, but let me love Thee for love's sake. Mirâ Bâi, the great queen, taught the doctrine of love for love's sake.

Our present consciousness is only a little bit of an infinite sea of mind. Do not be limited to this consciousness.

Three great things [are] to be desired to develop the soul: First, human birth; second, thirst for the highest; third, to find one who has reached the highest — a Mahâtmâ, one whose mind, word and deed are full of the nectar of virtue, whose only pleasure is in doing good to the universe, who looks upon others' virtues, be they only as a mustard seed, even as though they were a mountain, thus expanding his own self and helping others to expand. Thus is the Mahatma.

The word Yoga is the root of which our word yoke is a derivation — meaning "to join" — and Yoga means "joining ourselves with God" — joining me with my real Self.

All actions now involuntary or automatic were once voluntary, and our first step is to gain a knowledge of the automatic actions — the real idea being to revivify and make voluntary all automatic actions, to bring them into consciousness. Many Yogis can control the actions of their hearts.

To go back into consciousness and bring out things we have forgotten is ordinary power, but this can be heightened. All knowledge — all that — can be brought out of the inner consciousness, and to do this is Yoga. The majority of actions and thoughts is automatic, or acting behind consciousness. The seat of automatic action is in the medulla oblongata and down the spinal cord.

The question is, how to find our way back to our inner consciousness. We have come out through spirit, soul, mind, and body, and now we must go back from body to spirit. First, get hold of the air [breath], then the nervous system, then the mind, then the Atman, or spirit. But in this effort we must be perfectly sincere in desiring the highest.

The law of laws is concentration. First, concentrate all the nerve energies and all power lodged in the cells of the body into one force and direct it at will. Then bring the mind, which is thinner matter, into one center. The mind has layer after layer.

When the nerve force concentrated is made to pass through the spinal column, one layer of the mind is open. When it is concentrated in one bone [plexus, or "lotus"], another part of the world is open. So from world to world it goes until it touches the pineal gland in the center of the brain. This is the seat of conservation of potential energy, the source of both activity and passivity.

Start with the idea that we can finish all experience in this world, in this incarnation. We must aim to become perfect in this life, this very moment. Success only comes to that life amongst men who wants to do this, this very moment. It is acquired by him who says, "Faith, I wait upon faith come what may". Therefore, go on knowing you are to finish this very moment. Struggle hard and then if you do not succeed, you are not to blame. Let the world praise or blame you. Let all the wealth of the earth come to your feet, or let you be made the poorest on earth. Let death come this moment or hundreds of years hence. Swerve not from the path you have taken. All good thoughts are immortal and go to make Buddhas and Christs.

Law is simply a means of [your] expression [of] various phenomena brought into your mind. Law is your method of grasping material phenomena and bringing them into unity. All law is finding unity in variety. The only method of knowledge is concentration on the physical, mental, and spiritual planes; and concentrating the powers of the mind to discover one in many, is what is called knowledge.

Everything that makes for unity is moral, everything that makes for diversity is immoral. Know the One without a second, that is perfection. The One who manifests in all is the basis of the universe; and all religion, all knowledge, must come to this point.

The following are some of the disconnected notes taken by Miss Emma Thursby during the last of the Swami's Greenacre classes, delivered Sunday morning, August 12, 1894.

I am Existence Absolute Kundalini

Bliss Absolute Circle mother I am He, Shivoham

I am He, Shivoham

He is the learned man who sees that every man's property is nothing. Every woman his Mother.

Shanti — peace —

We meditate on the Glory of Hrim (A Bija Mantra, or seed word, for the Divine Mother.)

Mother

Buddhistic Prayer

I bow to all the saint[s] on Earth

I bow down to the founders of Religion

to all holy men and women

Prophets of Religion

who have been on Earth

Hindu prayer

I meditate on the Glory of the producer of this Universe may He enlighten our minds.

CHRIST'S MESSAGE TO THE WORLD

New Discoveries, Vol. 5, p. 379.

From Mr. Frank Rhodehamel's notes of a lecture delivered in San Francisco, California, on March 11, 1900.

Everything progresses in waves. The march of civilization, the progression of worlds, is in waves. All human activities likewise progress in waves — art, literature, science, religion.

Great waves succeed each other, and between these great waves is a quiet, a calm, a period of rest, a period of recuperation.

All manifest life seems to require a period of sleep, of calm, in which to gain added strength, renewed vigour, for the next manifestation, or awakening to activity. Thus is the march of all progress, of all manifest life — in waves, successive waves, [of] activity and repose. Waves succeed each other in an endless chain of progression.

Religion, like everything else, progresses in waves; and at the summit of each great wave stands an illumined soul, a mighty spiritual leader and teacher of men. Such a one was Jesus of Nazareth.

MOHAMMED'S MESSAGE TO THE WORLD

New Discoveries, Vol. 5, pp. 401-3. Cf. "Mohammed", Complete Works, I.

Excerpts of Ida Ansell's first transcript of Swami Vivekananda's San Francisco lecture delivered Sunday, March 25, 1900.

Mohammed

After stating that he would "take Mohammed and bring out the particular work of the great Arabian prophet", Swami Vivekananda continued his lecture.

Each great messenger not only creates a new order of things, but is himself the creation of a certain order of things. There is no such thing as an independent, active cause. All causes are cause and effect in turn. Father is father and son in turn. Mother is mother and daughter in turn. It is necessary to understand the surroundings and circumstances into which they [the great messengers] come...

This is the peculiarity of civilization. One wave of a race will go from its birthplace to a distant land and make a wonderful civilization. The rest will be left in barbarism. The Hindus came into India and the tribes of Central Asia were left in barbarism. Others came to Asia Minor and Europe. Then, you remember the coming out of Egypt of the Israelites. Their home was the Arabian desert. Out of that springs a new work...All civilizations grow that way. A certain race becomes civilized. Then comes a nomad race. Nomads are always ready to fight. They come and conquer a race. They bring better blood, stronger physiques. They take up the mind of the conquered race and add that to their body and push civilization still further. One race becomes cultured and civilized until the body is worn out. Then like a whirlwind comes a race strong in the physical, and they take up the arts and the sciences and the mind, and push civilization further. This must be. Otherwise the world would not be.

***

The moment a great man rises, they build a beautiful [mythology] around him. Science and truth is all the religion that exists. Truth is more beautiful than any mythology in the world...

The old Greeks had disappeared already, the whole nation [lay] under the feet of the Romans who were learning their science and art. The Roman was a barbarian, a conquering man. He had no eye for poetry or art. He knew how to rule and how to get everything centralized into that system of Rome and to enjoy that. That was sweet. And that Roman Empire is gone, destroyed by all sorts of difficulties, luxury, a new foreign religion, and all that. Christianity had been already six hundred years in the Roman Empire...

Whenever a new religion tries to force itself upon another race, it succeeds if the race is uncultured. If it [the race] is cultured, it will destroy the [religion]...The Roman Empire was a case in point, and the Persian people saw that. Christianity was another thing with the barbarians in the north. [But] the Christianity of the Roman Empire was a mixture of everything, something from Persia, from the Jews, from India, from Greece, everything.

* * *

The race is always killed by [war]. War takes away the best men, gets them killed, and the cowards are left at home. Thus comes the degeneration of the race...Men became small. Why? All the great men became [warriors]. That is how war kills races, takes their best into the battlefields.

Then the monasteries. They all went to the desert, to the caves for meditation. The monasteries gradually became the centres of wealth and luxury...

The Anglo-Saxon race would not be Anglo-Saxon but for these monasteries. Every weak man was worse than a slave....In that state of chaos these monasteries were centres of light and protection.

Where [cultures] differ very much they do not quarrel. All these warring, jarring elements [were originally] all one.

In the midst of all this chaos was born the prophet...

[This concluded the first part of the Swami's lecture. Vide "Mohammed"]

CLASS LESSONS IN MEDITATION BY SWAMI VIVEKANANDA

New Discoveries, Vol. 6, p. 10.

Mr. Frank Rhodehamel's notes of a class delivered in San Francisco, California, on Monday, March 26, 1900.

The first point is the position. Sit with the spine perfectly free, with the weight resting on the hips. The next step is breathing. Breathe in the left nostril and out the right. Fill the lungs full and eject all the breath. Clear the lungs of all impure air. Breathe full and deep. The next thing is to think of the body as luminous, filled with light. The next thing is to concentrate on the base of the spine, not from the outside, but look down the spinal column inside to the base of the spine.

THE GITA

New Discoveries, Vol. 6, pp. 175-76.

Mr. Frank Rhodehamel's notes of a Bhagavad-Gitâ class delivered Thursday, May 24, 1900, in San Francisco, California

The Gitâ is the gist of the Vedas. It is not our Bible; the Upanishads are our Bible. It [the Gita] is the gist of the Upanishads and harmonizes the many contradictory parts of the Upanishads.

The Vedas are divided into two portions — the work portion and the knowledge portion. The work portion contains ceremonials, rules as to eating, living, doing charitable work, etc. The knowledge came afterwards and was enunciated by kings.

The work portion was exclusively in the hands of the priests and pertained entirely to the sense life. It taught to do good works that one might go to heaven and enjoy eternal happiness. Anything, in fact, that one might want could be provided for him by the work or ceremonials. It provided for all classes of people good and bad. Nothing could be obtained through the ceremonials except by the intercession of the priests. So if one wanted anything, even if it was to have an enemy killed, all he had to do was to pay the priest; and the priest through these ceremonials would procure the desired results. It was therefore in the interests of the priests that the ceremonial portion of the Vedas should be preserved. By it they had their living. They consequently did all in their power to preserve that portion intact. Many of these ceremonials were very complicated, and it took years to perform some of them.

The knowledge portion came afterwards and was promulgated exclusively by kings. It was called the Knowledge of Kings. The great kings had no use for the work portion with all its frauds and superstitions and did all in their power to destroy it. This knowledge consisted of a knowledge of God, the soul, the universe, etc. These kings had no use for the ceremonials of the priests, their magical works, etc. They pronounced it all humbug; and when the priests came to them for gifts, they questioned the priests about God, the soul, etc., and as the priests could not answer such questions they were sent away. The priests went back to their fathers to enquire about the things the kings asked them, but could learn nothing from them, so they came back again to the kings and became their disciples. Very little of the ceremonials are followed today. They have been mostly done away with, and only a few of the more simple ones are followed today.

Then in the Upanishads there is the doctrine of Karma. Karma is the law of causation applied to conduct. According to this doctrine we must work forever, and the only way to get rid of pain is to do good works and thus to enjoy the good effects; and after living a life of good works, die and go to heaven and live forever in happiness. Even in heaven we could not be free from Karma, only it would be good Karma, not bad.

The philosophical portion denounces all work however good, and all pleasure, as loving and kissing wife, husband or children, as useless. According to this doctrine all good works and pleasures are nothing but foolishness and in their very nature impermanent. "All this must come to an end sometime, so end it now; it is vain." So says the philosophical portion of the Upanishads. It claims all the pain in the world is caused by ignorance, therefore the cure is knowledge.

This idea of one being held down fast by past Karma, or work, is all nonsense. No matter how dense one may be, or how bad, one ray of light will dissipate it all. A bale of cotton, however large, will be utterly destroyed by a spark. If a room has been dark for untold ages, a lamp will end it all. So with each soul, however benighted he may be, he is not absolutely bound down by his past Karma to work for ages to come. "One ray of Divine Light will free him, reveal to him his true nature."

Well, the Gita harmonizes all these conflicting doctrines. As to Krishna, whether or not he ever lived, I do not know. "A great many stories are told of him, but I do not believe them."

"I doubt very much that he ever lived and think it would be a good thing if he never did. There would have been one less god in the world."

THE GITA — I

New Discoveries, Vol. 6, pp. 205-7. Cf. Ida Ansell's notes of "The Gita I", Complete Works, I.

Mr. Frank Rhodehamel's notes of a Bhagavad-Gîtâ lecture delivered Saturday, May 26, 1900, in San Francisco, California.

The Gîtâ is to the Hindus what the New Testament is to the Christians. It is about five thousand years old, and the day of religious celebrations with the Hindus is the anniversary of the Battle of Kurukshetra about five thousand years ago. As I said, the Vedas are divided into two great divisions, the philosophical and the Karmakânda, or work portion.

Between the kings, who promulgated the philosophic portion, and the priests a great conflict arose. The priests had the people on their side because they had all the utility which appealed to the popular mind. The kings had all the spirituality and none of the economic element; but as they were powerful and the rulers of the nation, the struggle was a hard and bitter one. The kings gradually gained a little ground, but their ideas were too elevated for the masses, so the ceremonial, or work portion, always had the mass of the people.

Always remember this, that whenever a religious system gains ground with the people at large, it has a strong economic side to it. It is the economic side of a religion that finds lodgement with the people at large, and never its spiritual, or philosophic, side. If you should preach the grandest philosophy in the streets for a year, you would not have a handful of followers. But you could preach the most arrant nonsense, and if it had an economic element, you would have the whole people with you.

None knows by whom the Vedas were written; they are so ancient. According to the orthodox Hindus, the Vedas are not the written words at all, but they consist of the words themselves orally spoken with the exact enunciation and intonation. This vast mass of religion has been written and consists of thousands upon thousands of volumes. Anyone who knows the precise pronunciation and intonation knows the Vedas, and no one else. In ancient times certain royal families were the custodians of certain parts of the Vedas. The head of the family could repeat every word of every volume he had, without missing a word or an intonation. These men had giant intellects, wonderful memories.

The strictly orthodox believers in the Vedas, the Karmakanda, did not believe in God, the soul or anything of the sort, but that we as we are were the only beings in the universe, material or spiritual. When they were asked what the many allusions to God in the Vedas mean, they say that they mean nothing at all; that the words properly articulated have a magical power, a power to create certain results. Aside from that they have no meaning.

Whenever you suppress a thought, you simply press it down out of sight in a coil, like a spring, only to spring out again at a moment's notice with all the pent up force as the result of the suppression, and do in a few moments what it would have done in a much longer period.

Every ounce of pleasure brings its pound of pain. It is the same energy that at one time manifests itself as pleasure and at another time as pain. As soon as one set of sensations stops, another begins. But in some cases, in more advanced persons, one may have two, yes, or even a hundred different thoughts enter into active operation at the same time. When one thought is suppressed, it is merely coiled up ready to spring forth with pent up fury at any time.

"Mind is of its own nature. Mind activity means creation. The thought is followed by the word, and the word by the form. All of this creating will have to stop, both mental and physical, before the mind can reflect the soul."

"My old master (Shri Ramakrishna.) could not write his own name without making a mistake. He made three mistakes in spelling, in writing his own name."

"Yet that is the kind of man at whose feet I sat."

"You will break the law of nature but once, and it will be the last time. Nature will then be nothing to you."

THE GITA — III

New Discoveries, Vol. 6, pp. 213-16. Cf. Ida Ansell's notes of "The Gita III", Complete Works, I.

Mr. Frank Rhodehamel's notes of the Bhagavad-Gitâ lecture delivered Tuesday, May 29, 1900, in San Francisco, California.

1. "If you know everything, disturb not the childlike faith of the innocent."

2. "Religion is the realization of Spirit as Spirit.

Not spirit as matter."

3. "You are spirit. Realize yourselves as spirit. Do it any way you can."

4. "Religion is a growth": each one must experience it himself.

5. "Everyone thinks 'my method is the best'. That is so, but it is the best for you."

6. "Spirit must stand revealed as spirit."

7. "There never was a time when spirit could be identified with matter."

8. "What is real in nature is the spirit."

9. "Action is in nature."

10. "In the beginning there was That Existence. He looked and everything was created.'"

11. "Everyone works according to his own nature."

12. "You are not bound by law. That is in your nature. The mind is in nature and is bound by law."

13. "If you want to be religious, keep out of religious arguments."

14. "Governments, societies, etc., are evils." "All societies are based on bad generalizations." "A law is that which cannot be broken."

15. "Better never love, if that love makes us hate others."

16. "The sign of death is weakness; the sign of life is strength."

The following numbered paragraphs are correlated with the preceding numbered sentences.

4. The Christian believes that Jesus Christ died to save him. With you it is belief in a doctrine, and this belief constitutes your salvation. With us, doctrine has nothing whatever to do with salvation. Each one may believe in whatever doctrine he likes or in no doctrine. With us realization is religion, not doctrine. What difference does it make to you whether Jesus Christ lived at a certain time? What has it to do with you that Moses saw God in a burning bush? The fact that Moses saw God in the burning bush does not constitute your seeing Him, does it? If it does, then the fact that Moses ate is enough for you; you ought to stop eating. One is just as sensible as the other. Records of great spiritual men of the past do us no good whatever except that they urge us onward to do the same, to experience religion ourselves. Whatever Christ or Moses or anybody else did does not help us in the least except to urge us on.

5. Each one has a special nature peculiar to himself which he must follow and through which he will find his way to freedom. Your teacher should be able to tell you what your particular path in nature is and to put you in it. He should know by your face where you belong and should be able to indicate it to you. We should never try to follow another's path for that is his way, not yours. When that path is found, you have nothing to do but fold your arms and the tide will carry you to freedom. Therefore when you find it, never swerve from it. Your way is the best for you, but that is no sign it is the best for another.

6. The truly spiritual see spirit as spirit, not as matter. Spirit as such can never become matter, though matter is spirit at a low rate of vibration. It is spirit that makes nature move; it is the Reality in nature, so action is in nature but not in the spirit. Spirit is always the same, changeless, eternal. Spirit and matter are in reality the same, but spirit, as such, never becomes matter, and matter, as such, never becomes spirit. Matter, as such, never becomes spirit as such, for it is simply a mode of spirit, or spirit at a low rate of vibration. You take food and it becomes mind, and mind in turn becomes the body. Thus mind and body, spirit and matter are distinct though either may give place to the other; but they are not to be identified.

8. "What is real in nature is the Spirit." The spirit is the life in all action in nature. It is the spirit that gives nature its reality and power of action.

9. "Action is in nature." "The spirit never acts. Why should it?" It merely is, and that is sufficient. It is pure existence absolute and has no need of action.

12. All nature is bound by law, the law of its own action; and this law can never be broken. If you could break a law of nature, all nature would come to an end in an instant. There would be no more nature. He who attains freedom breaks the law of

nature and for him nature fades away and has no more power over him. Each one will break the law but once and forever and that will end his trouble with nature. "You are not bound by law. That is in your nature. The mind is in nature and is bound by law."

14. The moment you form yourselves into an organization, you begin to hate everybody outside of that organization. When you join an organization you are putting bonds upon yourself, you are limiting your own freedom. Why should you form yourselves into an order having rules and regulations, thus limiting every one as to his independent action? If one breaks a law of an order or society he is hated by the rest. What right has anyone to lay down rules and laws governing others? Such laws are not laws at all. If it were a law it could not be broken. The fact that these so-called laws are broken shows clearly they are not laws.

GITA CLASS

New Discoveries, Vol. 6, pp. 275-76.

Sister Nivedita's notes of a New York Bhagavad-Gitâ class, recorded in a June 16, 1900 letter to Miss Josephine MacLeod.

This morning the lesson on the Gitâ was grand. It began with a long talk on the fact that the highest ideals are not for all. Non-resistance is not for the man who thinks the replacing of the maggot in the wound by the leprous saint with "Eat, Brother!" disgusting and horrible. Non-resistance is practised by a mother's love towards an angry child. It is a travesty in the mouth of a coward, or in the face of a lion.

Let us be true. Nine-tenths of our life's energy is spent in trying to make people think us that which we are not. That energy would be more rightly spent in becoming that which we would like to be. And so it went — beginning with the salutation to an incarnation:

Salutation to thee — the Guru of the universe,
Whose footstool is worshipped by the gods.
Thou one unbroken Soul,
Physician of the world's diseases.
Guru of even the gods,
To thee our salutation.

Thee we salute. Thee we salute. Thee we salute. In the Indian tones — by Swami himself.

There was an implication throughout the talk that Christ and Buddha were inferior to Krishna — in the grasp of problems — inasmuch as they preached the highest ethics as a world path, whereas Krishna saw the right of the whole, in all its parts — to its own differing ideals.

REMARKS FROM VARIOUS LECTURES

New Discoveries, Vol. 6, pp. 209-10.

Mr. Frank Rhodehamel's random lecture notes, most of which seem to pertain to chapter two of the Bhagavad-Gitâ.

"Spirituality can never be attained until materiality is gone." The first discourse in the Gita can be taken allegorically. "The Vedas only teach of things in nature, only teach of nature." We are always letting sentiment usurp the place of duty, and flattering ourselves that we are acting in response to true love. We must get beyond emotionalism if we would be able to renounce. Emotion belongs to the animals. They are creatures of emotion entirely. It is not sacrifice of a high order to die for one's young. The animals do that, and just as readily as any human mother ever did. It is no sign of real love to do that; merely blind emotion.

We are forever trying to make our weakness look like strength, our sentiment like love, our cowardice like courage, etc.

Say to your soul in regard to vanities, weaknesses, etc., "This does not befit thee. This does not befit thee".

WRITINGS: PROSE AND POEMS

THE ETHER[1]

This article first appeared anonymously in the February 1895 issue of the New York Medical Times, a prestigious monthly medical journal founded and edited by Dr. Egbert Guernsey.

Classification or grouping of phenomena by their similarities is the first step in scientific knowledge — perhaps it is all. An organized grouping, revealing to us a similarity running through the whole group, and a conviction that under similar circumstances the group will arrange itself in the same form — stretched over all time, past, present and future — is what we call law.

This finding of unity in variety is really what we call knowledge. These different groups of similars are stowed away in the pigeon-holes of the mind, and when a new fact comes before us we begin to search for a similar group already existing in one of the pigeon-holes of the mind. If we succeed in finding one ready-made, we take the newcomer in immediately. If not, we either reject the new fact, or wait till we find more of his kind, and form a new place for the group.

Facts which are extraordinary thus disturb us; but and when we find many like them, they cease to disturb, even when our knowledge about their cause remains the same as before.

The ordinary experiences of our lives are no less wonderful than any miracles recorded in any sacred book of the world; nor are we any more enlightened as to the cause of these ordinary experiences than of the so-called miracles. But the miraculous is "extraordinary", and the everyday experience is "ordinary". The "extraordinary" startles the mind, the "ordinary" satisfies.

The field of knowledge is so varied, and the more the difference is from the centre, the more widely the radii diverge.

At the start the different sciences were thought to have no connection whatever with each other; but as more and more knowledge comes in — that is, the more and more we come nearer the centre — the radii are converging more and more, and it seems that they are on the eve of finding a common centre. Will they ever find it?

The study of the mind was, above all, the science to which the sages of India and Greece had directed their attention. All religions are the outcome of the study of the inner man. Here we find the attempt at finding the unity, and in the science of religion, as taking its stand upon general and massive propositions, we find the boldest and the most vigorous manifestation of this tendency at finding the unity.

Some religions could not solve the problem beyond the finding of a duality of causes, one good, the other evil. Others went as far as finding an intelligent personal cause, a few went still further beyond intellect, beyond personality, and found an infinite being.

In those, and only those systems which dared to transcend beyond the personality of a limited human consciousness, we find also an attempt to resolve all physical phenomena into unity.

The result was the "Akâsha" of the Hindus and the "Ether" of the Greeks.

This "Akasha" was, after the mind, the first material manifestation, said the Hindu sages, and out of this "Akasha" all this has been evolved.

History repeats itself; and again during the latter part of the nineteenth century, the same theory is coming with more vigour and fuller light.

It is being proved more clearly than ever that as there is a co-relation of physical forces there is also a co-relation of different [branches of] knowledge, and that behind all these general groups there is a unity of knowledge.

It was shown by Newton[2] that if light consisted of material particles projected from luminous bodies, they must move faster in solids and liquids than in air, in order that the laws of refraction might be satisfied.

---

1. Reprinted in New Discoveries, Vol. 3, pp. 55-59. Because the Swami's original handwritten article is unavailable, we have made the spelling, punctuation and grammar of his published version conform to the style of the *Complete Works*. — Publisher.

2. Isaac Newton, 1642 – 1727.

Huyghens[1], on the other hand, showed that to account for the same laws on the supposition that light consisted in the undulating motion of an elastic medium, it must move more slowly in solids and fluids than in gases. Fizeau[2] and Foucault[3] found Huyghens's predictions correct.

Light, then, consists in the vibrating motion of a medium, which must, of course, fill all space. This is called the ether.

In the fact that the theory of a cosmic ether explains fully all the phenomena of radiation, refraction, diffraction and polarization of light is the strongest argument in favour of the theory.

Of late, gravitation, molecular action, magnetic, electric, and electro-dynamic attractions and repulsions have thus been explained.

Sensible and latent heat, electricity and magnetism themselves have been of late almost satisfactorily explained by the theory of the all-pervading ether.

Zöllner[4], however, basing his calculations upon the data supplied by the researches of Wilhelm Weber[5], thinks that the transmission of life force between the heavenly bodies is effected both ways, by the undulation of a medium and by the actual evidence of particles.

Weber found that the molecules, the smallest particles of bodies, were composed of yet smaller particles, which he called the electric particles, and which in the molecules are in a constant circular motion. These electric particles are partly positive, partly negative.

Those of the same electricity repulse those of different electricity; attracting each other, each molecule contains the same amount of electric particles, with a small surplus of either positive or negative quickly changing the balance.

Upon this Zöllner builds these propositions:

1. Christian Huyghens, 1629 – 1695.
2. Armand Hippolyte Louis Fizeau, 1819 – 1896.
3. Jean Bernard Léon Foucault, 1819 – 1868.
4. Johann K. F. Zöllner, 1834 – 1882.
5. Wilhelm Eduard Weber, 1804 – 1891.

(1) The molecules are composed of a very great number of particles—the so-called electric particles, which are in constant circular motion around each other within the molecule.

(2) If the inner motion of a molecule increases over a certain limit, then electric particles are emitted. They then travel from one heavenly body through space until they reach another heavenly body, where they are either reflected or absorbed by other molecules.

(3) The electric particles thus traversing space are the ether of the physicist.

(4) These ether particles have a twofold motion: first, their proper motion; second, an undulatory motion, for which they receive the impulse from the ether particles rotating in the molecules.

(5) The motion of the smallest particles corresponds to that of the heavenly bodies.

The corollary is:

The law of attraction which holds good for the heavenly bodies also holds good for the smallest particles.

Under these suppositions, that which we call space is really filled with electric particles, or ether.

Zöllner also found the following interesting calculation for the electric atoms:

Velocity: 50,143 geographical miles per second.

Amount of ether particles in a water molecule: 42,000 million.

Distance from each other: 0.0032 millimeter.

So far as it goes, then, the theory of a universal cosmic ether is the best at hand to explain the various phenomena of nature.

As far as it goes, the theory that this ether consists of particles, electric or otherwise, is also very valuable. But on all suppositions, there must be space between two particles of ether, however small; and what fills this inter-ethereal space? If particles still finer, we require still more fine ethereal particles to fill up the vacuum between every two of them, and so on.

Thus the theory of ether, or material particles in space, though accounting for the phenomena in space, cannot account for space itself.

And thus we are forced to find that the ether which comprehends the molecules explains the molecular phenomena, but itself cannot explain space because we cannot but think of ether as in space. And, therefore, if there is anything which will explain this space, it must be something that comprehends in its infinite being the infinite space itself. And what is there that can comprehend even the infinite space but the Infinite Mind?

NOTES[6]

An undated and untitled, one-page manuscript in Swami Vivekananda's own handwriting.

My nerves act on my brain—the brain sends back a reaction which, on the mental side, is this world.

Something—x—acts on the brain through the nerves, the reaction is this world.

Why not the x be also in the body—why outside?

Because we find the already created outside world (as the result of a previous reaction of the brain) acts on us calling on a further reaction.

Thus inside becomes outside and creates another action, which interior action created another reaction, which again becomes outside and again acts inside.

The only way of reconciling idealism and realism is to hold that one brain can be affected by the world created as reaction by another brain from inside, i.e., the mixture x + mind which one brain throws out can affect another, to which it's similarly external.

Therefore as soon as we come within the influence of this hypnotic circle, or influence, created by hundreds of preceding brains we begin to feel this world as they see it.

Mind is only a phase of matter, i.e., of the ever-changing phenomena of which matter and mind are different states or views. There must be something in whose presence this eternal, phenomenal net is spread—that is the Substance, the Brahman.

---
6. *New Discoveries*, Vol. 3, pp. 440-41.

LECTURE NOTES

New Discoveries, Vol. 4, pp. 213-14.

Probably at the turn of the century, Miss Ellen Waldo gave these undated notes in Swami Vivekananda's handwriting to her friend Sister Devamata, a member of the Boston Vedanta Centre, where they were later made available for publication.

Man will need a religion so long as he is constituted as at present. The forms will change from time to time.

The dissatisfaction with the senses.

The yearning beyond.

There were encroachments of religion on the domains of physical science — these [encroachments] religion is giving up every day. Yet there is a vast field covered by religion where physical science[s] are mute.

The [vain?] attempt to keep man strictly within the limits of the senses — Because — there are men who catch a glimpse now and then of the infinite beyond.

The types of men.

The worker — the mystic the emotional the intellectual. Each type is necessary for the well — being of society. The dangers of each —

A mixture minimizes the danger.

The East is too full of mystics and meditative the West of workers — An exchange will be for the good of both.

The necessity of religion —

The four types of men

that come to religion —

the basis of Unity — the Divinity

in man. Why use this term?

the western Society has work

and intellectual philosophy —

But work must not be destructive

of others.

Philosophy — must not be only dry intellectuality.

MACROCOSM AND MICROCOSM

The Life of Swami Vivekananda, Vol. I. p. 250.

After his experience of the macrocosm within the microcosm while absorbed in meditation under the peepul tree at Kakrighat, in 1890, Swami Vivekananda jotted down in Bengali fragments of his realization in his notebook.

In the beginning was the Word etc.

The microcosm and the macrocosm are built on the same plan. Just as the individual soul is encased in the living body, so is the universal Soul in the Living Prakriti [Nature] — the objective universe. Shivâ [i.e. Kâli] is embracing Shiva: this is not a fancy. This covering of the one [Soul] by the other [Nature] is analogous to the relation between an idea and the word expressing it: they are one and the same; and it is only by a mental abstraction that one can distinguish them. Thought is impossible without words. Therefore, in the beginning was the Word etc.

This dual aspect of the Universal Soul is eternal. So what we perceive or feel is this combination of the Eternally Formed and the Eternally Formless.

SWAMI VIVEKANANDA'S FOOTNOTES TO THE IMITATION OF CHRIST[1]

In 1889, Swami Vivekananda translated into Bengali selections from Book I, chapters 1-6 of Thomas à Kempis's The Imitation of Christ. They were published along with a preface in a now-defunct Bengali monthly magazine, Sâhitya Kalpadruma. The Swami's preface and Bengali translation, entitled "Ishânusharana"[2], were later published in the Bengali Complete Works (first edition), VI, pp. 16-28. However, only the preface to The Imitation of Christ was published in the English edition of the Complete Works, VIII.

Swami Vivekananda's partial Bengali translation of The Imitation of Christ includes as footnotes quotations from Hindu scriptures that parallel à Kempis's ideas, comments or commentary. For the sake of clarity, these footnotes (numbered 1 through 17) have been appended to their respective verses in The Imitation of Christ (indicated in parentheses), arranged under their appropriate chapter headings in the book, and reproduced here in bold.

Many of the Sanskrit footnotes to the Bengali translation were later rendered into English during the course of Swami Vivekananda's lecturing or writing. For the sake of interest, these English translations have also been added to the Swami's restored footnote text. Otherwise, Sanskrit verses have been translated by the Publisher for the convenience of the reader.

—Publisher

BOOK I[3]

Chapter 1

Of the Imitation of Christ and Contempt of all the Vanities of the World

1. "He that followeth Me, walketh not in darkness", saith the Lord [John 8.12]. (The Imitation of Christ V.1.)

Swami Vivekananda's Footnote: Bhagavad-Gita 7.14

देवी ह्येषा गुणमयी मम माया दुरत्यया ।
मामेव ये प्रपद्यन्ते मायामेतां तरन्ति ते ॥

Swami Vivekananda's Translation: This My Mâyâ is divine, made up of qualities and very difficult to cross. Yet those who come unto Me, cross the river of life[4].

---

1. *Prabuddha Bharata*, September 1982, pp. 390-93.

2. In Bengali, the word Ishâ means Christ and Anusharana, "to follow"; hence Ishânusharana means "to follow Christ".

3. Verses are cited from Thomas à Kempis's *Of the Imitation of Christ* (London: Oxford University Press, 1961.) This translation—based on that of F. B. (the Jesuit Anthony Hoskins), which first appeared c. 1613—has been lightly edited in order to conform to the grammar, punctuation and style of the *Complete Works* — Publisher.

4. Vide "Maya and Freedom", *Complete Works*, II:123.

2. Let therefore our chief endeavour be to meditate upon the life of Jesus Christ. (The Imitation of Christ V.1.)

Swami Vivekananda's Footnote: Adhyâtma Râmâyana, Uttara-Kanda 5.54 (RamaGita)

ध्यात्वैवमात्मानमहर्निशं मुनिः।
तिष्ठेत्सदा मुक्तसमस्तबन्धनः ॥

Publisher's Translation: Thus meditating upon the Self day and night, let the sage abide free from all bondage.

3. The doctrine of Christ exceedeth all the doctrines of holy men; and he that hath the Spirit will find therein the hidden manna. (The Imitation of Christ V.2.)

Swami Vivekananda's Footnote:

When the Israelites were afflicted by want of food in a desert, God showered on them a kind of "manna".

4. But it falleth out, that many who often hear the Gospel of Christ, are yet but little affected, because they are void of the Spirit of Christ. But whosoever would fully and feelingly understand the words of Christ, must endeavour to conform his life wholly to the life of Christ. (The Imitation of Christ V.2.)

Swami Vivekananda's Footnote (a): Bhagavad-Gita 2.29

श्रुत्वाप्येनं वेद न चैव कश्चित् ।

Swami Vivekananda'S Translation: Others, hearing of It, do not understand[5].

Swami Vivekananda's Footnote (b): Vivekachudâmani 62.

न गच्छति विना पानं व्याधिरौषधशब्दतः ।
विनापरोक्षानुभवं ब्रह्मशब्देर्न मुच्यते ॥

Publisher's Translation: A disease does not leave the body by simply repeating the name of the medicine; one must take the medicine. Similarly, liberation does not come by merely saying the word Brahman. Brahman must be experienced.

Swami Vivekananda's Footnote (c): Mahabharata(critical edition) 12.309.91.

श्रुतेन किं येन न धर्ममाचरेत् ।

Publisher's Translation: Of what avail is reading the Vedas without practising religion?

5. What will it avail thee to dispute profoundly of the Trinity if thou be void of humility and art thereby displeasing to the Trinity? (The Imitation of Christ V.3.)

Swami Vivekananda's Footnote:

According to the Christians, God the Father, Holy Ghost, and God the Son are One in three and Three in One.

6. Surely great words do not make a man holy and just; but a virtuous life maketh him dear to God. (The Imitation of Christ V.3.)

Swami Vivekananda's Footnote: Vivekachudamani 58.

वाग्वैखरी शब्दझरी शास्त्रव्याख्यानकौशलम्।
वैदुष्यं विदुषां तद्वद् भुक्तये न तु मुक्तये॥

Swami Vivekananda's Translation: Wonderful methods of joining words, rhetorical powers, and explaining texts of the books in various ways — these are only for the enjoyment of the learned, and not religion[6].

7. If thou didst know the whole Bible by heart and the sayings of all the philosophers, what would it profit thee without the love of God and without grace? (The Imitation of Christ V.3.)

Swami Vivekananda's Footnote: [reference only]
—I Corinthians 13.2.

8. "Vanity of vanities, all is vanity" (Eccles.) except to love God and to serve Him only. (The Imitation of Christ V.3.)

Swami Vivekananda's Footnote: Maniratnamâlâ

के सन्तः सन्तोऽखिलनीतिरागाः ।
अपास्तमोहाः श्रवितत्त्वनिष्ठाः ॥

Publisher's Translation: They alone are holy men (Sâdhus) who are devoid of any longing for worldly objects, free from delusion and are devoted to the truth of Shiva.

---
5. Vide "The Gita II", *Complete Works*, I.

6. Vide "Realization", *Complete Works*, II:164

9. Call often to mind that proverb "The eye is not satisfied with seeing, nor the ear filled with hearing". (The Imitation of Christ V.5.)

Swami Vivekananda's Footnote: [reference only] —Eccles. 1.8.

10. Endeavour, therefore, to withdraw thy heart from the love of visible things and to turn thyself to the invisible. For they that follow their lusts stain their own consciences and lose the grace of God. (The Imitation of Christ V.5.)

Swami Vivekananda's Footnote: Mahabharata, 2.63.

(Yayatigatha)

न जातु कामः कामानुपभोगेन शाम्यति ।
हविषा कृष्णवर्त्मेव भूय एवाभिवर्धते ॥

Swami Vivekananda's Translation: Desire is never satisfied by the enjoyment of desires; it only increases the more, as fire when butter is poured upon it[1].

Chapter 3

Of the Doctrine of Truth

11. What availeth it to cavil and dispute much about dark and hidden things; for ignorance of which we shall not be reproved at the day of judgement?(The Imitation of Christ V.1.)

Swami Vivekananda's Footnote:

According to the Christian view, God will judge all beings on the last day (the day of the dissolution of the world), and will award heaven or hell according to the virtues or vices of different individuals.

12. He to whom the Eternal Word speaketh is delivered from many an opinion.(The Imitation of Christ V.2.)

Swami Vivekananda's Footnote:

This Word is somewhat similar to the Maya of the Vedantists. This Itself was manifested in the form of Christ.

Chapter 5

Of the Reading of Holy Scriptures

13. Truth, not eloquence, is to be sought for in Holy Scripture. Each part of the Scripture is to be read with the same Spirit wherewith it was written. (The Imitation of Christ V.1.)

Swami Vivekananda's Footnote: Katha Upanishad 1.2.9.

नैषा तर्केण मतिरापनेया ।

Swami Vivekananda's Translation: Neither is the mind to be disturbed by vain arguments, for it is no more a question of argument; it is a question of fact[2].

14. Let not the authority of the writer offend thee, whether he be of great or small learning; but let the love of pure truth draw thee to read. (The Imitation of Christ V.1.)

Swami Vivekananda's Footnote: Laws of Manu 2.238.

आददीत शुभां विद्यां प्रयत्नादवरादपि ।

Swami Vivekananda's Translation: Learn supreme knowledge with service even from the man of low birth[3].

Chapter 6

Of Inordinate Affections

15. Whensoever a man desireth anything inordinately, he becometh presently disquieted in himself. (The Imitation of Christ V.1.)

Swami Vivekananda's Footnote: Bhagavad-Gita 2.67.

इन्द्रियाणां हि चरतां यन्मनोऽनु विधीयते ।
तदस्य हरति प्रज्ञां वायुर्नावमिवाम्भसि ॥

Swami Vivekananda's Translation: For the mind which follows in the wake of the wandering senses carries away his discrimination as a wind (carries away from its course) a boat on the waters.

---

1. Vide "Maya and Illusion", *Complete Works*, II.

2. Vide "Realization", Complete Works, II:162

3. Vide "The Common Bases of Hinduism", *Complete Works*, III. 381-382

16. The proud and covetous can never rest. The poor and humble in spirit live together in all peace.

The man that is not yet perfectly dead to himself, is quickly tempted and overcome in small and trifling things. (The Imitation of Christ V.1.)

Swami Vivekananda's Footnote: Bhagavad-Gita 2.62-63.

ध्यायतो विषयान्पुंसः संगस्तेषूपजायते ।
संगात्संजायते कामः कामात्क्रोधोऽभिजायते ॥
क्रोधाद्भवति संमोहः संमोहात्स्मृतिविभ्रमः ।
स्मृतिभ्रंशाद् बुद्धिनाशो बुद्धिनाशात्प्रणश्यति ॥

Publisher's Translation: By thinking about sense objects, attachment to them is formed. From attachment comes longing, and longing breeds anger. From anger comes delusion, and from delusion, confused memory. From confused memory comes the ruin of discrimination; and from the ruin of discrimination, a man perishes.

17. There is then no peace in the heart of a carnal man, nor in him that is addicted to outward things, but in the spiritual and devout man. (The Imitation of Christ V.2.)

Swami Vivekananda's Footnote: Bhagavad-Gita 2.60.

यततो ह्यपि कौन्तेय पुरुषस्य विपश्चितः ।
इन्द्रियाणि प्रमाथीनि हरन्ति प्रसभं मनः ॥

Publisher's Translation: The turbulent senses, O son of Kunti, violently carry away the mind of even a wise man striving after perfection.

THE PLAGUE MANIFESTO

Om Salutations to Bhagavan Shri Ramakrishna!

Brothers of Calcutta!

1. We feel happy when you are happy, and we suffer when you suffer. Therefore, during these days of extreme adversity, we are striving and ceaselessly praying for your welfare and an easy way to save you from disease and the fear of an epidemic.

2. If that grave disease — fearing which both the high and the low, the rich and the poor are all fleeing the city — ever really comes in our midst, then even if we perish while serving and nursing you, we will consider ourselves fortunate because you are all embodiments of God. He who thinks otherwise — out of vanity, superstition or ignorance — offends God and incurs great sin. There is not the slightest doubt about it.

3. We humbly pray to you — please do not panic due to unfounded fear. Depend upon God and calmly try to find the best means to solve the problem. Otherwise, join hands with those who are doing that very thing.

4. What is there to fear? The terror that has entered people's hearts due to the occurrence of the plague has no real ground. Through God's will, nothing of the terrible form that plague takes, as seen in other places, has occurred in Calcutta. The government authorities have also been particularly helpful to us. So what is there to fear?

5. Come, let us give up this false fear and, having faith in the infinite compassion of God, gird our loins and enter the field of action. Let us live pure and clean lives. Disease, fear of an epidemic, etc., will vanish into thin air by His grace.

6. (a) Always keep the house and its premises, the rooms, clothes, bed, drain, etc., clean.

(b) Do not eat stale, spoiled food; take fresh and nutritious food instead. A weak body is more susceptible to disease.

(c) Always keep the mind cheerful. Everyone will die once. Cowards suffer the pangs of death again and again, solely due to the fear in their own minds.

(d) Fear never leaves those who earn their livelihoods by unethical means or who cause harm to others. Therefore, at this time when we face the great fear of death, desist from all such behaviour.

(e) During the period of epidemic, abstain from anger and from lust — even if you are householders.

(f) Do not pay any heed to rumours.

(g) The British government will not vaccinate anyone by force. Only those who are willing will be vaccinated.

(h) There will be no lack of effort in treating the afflicted patients in our hospital under our special care and supervision, paying full respect to religion, caste and the modesty (Purdah) of women. Let the wealthy run away! But we are poor; we understand the heartache of the poor. The Mother of the Universe is Herself the support of the helpless. The Mother is assuring us: "Fear not! Fear not!"

7. Brother, if there is no one to help you, then send information immediately to the servants of Shri Bhagavan Ramakrishna at Belur Math. There will be no dearth of help that is physically possible. By the grace of the Mother, monetary help will also be possible.

— N. B. In order to remove the fear of the epidemic, you should sing Nâma Sankirtanam [the name of the Lord] every evening and in every locality.

ONE CIRCLE MORE

A fragmentary poem composed at Ridgely Manor, in 1899.

One circle more the spiral path of life ascends
And time's restless shuttle — running back and fro
Through maze of warp and woof of shining
   threads of life — spins out a stronger piece. (Cf. a slightly different version of the first three lines of this poem which appeared in Swami Vivekananda's own handwriting on the left-hand side of the folded letter paper containing the original draft (Vide the facsimile): One circle more the spiral path of life ascends And Time's restless shuttle running back and fro through maze of warp and woof spins out a stronger piece.)

Hand in hand they stand — and try to fathom depths whence springs eternal love, each in other's eyes; and find no hold o'er that age but brings the youth anew — and time — the good, the pure, the true.

FACSIMILE

One circle more the spiral path of life ascends
And Time's restless shuttle running back and fro
through maze of warp and woof spins out a stronger piece.

RAILROAD STATION,
W. U. TELEGRAPH AND P. O. STONERIDGE.
NATIONAL EXPRESS OFFICES, ULSTER CO., N. Y.
BINNEWATER, ULSTER CO., N. Y.

AN UNTITLED POEM ON SHRI RAMAKRISHNA

Complete Works (Bengali edition), VI, p. 256.

He who was praised by the Brâhmanas, those knowers of the Vedas who made the sky reverberate with the sacred sounds of the sacrifice and caused the darkness of delusion to vanish through well-performed rituals and the knowledge known as Vedanta — he whose greatness was sung in the sweet chants of the Sâma-Veda etc., with voices thundering like clouds (In Indian mythology clouds can cause both thunder and lightning.) — to that Shri Ramakrishna, I offer my eternal worship.

AN UNFINISHED POEM

New Discoveries, Vol. 3. p. 490. This undated poem is preserved in the archives of the Vedanta Centre, Cohasset, Massachusetts. Cf. "My Play is Done", [6]Complete Works, VI.

From life to life I am waiting here at the gates — they open not.

My tongue is parched with ceaseless prayers and dim my eyes have grown

With constant straining through the gloom to catch one ray long sought;

My heart is seized with dark despair, all hope well-nigh has flown.

———

And standing on life's narrow ridge, beneath the chasm I see —

Strife and sorrow, darkness deep of whirling life and death,

Of mad commotion, struggles vain, of folly roaming free.

On one side this dark abyss — I shudder to see it even —

On the other this wall…

BHARTRIHARI'S VERSES ON RENUNCIATION

This is Swami Vivekananda's free translation of verses from Bhartrihari's Sanskrit poem Vairâgya Shatakam.

The Swami's translation is from Sister Nivedita's Unpublished Notes of Some Wanderings with the Swami Vivekananda — selected verses recorded almost verbatim, but not necessarily in Bhartrihari's order, by Sister Nivedita as Swami Vivekananda translated them orally for some of his Western disciples during a Himalayan pilgrimage in 1898.

For the researcher's benefit, verses 14-15, 18, 24-26, 31, and 33 have been footnoted as corresponding verses taken from Swami Vivekananda's original handwritten translation, which was given to the Vedanta Society of Southern California by Miss Josephine MacLeod, shortly before her passing away in 1948. This footnoted handwritten version was first published in the collection of poetry entitled In Search of God and Other Poems (Mayavati: Advaita Ashrama, 1968).

Stylistic differences in Swami Vivekananda's overall translation of Bhartrihari's poem are due to those variations inherent in the two aforementioned sources. Obvious typographical and punctuation errors have been corrected.

The verse numbers, as available, correspond to Bhartrihari's numbering.

— Publisher

BHARTRIHARI'S VERSES ON RENUNCIATION

A translation of verses from Bhartrihari's Sanskrit poem Vairagya Shatakam.

I have travelled in many countries, hard to travel in, And got no result;

Giving up pride of birth and position,

I have served all.

Like a crow stealing into a kitchen,

With fear I have eaten the bread of others in their homes, Yet thou, Desire, who leadest to evil deeds,

Leavest me not!

(Verse 2)

I have crossed oceans to find wealth.

I have blasted mountains to get jewels.

I have spent whole nights in graveyards repeating Mantras

And have obtained — not the broken cowrie of blessedness

Ah, Desire, give me up now.

(Verse 3)

I have borne the wicked words of the wicked;

To please fools, when my heart is weeping,

my lips ever laughed.

Stopping my judgment, I have with folded hands

Stood before unworthy persons.

Even now, my Desire, why do you make me dance like a fool?

(Verse 4)

For this life, which is like a drop of water on a lotus leaf,

We have not enjoyed, but enjoyments have enjoyed

us. We did not penance, but penances burnt us up.
Time did not fly, yet we are gone.
We become decrepit with age, but not so Desire.
Infirmity assails us, the skin wrinkles,
The hair whitens, the body becomes crooked,
Old age comes on.
Desire alone grows younger every day.

(Verses 5-8)

Hope is the name of this river, whose water is Desire, And Thirst the waves thereof.
Passion is the crocodile living in that water,
Vain resolves are the birds that reside
In the tree of virtue on the shores and kill it. But there are the whirlpools of Delusion
And Despondence, the high banks.
The great Yogis are blissful because they,
With their pure minds, never crossed this river.

(Verse 10)

Blessed are they that, living even in the caves of mountains,
Meditate on the supreme Light.
Even the birds will fearlessly drink of the tears of pleasure
That flow from their eyes.
Alas, (Here Swami Vivekananda's handwritten translation begins.) our minds grow familiar, even in imagination,
With palaces and pleasure — gardens,
And thus our lives fleet by.

(Verse 14)

Even when the only food is gained by begging, and that is tasteless;
One's bed, the dry earth;
One's whole family, his own body;
His only clothing, a ragged bit of cloth —
Alas, alas, the desire for enjoyment does not leave a man.

(Verse 15)

Not knowing the power of flame, the insect falls into it. The fish swallows the bait, not knowing the hook inside. That, well aware of the vanity and dangers of the world, We cannot give it up —
Such is the power of Delusion.

(Verse 18)

Have such places in the Himalayas become extinct
That a man should go begging at others' doors?
Have the roots in the mountain forests all disappeared? Are the springs all dry?
Are the trees all withered that bear sweet fruits
And bark for garments
That a man should look with fear on the face of a fool, Whose head is turned by a little wealth?
(Lit., "Whose eyebrows are dancing with the wind of the pride of a little wealth".)

(Verses 24-25)

Arise! Let us go into the forest
Where pure roots and fruits will be our food,
Pure water our only drink,
Pure leaves our bed,
And where the little-minded, the thoughtless,
And those whose hearts are cramped with wealth
Do not exist.

(Verse 26)

In enjoyment is the fear of disease;
In high birth, the fear of losing caste;
In wealth, the fear of tyrants;
In honour, the fear of losing her;
In strength, the fear of enemies;
In beauty, the fear of the other sex;
In knowledge, the fear of defeat;
In virtue, the fear of scandal;
In the body, the fear of death.
In this life, all is fraught with fear.
Renunciation alone is fearless.

(Verse 31)

The root of health has always round about it
A thousand worms in the form of dangers and

disease. Where fortune falls, open a hundred gates of danger. Whosoever is born, him death will surely swallow. Say, where is that Providence who ever created
Anything that died not?
(Verse 33)

Life is like a wave upon the waters,
Youth only remains a few days.
Wealth is like a fancy of the mind,
It immediately vanishes.
Enjoyment is like a flash of lightning
amongst dark clouds.
Our most beloved one is only for a moment.
Knowing this, O man, give your heart unto Brahman To cross this ocean of life.
(Verse 36)

…Living in whom gods like Indra, Brahmâ and others appear like a blade of grass,
Whose anger can destroy the worlds in a moment.
O sage, know Him, that One Supreme
Who dies not,
And give not your mind to false enjoyment.
(Verse 40)

Ah, where is happiness in this life?
(At best it lasts but a hundred years, of which half is spent in sleep; of the other half, half in decrepitude; of what remains — one half goes in childhood and, of the rest, still half in serving others!)
O man, in this futile, wave-like life
Where is happiness?
(Verse 49)

Now you appear as child
And now as a youth, whose whole occupation is love. This moment poor, another wealthy,
Now a babe, and again a decrepit old man.
O actor man, at last you vanish from the stage
When death beckons you behind the scenes!
(Verse 50)

You are a king, but we have served Gurus,
Who are great in knowledge.
You are known by your wealth as a king,
We for our knowledge.
There is infinite difference between us and you,
Therefore we are not the persons to wait upon you,
O Kings!
(Verse 51)

Oh, when will that day come,
When in a forest, saying "Shiva", "Shiva",
My days shall pass?
A serpent and a garland the same,
The strong foe and the friend the same,
The flower-bed and the stone-bed the same,
A beautiful woman and a blade of grass the same!
(Verses 85, 90)

O Shiva, when shall I be able to cut
To the very roots of my Karma,
By becoming solitary, desireless, quiet —
My hands my only plate, and the cardinal points my clothing?
(Verse 99)

The fruits are sufficient food,
The waters of the mountain sufficient dinner,
The earth a sufficient bed,
And bark a sufficient garment —
These are all welcome.
Only I cannot bear the proud words of fools,
Whose organs are all disordered by the drink
Of the wine of new wealth!
(Verse 54)

What if you have got the wealth that fulfils every desire? If your foot is on the heads of your foes,
What of that?
If you have made all your love wealthy,
If your body remains a Kalpa (A periodic cycle of creation and dissolution.) — what of that?
The only thing to be desired is Renunciation

Which gives all love to Shiva.
(Verse 67)

Fear only life, that brings Birth and Death,
Have no love of friends, no lust, no attachment.
Alone, living alone in a forest,
What is more to be longed for than this Renunciation.
(Verse 68)

Going searching in the lower regions,
Going into the skies,
Travelling through all the worlds,
This is but the fickleness of the mind.
Ah, friend, you never remember the Lord
Who resides within you!
How can you get happiness?
(Verse 70)

What is there in the reading of Vedas,
The Shrutis, the Purânas and doing sacrifices?
Freedom alone takes off the weight
of this dreadful world,
And manifests Self-blessedness.
Here is the truth: the rest is all shop-keeping.
(Verse 71)

When the body is still healthy and diseaseless,
When old age has not yet attacked it,
When the organs have not yet lost their power,
And life is still full and undiminished,
Now, now, struggle on, rendering great help to yourself! My friend, it is useless to try to dig a well
In a house that is already on fire!
(Verse 75)

In Shiva, who is the Lord of this Universe,
Or Vishnu, its soul, I see no difference,
But still, my love is for Him
Who has the young moon on His forehead.
(Verse 84)

Oh when will that time come,
When in a beautiful full-moon night,
Sitting on the banks of some river,
And in a calm, yet high notes repeating
"Shiva! Shiva! Shiva!"
All my feelings will come out through the eyes
In the form of tears?
(Verse 85)

When, wearing only the Kaupina, (Loincloth.)
Lying on the sands of the holy Ganges in Benares,
When shall I weep aloud, "O Lord of ghouls",
Saying this, and whole days shall pass like moments?
(Verse 87)

When, bathing in the pure Ganges water,
Worshipping Thee, Omnipresent, with holy fruits and flowers,
Stretching myself on stones in a stony cave,
My whole soul shall go into meditation,
And according to the voice of my Guru,
I shall avoid all misery, and purify
The mind defiled with serving the rich.
(Verse 88)

This whole wide earth my bed,
My beautiful pillows my own two arms,
My wonderful canopy the blue sky,
And the cool evening air to fan me,
The moon and the stars my lamps,
And my beautiful wife, Renunciation, by my side, What king is there who can sleep like me in pleasure?
(Verse 94)

This Universe is only a little circle.
What is there to desire in it?
Will the ocean go into waves
By the jumping of a little [fish?]?
(Verse 92)

There was a time when I could see nothing but Women in this world:
And now that my eyes are opened,

I can see nothing but Brahman.
Beautiful are the rays of the moon,
Beautiful are the lawns in the forest,
Beautiful is the meeting of the good,
Beautiful is poetry, and
Beautiful is the face of the beloved.
But to me none of these are beautiful,
Knowing that they are evanescent.

    (Verse 79)

Oh mother earth, father wind,
Friend light, sweetheart water,
Brother sky,
Here take my last salutation
With folded hands!
For today I am melting away into Brahman,
Because my heart became pure,
And all delusion vanished
Thro' the power of your good company.

    (Verse 100)

Old age watches us, roaring like a tigress.
Disease, like enemies, is striking us often.
Life is flowing out like water from a broken jar.
Curious still how men do evil deeds in this world!

    (Verse 38)

Those beautiful cities.
Those mighty monarchs.
Those powerful nobles.
Those learned assemblies.
Those moon-faced women.
Those proud princes.
And those that sang their praises —
They have all been swept away from the memory of man.
My salutation, therefore, is to Time who works all these!

    (Verse 41)

The sun by his coming and going every hour is lessening the life of man.
Time flies without our knowledge,
Crushed as we are by the load of many works.
Seeing the evils of Birth, Old Age, Danger, and Death We are not afraid.
Ah me, drinking the wine of delusion,
The world has become mad.

    (Verse 43)

I have not learnt that knowledge which defeats all opponents!
Nor have been able, at the point of the sword,
Which can cut thro' an elephant's back,
To send our glory even unto the skies;
Nor, under the light of the full moon,
Drunk the nectar of the budding lips of the Beloved. My youth is gone fruitless
Like a lamp in an empty house.

    (Verse 46)

CONVERSATIONS AND INTERVIEWS

FIRST MEETING WITH MADAME EMMA CALVE

New Discoveries, Vol. 1, pp. 484-86.

The story of the first meeting of Swami Vivekananda and Madame Emma Calvé, as told in Calvé's autobiography, My Life.

…[Swami Vivekananda] was lecturing in Chicago one year when I was there; and as I was at that time greatly depressed in mind and body, I decided to go to him.

…Before going I had been told not to speak until he addressed me. When I entered the room, I stood before him in silence for a moment. He was seated in a noble attitude of meditation, his robe of saffron yellow falling in straight lines to the floor, his head swathed in a turban bent forward, his eyes on the ground. After a pause he spoke without looking up.

"My child", he said, "what a troubled atmosphere you have about you. Be calm. It is essential".

Then in a quiet voice, untroubled and aloof, this man who did not even know my name talked to me of my secret problems and anxieties. He spoke of things that I thought were unknown even to my nearest friends. It seemed miraculous, supernatural.

"How do you know all this?" I asked at last. "Who has talked of me to you?"

He looked at me with his quiet smile as though I were a child who had asked a foolish question.

"No one has talked to me", he answered gently. "Do you think that it is necessary? I read in you as in an open book."

Finally it was time for me to leave.

"You must forget", he said as I rose. "Become gay and happy again. Build up your health. Do not dwell in silence upon your sorrows. Transmute your emotions into some form of external expression. Your spiritual health requires it. Your art demands it."

I left him deeply impressed by his words and his personality. He seemed to have emptied my brain of all its feverish complexities and placed there instead his clear and calming thoughts. I became once again vivacious and cheerful, thanks to the effect of his powerful will. He did not use any of the hypnotic or mesmeric influences. It was the strength of his character, the purity and intensity of his purpose that carried conviction. It seemed to me, when I came to know him better, that he lulled one's chaotic thoughts into a state of peaceful acquiescence, so that one could give complete and undivided attention to his words.

FIRST MEETING WITH JOHN D. ROCKEFELLER

An excerpt from Madame Verdier's journal quoted in the New Discoveries, Vol. 1, pp. 487-88.

As told by Madame Emma Calvé, to Madame Drinette Verdier.

Mr. X, in whose home Swamiji was staying in Chicago, was a partner or an associate in some business with John D. Rockefeller. Many times John D. heard his friends talking about this extraordinary and wonderful Hindu monk who was staying with them, and many times he had been invited to meet Swamiji but, for one reason or another, always refused. At that time Rockefeller was not yet at the peak of his fortune, but was already powerful and strong-willed, very difficult to handle and a hard man to advise.

But one day, although he did not want to meet Swamiji, he was pushed to it by an impulse and went directly to the house of his friends, brushing aside the butler who opened the door and saying that he wanted to see the Hindu monk.

The butler ushered him into the living room, and, not waiting to be announced, Rockefeller entered into Swamiji's adjoining study and was much surprised, I presume, to see Swamiji behind his writing table not even lifting his eyes to see who had entered.

After a while, as with Calvé, Swamiji told Rockefeller much of his past that was not known to any but himself, and made him understand that the money he had already accumulated was not his, that he was only a channel and that his duty was to do good to the world — that God had given him all his wealth in order that he might have an opportunity to help and do good to people.

Rockefeller was annoyed that anyone dared to talk to him that way and tell him what to do. He left the room in irritation, not even saying goodbye. But about a week after, again without being announced, he entered Swamiji's study and, finding him the same as before, threw on his desk a paper which told of his plans to donate an enormous sum of money toward the financing of a public institution.

"Well, there you are", he said. "You must be satisfied now, and you can thank me for it."

Swamiji didn't even lift his eyes, did not move. Then taking the paper, he quietly read it, saying: "It is for you to thank me". That was all. This was Rockefeller's first large donation to the public welfare.

A DUSKY PHILOSOPHER FROM INDIA

New Discoveries, Vol. 5, pp. 389-94.

To preserve the historical authenticity of the newspaper reports in this section, their original spelling has been largely retained; however, their punctuation has been made consistent with the style of the Complete Works. — Publisher.

An interview by Blanche Partington, San Francisco Chronicle, March 18, 1900.

…Bowing very low in Eastern fashion on his entrance to the room, then holding out his hand in good American style, the dusky philosopher from the banks of the Ganges gave friendly greeting to the representative of that thoroughly Occidental institution, the daily press.

…I asked for a picture to illustrate this article, and when someone handed me a certain "cut" which has been extensively used in lecture advertisements here, he uttered a mild protest against its use.

"But that does not look like you", said I.

"No, it is as if I wished to kill someone", he said smiling, "like — like —"

"Othello", I inserted rashly. But the little audience of friends only smiled as the Swami made laughing recognition of the absurd resemblance of the picture to the jealous Moor. But I do not use that picture.

"Is it true, Swami", I asked, "that when you went home after lecturing in the Congress of Religions after the World's Fair, princes knelt at your feet, a half dozen of the ruling sovereigns of India dragged your carriage through the streets, as the papers told us? We do not treat our priests so".

"That is not good to talk of", said the Swami. "But it is true that religion rules there, not dollars."

"What about caste?"

"What of your Four Hundred?" he replied, smiling. "Caste in India is an institution hardly explicable or intelligible to the Occidental mind. It is acknowledged to be an imperfect institution, but we do not recognize a superior social result from your attempts at class distinction. India is the only country which has so far succeeded in imposing a permanent caste upon her people, and we doubt if an exchange for Western superstitions and evils would be for her advantage."

"But under such regime — where a man may not eat this nor drink that, nor marry the other — the freedom you teach would be impossible", I ventured.

"It is impossible", assented the Swami; "but until India has outgrown the necessity for caste laws, caste laws will remain". "Is it true that you may not eat food cooked by a foreigner — unbeliever?" I asked.

"In India the cook — who is not called a servant — must be of the same or higher caste than those for whom the food is cooked, as it is considered that whatever a man touches is impressed by his personality, and food, with which a man builds up the body through which he expresses himself, is regarded as being liable to such impression. As to the foods we eat, it is assumed that certain kinds of food nourish certain properties worthy of cultivation, and that others retard our spiritual growth. For instance, we do not kill to eat. Such food would be held to nourish the animal body, at the expense of the spiritual body, in which the soul is said to be clothed on its departure from this physical envelope, besides laying the sin of blood-guiltiness upon the butcher."

"Ugh!" I exclaimed involuntarily, an awful vision of reproachful little lambs, little chicken ghosts, hovering cow spirits — I was always afraid of cows anyway — rising up before me.

"You see", explained the Brahmin [Kshatriya], "the universe is all one, from the lowest insect to the highest Yogi. It is all one, we are all one, you and I are one —". Here the Occidental audience smiled, the unconscious monk chanting the oneness of things in Sanskrit and the consequent sin of taking any life.

…He was pacing up and down the room most of the time during our talk, occasionally standing over the register — it was a chill morning for this child of the sun — and doing with grace and freedom whatever occurred to him, even, at length, smoking a little.

"You, yourself, have not yet attained supreme control over all desires", I ventured. The Swami's frankness is infectious.

"No, madam", and he smiled the broad and brilliant smile of a child; "Do I look it?" But the Swami, from the land of hasheesh and dreams, doubtless did not connect my query with its smoky origin.

"Is it usual among the Hindoo priesthood to marry?" I ventured again.

"It is a matter of individual choice", replied this member of the Hindoo priesthood. "One does not marry that he may not be in slavery to a woman and children, or permit the slavery of a woman to him."

"But what is to become of the population?" urged the anti-Malthusian.

"Are you so glad to have been born?" retorted the Eastern thinker, his large eyes flashing scorn. "Can you conceive of nothing higher than this warring, hungry, ignorant world? Do not fear that the you may be lost, though the sordid, miserable consciousness of the now may go. What worth having [would be] gone?

"The child comes crying into the world. Well may he cry! Why should we weep to leave it? Have you thought" — here the sunny smile came back — "of the different modes of East and West of expressing the passing away? We say of the dead man, 'He gave up his body'; you put it, 'he gave up the ghost'. How can that be? Is it the dead body that permits the ghost to depart? What curious inversion of thought!"

"But, on the whole, Swami, you think it better to be comfortably dead than a living lion?" persisted the defender of populations.

"Swâhâ, Swaha, so be it!" shouted the monk.

"But how is it that under such philosophy men consent to live at all?"

"Because a man's own life is sacred as any other life, and one may not leave chapters unlearned", returned the philosopher. "Add power and diminish time, and the school days are shorter; as the learned professor can make the marble in twelve years which nature took centuries to form. It is all a question of time."

"India, which has had this teaching so long, has not yet learned her lesson?"

"No, though she is perhaps nearer than any other country, in that she has learned to love mercy."

"What of England in India?" I asked.

"But for English rule I could not be here now", said the monk, "though your lowest free-born American Negro holds higher position in India politically than is mine. Brahmin and coolie, we are all 'natives'. But it is all right, in spite of the misunderstanding and oppression. England is the Tharma [Karma?] of India, attracted inevitably by some inherent weakness, past mistakes, but from her blood and fibre will come the new national hope for my countrymen. I am a loyal subject of the Empress of India!" and here the Swami salaamed before an imaginary potentate, bowing very low, perhaps too low for reverence.

"But such an apostle of freedom — ", I murmured.

"She is the widow for many years, and such we hold in high worth in India", said the philosopher seriously. "As to freedom, yes, I believe the goal of all development is freedom, law and order. There is more law and order in the grave than anywhere else — try it."

"I must go", I said. "I have to catch a train".

"Thatis like all Americans", smiled the Swami, and I had a glimpse of all eternity in his utter restfulness. "You must catch this car or that train always. Is there not another, later?"

But I did not attempt to explain the Occidental conception of the value of time to this child of the Orient, realizing its utter hopelessness and my own renegade sympathy. It must be delightful beyond measure to live in the land of "time enough". In the Orient there seems time to breathe, time to think, time to live; as the Swami says, what have we in exchange? We live in time; they in eternity.

"WE ARE HYPNOTIZED INTO WEAKNESS BY OUR SURROUNDINGS"

New Discoveries, Vol. 5, pp. 396-98.

An interview by the San Francisco Examiner, March 18, 1900.

Hindoo Philosopher Who Strikes at the Root of Some

Occidental Evils and Tells How We Must Worship God

Simply and Not with Many Vain Prayers.

...

One American friend he may be assured of — the Swami is a charming person to interview.

Pacing about the little room where he is staying, he kept the small audience of interviewer and friend entertained for a couple of hours.

"Tell you about the English in India? But I do not wish to talk of politics. But from the higher standpoint, it is true that but for the English rule I could not be here. We natives know that it is through the intermixture of English blood and ideas that the salvation of India will come. Fifty years ago, all the literature and religion of the race were locked up in the Sanskrit language; today the drama and the novel are written in the vernacular, and the literature of religion is being translated. That is the work of the English, and it is unnecessary, in America, to descant upon the value of the education of the masses."

"What do you think of the Boers War?" was asked.

"Oh! Have you seen the morning paper? But I do not wish to discuss politics. English and Boers are both in the wrong. It is terrible — terrible — the bloodshed! English will conquer, but at what fearful cost! She seems the nation of Fate."

And the Swami with a smile, began chanting the Sanskrit for an unwillingness to discuss politics.

Then he talked long of ancient Russian history, and of the wandering tribes of Tartary, and of the Moorish rule in Spain, and displaying an astonishing memory and research. To this childlike interest in all things that touch him is doubtless due much of the curious and universal knowledge that he seems to possess.

MARRIAGE

New Discoveries, Vol. 5, p. 138.

From Miss Josephine MacLeod's February 1908 letter to Mary Hale, in which she described Swami Vivekananda's response to Alberta Sturges's question:

ALBERTA STURGES: Is there no happiness in marriage?

SWAMI VIVEKANANDA: Yes, Alberta, if marriage is entered into as a great austerity — and everything is given up — even principle!

LINE OF DEMARCATION

New Discoveries, Vol. 5, p. 225.

From Mrs. Alice Hansbrough's reminiscences of a question-answer exchange following the class entitled "Hints on Practical Spirituality":

Q: Swami, if all things are one, what is the difference between a cabbage and a man?

A: Stick a knife into your leg, and you will see the line of demarcation.

GOD IS!

New Discoveries, Vol. 5, p. 276.

Alice Hansbrough's record of a question-answer session after a class lecture:

Q: Then, Swami, what you claim is that all is good?

A: By no means. My claim is that all is not — only God is! That makes all the difference.

RENUNCIATION

New Discoveries, Vol. 6, p. 11-12.

From Alice Hansbrough's reminiscences of a question-answer session following one of Swami Vivekananda's San Francisco classes pertaining to renunciation:

WOMAN STUDENT: Well, Swami, what would become of the world if everyone renounced?

SWAMI VIVEKANANDA: Madam, why do you come to me with that lie on your lips? You have never considered anything in this world but your own pleasure!

SHRI RAMAKRISHNA'S DISCIPLE

New Discoveries, Vol. 6, p. 12.

Mrs. Edith Allan described a teacher-student exchange in one of Swami Vivekananda's San Francisco classes:

SWAMI VIVEKANANDA: I am the disciple of a man who could not write his own name, and I am not worthy to undo his shoes. How often have I wished I could take my intellect and throw it into the Ganges!

STUDENT: But, Swami, that is the part of you I like best.

SWAMI VIVEKANANDA: That is because you are a fool, Madam — like I am.

THE MASTER'S DIVINE INCARNATION

New Discoveries, Vol. 6, p. 17.

From Mrs. Edith Allan's reminiscences:

SWAMI VIVEKANANDA: I have to come back once more. The Master said I am to come back once more with him.

MRS. ALLAN: You have to come back because Shri Ramakrishna says so?

SWAMI VIVEKANANDA: Souls like that have great power, Madam.

A PRIVATE ADMISSION

New Discoveries, Vol. 6, p. 121.

From Mrs. Edith Allan's reminiscences of Swami Vivekananda's stay in northern California, 1900:

WOMAN STUDENT: Oh, if I had only lived earlier, I could have seen Shri Ramakrishna!

SWAMI VIVEKANANDA (turning quietly to her): You say that, and you have seen me?

A GREETING

New Discoveries, Vol. 6, p. 136.

From Mr. Thomas Allan's reminiscences of Swami Vivekananda's visit to Alameda, California, 1900:

MR. ALLAN: Well, Swami, I see you are in Alameda!

SWAMI VIVEKANANDA: No, Mr. Allan, I am not in Alameda; Alameda is in me.

"THIS WORLD IS A CIRCUS RING"

New Discoveries, Vol. 6, p. 156.

From Mrs. Alice Hansbrough's reminiscences of Swami Vivekananda's conversation with Miss Bell at Camp Taylor, California, in May 1900:

MISS BELL: This world is an old schoolhouse where we come to learn our lessons.

SWAMI VIVEKANANDA: Who told you that? [Miss Bell could not remember.] Well, I don't think so. I think this world is a circus ring in which we are the clowns tumbling.

MISS BELL: Why do we tumble, Swami?

SWAMI VIVEKANANDA: Because we like to tumble. When we get tired, we will quit.

ON KALI

The Complete Works of Sister Nivedita, Vol. I, p. 118.

Sister Nivedita's reminiscence of a conversation with Swami Vivekananda at the time she was learning the Kâli worship:

SISTER NIVEDITA: Perhaps, Swamiji, Kali is the vision of Shiva! Is She?

SWAMI VIVEKANANDA: Well! Well! Express it in your own way. Express it in your own way!

TRAINING UNDER SHRI RAMAKRISHNA

The Complete Works of Sister Nivedita, Vol. I, pp. 159-60.

While on board a ship to England, Swami Vivekananda was touched by the childlike devotion of the ship's servants:

SWAMI VIVEKANANDA: You see, I love our Mohammedans!

SISTER NIVEDITA: Yes, but what I want to understand is this habit of seeing every people from their strongest aspect. Where did it come from? Do you recognize it in any historical character? Or is it in some way derived from Shri Ramakrishna?

SWAMI VIVEKANANDA: It must have been the training under Ramakrishna Paramahamsa. We all went by his path to some extent. Of course it was not so difficult for us as he made it for himself. He would eat and dress like the people he wanted to understand, take their initiation, and use their language. "One must learn", he said, "to put oneself into another man's very soul". And this method was his own! No one ever before in India became Christian and Mohammedan and Vaishnava, by turn!

EXCERPTS FROM SISTER NIVEDITA'S BOOK

NOTES OF SOME WANDERINGS WITH SWAMI VIVEKANANDA

Excerpts from the book by Sister Nivedita

Note: In the following work only those extracts which present Swami Vivekananda's ideas or direct quotations have been printed. Descriptions marking the background context of these talks have also been retained for the sake of clarity and continuity. Ellipses mark the deleted portions. Spelling and punctuation have been made to conform to the style of the Complete Works. — Publisher

FOREWORD

PERSONS: The Swami Vivekananda, Gurubhais, (Spiritual brethren; disciples of one and the same master are so called.) and a party of European guests and disciples, amongst whom were Dhira Mata, the "Steady Mother" [Mrs. Ole Bull]; one whose name was Jaya [Miss Josephine MacLeod]; and Sister Nivedita. (Dhira Mata and Jaya were Americans; Nivedita was British. — Publisher.)

PLACE: Different parts of India.

TIME: The year 1898.

Beautiful have been the days of this year. In them the Ideal has become the Real. First in our riverside cottage at Belur; then in the Himalayas, at Naini Tal and Almora; afterwards wandering here and there through Kashmir — everywhere have come hours never to be forgotten, words that will echo through our lives forever, and once, at least, a glimpse of the Beatific Vision.

It has been all play.

We have seen a love that would be one with the humblest and most ignorant, seeing the world for the moment through his eyes, as if criticism were not; we have laughed over the colossal caprice of genius; we have warmed ourselves at heroic fires; and we have been present, as it were, at the awakening of the Holy Child.

But there has been nothing grim or serious about any of these things. Pain has come close to all of us. Solemn anniversaries have been and gone. But sorrow was lifted into a golden light, where it was made radiant and did not destroy.

Fain, if I could, would I describe our journeys. Even as I write I see the irises in bloom at Baramulla; the young rice beneath the poplars at Islamabad; starlight scenes in Himalayan forests; and the royal beauties of Delhi and the Taj. One longs to attempt some memorial of these. It would be worse than useless. Not, then, in words, but in the light of memory they are enshrined forever, together with the kindly and gentle folk who dwell among them and whom we trust always to have left the gladder for our coming.

We have learnt something of the mood in which new faiths are born and of the persons who inspire such faiths. For we have been with one who drew all men to him — listening to all, feeling with all and refusing none. We have known a humility that wiped out all littleness, a renunciation that would die for scorn of oppression and pity of the oppressed, a love that would bless even the oncoming feet of torture and of death. We have joined hands with that woman who washed the feet of the Lord with her tears and wiped them with the hairs of her head. We have lacked not the occasion, but her passionate consciousness of self.

Seated under a tree in the garden of dead emperors there came to us a vision of all the rich and splendid things of Earth, offering themselves as a shrine for the great of soul. The storied windows of cathedrals and the jewelled thrones of kings, the banners of great captains and the vestments of the priests, the pageants of cities and the retreats of the proud — all came and all were rejected.

In the garments of the beggar, despised by the alien, worshipped by the people, we have seen him; and only the bread of toil, the shelter of cottage roofs, and the common road across the cornfields seem real enough for the background to this life....Amongst his own the ignorant loved him as much as scholars and statesmen. The boatmen watched the river, in his absence, for his return, and servants disputed with guests to do him service. And through it all the veil of playfulness was never dropped. "They played with the Lord" and instinctively they knew it.

To those who have known such hours, life is richer and sweeter, and in the long nights even the wind in the palm trees seems to cry: "Mahadeva! Mahadeva! Mahadeva!"

CHAPTER I

THE HOUSE ON THE GANGES

PLACE: A cottage at Belur, beside the Ganges.
TIME: March to May, 1898.

Of the home by the Ganges the Master had said to one, "You will find that little house of Dhira Mata like heaven, for it is all love, from beginning to end.

It was so indeed. Within, an unbroken harmony, and without, everything alike beautiful — the green stretch of grass, the tall cocoanut palms, the little brown villages in the jungle, and the Nilkantha that built her nest in a tree — top beside us, on purpose to bring us the blessings of Shiva. In the morning the shadows lay behind the house, but in the afternoons we could sit in front worshipping the Ganges herself — great leonine mother! — and in sight of Dakshineswar.

There came one and another with traditions of the past, and we learnt of the Master's eight years' wanderings; of the name changed from village to village; of the Nirvikalpa Samâdhi; and of that sacred sorrow, too deep for words or for common sight, that one who loved had alone seen. And there too came the Master himself, with his stories of Umâ and Shiva, of Râdhâ and Krishna, and his fragments of song and poetry.

It seemed as if he knew that the first material of a new consciousness must be a succession of vivid but isolated experiences, poured out without proper sequence so as to provoke the mind of the learner to work for its own conception of order and relation...For the most part it was the Indian religions that he portrayed for us—today dealing with one and tomorrow with another — his choice guided, seemingly, by the whim of the moment. But it was not religion only that he poured out upon us. Sometimes it would be history. Again, it would be folk-lore. On still another occasion it would be the manifold anomalies and inconsistencies of race, caste and custom. In fact India herself became, as heard in him, as the last and noblest of the Purânas, uttering itself through his lips.

Another point in which he had caught a great psychological secret was that of never trying to soften for us that which would at first sight be difficult or repellent. In matters Indian he would rather put forward, in its extreme form at the beginning of our experience, all that might seem impossible for European minds to enjoy. Thus he would quote, for instance, some verses about Gauri and Shankar in a single form:

On one side grows the hair in long black curls,
And on the other, corded like rope.

On one side are seen the beautiful garlands,

On the other, bone earrings and snake-like coils.
One side is white with ashes, like the snow mountains, The other, golden as the light of dawn.

For He, the Lord, took a form,

And that was a divided form,

Half-woman and half-man

...

Whatever might be the subject of the conversation, it ended always on the note of the infinite...He might appear to take up any subject — literary, ethnological or scientific — but he always made us feel it as an illustration of the Ultimate Vision. There was for him nothing secular. He had a loathing for bondage and a horror of those who "cover chains with flowers", but he never failed to make the true critic's distinction between this and the highest forms of art.

One day we were receiving European guests and he entered into a long talk about Persian poetry. Then suddenly, finding himself quoting the poem that says, "For one mole on the face of my Beloved, I would give all the wealth of Samarkand!" he turned and said energetically, "I would not give a straw, you know, for the man who was incapable of appreciating a love song!" His talk too teemed with epigrams.

It was that same afternoon, in the course of a long political argument, that he said, "In order to become a nation, it appears that we need a common hate as well as a common love".

Several months later he remarked that before one who had a mission he never talked of any of the gods save Uma and Shiva. For Shiva and the Mother made the great workers. Yet I have sometimes wondered if he knew at this time how the end of every theme was Bhakti. Much as he dreaded the luxury of spiritual emotion for those who might be enervated by it, he could not help giving glimpses of what it meant to be consumed with the intoxication of God. And so he would chant for us such poems as:

They have made Radha queen, in the beautiful groves of Vrindaban.

At her gate stands Krishna, on guard.

His flute is singing all the time:

Radha is about to distribute infinite wealth of love. Though I am guard, all the world may enter.

Come all ye who thirst! Say only 'Glory unto Radha!' Enter the region of love!

Or he would give us the great antiphonal Chorus of the Cowherds, written by his friend: (The Bengali dramatist Girish Chandra Ghosh.)

Men: Thou art the Soul of souls,

Thou yellow-garbed,

With thy blue eyes.

Women: Thou dark One! Thou

Shepherd of Vrindaban!

Kneeling at the feet of the Shepherdesses.

Men: My soul sings the praise of the glory of the Lord,

Who took the human form.

Women: Thy beauty for us, the Gopis.

Men: Thou Lord of Sacrifice.

Saviour of the weak.

Women: Who lovest Radha and thy body floats on its own tears.

...

MARCH 25

…At this time the Swami kept the custom of coming to the cottage early and spending the morning hours there, and again returning in the late afternoon. On the second morning of this visit, however — Friday, the Christian feast of the Annunciation — he took us all three back to the Math, and there in the worship-room was held a little service of initiation where one was made a Brahmachârini. That was the happiest of mornings.

After the service we were taken upstairs. The Swami put on the ashes and bone-earrings and matted locks of a Shiva-Yogi and sang and played to us — Indian music on Indian instruments — for an hour.

And in the evening in our boat on the Ganges, he opened his heart to us and told us much of his questions and anxieties regarding the trust that he held from his own Master.

Another week and he was gone to Darjeeling; and till the day that the plague declaration brought him back, we saw him again no more.

MAY 3

Then two of us met him in the house of our Holy Mother. The political sky was black. It seemed as if a storm were about to burst…Plague, panic and riot were doing their fell work. And the Master turned to the two and said, "There are some who scoff at the existence of Kâli. Yet today She is out there amongst the people. They are frantic with fear, and the soldiery have been called to deal out death. Who can say that God does not manifest Himself as evil as well as good? But only the Hindu dares to worship Him in the evil".

He had come back and the old life was resumed once more, as far as could be, seeing that an epidemic was in prospect and that measures were on hand to give the people confidence. As long as this possibility darkened the horizon, he would not leave Calcutta. But it passed away, and those happy days with it, and the time came that we should go.

CHAPTER II

AT NAINI TAL AND ALMORA

PERSONS: The Swami Vivekananda, Gurubhâis, and a party of Europeans and disciples, amongst whom were Dhira Mata, the "Steady Mother"; one whose name was Jaya; and Nivedita.

PLACE: The Himalayas.

TIME: May 11 to May 25, 1898.

We were a large party, or, indeed, two parties, that left Howrah station on Wednesday evening and on Friday morning came in sight of the Himalayas...

Naini Tal was made beautiful by three things — the Master's pleasure in introducing to us his disciple the Raja of Khetri; the dancing girls who met us and asked us where to find him, and were received by him in spite of the remonstrances of others; and by the Mohammedan gentleman who said, "Swamiji, if in after-times any claim you as an Avatâra, an especial incarnation of the Deity — remember that I, a Mohammedan, am the first!"

It was here too that we heard a long talk on Ram Mohan Roy in which he pointed out three things as the dominant notes of this teacher's message — his acceptance of the Vedanta, his preaching of patriotism, and the love that embraced the Mussulman equally with the Hindu. In all these things he claimed himself to have taken up the task that the breadth and foresight of Ram Mohan Roy had mapped out.

The incident of the dancing girls occurred in consequence of our visit to the two temples at the head of the tarn...Here, offering worship, we found two nautch-women. When they had finished, they came up to us, and we, in broken language, entered into conversation with them. We took them for respectable ladies of the town and were much astonished later at the storm which had evidently passed over the Swami's audience at his refusal to have them turned away. Am I mistaken in thinking that it was in connection with these dancing-women of Naini Tal that he first told us the story, many times repeated, of the nautch-girl of Khetri? He had been angry at the invitation to see her, but being prevailed upon to come, she sang:

O Lord, look not upon my evil qualities!
Thy name, O Lord, is Same-Sightedness.
Make us both the same Brahman!

One piece of iron is the knife in the hand of the butcher, And another piece of iron is the image in the temple. But when they touch the philosopher's stone,

Both alike turn to gold!
One drop of water is in the sacred Jamuna,
And one is foul in a ditch by the roadside.
But when they fall into the Ganges,
Both alike become holy!
So, Lord, look not upon my evil qualities!
Thy name, O Lord, is Same-Sightedness.
Make us both the same Brahman!

And then, said the Master of himself, the scales fell from his eyes, and seeing that all are indeed one, he condemned no more...

It was late in the afternoon when we left Naini Tal for Almora, and night overtook us while still travelling through the forest...till we reached a quaintly placed Dak bungalow, on the mountain side in the midst of trees. There after some time Swamiji arrived with his party, full of fun and keen in his appreciation of everything that concerned the comfort of his guests...

From the day that we arrived at Almora the Swami renewed his habit of coming over to us at our early breakfast and spending some hours in talk. Then and always he was an exceedingly light sleeper, and I imagine that his visit to us, early as the hour might be, was often paid during the course of his return with his monks from a still earlier walk. Sometimes, but rarely, we saw him again in the evening, either meeting him when out for a walk or going ourselves to Captain Sevier's, where he and his party were staying, and seeing him there. And once he came at that time to call on us.

Into these morning talks at Almora a strange new element, painful but salutary to remember, had crept. There appeared to be on the one side a curious bitterness and distrust, and on the other, irritation and defiance. The youngest of the Swami's disciples at this time, it must be remembered, was an English woman, and of how much this fact meant intellectually — what a strong bias it implied, and always does imply, in the reading of India, what an idealism of the English race and all their deeds and history — the Swami himself had had no conception till the day after her initiation at the monastery. Then he had asked her some exultant question, as to which nation she now belonged, and had been startled to find with what a passion of loyalty and worship she regarded the English flag, giving to it much of the feeling that an Indian woman would give to her Thakur. His surprise and disappointment at the moment were scarcely perceptible. A startled look, no more. Nor did his discovery of the superficial way in which this disciple had joined herself with his people in any degree affect his confidence and courtesy during the remaining weeks spent in the plains.

But with Almora it seemed as if a going-to-school had commenced...It was never more than this; never the dictating of opinion or creed; never more than emancipation from partiality. Even at the end of the terrible experience when this method, as regarded race and country, was renounced, never to be taken up systematically again, the Swami did not call for any confession of faith, any declaration of new opinion. He dropped the whole question. His listener went free. But he had revealed a different standpoint in thought and feeling, so completely and so strongly as to make it impossible for her to rest, until later, by her own labours, she had arrived at a view in which both these partial presentments stood rationalized and accounted for.

"Really, patriotism like yours is sin!" he exclaimed once, many weeks later, when the process of obtaining an uncoloured judgement on some incident had been more than commonly exasperating. "All that I want you to see is that most people's actions are the expression of self-interest, and you constantly oppose to this the idea that a certain race are all angels. Ignorance so determined is wickedness!"...

These morning talks at Almora, then, took the form of assaults upon deep-rooted preconceptions — social, literary and artistic — or of long comparisons of Indian and European history and sentiments, often containing extended observations of very great value. One characteristic of the Swami was the habit of attacking the abuses of a country or society openly and vigorously when he was in its midst, whereas after he had left it, it would often seem as if nothing but its virtues were remembered by him. He was always testing his disciples, and the manner of these particular discourses was probably adopted in order to put to the proof the courage and sincerity of one who was both woman and European.

CHAPTER III

MORNING TALKS AT ALMORA

PLACE: Almora.
TIME: May and June, 1898.

The first morning the talk was that of the central ideals of civilization — in the West, truth; in the East, chastity. He justified Hindu marriage customs as springing from the pursuit of this ideal and from the woman's need of protection, in combination. And he traced out the relation of the whole subject to the philosophy of the Absolute.

Another morning he began by observing that as

there were four main castes — Brahmin, Kshatriya, Bâniyâ [Vaishya], Shudra — so there were four great national functions: the religious or priestly, fulfilled by the Hindus; the military, by the Roman Empire; the mercantile, by England today; and the democratic, by America in the future. And here he launched off into a glowing prophetic forecast of how America would yet solve the problems of the Shudra — the problems of freedom and co-operation — and turned to relate to a non-American listener the generosity of the arrangements which that people had attempted to make for their aborigines.

Again it would be an eager résumé of the history of India or of the Moguls, whose greatness never wearied him. Every now and then throughout the summer he would break out into descriptions of Delhi and Agra. Once he described the Taj as "a dimness, and again a dimness, and there — a grave!"

Another time he spoke of Shah Jehan, and then, with a burst of enthusiasm: "Ah! He was the glory of his line! A feeling for and discrimination of beauty that are unparalleled in history. And an artist himself! I have seen a manuscript illuminated by him which is one of the art treasures of India. What a genius!"

Oftener still, it was Akbar of whom he would tell, almost with tears in his voice and a passion easier to understand, beside that undomed tomb, open to sun and wind — the grave of Secundra at Agra.

But all the more universal forms of human feeling were open to the Master. In one mood he talked of China as if she were the treasure-house of the world, and told us of the thrill with which he saw inscriptions in old Bengali (Kutil?) characters over the doors of Chinese temples.

Few things could be more eloquent of the vagueness of Western ideas regarding Oriental peoples than the fact that one of his listeners alleged untruthfulness as a notorious quality of that race…The Swami would have none of it. Untruthfulness! Social rigidity! What were these, except very, very relative terms? And as to untruthfulness in particular, could commercial life or social life or any other form of co-operation go on for a day if men did not trust men? Untruthfulness as a necessity of etiquette? And how was that different from the Western idea? Is the Englishman always glad and always sorry at the proper place? But there is still a difference of degree? Perhaps — but only of degree!

Or he might wander as far afield as Italy, that "greatest of the countries of Europe — land of religion and of art; alike of imperial organization and of Mazzini; mother of ideas, of culture and of freedom!

One day it was Shivaji and the Mahrattas and the year's wandering as a Sannyâsin that won him home to Raigarh. "And to this day", said the Swami, "authority in India dreads the Sannyasin, lest he conceals beneath his yellow garb another Shivaji".

Often the enquiry "Who and what are the Aryans?" absorbed his attention; and holding that their origin was complex, he would tell us how in Switzerland he had felt himself to be in China, so like were the types. He believed too that the same was true of some parts of Norway. Then there were scraps of information about countries and physiognomies, an impassioned tale of the Hungarian scholar who traced the Huns to Tibet, and lies buried in Darjeeling and so on…

Sometimes the Swami would deal with the rift between Brahmins and Kshatriyas, painting the whole history of India as a struggle between the two and showing that the latter had always embodied the rising, fetter-destroying impulses of the nation. He could give excellent reason too for the faith that was in him that the Kâyasthas of modern Bengal represented the pre-Mauryan Kshatriyas. He would portray the two opposing types of culture: the one, classical, intensive and saturated with an ever-deepening sense of tradition and custom; the other, defiant, impulsive and liberal in its outlook. It was part of a deep-lying law of the historic development that Râma, Krishna and Buddha had all arisen in the kingly, and not in the priestly caste. And in this paradoxical moment Buddhism was reduced to a caste-smashing formula — "a religion invented by the Kshatriyas" as a crushing rejoinder to Brahminism!

That was a great hour indeed when he spoke of Buddha; for, catching a word that seemed to identify him with its anti—Brahminical spirit, an uncomprehending listener said, "Why, Swami, I did not know that you were a Buddhist!

"Madam", he said, rounding on her, his whole face aglow with the inspiration of that name, "I am the servant of the servants of the servants of Buddha. Who was there ever like him? — the Lord — who never performed one action for himself — with a heart that embraced the whole world! So full of pity that he — prince and monk — would give his life to save a little goat! So loving that he sacrificed himself to the hunger of a tigress! — to the hospitality of a pariah and blessed him! And he came into my room when I was a boy and I fell at his feet! For I knew it was the Lord Himself!

Many times he spoke of Buddha in this fashion, sometimes at Belur and sometimes afterwards. And once he told us the story of Ambâpâli, the beautiful courtesan who feasted him…

National feeling did not have it all its own way. For one morning when the chasm seemed to be widest, there was a long talk on Bhakti — that perfect identity with the Beloved that the devotion of Ray Ramananda, the Bengali nobleman, before Chaitanya so beautifully illustrates:

Four eyes met. There were changes in two souls. And now I cannot remember whether he is a man

And I a woman, or he a woman and I a man!

All I know is, there were two, Love came, and there is one!

It was that same morning that he talked of the Babists of Persia, in their era of martyrdom — of the woman who inspired and the man who worshipped and worked. And doubtless then he expatiated on that theory of his — somewhat quaint and surprising to unaccustomed minds, not so much for the matter of the statement as for the explicitness of the expression — of the greatness and goodness of the young, who can love without seeking personal expression for their love, and their high potentiality.

Another day coming at sunrise when the snows could be seen, dawn-lighted, from the garden, it was Shiva and Umâ on whom he dwelt — and that was Shiva up there, the white snow-peaks, and the light that fell upon Him was the Mother of the World! For a thought on which at this time he was dwelling much was that God is the Universe — not within it or outside it and not the universe God or the image of God, but He it, and the All.

Sometimes all through the summer he would sit for hours telling us stories, those cradle-tales of Hinduism whose function is not at all that of our nursery fictions, but much more like the man-making myths of the old Hellenic world. Best of all these I thought was the story of Shuka, and we looked on the Shiva-mountains and the bleak scenery of Almora the evening we heard it for the first time…

Shuka was indeed the Swami's saint. He was the type, to him, of that highest realization to which life and the world are merely play. Long after, we learned how Shri Ramakrishna had spoken of him in his boyhood as "my Shuka". And never can I forget the look, as of one gazing far into depths of joy, with which he once stood and quoted the words of Shiva in praise of the deep spiritual significance of the Bhagavad-Gitâ and of the greatness of Shuka: "I know the real meaning of the teachings of the Bhagavad-Gita, and Shuka knows, and perhaps Vyâsa knows — a little!"

Another day in Almora the Swami talked of the great humanizing lives that had arisen in Bengal, at the long inrolling wash of the first wave of modern consciousness on the ancient shores of Hindu culture. Of Ram Mohan Roy we had already heard from him at Naini Tal. And now of the Pundit Vidyâsâgar he exclaimed, "There is not a man of my age in northern India on whom his shadow has not fallen!" It was a great joy to him to remember that these men and Shri Ramakrishna had all been born within a few miles of each other.

The Swami introduced Vidyasagar to us now as "the hero of widow remarriage and of the abolition of polygamy". But his favourite story about him was of that day when he went home from the Legislative Council, pondering over the question of whether or not to adopt English dress on such occasions.

Suddenly someone came up to a fat Mogul who was proceeding homewards in leisurely and pompous fashion in front of him, with the news "Sir, your house is on fire!" The Mogul went neither faster nor slower for this information, and presently the messenger contrived to express a discreet astonishment, whereupon his master turned on him angrily. "Wretch!" he said. "Am I to abandon the gait of my ancestors because a few sticks happen to be burning?" And Vidyasagar, walking behind, determined to stick to the Châdar, Dhoti and sandals, not even adopting coat and slippers.

The picture of Vidyasagar going into retreat for a month for the study of the Shâstras, when his mother had suggested to him the remarriage of child-widows, was very forcible. "He came out of his retirement of opinion that they were not against such remarriage, and he obtained the signatures of the pundits that they agreed in this opinion. Then the action of certain native princes led the pundits to abandon their own signatures so that, had the government not determined to assist the movement, it could not have been carried — and now", added the Swami, "the difficulty has an economic rather than a social basis".

We could believe that a man who was able to discredit polygamy by moral force alone, was "intensely spiritual". And it was wonderful indeed to realize the Indian indifference to a formal creed when we heard how this giant was driven by the famine of 1864 — when 140,000 people died of hunger and disease — to have nothing more to do with God and become entirely agnostic in thought.

With this man, as one of the educators of Bengal, the Swami coupled the name of David Hare, the old Scotsman and atheist to whom the clergy of Calcutta refused Christian burial. He had died of nursing an old pupil through cholera. So his own boys carried his dead body and buried it in a swamp and made the grave a place of pilgrimage. That place has now become College Square, the educational centre, and his school is now within the university. And to this day Calcutta students make pilgrimage to the tomb.

On this day we took advantage of the natural turn of the conversation to cross-question the Swami as to the possible influence that Christianity might have exerted over himself. He was much amused to hear that such a statement had been hazarded, and told us with much pride of his only contact with missionary influences, in the person of his old Scotch master, Mr. Hastie. This hot-headed old man lived on nothing and regarded his room as his boys' home as much as his own. It was he who had first sent the Swami to Shri Ramakrishna, and towards the end of his stay in India he used to say, "Yes, my boy, you were right, you were right! — It is true that all is God!" "I am proud of him!" cried the Swami. "But I don't think you could say that he had Christianized me much!"...

We heard charming stories too on less serious subjects. There was the lodging-house in an American city, for instance, where he had had to cook his own food, and where he would meet in the course of operations "an actress who ate roast turkey every day, and a husband and wife who lived by making ghosts". And when the Swami remonstrated with the husband and tried to persuade him to give up deceiving people, saying, "You ought not to do this!" the wife would come up behind and say eagerly, "Yes, sir! That's just what I tell him; for he makes all the ghosts, and Mrs. Williams takes all the money!"

He told us also of a young engineer, an educated man, who, at a spiritualistic gathering, "when the fat Mrs. Williams appeared from behind the screen as his thin mother, exclaimed, 'Mother dear, how you have grown in the spirit-world!'"

"At this", said the Swami, "my heart broke, for I thought there could be no hope for the man". But never at a loss, he told the story of a Russian painter who was ordered to paint the picture of a peasant's dead father, the only description given being, "Man! Don't I tell you he had a wart on his nose?" When at last, therefore, the painter had made a portrait of some stray peasant and affixed a large wart to the nose, the picture was declared to be ready, and the son was told to come and see it. He stood in front of it, greatly overcome, and said, "Father! Father! How changed you are since I saw you last!" After this, the young engineer would never speak to the Swami again, which showed at least that he could see the point of a story. But at this the Hindu monk was genuinely astonished.

In spite of such general interests, however, the inner strife grew high, and the thought pressed on the mind of one of the older members of our party that the Master himself needed service and peace. Many times he spoke with wonder of the torture of life, and who can say how many signs there were of bitter need? A word or two was spoken — little, but enough — and he, after many hours, came back and told us that he longed for quiet and would go alone to the forests and find soothing.

And then, looking up, he saw the young moon shining above us, and he said, "The Mohammedans think much of the new moon. Let us also, with the new moon, begin a new life!" And he blessed his daughter with a great blessing so that she, thinking that her old relationship was broken, nor dreaming that a new and deeper life was being given to it, knew only that the hour was strange and passing sweet...

MAY 25

He went. It was Wednesday. And on Saturday he came back. He had been in the silence of the forests ten hours each day, but on returning to his tent in the evenings he had been surrounded with so much eager attendance as to break the mood, and he had fled. Yet he was radiant. He had discovered in himself the old-time Sannyasin, able to go barefoot and endure heat, cold and scanty fare, unspoilt by the West...

JUNE 2

And then, as we sat working on Friday morning the telegram came, a day late, that said: "Goodwin died last night at Ootacamund". Our poor friend had, it appeared, been one of the first victims of what was to prove an epidemic of typhoid fever. And it seemed that with his last breath he had spoken of the Swami and longed for his presence by his side.

JUNE 5

On Sunday evening the Swami came home. Through our gate and over the terrace his way brought him, and there we sat and talked with him a moment. He did not know our news, but a great darkness hung over him already, and presently he broke the silence to remind us of that saint who had called the cobra's bite "messenger from the Beloved", one whom he had loved second only to Shri Ramakrishna himself. "I have just", he said, "received a letter that says: 'Pavhari Baba has completed all his sacrifices with the sacrifice of his own body. He has burnt himself in his sacrificial fire'". "Swami!" exclaimed someone from amongst his listeners. "Wasn't that very wrong?"

"How can I tell?" said the Swami, speaking in great agitation. "He was too great a man for me to judge. He knew himself what he was doing."

Very little was said after this, and the party of monks passed on. Not yet had the other news been broken.

JUNE 6

Next morning he came early in a great mood. He had been up, he said afterwards, since four. And one went out to meet him and told him of Mr. Goodwin's death. The blow fell quietly. Some days later he refused to stay in the place where he had received it, and complained of the weakness that brought the image of his most faithful disciple constantly into his mind. It was no more manly, he protested, to be thus ridden by one's memory than to retain the characteristics of the fish or the dog. Man must conquer this illusion and know that the dead are here beside us and with us as much as ever. It is their absence and separation that are a myth. And then he would break out again with some bitter utterance against the folly of imagining Personal Will to guide the universe. "As if", he exclaimed, "it would not be one's right and duty to fight such a God and slay Him for killing Goodwin! And Goodwin, if he had lived, could have done so much!" And in India one was free to recognize this as the most religious, because the most unflinchingly truthful, mood of all!

And while I speak of this utterance, I may perhaps put beside it another that I heard a year later, spoken out of the same fierce wonder at the dreams with which we comfort ourselves. "Why!" he said then. "Every petty magistrate and officer is allowed his period of retirement and rest. Only God, the Eternal Magistrate, must sit judging forever and never go free!"

But in these first hours the Swami was calm about his loss, and sat down and chatted quietly with us. He was full that morning of Bhakti passing into asceticism, the divine passion that carries the soul on its high tides far out of reach of persons, yet leaves it again struggling to avoid those sweet snares of personality.

What he said that morning of renunciation proved a hard gospel to one of those who listened, and when he came again she put it to him as her conviction that to love without attachment involved no pain, and was in itself ideal.

He turned on her with a sudden solemnity. "What is this idea of Bhakti without renunciation?" he said. "It is most pernicious!" And standing there for an hour or more, he talked of the awful self-discipline that one must impose on oneself if one would indeed be unattached, of the requisite nakedness of selfish motives, and of the danger that at any moment the most flower-like soul might have its petals soiled with the grosser stains of life. He told the story of an Indian nun who was asked when a man could be certain of safety on this road, and who sent back for answer a little plate of ashes. For the fight against passion was long and fierce, and at any moment the conqueror might become the conquered...

...Weeks afterwards in Kashmir, when he was again talking in some kindred fashion, one of us ventured to ask him if the feeling he thus roused were not that worship of pain that Europe abhors as morbid.

"Is the worship of pleasure, then, so noble?" was his immediate answer. "But indeed", he added after a pause, "we worship neither pain nor pleasure. We seek through either to come at that which transcends them both".

JUNE 9

This Thursday morning there was a talk on Krishna. It was characteristic of the Swami's mind, and characteristic also of the Hindu culture from which he had sprung, that he could lend himself to the enjoyment and portrayal of an idea one day that the next would see submitted to a pitiless analysis and left slain upon the field. He was a sharer to the full in the belief of his people that, provided an idea was spiritually true and consistent, it mattered very little about its objective actuality. And this mode of thought had first been suggested to him in his boyhood by his own master. He had mentioned some doubt as to the authenticity of a certain religious history. "What!" said Shri Ramakrishna. "Do you not then think that those who could conceive such ideas must have been the thing itself?"

The existence of Krishna, then, like that of Christ, he often told us "in the general way" he doubted. Buddha and Mohammed alone amongst religious teachers had been fortunate enough to have "enemies as well as friends", so that their historical careers were beyond dispute. As for Krishna, he was the most shadowy of all. A poet, a cowherd, a great ruler, a warrior and a sage had all perhaps been merged in one beautiful figure holding the Gitâ in his hand.

But today Krishna was "the most perfect of the Avatâras". And a wonderful picture followed of the charioteer who reined in his horses while he surveyed the field of battle and in one brief glance noted the disposition of the forces, at the same moment that he commenced to utter to his royal pupil the deep spiritual truths of the Gita.

And indeed as we went through the countrysides of northern India this summer, we had many chances of noting how deep this Krishna myth had set its mark upon the people. The songs that dancers chanted as they danced in the roadside hamlets were all of Râdhâ and Krishna. And the Swami was fond of a statement, as to which we, of course, could have no opinion, that the Krishna-worshippers of India had exhausted the possibilities of the romantic motive in lyric poetry...

But throughout these days the Swami was fretting to be away and alone. The place where he had heard of Mr. Goodwin's loss was intolerable to him, and letters to be written and received constantly renewed the wound. He said one day that Shri Ramakrishna, while seeming to be all Bhakti, was really within all Jnana; but he himself, apparently all Jnana, was full of Bhakti, and that thereby he was apt to be as weak as any woman.

One day he carried off a few faulty lines of someone's writing and brought back a little poem, which was sent to the widowed mother as his memorial of her son…[Vide "Requiescat in Pace", Complete Works, IV]

And then, because there was nothing left of the original and he feared that she who was corrected (because her lines had been "in three metres") might be hurt, he expatiated, long and earnestly upon the theme, that it was so much greater to feel poetically than merely to string syllables together in rhyme and metre.

He might be very severe on a sympathy or an opinion that seemed in his eyes sentimental or false. But an effort that failed found always in the Master its warmest advocate and tenderest defence.

And how happy was that acknowledgment of the bereaved mother to him when in the midst of her sorrow she wrote and thanked him for the character of his influence over the son who had died so far away!

JUNE 10

It was our last afternoon at Almora that we heard the story of the fatal illness of Shri Ramakrishna. Dr. Mahendra Lal Sarkar had been called in and had pronounced the disease to be cancer of the throat, leaving the young disciples with many warnings as to its infectious nature. Half an hour later "Naren", as he then was, came in and found them huddled together discussing the dangers of the case. He listened to what they had been told and then, looking down, saw at his feet the cup of gruel that had been partly taken by Shri Ramakrishna and which must have contained in it the germs of the fatal discharges of mucus and pus, as it came out in his baffled attempts to swallow the thing on account of the stricture of the food-passage in the throat. He picked it up and drank from it before them all. Never was the infection of cancer mentioned amongst the disciples again.

CHAPTER IV

ON THE WAY TO KATHGODAM

JUNE 11

On Saturday morning we left Almora. It took us two days and a half to reach Kathgodam…

Somewhere en route near a curious old water-mill and deserted forge, the Swami told Dhira Mata of a legend that spoke of this hill-side as haunted by a race of centaur-like phantoms, and of an experience known to him by which one had first seen forms there and only afterwards heard the folk tale.

The roses were gone by this time, but a flower was in bloom that crumbled at a touch, and he pointed this out because of its wealth of associations in Indian poetry.

JUNE 12

On Sunday afternoon we rested near the plains in what we took to be an out-of-the-way hotel above a lake and fall, and there he translated for us the Rudra prayer:

From the unreal lead us to the Real.

From darkness lead us unto light.

From death lead us to immortality.

Reach us through and through our self.

And evermore protect us — O Thou Terrible! — From ignorance, by Thy sweet, compassionate face.

He hesitated a long time over the fourth line, thinking of rendering it, "Embrace us in the heart of our heart". But at last he put his perplexity to us, saying shyly, "The real meaning is, Reach us through and through our self". He had evidently feared that this sentence, with its extraordinary intensity, might not make good sense in English…I have understood that a more literal rendering would be, "O Thou who art manifest only unto Thyself, manifest Thyself also unto us!" I now regard his translation as a rapid and direct transcript of the experience of Samâdhi itself. It tears the living heart out of the Sanskrit, as it were, and renders it again in an English form.

It was indeed an afternoon of translations, and he gave us fragments of the great benediction after mourning, which is one of the most beautiful of the Hindu sacraments:

The blissful winds are sweet to us.
The seas are showering bliss on us.
May the corn in our fields bring bliss to us.
May the plants and herbs bring bliss to us.
May the cattle give us bliss.
O Father in Heaven, be Thou blissful unto us!
Thy very dust of the earth is full of bliss.
And then, the voice dying down into meditation:
It is all bliss — all bliss — all bliss.

And again we had Suradâsa's song, which the Swami heard from the nautch-girl at Khetri:

O Lord, look not upon my evil qualities!
Thy name, O Lord, is Same-Sightedness.
Make of us both the same Brahman!...

Was it that same day or some other that he told us of the old Sannyâsin in Benares who saw him annoyed by troops of monkeys and, afraid that he might turn and run, shouted, "Always face the brute!"?

Those journeys were delightful. We were always sorry to reach a destination. At this time it took us a whole afternoon to cross the Terai by rail — that strip of malarial country on which, as he reminded us, Buddha had been born.

As we had come down the mountain roads, we had met parties of country-folk fleeing to the upper hills with their families and all their goods, to escape the fever which would be upon them with the rains. And now in the train there was the gradual change of vegetation to watch and the Master's pleasure, greater than that of any proprietor, in showing us the wild peacocks, or here and there an elephant or a train of camels...

CHAPTER V

ON THE WAY TO BARAMULLA

PERSONS: The Swami Vivekananda, Gurubhais, and a party of Europeans and disciples, amongst whom were Dhira Mata, the "Steady Mother"; one whose name was Jaya; and Nivedita.

PLACE: From Bareilly to Baramulla, Kashmir.

TIME: June 14 to 20, 1898.

JUNE 14

We entered the Punjab next day, and great was the Swami's excitement at the fact. It almost seemed as if he had been born there, so close and special was his love for this province. He talked of the girls at their spinning wheels listening to the "So'ham! So'ham!" — I am He! I am He! Then, by a swift transition he turned to the far past and unrolled for us the great historic panorama of the advance of the Greeks on the Indus, the rise of Chandragupta and the development of the Buddhistic empire. He was determined this summer to find his way to Attock and see with his own eyes the spot at which Alexander was turned back. He described to us the Gandhara sculptures, which he must have seen in the Lahore Museum the year before, and lost himself in indignant repudiation of the absurd European claim that India had ever sat at the feet of Greece in things artistic.

Then there were flying glimpses of long-expected cities — Ludhiana, where certain trusty English disciples had lived as children; Lahore, where his Indian lectures had ended; and so on. We came too upon the dry gravel beds of many rivers and learnt that the space between one pair was called the Doab and the area containing them all, the Punjab.

It was at twilight, crossing one of these stony tracts, that he told us of that great vision which came to him years ago, while he was still new to the ways of the life of a monk, giving back to him, as he always afterwards believed, the ancient mode of Sanskrit chanting.

"It was evening", he said, "in that age when the Aryans had only reached the Indus. I saw an old man seated on the bank of the great river. Wave upon wave of darkness was rolling in upon him, and he was chanting from the Rig-Veda. Then I awoke and went on chanting. They were the tones that we used long ago".

…Those who were constantly preoccupied with imagination regarding their own past always aroused his contempt. But on this occasion of telling the story, he gave a glimpse of it from a very different point of view.

"Shankarâchârya", he was saying, "had caught the rhythm of the Vedas, the national cadence. Indeed I always imagine", he went on suddenly with dreamy voice and far-away look, "I always imagine that he had some vision such as mine when he was young, and recovered the ancient music that way. Anyway, his whole life's work is nothing but that, the throbbing of the beauty of the Vedas and Upanishads"…

From Rawalpindi to Murree we went by tonga, and there we spent some days before setting out for Kashmir. Here the Swami came to the conclusion that any effort which he might make to induce the orthodox to accept a European as a fellow-disciple, or in the direction of woman's education, had better be made in Bengal. The distrust of the foreigner was too strong in Punjab to admit of work succeeding there. He was much occupied by this question from time to time, and would sometimes remark on the paradox presented by the Bengali combination of political antagonism to the English, and readiness to love and trust…

JUNE 18

Most of the afternoon we were compelled by a storm to spend indoors;, and a new chapter was opened at Dulai in our knowledge of Hinduism, for the Swami told us gravely and frankly of its modern abuses and spoke of his own uncompromising hostility to those evil practices which pass under the name of Vâmâchâra.

When we asked how Shri Ramakrishna — who never could bear to condemn the hope of any man — had looked at these things, he told us that "the old man" had said, "Well, well! But every house may have a scavengers' entrance!" And he pointed out that all sects of diabolism in any country belonged to this class…

JUNE 19

We took it in turns to drive with the Swami in his tonga, and this next day seemed full of reminiscence.

He talked of Brahmavidyâ, the vision of the One, the Alone — Real, and told how love was the only cure for evil. He had had a schoolfellow who grew up and became rich, but lost his health. It was an obscure disease, sapping his energy and vitality daily, yet altogether baffling the skill of the doctors. At last, because he knew that the Swami had always been religious, and men turn to religion when all else fails, he sent to beg him to come to him. When the Master reached him a curious thing happened. There came to his mind a text: "Him the Brahmin conquers who thinks that he is separate from the Brahmin. Him the Kshatriya conquers who thinks that he is separate from the Kshatriya. And him the universe conquers who thinks that he is separate from the universe". And the sick man grasped this and recovered. "And so", said the Swami, "though I often say strange things and angry things, yet remember that in my heart I never seriously mean to preach anything but love! All these things will come right only when we realize that we love each other".

Was it then, or the day before, that talking of the great God, he told us how when he was a child his mother would sigh over his naughtiness and say, "So many prayers and austerities, and instead of a good soul, Shiva has sent me you!" till he was hypnotized into a belief that he was really one of Shiva's demons. He thought that for a punishment he had been banished for a while from Shiva's heaven, and that his one effort in life must be to go back there.

His first act of sacrilege, he told us once, had been committed at the age of five when he embarked on a stormy argument with his mother, to the effect that when his right hand was soiled with eating, it would be cleaner to lift his tumbler of water with the left. For this or similar perversities her most drastic remedy was to put him under the water tap and, while cold water was pouring over his head, to say "Shiva! Shiva!" This, he said, never failed of its effect. The prayer would remind him of his exile, and he would say to himself, "No, no, not this time again!" and so return to quiet and obedience.

He had a surpassing love for Mahâdeva, and once he said of the Indian women of the future that if, amidst their new tasks, they would only remember now and then to say "Shiva! Shiva!" it would be worship enough. The very air of the Himalayas was charged for him with the image of that "eternal meditation" that no thought of pleasure could break. And he understood, he said, for the first time this summer, the meaning of the nature-story that made the Ganges fall on the head of the great God, and wander in and out amongst His matted locks before She found an outlet on the plains below. He had searched long, he said, for the words that the rivers and waterfalls uttered, amongst the mountains, before he had realized that it was the eternal cry "Bom! Bom! Hara! Hara!"

"Yes!" he said of Shiva one day, "He is the great God — calm, beautiful, and silent! And I am His great worshipper".

Again his subject was marriage, as the type of the soul's relation to God. "This is why", he exclaimed, "though the love of a mother is in some ways greater, yet the whole world takes the love of man and woman as the type. No other has such tremendous idealizing power. The beloved actually becomes what he is imagined to be. This love transforms its object".

Then the talk strayed to national types, and he spoke of the joy with which the returning traveller greets once more the sight of the men and women of his own country. The whole of life has been a subconscious education to enable one to understand in these every faintest ripple of expression in face and form.

And again we passed a group of Sannyâsins going on foot, and he broke out into fierce invective against asceticism as "savagery" …But the sight of wayfarers doing slow miles on foot in the name of their ideals seemed to rouse in his mind a train of painful associations, and he grew impatient on behalf of humanity at "the torture of religion". Then again the mood passed as suddenly as it had arisen and gave place to the equally strong statement of the conviction that were it not for this "savagery", luxury would have robbed man of all his manliness.

We stopped that evening at Uri Dak bungalow, and in the twilight we all walked in the meadows and the bazaar. How beautiful the place was! A little mud fortress — exactly of the European feudal pattern — overhung the footway as it swept into a great open theatre of field and hill. Along the road above the river lay the bazaar, and we returned to the bungalow by a path across the fields, past cottages in whose gardens the roses were in bloom. As we came, too, it would happen that here and there some child more venturesome than others would play with us.

JUNE 20

The next day, driving through the most beautiful part of the pass and seeing cathedral rocks and an old ruined temple of the sun, we reached Baramulla. The legend is that the Vale of Kashmir was once a lake and that at this point the Divine Boar pierced the mountains with his tusks and let the Jhelum go free. Another piece of geography in the form of myth. Or is it also prehistoric history?

CHAPTER VI

THE VALE OF KASHMIR

PERSONS: The Swami Vivekananda and a party of Europeans and disciples, amongst whom were Dhira Mata, the "Steady Mother"; one whose name was Jaya; and Nivedita.

PLACE: The River Jhelum-Baramulla to Srinagar.

TIME: June 20 to June 22.

"It is said that the Lord Himself is the weight on the side of the fortunate!" cried the Swami in high glee, returning to our room at the Dak bungalow and sitting down with his umbrella on his knees. As he had brought no companion, he had himself to perform all the ordinary little masculine offices, and he had gone out to hire Dungas [houseboats] and do what was necessary. But he had immediately fallen in with a man who, on hearing his name, had undertaken the whole business and sent him back free of responsibility.

So we enjoyed the day. We drank Kashmiri tea out of a Samovar and ate the jam of the country, and at about four o'clock we entered into possession of a flotilla of Dungas, three in number, on which presently we set forth for Srinagar. The first evening, however, we were moored by the garden of the Swami's friend...

We found ourselves next day in the midst of a beautiful valley ringed round with snow mountains. This is known as the Vale of Kashmir, but it might be more accurately described, perhaps, as the Vale of Srinagar...

That first morning, taking a long walk across the fields, we came upon an immense chennaar tree standing in the midst of a wide pasture. It really looked as if the passage through it might shelter the proverbial twenty cows! The Swami fell to architectural visions of how it might be fitted up as a dwelling-place for a hermit. A small cottage might in fact have been built in the hollow of this living tree. And then he talked of meditation, in a way to consecrate every chennaar we should ever see.

We turned with him into the neighbouring farmyard. There we found, seated under a tree, a singularly handsome elderly woman. She wore the crimson coronet and white veil of the Kashmiri wife and sat spinning wool, while round her, helping her, were her two daughters-in-law and their children. The Swami had called at this farm once before in the previous autumn and had often spoken since of the faith and pride of this very woman. He had begged for water, which she had at once given him.

Then, before going, he had asked her quietly, "And what, Mother, is your religion?" "I thank God, sir!" had rung out the old voice in pride and triumph. "By the mercy of the Lord, I am a Mussulman!" The whole family received him now as an old friend and were ready to show every courtesy to the friends he had brought.

The journey to Srinagar took two to three days, and one evening, as we walked in the fields before supper, one who had seen the Kalighat complained to the Master of the abandonment of feeling there, which had jarred on her. "Why do they kiss the ground before the image?" she exclaimed. The Swami had been pointing to the crop of Til — which he thought to have been the original of the English dill — and calling it "the oldest oil-bearing seed of the Aryans". But at this question he dropped the little blue flower from his hands, and a great hush came over his voice as he stood still and said, "Is it not the same thing to kiss the ground before that image as to kiss the ground before these mountains?"

Our master had promised that before the end of the summer he would take us into retreat and teach us to meditate...It was decided that we should first see the country and afterwards make the retreat.

The first evening in Srinagar we dined out with some Bengali officials, and in the course of conversation one of the Western guests maintained that the history of every nation illustrated and evolved certain ideals to which the people of that nation should hold themselves true. It was very curious to see how the Hindus present objected to this. To them it was clearly a bondage to which the mind of man could not permanently submit itself. Indeed, in their revolt against the fetters of the doctrine, they appeared to be unable to do justice to the idea itself. At last the Swami intervened. "I think you must admit", he said, "that the ultimate unit is psychological. This is much more permanent than the geographical". And then he spoke of cases known to us all, of one of whom he always thought as the most typical "Christian" he had ever seen, yet she was a Bengali woman, and of another, born in the West, who was "a better Hindu than himself". And was not this, after all, the ideal state of things, that each should be born in the other's country to spread the given ideal as far as it could be carried?

CHAPTER VII

LIFE AT SRINAGAR

PLACE: Srinagar.
TIME: June 22 to July 15, 1898.

In the mornings we still had long talks as before — some-times it would be the different religious periods through which Kashmir had passed, or the morality of Buddhism, or the history of Shiva-worship, or perhaps the position of Srinagar under Kanishka.

Once he was talking with one of us about Buddhism, and he suddenly said, "The fact is, Buddhism tried to do, in the time of Ashoka, what the world never was ready for till now!" He referred to the federalization of religions. It was a wonderful picture, this, of the religious imperialism of Ashoka, broken down time and again by successive waves of Christianity and Mohammedanism, each claiming exclusive rights over the conscience of mankind and finally to seem to have a possibility, within measurable distance of time, today!

Another time the talk was of Genghis, or Chenghis, Khan, the conqueror from Central Asia. "You hear people talk of him as a vulgar aggressor", he cried passionately, "but that is not true! They are never greedy or vulgar, these great souls! He was inspired with the thought of unity, and he wanted to unify his world. Yes, Napoleon was cast in the same mould. And another, Alexander. Only those three, or perhaps one soul manifesting itself in three different conquests!" And then he passed on to speak of that one soul whom he believed to have come again and again in religion, charged with the divine impulse to bring about the unity of man in God.

At this time the transfer of the Prabuddha Bharata from Madras to the newly established Ashrama at Mayavati was much in all our thoughts. The Swami had always had a special love for this paper, as the beautiful name he had given it indicated. He had always been eager too for the establishment of organs of his own. The value of the journal in the education of modern India was perfectly evident to him, and he felt that his master's message and mode of thought required to be spread by this means as well as by preaching and by work. Day after day, therefore, he would dream about the future of his papers, as about the work in its various centres. Day after day he would talk of the forthcoming first number under the new editorship of Swami Swarupananda. And one afternoon he brought to us, as we sat together, a paper on which he said he had "tried to write a letter, but it would come this way!" ...[Vide To the Awakened India", Complete Works, IV]

JUNE 26

The Master was longing to leave us all and go away into some place of quiet, alone. But we, not knowing this, insisted on accompanying him to the Coloured Springs, called "Kshir Bhavâni", or "Milk of the Mother". It was said to be the first time that Christian or Mohammedan had ever landed there, and we can never be thankful enough for the glimpse we had of it since afterwards it was to become the most sacred of all names to us. . .

JUNE 29

Another day we went off quietly by ourselves and visited the Takt-i-Suleiman, a little temple very massively built on the summit of a small mountain two or three thousand feet high. It was peaceful and beautiful, and the famous Floating Gardens could be seen below us for miles around. The Takt-i-Suleiman was one of the great illustrations of the Swami's argument when he would take up the subject of the Hindu love of nature as shown in the choice of sites for temples and architectural monuments. As he had declared, in London, that the saints lived on the hill-tops in order to enjoy the scenery, so now he pointed out — citing one example after another — that our Indian people always consecrated places of peculiar beauty and importance by making there their altars of worship. And there was no denying that the little Takt, crowning the hill that dominated the whole valley, was a case in point.

Many lovely fragments of those days come into mind, as:

Therefore, Tulasi, take thou care to live with all, for who can tell where, or in what garb, the Lord Himself may next come to thee?
One God is hidden in all these, the Torturer of all, the Awakener of all, the Reservoir of all being, the One who is bereft of all qualities.
There the sun does not shine, nor the moon, nor the stars.

There was the story of how Râvana was advised to take the form of Râma in order to cheat Sitâ. He answered, "Have I not thought of it? But in order to take a man's form you must meditate on him; and Rama is the Lord Himself; so when I meditate on him, even the position of Brahmâ becomes a mere straw. How, then, could I think of a woman?"

"And so", commented the Swami, "even in the commonest or most criminal life, there are these glimpses". It was ever thus. He was constantly interpreting human life as the expression of God, never insisting on the heinousness or wickedness of the act or a character.

"In that which is dark night to the rest of the world, there the man of self-control is awake. That which is life to the rest of the world is sleep to him."

Speaking of Thomas à Kempis one day, and of how he himself used to wander as a Sannyâsin with the Gitâ and the Imitation as his whole library, one word, he said, came back to him, inseparably associated with the name of the Western monk:

Silence! ye teachers of the world, and silence! ye prophets! Speak Thou alone, O Lord, unto my soul!

Again:

The soft Shirisha flower can bear the weight of humming bees, but not of birds —
So Umâ, don't you go and make Tapasyâ!
Come, Uma, come! delight and idol of my soul!
Be seated, Mother, on the lotus of my heart,
And let me take a long, long look at you.
From my birth up, I am gazing,
Mother, at your face —
Know you suffering what trouble,
and pain?
Be seated, therefore, Blessed One,
on the lotus of my heart,
And dwell there for evermore.

Every now and then there would be long talks about the Gita — "that wonderful poem, without one note in it of weakness or unmanliness." He said one day that it was absurd to complain that knowledge was not given to women or to Shudras. For the whole gist of the Upanishads was contained in the Gita. Without it, indeed, they could hardly be understood; and women and all castes could read the Mahâbhârata.

JULY 4

With great fun and secrecy the Swami and his one non-American disciple prepared to celebrate the Fourth of July. A regret had been expressed in his hearing that we had no American flag with which to welcome the other members of the party to breakfast on their national festival; and late on the afternoon of the third, he brought a Pundit Durzey [Brahmin tailor] in great excitement, explaining that this man would be glad to imitate it if he were told how. The stars and stripes were very crudely represented, I fear, on the piece of cotton that was nailed with branches of evergreens to the head of the dining—room—boat when the Americans stepped on board for early tea on Independence Day! But the Swami had postponed a journey in order to be present at the little festival, and he himself contributed a poem to the addresses that were now read aloud by way of greeting…[Vide "To the Fourth of July", Complete Works, V]

JULY 5

That evening someone pained him by counting the cherry-stones left on her plate, to see when she would be married. He somehow took the play in earnest and came the following morning surcharged with passion for the ideal renunciation.

JULY 6

"These shadows of home and marriage cross even my mind now and then!" he cried, with that tender desire to make himself one with the sinner that he so often showed. But it was across oceans of scorn for those who would glorify the householder that he sought on this occasion to preach the religious life. "Is it so easy", he exclaimed, "to be Janaka? To sit on a throne absolutely unattached? Caring nothing for wealth or fame, for wife or child? One after another in the West has told me that he had reached this. But I could only say, 'Such great men are not born in India'!"

And then he turned to the other side.

"Never forget", he said to one of his hearers, "to say to yourself, and to teach to your children: as is the difference between a firefly and the blazing sun, between the infinite ocean and a little pond, between a mustard-seed and the mountain of Meru, such is the difference between the householder and the Sannyasin!"

"Everything is fraught with fear: Renunciation alone is fearless."

"Blessed be even the fraudulent Sâdhus, and those who have failed to carry out their vows, inasmuch as they also have witnessed to the ideal and so are in some degree the cause of the success of others!"

"Let us never, never, forget our ideal!"

At such moments he would identify himself entirely with the thought he sought to demonstrate, and in the same sense in which a law of nature might be deemed cruel or arrogant, his exposition might have those qualities. Sitting and listening, we felt ourselves brought face to face with the invisible and absolute.

All this was on our return to Srinagar from the real Fourth of July celebration, which had been a visit to Dahl Lake...

At nine o'clock on the evening of the following Sunday, July the 10th, the first two [Dhira Mata and Jaya] came back unexpectedly, and presently, from many different sources, we gathered the news that the Master had gone to Amarnath by the Sonamarg route and would return another way. He had started out penniless, but that could give no concern to his friends, in a Hindu native state...

JULY 15

What were we setting out for? We were just moving to go down the river on Friday, and it was close on five in the afternoon when the servants recognized some of their friends in the distance, and word was brought that the Swami's boat was coming towards us.

An hour later he was with us, saying how pleasant it was to be back. The summer had been unusually hot and certain glaciers had given way, rendering the Sonamarg route to Amarnath impracticable. This fact had caused his return.

But from this moment dated the first of three great increments of joy and realization that we saw in him during our months in Kashmir. It was almost as if we could verify for ourselves the truth of that saying of his Guru: "There is indeed a certain ignorance. It has been placed there by my Holy Mother that her work may be done. But it is only like a film of tissue paper. It might be rent at any moment".

CHAPTER VIII

THE TEMPLE OF PANDRENTHAN

PERSONS: The Swami Vivekananda and a party of Europeans and disciples, amongst whom were Dhira Mata, the "Steady Mother"; one whose name was Jaya; and Nivedita.

PLACE: Kashmir.

TIME: July 16 to 19, 1898.

JULY 16

It fell to the lot of one of the Swami's disciples next day to go down the river with him in a small boat. As it went, he chanted one song after another of Râmprasâd, and now and again he would translate a verse:

> I call upon thee, Mother.
> For though his mother strikes him,
> The child cries, "Mother! Oh, Mother!"
> Though I cannot see Thee,
> I am not a lost child!
> I still cry, "Mother! Mother!"

And then with the haughty dignity of an offended child, some-thing that ended, "I am not the son to call any other woman 'Mother'!"

JULY 17

It must have been next day that he came into Dhira Mata's Dunga and talked of Bhakti. First it was that curious Hindu thought of Shiva and Umâ in one. It is easy to give the words, but without the voice how comparatively dead they seem! And then there were the wonderful surroundings — picturesque Srinagar, tall Lombardy poplars and distant snows. There in that river-valley, some space from the foot of the great mountains, he chanted to us how "the Lord took a form and that was a divided form, half woman and half man. On one side, beautiful garlands; on the other, bone earrings and coils of snakes. On one side, the hair black, beautiful and in curls; on the other, twisted like rope". And then passing immediately into the other form of the same thought, he quoted:

> God became Krishna and Râdhâ —
> Love flows in thousands of coils.
> Whoso wants, takes it.
> Love flows in thousands of coils —
> The tide of love and loving past,
> And fills the soul with bliss and joy!

So absorbed was he that his breakfast stood unheeded long after it was ready, and when at last he went reluctantly — saying, "When one has all this Bhakti what does one want with food?" — it was only to come back again quickly and resume the subject.

But either now or at some other time he said that he did not talk of Radha and Krishna where he looked for deeds. It was Shiva who made stern and earnest workers, and to Him the labourer must be dedicated.

The next day he gave us a quaint saying of Shri Ramakrishna, comparing the critics of others to bees or flies, according as they chose honey or wounds.

And then we were off to Islamabad, and really, as it proved, to Amarnath.

JULY 19

The first afternoon, in a wood by the side of the Jhelum, we discovered the long — sought temple of Pandrenthan (Pandresthan, place of the Pândavas?).

It was sunk in a pond, and this was thickly covered with scum out of which it rose, a tiny cathedral of the long ago, built of heavy grey limestone. The temple consisted of a small cell with four doorways opening to the cardinal points. Externally it was a tapering pyramid — with its top truncated, to give foot-hold to a bush — supported on a four-pierced pedestal. In its architecture, trefoil and triangular arches were combined in an unusual fashion with each other and with the straight-lined lintel. It was built with marvellous solidity, and the necessary lines were somewhat obscured by heavy ornament…

For all but the Swami himself, this was our first peep at Indian archaeology. So when he had been through it, he taught us how to observe the interior.

In the centre of the ceiling was a large sun-medallion, set in a square whose points were the points of the compass. This left four equal triangles at the corners of the ceiling, which were filled with sculpture in low relief, male and female figures intertwined with serpents, beautifully done. On the wall were empty spaces, where seemed to have been a band of topes.

Outside, carvings were similarly distributed. In one of the trefoil arches — over, I think, the eastern door — was a fine image of the Teaching Buddha, standing, with his hand uplifted. Running round the buttresses was a much-defaced frieze of a seated woman with a tree — evidently Mâyâ Devi, the mother of Buddha. The three other door-niches were empty, but a slab by the pond-side seemed to have fallen from one, and this contained a bad figure of a king, said by the country-people to represent the sun.

The masonry of this little temple was superb and probably accounted for its long preservation. A single block of stone would be so cut as to correspond not to one brick in a wall, but to a section of the architect's plan. It would turn a corner and form part of two distinct walls, or sometimes even of three. This fact made one take the building as very, very old, possibly even earlier than Marttanda. The theory of the workmen seemed so much more that of carpentering than of building! The water about it was probably an overflow into the temple-court from the sacred spring that the chapel itself may have been placed, as the Swami thought, to enshrine.

To him, the place was delightfully suggestive. It was a direct memorial of Buddhism, representing one of the four religious periods into which he had already divided the history of Kashmir: (1) tree and snake worship, from which dated all the names of the springs ending in Nag, as Verinag, and so on; (2) Buddhism; (3) Hinduism, in the form of sun worship; and (4) Mohammedanism.

Sculpture, he told us, was the characteristic art of Buddhism, and the sun-medallion, or lotus, one of its commonest ornaments. The figures with the serpents referred to pre-Buddhism. But sculpture had greatly deteriorated under sun worship, hence the crudity of the Surya figure…

It was the time of sunset — such a sunset! The mountains in the west were all a shimmering purple. Further north they were blue with snow and cloud. The sky was green and yellow and touched with red — bright flame and daffodil colours, against a blue and opal background. We stood and looked, and then the Master, catching sight of the throne of Solomon — that little Takt which we already loved — exclaimed, "What genius the Hindu shows in placing his temples! He always chooses a grand scenic effect! See! The Takt commands the whole of Kashmir. The rock of Hari Parbat rises red out of blue water, like a lion couchant, crowned. And the temple of Marttanda has the valley at its feet!"

Our boats were moored near the edge of the wood, and we could see that the presence of the silent chapel, of the Buddha, which we had just explored, moved the Swami deeply. That evening we all foregathered in Dhira Mata's houseboat, and a little of the conversation has been noted down.

Our master had been talking of Christian ritual as derived from Buddhist, but one of the party would have none of the theory.

"Where did Buddhist ritual itself come from?" she asked.

"From Vedic", answered the Swami briefly."

Or as it was present also in southern Europe, is it not better to suppose a common origin for it and the Christian and the Vedic rituals?"

"No! No!" he replied. "You forget that Buddhism was entirely within Hinduism! Even caste was not attacked — it was not yet crystallized, of course! — and Buddha merely tried to restore the ideal. He who attains to God in this life, says Manu, is the Brahmin. Buddha would have had it so, if he could."

"But how are Vedic and Christian rituals connected?" persisted his opponent. "How could they be the same? You have nothing even corresponding to the central rite of our worship!"

"Why, yes!" said the Swami. "Vedic ritual has its Mass, the offering of food to God; your Blessed Sacrament, our Prasâdam. Only it is offered sitting, not kneeling, as is common in hot countries. They kneel in Tibet. Then too Vedic ritual has its lights, incense, music."

"But", was the somewhat ungracious argument, "has it any common prayer?" Objections urged in this way always elicited some bold paradox which contained a new and unthought-of generalization.

He flashed down on the question. "No! And neither has Christianity! That is pure Protestantism and Protestantism took it from the Mohammedans, perhaps through Moorish influence!

"Mohammedanism is the only religion that has

completely broken down the idea of the priest. The leader of prayer stands with his back to the people, and only the reading of the Koran may take place from the pulpit. Protestantism is an approach to this.

"Even the tonsure existed in India, in the shaven head. I have seen a picture of Justinian receiving the Law from two monks, in which the monks' heads are entirely shaven. The monk and nun both existed in pre-Buddhistic Hinduism. Europe gets her orders from the Thebaid."

"At that rate, then, you accept Catholic ritual as Aryan!"

"Yes, almost all Christianity is Aryan, I believe. I am inclined to think Christ never existed. I have doubted that ever since I had my dream — that dream off Crete! Indian and Egyptian ideas met at Alexandria and went forth to the world, tinctured with Judaism and Hellenism, as Christianity.

"The Acts and Epistles, you know, are older than the Gospels, and S. John is spurious. The only figure we can be sure of is S. Paul, and he was not an eye-witness, and according to his own showing was capable of Jesuitry — 'by all means save souls' — isn't it?

"No! Buddha and Mohammed, alone amongst religious teachers, stand out with historic distinctness — having been fortunate enough to have, while they were living, enemies as well as friends. Krishna — I doubt; a Yogi, a shepherd, and a great king have all been amalgamated in one beautiful figure, holding the Gîtâ in his hand.

"Renan's life of Jesus is mere froth. It does not touch Strauss, the real antiquarian. Two things stand out as personal living touches in the life of Christ — the woman taken in adultery, the most beautiful story in literature, and the woman at the well. How strangely true is this last to Indian life! A woman coming to draw water finds, seated at the well-side, a yellow-clad monk. He asks her for water. Then he teaches her and does a little mind-reading and so on. Only in an Indian story, when she went to call the villagers to look and listen, the monk would have taken his chance and fled to the forest!

"On the whole, I think old Rabbi Hillel is responsible for the teachings of Jesus, and an obscure Jewish sect of Nazarenes — a sect of great antiquity — suddenly galvanized by S. Paul, furnished the mythic personality as a centre of worship.

"The resurrection, of course, is simply spring-cremation. Only the rich Greeks and Romans had had cremation anyway, and the new sun-myth would only stop it amongst the few.

"But Buddha! Buddha! Surely he was the greatest man who ever lived. He never drew a breath for himself. Above all, he never claimed worship. He said, 'Buddha is not a man, but a state. I have found the door. Enter, all of you!'

"He went to the feast of Ambâpâli, 'the sinner'. He dined with the pariah, though he knew it would kill him, and sent a message to his host on his death-bed, thanking him for the great deliverance. Full of love and pity for a little goat, even before he had attained the truth! You remember how he offered his own head, that of prince and monk, if only the king would spare the kid that he was about to sacrifice, and how the king was so struck by his compassion that he saved its life? Such a mixture of rationalism and feeling was never seen! Surely, surely, there was none like him!"

CHAPTER IX

WALKS AND TALKS BESIDE THE JHELUM

PERSONS: The Swami Vivekananda and a party of Europeans and disciples, amongst whom were Dhira Mata, the "Steady Mother"; one whose name was Jaya; and Nivedita.

PLACE: Kashmir.

TIME: July 20 to July 29, 1898.

JULY 20

That morning the river was broad and shallow and clear, and two of us walked with the Swami across the fields and along the banks about three miles. He began by talking of the sense of sin, how it was Egyptian, Semitic and Aryan. It appears in the Vedas, but quickly passes out. The devil is recognized there as the Lord of Anger. Then, with the Buddhists he became Mara, the Lord of Lust, and one of the most loved of the Lord Buddha's titles was "Conqueror of Mara". (Vide the Sanskrit lexicon Amarkosha that Swami learnt to patter as a child of four!) But while Satan is the Hamlet of the Bible, in the Hindu scriptures the Lord of Anger never divides creation. He always represents defilement, never duality.

Zoroaster was a reformer of some old religion. Even Ormuzd and Ahriman with him were not supreme; they were only manifestations of the Supreme. That older religion must have been Vedantic. So the Egyptians and Semites cling to the theory of sin while the Aryans, as Indians and Greeks, quickly lose it. In India righteousness and sin become Vidyâ and Avidyâ — both to be transcended. Amongst the Aryans, Persians and Europeans become Semitized by religious ideas; hence the sense of sin.

And then the talk drifted, as it was always so apt to do, to questions of the country and the future. What idea must be urged on a people to give them strength? The line of their own development runs in one way, A. Must the new accession of force be a compensating one, B? This would produce a development midway between the two, C — a geometrical alteration merely. But it was not so.

National life was a question of organic forces. We must reinforce the current of that life itself, and leave it to do the rest. Buddha preached renunciation, and India heard. Yet within a thousand years she had reached her highest point of national prosperity. The national life in India has renunciation as its source. Its highest ideals are service and Mukti. The Hindu mother eats last. Marriage is not for individual happiness, but for the welfare of the nation and the caste. Certain individuals of the modern reform, having embarked on an experiment which could not solve the problem, "are the sacrifices over which the race has to walk".

And then the trend of conversation changed again and became all fun and merriment, jokes and stories. And as we laughed and listened, the boats came up and talk was over for the day.

The whole of that afternoon and night the Swami lay in his boat, ill. But next day, when we landed at the temple of Bijbehara — already thronged with Amarnath pilgrims — he was able to join us for a little while. "Quickly up and quickly down", as he said of himself, was always his characteristic. After that he was with us most of the day, and in the afternoon we reached Islamabad...

In the dusk that evening one came into the little group amongst the apple trees and found the Master engaged in the rarest of rare happenings, a personal talk with Dhira Mata and her whose name was Jaya. He had taken two pebbles into his hand and was saying how, when he was well, his mind might direct itself to this and that, or his will might seem less firm; but let the least touch of pain or illness come, let him look death in the face for a while, and "I am as hard as that (knocking the stones together), for I have touched the feet of God".

And one remembered, apropos of this coolness, the story of a walk across the fields in England, where he and an Englishman and woman had been pursued by an angry bull. The Englishman frankly ran and reached the other side of the hill in safety. The woman ran as far as she could and then sank to the ground, incapable of further effort. Seeing this, and unable to aid her, the Swami — thinking "So this is the end, after all" — took up his stand in front of her, with folded arms. He told afterwards how his mind was occupied with a mathematical calculation as to how far the bull would be able to throw. But the animal suddenly stopped a few paces off and then, raising his head, retreated sullenly.

A like courage — though he himself was far from thinking of these incidents — had shown itself in his early youth when he quietly stepped up to a runaway horse and caught it in the streets of Calcutta, thus saving the life of the woman who occupied the carriage behind.

The talk drifted on, as we sat on the grass beneath the trees, and became, for an hour or two, half grave, half gay. We heard much of the tricks the monkeys could play in Vrindaban. And we elicited stories of two separate occasions in his wandering life when he had had clear previsions of help which had been fulfilled. One of these I remember. It may possibly have occurred at the time when he was under the vow to ask for nothing, and he had been several days (perhaps five) without food. Suddenly, as he lay almost dying of exhaustion in a railway-station, it flashed into his mind that he must rise up and go out along a certain road and that there he would meet a man bringing him help. He obeyed and met one carrying a tray of food. "Are you he to whom I was sent?" said this man, coming up to him and looking at him closely.

Then a child was brought to us, with its hand badly cut, and the Swami applied an old wives' cure. He bathed the wound with water and then laid on it, to stop the bleeding, the ashes of a piece of calico. The villagers were soothed and consoled, and our gossip was over for the evening.

JULY 23

The next morning a motley gathering of coolies assembled beneath the apple-trees and waited some hours to take us to the ruins of Marttanda. It had been a wonderful old building — evidently more abbey than temple — in a wonderful position; and its great interest lay in the obvious agglomeration of styles and periods in which it had grown up…Its presence is a perpetual reminder that the East was the original home of monasticism. The Swami was hard at work in an instant on observations and theorics, pointing out the cornice that ran along the nave from the entrance to the sanctuary, to the west, surmounted by the high trefoils of the two arches and also by a frieze; or showing us the panels containing cherubs; and before we had done, had picked up a couple of coins. The ride back through the sunset light was charming. From all these hours, the day before and the day after, fragments of talk come back to me.

"No nation, not Greek or another, has ever carried patriotism so far as the Japanese. They don't talk, they act — give up all for country. There are noblemen now living in Japan as peasants, having given up their princedoms without a word to create the unity of the empire.[7]* And not one traitor could be found in the Japanese war. Think of that!"

Again, talking of the inability of some to express feeling, "Shy and reserved people, I have noticed, are always the most brutal when roused".

Again, evidently talking of the ascetic life and giving the rules of Brahmacharya — "The Sannyâsin who thinks of gold, to desire it, commits suicide", and so on.

JULY 24

The darkness of night and the forest, a great pine-fire under the trees, two or three tents standing out white in the blackness, the forms and voices of many servants at their fires in the distance, and the Master with three disciples, such is the next picture…Suddenly the Master turned to one member of the party and said, "You never mention your school now. Do you sometimes forget it? You see", he went on, "I have much to think of. One day I turn to Madras and think of the work there. Another day I give all my attention to America or England or Ceylon or Calcutta. Now I am thinking about yours".

At that moment the Master was called away to dine, and not till he came back could the confidence he had invited be given.

He listened to it all, the deliberate wish for a tentative plan, for smallness of beginnings, and the final inclination to turn away from the idea of inclusiveness and breadth and to base the whole of an educational effort on the religious life and on the worship of Shri Ramakrishna.

"Because you must be sectarian to get that enthusiasm, must you not?" he said. "You will make a sect in order to rise above all sects. Yes I understand".

There would be obvious difficulties. The thing sounded on this scale almost impossible for many reasons. But for the moment the only care need be to will rightly; and if the plan was sound, ways and means would be found to hand, that was sure.

He waited a little when he had heard it all, and then he said, "You ask me to criticize, but that I cannot do. For I regard you as inspired, quite as much inspired as I am. You know that's the difference between other religions and us. Other people believe their founder was inspired, and so do we. But so am I also, just as much so as he, and you as I; and after you, your girls and their disciples will be. So I shall help you to do what you think best".

Then he turned to Dhira Mata and to Jaya and spoke of the greatness of the trust that he would leave in the hands of that disciple who should represent the interests of women when he should go West, of how it would exceed the responsibility of work for men. And he added, turning to the worker of the party, "Yes, you have faith, but you have not that burning enthusiasm that you need. You want to be consumed [with] energy. Shiva! Shiva!" And so, invoking the blessing of Mahâdeva, he said goodnight and left us, and we presently went to bed.

JULY 25

The next morning we breakfasted early in one of the tents and went on to Achhabal. One of us had had a dream of old jewels lost and restored, all bright and new. But the Swami, smiling, stopped the tale, saying, "Never talk of a dream as good as that!"

At Achhabal we found more gardens of Jehangir. Was it here or at Verinag that had been his favourite resting-place?

We roamed about the gardens and bathed in a still pool opposite the Pathan Khan's Zenana, and then we lunched in the first garden and rode down in the afternoon to Islamabad.

As we sat at lunch, the Swami invited his daughter to go to the cave of Amarnath with him and be dedicated to Shiva. Dhira Mata smiled permission, and the next half-hour was given to pleasure and congratulations. It had already been arranged that we were all to go to Pahalgam and wait there for the Swami's return from the pilgrimage. So we reached the boats that evening, packed and wrote letters, and next day in the afternoon started for Bawan.

CHAPTER IX

THE SHRINE OF AMARNATH

PLACE: Kashmir.
TIME: July 29 to August 8, 1898.

JULY 29

From this time we saw very little of the Swami. He was full of enthusiasm about the pilgrimage and lived mostly on one meal a day, seeking no company much, save that of Sâdhus. Sometimes he would come to a camping-ground, beads in hand. Tonight two of the party went roaming about Bawan, which was like a village fair, all modified by a religious tendency centering in the sacred springs. Afterwards with Dhira Mata it was possible to go and listen at the tent door to the crowd of Hindi-speaking Sadhus who were plying the Swami with questions.

On Thursday we reached Pahalgam and camped down at the lower end of the valley. We found that the Swami had to encounter high opposition over the question of our admission at all. He was supported by the Naked Swamis, one of whom said, "It is true you have this strength, Swamiji, but you ought not to manifest it!" He yielded at the word. That afternoon, however, he took his daughter round the camp to be blessed, which really meant to distribute alms — and whether because he was looked upon as rich or because he was recognized as strong, the next day our tents were moved up to a lovely knoll at the head of the camp...

JULY 30

How beautiful was the route to the next halt, Chandanwari! There we camped on the edge of a ravine. It rained all afternoon, and I was visited by the Swami only for a five-minutes' chat. But I received endless touching little kindnesses from the servants and other pilgrims...

Close to Chandanwari the Swami insisted on my doing my first glacier on foot and took care to point out every detail of interest. A tremendous climb of some thousands of feet was the next experience. Then a long walk along a narrow path that twisted round mountain after mountain, and finally another steep climb. At the top of the first mountain, the ground was simply carpeted with edelweiss. Then the road passed five hundred feet above Sheshnag with its sulky water, and at last we camped in a cold damp place amongst the snow-peaks, 18,000 feet high. The firs were far below, and all afternoon and evening the coolies had to forage for juniper in all directions. The Tahsildar's, Swami's and my own tents were all close together, and in the evening a large fire was lighted in front. But it did not burn well, and many feet below lay the glacier. I did not see the Swami after we camped.

Panchatarani — the place of the five streams — was not nearly such a long march. Moreover, it was lower than Sheshnag, and the cold was dry and exhilarating. In front of the camp was a dry riverbed, all gravel, and through this ran five streams, in all of which it was the duty of the pilgrim to bathe, walking from one to the other in wet garments. Contriving to elude observation completely, Swamiji nevertheless fulfilled the law to the last letter in this respect…

At these heights we often found ourselves in great circles of snow-peaks, those mute giants that have suggested to the Hindu mind the idea of the ash-encovered God.

AUGUST 2

On Tuesday, August the 2nd, the great day of Amarnath, the first batch of pilgrims must have left the camp at two! We left by the light of the full moon. The sun rose as we went down the narrow valley. It was not too safe at this part of the journey. But when we left our Dandies and began to climb, the real danger began…Then, having at last reached the bottom of the farther slope, we had to toil along the glacier mile after mile to the cave…

The Swami, exhausted, had by this time fallen behind…He came at last and with a word sent me on; he was going to bathe. Half an hour later he entered the cave. With a smile he knelt first at one end of the semi-circle, then at the other. The place was vast, large enough to hold a cathedral; and the great ice-Shiva, in a niche of deepest shadow, seemed as if throned on its own base. A few minutes passed, and then he turned to leave the cave.

To him, the heavens had opened. He had touched the feet of Shiva. He had had to hold himself tight, he said afterwards, lest he "should swoon away". But so great was his physical exhaustion that a doctor said afterwards that his heart ought to have stopped beating, but had undergone a permanent enlargement instead. How strangely near fulfilment had been those words of his Master, "When he realizes who and what he is, he will give up this body!"

"I have enjoyed it so much!" he said half an hour afterwards, as he sat on a rock above the streamside, eating lunch with the kind Naked Swami and me. "I thought the ice Linga was Shiva Himself. And there were no thievish Brahmins, no trade, nothing wrong. It was all worship. I never enjoyed any religious place so much!"

Afterwards he would often tell of the overwhelming vision that had seemed to draw him almost into its vertex. He would talk of the poetry of the white ice-pillar; and it was he who suggested that the first discovery of the place had been by a party of shepherds, who had wandered far in search of their flocks one summer day and had entered the cave to find themselves before the unmelting ice, in the presence of the Lord Himself. He always said too that the grace of Amarnath had been granted to him there, not to die till he himself should give consent. And to me he said, "You do not now understand. But you have made the pilgrimage, and it will go on working. Causes must bring their effects. You will understand better afterwards. The effects will come".

How beautiful was the road by which we returned next morning to Pahalgam! We struck tents that night immediately on our return to them and camped later for the night in a snowy pass a whole stage further on. We paid a coolie a few annas here to push on with a letter; but when we actually arrived next afternoon we found that this had been quite unnecessary, for all morning long relays of pilgrims had been passing the tents and dropping in, in the most friendly manner, to give the others news of us and our impending arrival. In the morning we were up and on the way long before dawn. As the sun rose before us, while the moon went down behind, we passed above the Lake of Death, into which about forty pilgrims had been buried one year by an avalanche which their hymns had started. After this we came to the tiny goat-path down the face of a steep cliff by which we were able to shorten the return journey so much. This was little better than a scramble, and everyone had perforce to do it on foot. At the bottom the villagers had something like breakfast ready. Fires were burning, Chapatties baking, and tea was ready to be served out. From this time on parties of pilgrims would leave the main body at each parting of the ways, and the feeling of solidarity that had grown up amongst us all throughout the journey became gradually less and less.

That evening on the knoll above Pahalgam, where a great fire of pine-logs was lighted and Dhurries spread, we all sat and talked. Our friend the Naked Swami joined us and we had plenty of fun and nonsense, but presently, when all had gone save our own little party, we sat on with the great moon overhead and the towering snows and rushing rivers and the mountain-pines. And the Swami talked of Shiva and the cave and the great verge of vision.

AUGUST 8

We started for Islamabad next day, and on Monday morning as we sat at breakfast, we were towed safely into Srinagar.

CHAPTER IX

AT SRINAGAR ON THE RETURN JOURNEY

PERSONS: The Swami Vivekananda and a party of Europeans and disciples, amongst whom were Dhira Mata, the "Steady Mother"; one whose name was Jaya; and Nivedita.

PLACE: Kashmir — Srinagar.
TIME: August 9 to August 13, 1898.

AUGUST 9

At this time the Master was always talking of leaving us. And when I find the entry "The river is pure that flows, the monk is pure that goes", I know exactly what it means — the passionate outcry "I am always so much better when I have to undergo hardships and beg my bread", the longing for freedom and the touch of the common people, the picture of himself making a long circuit of the country on foot and meeting us again at Baramulla for the journey home.

His family of boat-people, whom he had staunchly befriended through two seasons, left us today. Afterwards he would refer to the whole incident of their connection with him as proof that even charity and patience could go too far.

AUGUST 10

It was evening, and we all went out to pay some visit. On the return he called his disciple Nivedita to walk with him across the fields. His talk was all about the work and his intentions in it. He spoke of the inclusiveness of his conception of the country and its religions; of his own distinction as being solely in his desire to make Hinduism active, aggressive, a missionary faith; of "don't-touch-ism" as the only thing he repudiated. Then he talked with depth of feeling of the gigantic spirituality of many of those who were most orthodox. India wanted practicality, but she must never let go her hold on the old meditative life for that. "To be as deep as the ocean and as broad as the sky", Shri Ramakrishna has said, was the ideal. But this profound inner life in the soul encased within orthodoxy is the result of an accidental, not an essential, association. "And if we set ourselves right here, the world will be right, for are we not all one? Ramakrishna Paramahamsa was alive to the depths of his being, yet on the outer plane he was perfectly active and capable."

And then of that critical question of the worship of his own master, "My own life is guided by the enthusiasm of that great personality, but others will decide for themselves how far this is true for them. Inspiration is not filtered out to the world through one man".

AUGUST 11

There was occasion this day for the Swami to rebuke a member of this party for practising palmistry. It was a thing he said that everyone desired, yet all India despised and hated. Yes, he said, in reply to a little special pleading, even of character-reading he disapproved. "To tell you the truth, I should have thought even your incarnation more honest if he and his disciples had not performed miracles. Buddha unfrocked a monk for doing it." Later, talking on the subject to which he had now transferred his attention, he spoke with horror of the display of the least of it as sure to bring a terrible reflex.

AUGUST 12 AND 13

The Swami had now taken a Brahmin cook. Very touching had been the arguments of the Amarnath Sâdhus against his willingness to let even a Mussulman cook for him. "Not in the land of Sikhs at least, Swamiji", they had said, and he had at last consented. But for the present he was worshipping his little Mohammedan boat-child as Umâ. Her whole idea of love was service, and the day he left Kashmir she, tiny one, was fain to carry a tray of apples for him all the way to the tonga herself. He never forgot her, though he seemed quite indifferent at the time. In Kashmir itself he was fond of recalling the time when she saw a blue flower on the towing path and sitting down before it, and striking it this way and that, "was alone with that flower for twenty minutes".

There was a piece of land by the riverside on which grew three chennaars, towards which our thoughts turned with peculiar love at this time. For the Mahârâjâ was anxious to give it to Swamiji, and we all pictured it as a centre of work in the future — work which should realize the great idea of "by the people, for the people, as a joy to worker and to served".

In view of Indian feeling about a homestead blessed by women, it had been suggested that we should go and annex the site by camping there for a while. One of our party, moreover, had a personal wish for special quiet at this time. So it was decided that we should establish "a women's Math", as it were, before the Maharaja should require the land to confer it on the Swami. And this was possible because the spot was one of the minor camping grounds used by Europeans.

CHAPTER IX

THE CAMP UNDER THE CHENNAARS

PERSONS: The Swami Vivekananda and a party of Europeans and disciples, amongst whom were Dhira Mata, the "Steady Mother"; one whose name was Jaya; and Nivedita.

PLACE: Kashmir — Srinagar.

TIME: August 14 to August 20, 1898.

AUGUST 14

It was Sunday morning and next afternoon the Swami was prevailed on to come up to tea with us in order to meet a European guest who seemed to be interested in the subject of Vedanta. He had been little inclined to concern himself with the matter, and I think his real motive in accepting was probably to afford his too-eager disciples an opportunity of convincing themselves of the utter futility of all such attempts as this. Certainly he took infinite pains with the enquirer and, as certainly, his trouble was wasted.

I remember his saying, amongst other things, "How I wish a law could be broken. If we were really able to break a law we should be free. What you call breaking the law is really only another way of keeping it". Then he tried to explain a little of the superconscious life. But his words fell on ears that could not hear.

AUGUST 16

On Tuesday he came once more to our little camp to the midday meal. Towards the end it began to rain heavily enough to prevent his return, and he took up Tod's History of Rajasthan, which was lying near, and drifted into talk of Mirâ Bâi. "Two-thirds of the national ideas now in Bengal", he said, "have been gathered from this book".

But the episode of Mira Bai, the queen who would not be queen, but would wander the world with the lovers of Krishna, was always his favourite, even in Tod. He talked of how she preached submission, prayerfulness, and service to all in contrast to Chaitanya, who preached love to the name of God, and mercy to all.

Mira Bai was always one of his great patronesses. He would put into her story many threads with which one is now familiar in other connections, such as the conversation of two great robbers, and the end by an image of Krishna opening and swallowing her up. I heard him on one occasion recite and translate one of her songs to a woman. I wish I could remember the whole, but it began in his rendering with the words "Cling to it, cling to it, cling to it, Brother", and ended with "If Ankâ and Bankâ, the robber brothers; Sujan, the fell butcher; and the courtesan who playfully taught her parrot to repeat the name of the Lord Krishna were saved, there is hope for all".

Again, I have heard him tell that marvellous tale of Mira Bai in which on reaching Vrindaban, she sent for a certain famous Sâdhu.[6]* He refused to go on the ground that women might not see men in Vrindaban. When this had happened three times, Mira Bai went to him herself saying that she had not known that there were such beings as men there; she had supposed that Krishna alone existed. And when she saw the astonished Sadhu, she unveiled herself completely, with the words "Fool, do you call yourself a man?" And as he fell prostrate before her with a cry of awe, she blessed him as a mother blesses her child.

Today the Swami passed on to the talk of Akbar and sang us a song of Tânsen, the poet-laureate of the emperor:

Seated on the throne, a god amongst men,
Thou, the Emperor of Delhi.
Blessed was the hour, the minute, the second,
When thou ascendest the throne,
O God amongst men,
Thou, the Lord of Delhi.
Long live thy crown, thy sceptre, thy throne,
O God amongst men,
Thou, Emperor of Delhi.
Live long, and remain awakened always,
O son of Humayoon,
Joy of the sun, God amongst men,
Thou, the Emperor of Delhi!

Then the talk passed to "our national hero" Pratâp Singh, who never could be brought to submission. Once indeed he was tempted to give in, at that moment when having fled from Chitore and the queen herself having cooked the scanty evening meal, a hungry cat swooped down on that cake of bread which was the children's portion, and the King of Mewar heard his babies cry for food. Then, indeed, the strong heart of the man failed him. The prospect of ease and relief tempted him. And for a moment he thought of ceasing from the unequal conflict and sending his alliance to Akbar, only for an instant. The Eternal Will protects its own. Even as the picture passed before his mind, there appeared a messenger with those despatches from a famous Rajput chief that said, "There is but one left amongst us who has kept his blood free from admixture with the alien. Let it never be said that his head has touched the dust". And the soul of Pratap drew in the long breath of courage and renewed faith; and he arose and swept the country of its foes and made his own way back to Udaipur.

Then there was the wonderful tale of the virgin princess Krishna Kumâri, whose hand was sought by various royal suitors at once. And when three armies were at the gate, her father could think of nothing better than to give her poison. The task was entrusted to her uncle, and he entered her room, as she lay asleep, to do it. But at the sight of her beauty and youth, remembering her too as a baby, the soldier's heart failed him, and he could not perform his task. But she was awakened by some sound, and being told what was proposed, stretched out her hand for the cup and drank the poison with a smile. And so on, and so on. For the stories of Rajput heroes in this kind are endless.

AUGUST 20

On Saturday the Swami and he whose name was Soong went to the Dahl Lake to be the guests of the American consul and his wife for a couple of days. They returned on Monday, and on Tuesday the Swami came up to the new Math, as we called it, and had his boat moved close by ours so that he could be with us for a few days before leaving for Ganderbal.

CONCLUDING WORDS OF THE EDITOR

From Ganderbal the Swami returned by the first week of October and announced his intention of leaving for the plains in a few days for urgent reasons. The European party had already made plans to visit the principal cities of northern India, e.g., Lahore, Delhi, Agra, etc., as soon as the winter set in. So both parties decided to return together and came to Lahore. From here the Swami and his party returned to Calcutta, leaving the rest to carry out their plans for sight-seeing in northern India.

SAYINGS AND UTTERANCES

LIST OF ABBREVIATIONS

In this section, only Swami Vivekananda's direct words have been placed within quotation marks. References have been identified by the following abbreviations:

ND → Burke, Marie Louise. Swami Vivekananda in the West: New Discoveries. 6 vols. Calcutta: Advaita Ashrama, 1983-87.

CWSN → Nivedita, Sister. The Complete Works of Sister Nivedita. Vol. 1. Calcutta: Advaita Ashrama, 1982.

LSN → Nivedita, Sister. Letters of Sister Nivedita. 2 vols. Compiled and edited by Sankari Prasad Basu. Calcutta: Nababharat Publishers, 1982.

VIN → Basu, Sankari Prasad and Ghosh, Sunil Bihari, eds. Vivekananda in Indian Newspapers: 1893-1902. Calcutta: Dineshchandra Basu, Basu Bhattacharya and Co., 1969.

* * * * *

1. From Mrs. Prince Woods's description of Swami Vivekananda's departure from the Woods's residence in Salem, Massachusetts, in August 1893. Swami Vivekananda gave his staff, his most precious possession, to Dr. Woods, who was at that time a young medical student, and his trunk and his blanket to Mrs. Kate T. Woods, saying:

"Only my most precious possessions should I give to my friends who have made me at home in this great country." (ND 1: 42)

2. On the back of Swami Vivekananda's transcription from Louis Rousselet's book India and Its Native Princes —Travels in Central India and in the Presidencies of Bombay and Bengal, dated February 11, 1894:

"I say there is but one remedy for one too anxious for the future — to go down on his knees." (ND 1: 225)

3. An extract from a prayer Swami Vivekananda delivered at the Chicago World's Parliament of Religions:

"Thou art He that beareth the burdens of the universe; help me to bear the little burden of this life." (ND 2: 32)

4. An extract from another prayer offered by Swami Vivekananda at the Chicago World's Parliament of Religions:

"At the head of all these laws, in and through every particle of matter and force, stands One through whose command the wind blows, the fire burns, the clouds rain, and death stalks upon the earth. And what is His nature? He is everywhere the pure and formless One, the Almighty and the All Merciful. Thou art our Father. Thou art our beloved Friend." (ND 2: 33)

5. From Mary T. Wright's journal entry dated Saturday, May 12, 1894:

The widows of high caste in India do not marry, he said; only the widows of low caste may marry, may eat, drink, dance, have as many husbands as they choose, divorce them all, in short enjoy all the benefits of the highest society in this country...

"When we are fanatical", he said, "we torture ourselves, we throw ourselves under huge cars, we cut our throats, we lie on spiked beds; but when you are fanatical you cut other people's throats, you torture them by fire and put them on spiked beds! You take very good care of your own skins!" (ND 2: 58-59)

6. An 1894 extract from the Greenacre Voice, quoting one of the Swami's teachings delivered at Greenacre, Maine:

"You and I and everything in the universe are that Absolute, not parts, but the whole. You are the whole of that Absolute." (ND 2: 150)

7. In a March 5, 1899 letter from Sister Nivedita to Miss Josephine MacLeod:

"I am at heart a mystic, Margot, all this reasoning is only apparent — I am really always on the lookout for signs and things — and so I never bother about the fate of my initiations. If they want to be Sannyâsins badly enough I feel that the rest is not my business. Of course it has its bad side. I have to pay dearly for my blunder sometimes — but it has one advantage. It has kept me still a Sannyasin through all this — and that is my ambition, to die a real Sannyasin as Ramakrishna Paramahamsa actually was — free from lust — and desire of wealth, and thirst for fame. That thirst for fame is the worst of all filth." (ND 3: 128-29)

8. From John Henry Wright's March 27, 1896 letter to Mary Tappan Wright, in which Swami Vivekananda stated that England is just like India with its castes:

"I had to have separate classes for the two castes. For the high caste people — Lady This and Lady That, Honourable This and Honourable That — I had classes in the morning; for the low caste people, who came pell-mell, I had classes in the evening." (ND 4: 73)

9. While Swami Vivekananda was offering flowers at the feet of the Virgin Mary in a small chapel in Switzerland in the summer of 1896, he said:

"For she also is the Mother." (ND 4: 276)

10. From Mr. J. J. Goodwin's October 23, 1896 letter to Mrs. Ole Bull, quoting Swami Vivekananda's conversation at Greycoat Gardens in London

"It is very good to have a high ideal, but don't make it too high. A high ideal raises mankind, but an impossible ideal lowers them from the very impossibility of the case." (ND 4: 385)

11. A November 20, 1896 entry from Swami Abhedananda's diary, quoting Swami Vivekananda's observation of the English people:

"You can't make friends here without knowing their customs, behaviour, politics. You have to know the manners of the rich, the cultured and the poor." (ND 4: 478)

12. In Mr. J. J. Goodwin's November 11, 1896 letter to Mrs. Ole Bull, quoting Swami Vivekananda's unpublished statement toward the end of "Practical Vedanta — IV":

"A Jiva can never attain absolutely to Brahman until the whole of Mâyâ disappears. While there is still a Jiva left in Maya, there can be no soul absolutely free…Vedantists are divided on this point." (ND 4: 481)

13. From Swami Saradananda's letter to a brother-disciple, concerning Swami Vivekananda's last days:

Sometimes he would say, "Death has come to my bedside; I have been through enough of work and play; let the world realize what contribution I have made; it will take quite a long time to understand that". (ND 4: 521)

14. In an October 13, 1898 letter to Mrs. Ashton Jonson, written from Kashmir, Sister Nivedita described Swami Vivekananda's spiritual mood:

To him at this moment "doing good" seems horrible. "Only the Mother does anything. Patriotism is a mistake. Everything is a mistake. It is all Mother…All men are good. Only we cannot reach all…I am never going to teach any more. Who am I that I should teach anyone? …Swamiji is dead and gone." (ND 5: 3-4)

15. From Mr. Sachindranath Basu's letter recounting Swami Vivekananda's closing remarks in his talk to swamis and novices assembled at Belur Math, June 19, 1899:

"My sons, all of you be men. This is what I want! If you are even a little successful, I shall feel my life has been meaningful." (ND 5: 17)

16. During an evening talk with Swami Saradananda in the spring of 1899:

"Men should be taught to be practical, physically strong. A dozen such lions will conquer the world, not millions of sheep. Men should not be taught to imitate a personal ideal, however great." (ND 5: 17)

17. From Mrs. Mary C. Funke's reminiscences of her August 1899 voyage to America with Swamis Vivekananda and Turiyananda:

"And if all this Maya is so beautiful, think of the wondrous beauty of the Reality behind it!" (ND 5: 76)

"Why recite poetry when there [pointing to sea and sky] is the very essence of poetry?" (Ibid.)

18. In Miss Josephine MacLeod's September 3,

1899 letter to Mrs. Ole Bull:

"In one's greatest hour of need one stands alone." (ND 5: 122)

19. From Sister Nivedita's October 27, 1899 diary entry at Ridgely Manor, in which Swami Vivekananda expressed his concern for Olea Bull Vaughn:

"Nightmares always begin pleasantly — only at the worst point [the] dream is broken — so death breaks [the] dream of life. Love death." (ND 5: 138)

20. In a December 1899 letter from Miss Josephine MacLeod to Sister Nivedita:

"All the ideas the Californians have of me emanated from Chicago." (ND 5: 179)

21. From Mrs. Alice Hansbrough's reminiscences which quoted Swami Vivekananda as telling Mr. Baumgardt:

"I can talk on the same subject, but it will not be the same lecture." (ND 5: 230)

22. Mrs. Alice Hansbrough's reminiscences relating Swami Vivekananda's response to her sight-seeing attempts:

"Do not show me sights. I have seen the Himalayas! I would not go ten steps to see sights; but I would go a thousand miles to see a [great] human being!" (ND 5: 244)

23. From Mrs. Alice Hansbrough's reminiscences relating Swami Vivekananda's interest in the problem of child training:

He did not believe in punishment. It had never helped him, he said, and added, "I would never do anything to make a child afraid". (ND 5: 253)

24. Mrs. Alice Hansbrough's record of Swami Vivekananda's explanation of God to seventeen-year-old Ralph Wyckoff:

"Can you see your own eyes? God is like that. He is as close as your own eyes. He is your own, even though you can't see Him." (ND 5: 254)

25. Mrs. Alice Hansbrough's reminiscences regarding Swami Vivekananda's opinion of the low-caste English soldiers who occupied India:

"If anyone should despoil the Englishman's home, the Englishman would kill him, and rightly so. But the Hindu just sits and whines!

"Do you think that a handful of Englishmen could rule India if we had a militant spirit? I teach meat-eating throughout the length and breadth of India in the hope that we can build a militant spirit!" (ND 5: 256)

26. Mrs. Alice Hansbrough's reminiscences of a picnic in Pasadena, California when a Christian Science woman suggested to Swami Vivekananda that one should teach people to be good:

"Why should I desire to be 'good'? All this is His handiwork [waving his hand to indicate the trees and the countryside]. Shall I apologize for His handiwork? If you want to reform John Doe, go and live with him; don't try to reform him. If you have any of the Divine Fire, he will catch it." (ND 5: 257)

27. From Mrs. Alice Hansbrough's reminiscences:

"When once you consider an action, do not let anything dissuade you. Consult your heart, not others, and then follow its dictates." (ND 5: 311)

28. From Mr. Frank Rhodehamel's notes taken during a March 1900 lecture in Oakland, California:

"Never loved a husband the wife for the wife's sake, or the wife the husband for the husband's sake. It is God in the wife the husband loves, and God in the husband the wife loves. (Cf. Brihadâranyaka Upanishad II.4.5.) It is God in everyone that draws us to that one in love. [It is] God in everything, in everybody that makes us love. God is the only love…In everyone is God, the Atman; all else is but dream, an illusion." (ND 5: 362)

29. From Mr. Frank Rhodehamel's notes taken during a March 1900 lecture in Oakland, California:

Oh, if you only knew yourselves! You are souls; you are gods. If ever I feel [that I am] blaspheming, it is when I call you man." (ND 5: 362)

30. An excerpt from Mr. Thomas J. Allan's remi-

niscences of Swami Vivekananda's March 1900 San Francisco lecture series on India:

"Send us mechanics to teach us how to use our hands, and we will send you missionaries to teach you spirituality." (ND 5: 365)

31. Mrs. Edith Allan's reminiscences of Swami Vivekananda's philosophical observations while cooking at the Turk Street flat:

"'The Lord dwells in the hearts of all beings, O Arjuna, by His illusive power causing all beings to revolve as though mounted on a potter's wheel.' [Bhagavad-Gitâ XVIII.61] This has all happened before, like the throw of a dice, so it is in life; the wheel goes on and the same combination comes up; that pitcher and glass have stood there before, so, too, that onion and potato. What can we do, Madam, He has us on the wheel of life." (ND 6: 17)

32. From Mrs. Edith Allan's reminiscences of an after-lunch conversation:

"The Master said he would come again in about two hundred years — and I will come with him. When a Master comes, he brings his own people." (ND 6: 17)

33. Mrs. Edith Allan's reminiscences of Swami Vivekananda's "kitchen" counsel while he was staying in San Francisco, California, in 1900:

"If I consider myself greater than the ant that crawls on the ground I am ignorant." (ND 6: 19)

"Madam, be broad—minded; always see two ways. When I am on the heights I say, 'Shivoham, Shivoham: I am He, I am He!' and when I have the stomachache I say, 'Mother have mercy on me!'" (Ibid.)

"Learn to be the witness. If two dogs are fighting on the street and I go out there, I get mixed up in the fight; but if I stay quietly in my room, I witness the fight from the window. So learn to be the witness." (Ibid.)

34. From Mr. Thomas J. Allan's reminiscences of a private talk with Swami Vivekananda in San Francisco, California, 1900:

"We do not progress from error to truth, but from truth to truth. Thus we must see that none can be blamed for what they are doing, because they are, at this time, doing the best they can. If a child has an open razor, don't try to take it from him, but give him a red apple or a brilliant toy, and he will drop the razor. But he who puts his hand in the fire will be burned; we learn only from experience." (ND 6: 42)

35. From Mrs. Alice Hansbrough's reminiscences of a walk home with Swami Vivekananda after one of his lectures in San Francisco in 1900:

"You have heard that Christ said, 'My words are spirit and they are life'. So are my words spirit and life; they will burn their way into your brain and you will never get away from them!" (ND 6: 57-58)

36. From Mrs. Alice Hansbrough's reminiscences in San Francisco, 1900 — referring to Swami Vivekananda's great heart:

"I may have to be born again because I have fallen in love with man." (ND 6: 79)

37. From Mrs. George Roorbach's reminiscences of Swami Vivekananda at Camp Taylor, California, in May 1900:

"In my first speech in this country, in Chicago, I addressed that audience as 'Sisters and Brothers of America', and you know that they all rose to their feet. You may wonder what made them do this, you may wonder if I had some strange power. Let me tell you that I did have a power and this is it — never once in my life did I allow myself to have even one sexual thought. I trained my mind, my thinking, and the powers that man usually uses along that line I put into a higher channel, and it developed a force so strong that nothing could resist it." (ND 6: 155)

38. In a conversation with Swami Turiyananda, which probably took place in New York:

"The call has come from Above: 'Come away, just come away — no need of troubling your head to teach others'. It is now the will of the Grand Old Lady (The "Grand Old Lady" was a figure in a children's game, whose touch put one outside the game.) that the play should be over." (ND 6: 373)

39. In a July 1902 Prabuddha Bharata eulogy, "a

Western disciple" wrote:

The Swami had but scant sympathy with iconoclasts, for as he wisely remarked, "The true philosopher strives to destroy nothing, but to help all". (VIN: 638)

40. Sister Nivedita's reminiscences of Swami Vivekananda in an October 9, 1899 letter to Miss Josephine MacLeod:

He has turned back on so much — "Let your life in the world be nothing but a thinking to yourself". (LSN I: 213)

41. Swami Vivekananda's luncheon remarks to Mrs. Ole Bull, recorded by Sister Nivedita in an October 18, 1899 letter to Miss Josephine MacLeod:

"You see, there is one thing called love, and there is another thing called union. And union is greater than love.

"I do not love religion. I have become identified with it. It is my life. So no man loves that thing in which his life has been spent, in which he really has accomplished something. That which we love is not yet ourself. Your husband did not love music for which he had always stood. He loved engineering in which as yet he knew comparatively little. This is the difference between Bhakti and Jnana; and this is why Jnana is greater than Bhakti." (LSN I: 216)

42. Swami Vivekananda's remarks on his spiritual ministry, recorded in Sister Nivedita's October 15, 1904 letter to Miss Josephine MacLeod:

"Only when they go away will they know how much they have received." (LSN II: 686)

43. Sister Nivedita's reminiscences in a November 5, 1904 letter to Alberta Sturges (Lady Sandwich) of Swami Vivekananda's talk on renunciation while he was staying at Ridgely Manor:

"In India we never say that you should renounce a higher thing for a lower. It is better to be absorbed in music or in literature than in comfort or pleasure, and we never say otherwise." (LSN II: 690)

44. In Sister Nivedita's November 19, 1909 letter to Miss Josephine MacLeod:

"The fire burns if we plunge our hand in — whether we feel it or not — so it is with him who speaks the name of God." (LSN II: 1030)

45. Swami Vivekananda's reminiscences of Shri Ramakrishna, recorded in Sister Nivedita's July 6, 1910 letter to Dr. T. K. Cheyne:

"He could not imagine himself the teacher of anyone. He was like a man playing with balls of many colours, and leaving it to others to select which they would for themselves." (LSN II: 1110)

46. Sister Nivedita's reminiscences of a conversation with Swami Vivekananda at Ridgely Manor, recorded in an 1899 letter written from Ridgely Manor to Miss Josephine MacLeod:

I have never heard the Prophet talk so much of Shri Ramakrishna. He told us what I had heard before of [his master's] infallible judgement of men…

"And so", Swami said, "you see my devotion is the dog's devotion. I have been wrong so often and he has always been right, and now I trust his judgement blindly". And then he told us how he would hypnotize anyone who came to him and in two minutes know all about him, and Swami said that from this he had learnt to count our consciousness as a very small thing. (LSN II: 1263)

47. From Sister Nivedita's January 27, 1900 letter to Sister Christine:

Swami said today that he is beginning to see the needs of humanity in quite a different light — that he is already sure of the principle that is to help, but is spending hours every day in trying to solve the methods. That what he had known hitherto is for men living in a cave — alone, undisturbed — but now he will give "humanity something that will make for strength in the stress of daily life". (LSN II: 1264)

48. In a July 7, 1902 letter to Sister Christine, Sister Nivedita recorded one of Swami Vivekananda's remarks made while giving a class to the monks at

Belur Math on July 4, 1902:

"Do not copy me. Kick out the man who imitates." (LSN II: 1270)

49. The Swami's comment after he made a statement concerning the ideal of the freedom of the soul, which brought it into apparent conflict with the Western conception of the service of humanity as the goal of the individual:

"You will say that this does not benefit society. But before this objection can be admitted you will first have to prove that the maintenance of society is an object in itself." (CWSN 1: 19)

50. Sister Nivedita wrote:

He touched on the question of his own position as a wandering teacher and expressed the Indian diffidence with regard to religious organization or, as someone expresses it, "with regard to a faith that ends in a church". "We believe", he said, "that organization always breeds new evils".

He prophesied that certain religious developments then much in vogue in the West would speedily die, owing to love of money. And he declared that "Man proceeds from truth to truth, and not from error to truth". (CWSN 1: 19-20)

51. "The universe is like a cobweb and minds are the spiders; for mind is one as well as many." (CWSN 1: 21)

52. "Let none regret that they were difficult to convince! I fought my Master for six years with the result that I know every inch of the way! Every inch of the way!" (CWSN 1: 22)

53. Swami Vivekananda was elucidating to what heights of selflessness the path of love leads and how it draws out the very best faculties of the soul:

"Suppose there were a baby in the path of the tiger! Where would your place be then? At his mouth — any one of you — I am sure of it." (CWSN 1: 24)

54. "That by which all this is pervaded, know That to be the Lord Himself!" (CWSN 1: 27)

55. Concerning Swami Vivekananda's attitude toward religion:

Religion was a matter of the growth of the individual, "a question always of being and becoming". (CWSN 1: 28)

56. "Forgive when you also can bring legions of angels to an easy victory." While victory was still doubtful, however, only a coward to his thinking would turn the other cheek. (CWSN 1: 28-29)

57. "Of course I would commit a crime and go to hell forever if by that I could really help a human being!" (CWSN 1: 34)

58. To a small group, including Sister Nivedita, after a lecture:

"I have a superstition — it is nothing, you know, but a personal superstition! — that the same soul who came once as Buddha came afterwards as Christ." (CWSN 1: 35)

59. After Swami Vivekananda was told of Sister Nivedita's willingness to serve India:

"For my own part I will be incarnated two hundred times, if that is necessary, to do this work amongst my people that I have undertaken." (CWSN 1: 36)

60. Sister Nivedita's memory of an incident:

He was riding on one occasion with the Raja of Khetri, when he saw that his arm was bleeding profusely and found that the wound had been caused by a thorny branch which he had held aside for himself to pass. When the Swami expostulated, the Rajput laughed the matter aside. "Are we not always the defenders of the faith, Swamiji?" he said.

"And then", said the Swami, telling the story, "I was just going to tell him that they ought not to show such honour to the Sannyasin, when suddenly I thought that perhaps they were right after all. Who knows? Maybe I too am caught in the glare of this flashlight of your modern civilization, which is only for a moment".

" — I have become entangled", he said simply to one who protested that to his mind the wandering Sâdhu of earlier years, who had scattered his knowledge and changed his name as he went, had been greater than the abbot of Belur, burdened with much work and many cares. "I have become entangled." (CWSN 1: 43)

61. Sister Nivedita wrote:

One day he was talking in the West of Mirâ Bâi — that saint who once upon a time was Queen of Chitore — and of the freedom her husband had offered her if only she would remain within the royal seclusion. But she could not be bound. "But why should she not?" someone asked in astonishment. "Why should she?" he retorted. "Was she living down here in this mire?" (CWSN 1: 44)

62. As years went by, the Swami dared less and less to make determinate plans or dogmatize about the unknown:

"After all, what do we know? Mother uses it all. But we are only fumbling about." (CWSN 1: 44)

63. Quoting Swami Vivekananda, Sister Nivedita remembered:

Love was not love, it was insisted, unless it was "without a reason" or without a "motive"…(CWSN 1: 52)

64. About Swami Vivekananda, Sister Nivedita wrote:

When asked by some of his own people what he considered, after seeing them in their own country, to be the greatest achievement of the English, he answered "that they had known how to combine obedience with self-respect". (CWSN 1: 54)

65. Swami Sadananda reported that early in the morning, while it was still dark, Swami Vivekananda would rise and call the others, singing:

"Awake! Awake! all ye who would drink of the divine nectar!" (CWSN 1: 56)

66. Sister Nivedita remembered:

At this time [during the Swami's itinerant days, near Almora] he passed some months in a cave overhanging a mountain village. Only twice have I known him to allude to this experience. Once he said, "Nothing in my whole life ever so filled me with the sense of work to be done. It was as if I were thrown out from that life in caves to wander to and fro in the plains below". And again he said to someone, "It is not the form of his life that makes a Sadhu. For it is possible to sit in a cave and have one's whole mind filled with the question of how many pieces of bread will be brought to one for supper!" (CWSN 1: 61)

67. About his own poem "Kali the Mother":

"Scattering plagues and sorrows", he quoted from his own verses,

Dancing mad with joy,

Come, Mother, come!

For terror is Thy name!

Death — is in Thy breath.

And every shaking step

Destroys a world for e'er.

"It all came true, every word of it", he interrupted himself to say.

Who dares misery love.

Dance in Destruction's dance,

And hug the form of death,…

"To him the Mother does indeed come. I have proved it. For I have hugged the form of Death!" (CWSN 1: 98-99)

68. Sister Nivedita, referring to her plans for a girls' school:

Only in one respect was he [Swami Vivekananda] inflexible. The work for the education of Indian women, to which he would give his name, might be as sectarian as I chose to make it. "You wish through a sect to rise beyond all sects." (CWSN 1: 102)

69. Commenting on Sister Nivedita's visit to Gopaler-Ma's dwelling — a small cell:

"Ah! this is the old India that you have seen, the India of prayers and tears, of vigils and fasts, that is passing away, never to return!" (CWSN 1: 109)

70. About the aims of the Ramakrishna Order:

The same purpose spoke again in his definition of the aims of the Order of Ramakrishna — "to effect an exchange of the highest ideals of the East and the West and to realize these in practice"...(CWSN 1: 113)

71. After teaching Sister Nivedita the worship of Shiva, Swami Vivekananda then culminated it in an offering of flowers at the feet of the Buddha. He said, as if addressing each soul that would ever come to him for guidance:

"Go thou and follow Him, who was born and gave His life for others five hundred times before He attained the vision of the Buddha!" (CWSN 1: 114)

72. Upon returning from a pilgrimage in Kashmir:

"These gods are not merely symbols! They are the forms that the Bhaktas have seen!" (CWSN 1: 120)

73. Sister Nivedita's reminiscences of Swami Vivekananda's words heard long before:

"The Impersonal God seen through the mists of sense is personal." (CWSN 1: 120)

74. Swami Vivekananda's comment when he was reminded of the rareness of criminality in India:

"Would God it were otherwise in my land, for this is verily the virtuousness of death!" (CWSN 1: 123)

75. Swami Vivekananda said:

"The whole of life is only a swan song! Never forget those lines:

The lion, when stricken to the heart,

gives out his mightiest roar.

When smitten on the head, the cobra lifts its hood. And the majesty of the soul comes forth,

only when a man is wounded to his depths."

(CWSN 1: 124)

76. After hearing of the death of Shri Durga Charan Nag (Nag Mahashay):

"[He] was one of the greatest of the works of Ramakrishna Paramahamsa." (CWSN 1: 129)

77. About Shri Ramakrishna's transformative power, Swami Vivekananda said:

"Was it a joke that Ramakrishna Paramahamsa should touch a life? Of course he made new men and new women of those who came to him, even in these fleeting contacts!" (CWSN 1: 130)

78. While speaking on the true spirit of a Sannyasin, Swami Vivekananda said:

"I saw many great men in Hrishikesh. One case that I remember was that of a man who seemed to be mad. He was coming nude down the street, with boys pursuing and throwing stones at him. The whole man was bubbling over with laughter while blood was streaming down his face and neck. I took him and bathed the wound, putting ashes on it to stop the bleeding. And all the time with peals of laughter he told me of the fun the boys and he had been having, throwing the stones. 'So the Father plays', he said.

"Many of these men hide, in order to guard themselves against intrusion. People are a trouble to them. One had human bones strewn about his cave and gave it out that he lived on corpses. Another threw stones. And so on...

"Sometimes the thing comes upon them in a flash. There was a boy, for instance, who used to come to read the Upanishads with Abhedananda. One day he turned and said, 'Sir, is all this really true?'

"'Oh yes!' said Abhedananda, 'It may be difficult to realize, but it is certainly true'.

"And next day, that boy was a silent Sannyasin, nude, on his way to Kedarnath!

"What happened to him? you ask. He became silent!

"But the Sannyasin needs no longer to worship or to go on pilgrimage or perform austerities. What then is the motive of all this going from pilgrimage to pilgrimage, shrine to shrine, and austerity to austerity? He is acquiring merit and giving it to the world!" (CWSN 1: 133)

79. Referring to the story of Shibi Rana:

"Ah yes! These are the stories that are deep in our nation's heart! Never forget that the Sannyasin takes two vows: one to realize the truth and one to help the world — and that the most stringent of stringent requirements is that he should renounce any thought of heaven!" (CWSN 1: 134)

80. To Sister Nivedita:

"The Gîtâ says that there are three kinds of charity: the Tâmasic, the Râjasic and the Sâttvic. Tamasic charity is performed on an impulse. It is always making mistakes. The doer thinks of nothing but his own impulse to be kind. Rajasic charity is what a man does for his own glory. And Sattvic charity is that which is given to the right person, in the right way, and at the proper time. . .

"When it comes to the Sattvic, I think more and more of a certain great Western woman in whom I have seen that quiet giving, always to the right person in the right way, at the right time, and never making a mistake.

"For my own part, I have been learning that even charity can go too far. . .

"As I grow older I find that I look more and more for greatness in little things. I want to know what a great man eats and wears, and how he speaks to his servants. I want to find a Sir Philip Sidney (Sir Philip Sidney (1554-1586): English poet, soldier and politician.) greatness! Few men would remember the thirst of others, even in the moment of death.

"But anyone will be great in a great position! Even the coward will grow brave in the glare of the footlights. The world looks on. Whose heart will not throb? Whose pulse will not quicken till he can do his best?

"More and more the true greatness seems to me that of the worm doing its duty silently, steadily, from moment to moment and from hour to hour." (CWSN 1: 137)

81. Referring to the great individual — the divine incarnation, the Guru, and the Rishi:

"You do not yet understand India! We Indians are man — worshippers, after all! Our God is man!" (CWSN 1: 144)

82. On another occasion, Swami Vivekananda used the word "man-worshippers" in an entirely different sense:

"This idea of man—worship exists in nucleus in India, but it has never been expanded. You must develop it. Make poetry, make art, of it. Establish the worship of the feet of beggars as you had it in Mediaeval Europe. Make man-worshippers." (CWSN 1: 144-45)

83. To Sister Nivedita:

"There is a peculiar sect of Mohammedans who are reported to be so fanatical that they take each newborn babe and expose it, saying, 'If God made thee, perish! If Ali made thee, live!' Now this, which they say to the child, I say, but in the opposite sense, to you tonight: 'Go forth into the world and there, if I made you, be destroyed! If Mother made you, live'!" (CWSN 1: 151)

84. Long after Southern magnates in America had apologized to Vivekananda when they learned that he had been mistaken for a Negro and was thus refused admission into hotels, the Swami remarked to himself:

"What! rise at the expense of another! I didn't come to earth for that! …If I am grateful to my white-skinned Aryan ancestor, I am far more so to my yellow-skinned Mongolian ancestor and, most so of all, to the black-skinned Negritoid!" (CWSN 1: 153)

85. Commenting on the dungeon-cages of mediaeval prisoners on Mont-Saint-Michel:

(CWSN 1: 154)

"Oh, I know I have wandered over the whole earth, but in India I have looked for nothing save the cave in which to meditate!" (Ibid.)

86. Though he considered offspring of the Roman Empire to be brutal and the Japanese notion of marriage a horror, Swami Vivekananda nevertheless summed up the constructive ideals, never the defects, of a community:

"For patriotism, the Japanese! For purity, the Hindu! And for manliness, the European! There is no other in the world who understands, as does the Englishman, what should be the glory of a man!"

(CWSN 1: 160)

87. Swami Vivekananda said of himself before he left for America in 1893:

"I go forth to preach a religion of which Buddhism is nothing but a rebel child and Christianity, with all her pretensions, only a distant echo!" (CWSN 1: 161)

88. Describing the night Buddha left his wife to renounce the world, Swami Vivekananda said:

"What was the problem that vexed him? Why! It was she whom he was about to sacrifice for the world! That was the struggle! He cared nothing for himself!" (CWSN 1: 172)

89. After describing Buddha's touching farewell to his wife, the Swami said:

"Have you never thought of the hearts of the heroes? How they were great, great, great — and soft as butter?" (CWSN 1: 172)

90. Swami Vivekananda's description of Buddha's death and its similarity with that of Shri Ramakrishna's:

He told how the blanket had been spread for him beneath the tree and how the Blessed One had lain down, "resting on his right side like a lion" to die, when suddenly there came to him one who ran for instruction. The disciples would have treated the man as an intruder, maintaining peace at any cost about their Master's death-bed, but the Blessed One overheard, and saying, "No, no! He who was sent (Lit., "the Tathâgata". "A word", explained Swami Vivekananda, "which is very like your 'Messiah'".) is ever ready", he raised himself on his elbow and taught. This happened four times and then, and then only, Buddha held himself free to die. "But first he spoke to reprove Ananda for weeping. The Buddha was not a person but a realization, and to that any one of them might attain. And with his last breath he forbade them to worship any."

The immortal story went on to its end. But to one who listened, the most significant moment had been that in which the teller paused — at his own words "raised himself on his elbow and taught" — and said, in brief parenthesis, "I saw this, you know, in the case of Ramakrishna Paramahamsa". And there rose before the mind the story of one, destined to learn from that teacher, who had travelled a hundred miles, and arrived at Cossipore only when he lay dying. Here also the disciples would have refused admission, but Shri Ramakrishna intervened, insisting on receiving the new-comer, and teaching him. (CWSN 1: 175-176)

91. Commenting on the historic and philosophic significance of Buddhistic doctrine:

"Form, feeling, sensation, motion and knowledge are the five categories in perpetual flux and fusion. And in these lies Maya. Of any one wave nothing can be predicated, for it is not. It but was and is gone. Know, O Man, thou art the sea! Ah, this was Kapila's philosophy, but his great disciple [Buddha] brought the heart to make it live!" (CWSN 1: 176)

92. Concerning the Buddhist First Council and the dispute as to its President:

"Can you imagine what their strength was? One said it should be Ananda, because he had loved Him most. But someone else stepped forward and said no! for Ananda had been guilty of weeping at the death-bed. And so he was passed over!" (CWSN 1: 177)

93. Considering reincarnation a "scientific speculation" rather than an article of faith:

"Why, one life in the body is like a million years of confinement, and they want to wake up the memory of many lives! Sufficient unto the day is the evil thereof! ...Yes! Buddhism must be right! Reincarnation is only a mirage! But this vision is to be reached by the path of Advaita alone!" (CWSN 1: 180-81)

94. "Had I lived in Palestine, in the days of Jesus of Nazareth, I would have washed his feet, not with my tears, but with my heart's blood!" (CWSN 1: 189)

95. "For the Advaitin, therefore, the only motive is love...It is the Saviour who should go on his way rejoicing, not the saved!" (CWSN 1: 197-98)

96. On the necessity of restraint in a disciple's life:

"Struggle to realize yourself without a trace of emotion! …Watch the fall of the leaves, but gather the sentiment of the sight from within at some later time!" (CWSN 1: 207)

"Mind! No loaves and fishes! No glamour of the world! All this must be cut short. It must be rooted out. It is sentimentality—the overflow of the senses. It comes to you in colour, sight, sound, and associations. Cut it off. Learn to hate it. It is utter poison!" (Ibid., 207-208)

97. On the value of types:

"Two diffferent races mix and fuse, and out of them rises one strong distinct type. A strong and distinct type is always the physical basis of the horizon. It is all very well to talk of universalism, but the world will not be ready for that for millions of years!

"Remember! if you want to know what a ship is like, the ship has to be specified as it is — its length, breadth, shape, and material. And to understand a nation, we must do the same. India is idolatrous. You must help her as she is. Those who have left her can do nothing for her!" (CWSN 1: 209)

98. Describing the Indian ideal of Brahmacharya in the student's life, Swami Vivekananda said:

"Brahmacharya should be like a burning fire within the veins!" (CWSN 1: 216)

99. Concerning marriage by arrangement instead of choice, Swami Vivekananda said:

"There is such pain in this country! Such pain! Some, of course, there must always have been. But now the sight of Europeans with their different customs has increased it. Society knows that there is another way!

[To a European] "We have exalted motherhood and you, wifehood; and I think both might gain by some interchange.

"In India the wife must not dream of loving even a son as she loves her husband. She must be Sati. But the husband ought not to love his wife as he does his mother. Hence a reciprocated affection is not thought so high as one unreturned. It is 'shopkeeping'. The joy of the contact of husband and wife is not admitted in India. This we have to borrow from the West. Our ideal needs to be refreshed by yours. And you, in turn, need something of our devotion to motherhood." (CWSN 1: 221-22)

100. Speaking to a disciple with great compassion:

"You need not mind if these shadows of home and marriage cross your mind sometimes. Even to me, they come now and again!" (CWSN 1: 222)

101. On hearing of the intense loneliness of a friend:

"Every worker feels like that at times!" (CWSN 1: 222)

102. Concerning the Hindu and Buddhist monastic and non-monastic ideals:

"The glory of Hinduism lies in the fact that while it has defined ideals, it has never dared to say that any one of these alone was the one true way. In this it differs from Buddhism, which exalts monasticism above all others as the path that must be taken by all souls to reach perfection. The story given in the Mahâbhârata of the young saint who was made to seek enlightenment, first from a married woman and then from a butcher, is sufficient to show this. 'By doing my duty', said each one of these when asked, 'by doing my duty in my own station, have I attained this knowledge'. There is no career then which might not be the path to God. The question of attainment depends only, in the last resort, on the thirst of the soul." (CWSN 1: 223)

103. With reference to the idea that the lover always sees the ideal in the beloved, Swami Vivekananda responded to a girl's newly avowed love:

"Cling to this vision! As long as you can both see the ideal in one another, your worship and happiness will grow more instead of less." (CWSN 1: 224)

104. "The highest truth is always the simplest." (CWSN 1: 226)

105. Swami Vivekananda's remarks on American séances:

"Always the greatest fraud by the simplest means." (CWSN 1: 233)

106. On Western and Eastern views of a person as a body or a soul:

"Western languages declare that man is a body and has a soul; Eastern languages declare that he is a soul and has a body." (CWSN 1: 236-37)

107. Concerning Swami Vivekananda's reverence for his Guru:

"I can criticize even an Avatâra [divine incarnation] without the slightest diminution of my love for him! But I know quite well that most people are not so; and for them it is safest to protect their own Bhakti!" (CWSN 1: 252)

"Mine is the devotion of the dog! I don't want to know why! I am contented simply to follow!" (Ibid., 252-53)

108. "Ramakrishna Paramahamsa used to begin every day by walking about in his room for a couple of hours, saying 'Satchidânanda!' or 'Shivoham!' or some other holy word." (CWSN 1: 255)

109. A few months before his passing away, Swami Vivekananda said:

"How often does a man ruin his disciples by remaining always with them! When men are once trained, it is essential that their leader leaves them; for without his absence they cannot develop themselves!" (CWSN 1: 260)

110. A few days before his passing away, the Swami said:

"I am making ready for death. A great Tapasyâ and meditation has come upon me, and I am making ready for death." (CWSN 1: 261-62)

111. In Kashmir after an illness, Swami Vivekananda said as he lifted a couple of pebbles:

"Whenever death approaches me, all weakness vanishes. I have neither fear, nor doubt, nor thought of the external. I simply busy myself making ready to die. I am as hard as that [the pebbles struck one another in his hand] — for I have touched the feet of God!" (CWSN 1: 262)

NEWSPAPER REPORTS

PART I: AMERICAN NEWSPAPER REPORTS

To preserve the historical authenticity of these newspapers reports, their original spelling, grammar and punctuation have been retained. For the sake of clarity, Swami Vivekananda's original words have been placed in block quotations and titles supplied by the Publisher have been marked with asterisks. Whenever possible, the original news typescripts have been selected, rather than their belated foreign reprints.–Publisher

RESPONSE TO WELCOME[1]

Editorial synthesis of four Chicago newspaper reports from: Herald, Inter Ocean, Tribune, and Record, ca. September 11, 1893.[2]

[Sisters and Brothers of America,]

It fills my heart with joy unspeakable to rise in response to the grand words of welcome given to us by you. I thank you in the name of the most ancient order of monks the world has ever seen, of which Gautama was only a member. I thank you in the name of the Mother of religions, of which Buddhism and Jainism are but branches; and I thank you, finally, in the name of the millions and millions of Hindoo people of all castes and sects. My thanks also to some of the speakers on the platform who have told you that these different men from far-off nations will bear to the different lands the idea of toleration which they may see here. My thanks to them for this idea.

I am proud to belong to a religion which has taught the world both tolerance and universal acceptance. We believe not only in universal tolerance but we accept all religions to be true. I am proud to tell you that I belong to a religion in whose sacred language, the Sanskrit, the word exclusion is untranslatable. (Applause) I am proud to belong to a nation which has sheltered the persecuted and the refugees of all religions and all nations of the earth. I am proud to tell you that we have gathered in our bosom the purest remnant of the Israelites, a remnant of which came to southern India and took refuge with us in the very years in which their holy temple was shattered to pieces by Roman tyranny. I am proud to belong to the religion which has sheltered and is still fostering the remnant of the grand Zoroastrian nation. I will quote to you, brothers, a few lines from a hymn which every Hindoo child repeats every day. I feel that the very spirit of this hymn, which I remember to have repeated from my earliest boyhood, which is every day repeated by millions and millions of men in India, has at last come to be realized. "As the different streams, having their sources in different places, all mingle their water in the sea; O Lord, so the different paths which men take through different tendencies, various though they appear, crooked or straight, all lead to Thee."

The present convention, which is one of the most august assemblies ever held, is in itself an indication, a declaration to the world of the wonderful doctrine preached in the Gita: "Whosoever comes to Me, through whatsoever form I reach him, all are struggling through paths that in the end always lead to me." Sectarianism, bigotry and its horrible descendant fanaticism, have possessed long this beautiful earth. It has filled the earth with violence, drenched it often and often with human gore, destroyed civilization and sent whole nations into despair. But its time has come, and I fervently believe that the bell that tolled this morning in honor of the representatives of the different religions of the earth, in this parliament assembled, is the death-knell to all fanaticism (applause), that it is the death-knell to all persecution with the sword or the pen, and to all uncharitable feelings between brethren wending their way to the same goal, but through different ways.

---

1. *New Discoveries*, Vol. 1, pp. 83-84.

2. Cf. "Response to Welcome", *Complete Works*, I: 3-4, for a somewhat different version.

PARLOR TALK[1]

Chicago Record, September 11, 1893.

Four leaders of religious thought were sitting in Dr. Barrow's [Barrows's] parlor—the Jain, George Condin [Candlin], the missionary who has passed sixteen years in China, Swami Vivekananda, the learned Brahman[2] Hindoo, and Dr. John H. Barrows, the Chicago Presbyterian. These four talked as if they were brothers of one faith.[3]

The Hindoo is of smooth countenance. His rather fleshy face is bright and intelligent. He wears an orange turban and a robe of the same color. His English is very good. "I have no home," said he.

I travel about from one college to another in India, lecturing to the students. Before starting for America I had been for some time in Madras. Since arriving in this country I have been treated with utmost courtesy and kindness. It is very gratifying to us to be recognized in this Parliament, which may have such an important bearing on the religious history of the world. We expect to learn much and take back some great truths to our 15,000,000 faithful Brahmins.

RELIGION NOT THE CRYING NEED OF INDIA[4]

A verbatim transcript of the address, delivered at the Parliament of Religions, September 20, 1893][5] [Chicago Inter Ocean, September 21, 1893.

Suami Vivekananda

At the close of the reading of Mr. Headland's paper on "Religion in Peking" Dr. Momerie announced that the other speakers bulletined for the evening had failed to appear. It was but 9 o'clock, and the main auditorium and galleries were well filled. There was an outburst of applause as they caught sight of the Hindoo monk, Vivekananda, sitting in his orange robe and scarlet turban upon the platform. This popular Hindoo responded to the generous applause by saying that he did not come to speak to-night. He took occasion, however, to criticise many of the statements made in the paper by Mr. Headland. Referring to the poverty which prevails in China, he said that the missionaries would do better to work in appeasing hunger than in endeavoring to persuade the Chinese to renounce their faith of centuries and embrace Christianity at [as] the price of food. And then the Hindu stepped back on the platform and whispered to Bishop Keane, of the Catholic church, a moment. He then resumed his address by saying that Bishop Keane had told him that Americans would not be offended at honest criticism. He said he had heard of all the terrible things and horrible conditions which prevail in China but he had not heard that any asylums had been erected by Christians for remedying all these difficulties.

He said:

Christian brethren of America, you are so fond of sending out missionaries to save the souls of heathens. I ask you what have you done and are doing to save their bodies from starvation? (Applause). In India, there are 300,000,000 men and women living on an average of a little more than 50 cents a month. I have seen them living for years upon wild flowers. Whenever there was a little famine hundreds of thousands died of starvation. Christian missionaries come and offer life but only on condition that the Hindoos become Christians, abandoning the faith of their fathers and forefathers. Is it right? There are hundreds of asylums, but if the Mohammedans or the Hindoos go there they would be kicked out. There are thousands of asylums erected by Hindoos where anybody would be received. There are hundreds of churches that have been erected with the assistance of the Hindoos, but no Hindoo temples for which a Christian has given a penny.

What the East Needs

Brethren of America, the crying evil of the East is not religion. We have more than religion enough;

---

1. *New Discoveries*, Vol. I, pp. 60-61.

2. The Swami was a Kshatriya, not a Brahmin.

3. An unidentified talk (probably occurring on Sunday, September 10), of which there is no verbatim transcript available.

4. *New Discoveries*, Vol. 1, pp. 123-26.

5. Cf. "Religion Not the Crying Need of India", *Complete Works*, I: 20, for select quotations from the full address.

what they want is bread, but they are given a stone. (Applause). It is an insult to a suffering man dying of hunger to preach to him metaphysics. Therefore, if you wish to illustrate the meaning of "brotherhood" treat the Hindoo more kindly, even though he be a Hindoo and is faithful to his religion. Send missionaries to them to teach them how better to earn a better piece of bread and not to teach them metaphysical nonsense. (Great applause).

And then the monk said he was in ill health today and wished to be excused. But there were thunders of applause and cries of "Go on" and Mr.

Vivekananda continued.

The paper just read says something about the miserable and ignorant priest. The same may be said of India. I am one of those monks who have been described as beggarly. That is the pride of my life. (Applause). I am proud in that sense to be Christ-like. I eat what I have today and think not of tomorrow. "Behold the lilies of the field; they toil not, neither do they spin." The Hindoo carries that out literally. Many gentlemen present in Chicago sitting on this platform can testify that for the last twelve years I never knew whence my next meal was coming. I am proud to be a beggar for the sake of the Lord. The idea in the east is [that] to preach or teach anything for the sake of money is low and vulgar, but to teach the name of the Lord for pay is such a degradation as would cause the priest to lose caste and be spat upon. There is one suggestion in the paper that is true: If the priests of China and India were organized there is an enormous amount of potential energy which could be used for regeneration of society and humanity. I endeavored to organize it in India, but failed for lack of money. It may be I shall get the help I want in America.

But we know it is very hard for a heathen to get any help from "Christian people". (Great applause). I have heard so much of this land of freedom, of liberty and freedom of thought that I am not discouraged. I thank you, ladies and gentlemen.

And then the popular visitor bowed gracefully and sought to retire with a graceful smile, but the audience cried to him to proceed. Mr. Vivekananda, fairly bubbling with an expression of good nature, then explained the Hindoo theory of [re]incarnation. At the close of the address Dr. Momerie [a delegate from England] said that he now understood why the newspapers had well called this parliament an approach to the millennium...

THE CHICAGO LETTER[6]

New York Critic, November 11, 1893.

It was an outgrowth of the Parliament of Religions, which opened our eyes to the fact that the philosophy of the ancient creeds contains much beauty for the moderns. When we had once clearly perceived this, our interest in their exponents quickened, and with characteristic eagerness we set out in pursuit of knowledge. The most available means of obtaining it, after the close of the Parliament, was through the addresses and lectures of Suami Vivekananda, who is still in this city. His original purpose in coming to this country was to interest Americans in the starting of new industries among the Hindoos, but he has abandoned this for the present, because he finds that, as "the Americans are the most charitable people in the world," every man with a purpose comes here for assistance in carrying it out. When asked about the relative condition of the poor here and in India, he replied that our poor would be princes there, and that he had been taken through the worst quarter of the city only to find it, from the standpoint of his knowledge, comfortable and even pleasant.

A Brahmin of the Brahmins, Vivekananda gave up his rank to join the brotherhood of monks, where all pride of caste is voluntarily relinquished. And yet he bears the mark of race upon his person. His culture, his eloquence, and his fascinating personality have given us a new idea of Hindoo civilization. He is an interesting figure, his fine, intelligent, mobile face in its setting of yellows, and his deep, musical voice prepossessing one at once in his favor.[7] So it is not strange that he has been taken up by the lit-

---

[6]. *New Discoveries*, Vol. 1, pp. 162-63.

[7]. The Swami quoted this passage in his letter to Shri Haridas Viharidas Desai, written November 15, 1893 (Vide *Complete Works*, VIII: 327).

erary clubs, has preached and lectured in churches, until the life of Buddha and the doctrines of his faith have grown familiar to us. He speaks without notes, presenting his facts and his conclusions with the greatest art, the most convincing sincerity; and rising at times to a rich, inspiring eloquence. As learned and cultivated, apparently, as the most accomplished Jesuit, he has also something Jesuitical in the character of his mind; but though the little sarcasms thrown into his discourses are as keen as a rapier, they are so delicate as to be lost on many of his hearers. Nevertheless his courtesy is unfailing, for these thrusts are never pointed so directly at our customs as to be rude. At present he contents himself with enlightening us in regard to his religion and the words of its philosophers. He looks forward to the time when we shall pass beyond idolatry—now necessary in his opinion to the ignorant classes,—beyond worship, even, to a knowledge of the presence of God in nature, of the divinity and responsibility of man. "Work out your own salvation," he says with the dying Buddha; "I cannot help you. No man can help you. Help yourself."

RELIGIONS OF INDIA[1]

Viva Kananda, the Hindoo Orator Delivers an Interesting Lecture.[2]

Daily Cardinal, University of Wisconsin at Madison, November 21, 1893.

A crowded house greeted Viva Kananda at the Congregational Church last evening. The speaker was attired in native costume, which consisted of a cream turban, with yellow gown and cardinal sash.

The first part of the lecture was devoted to illustrating the many resemblances of Sanscrit [sic], the language of the Hindoos, to that of English. They have no word in their language which means salvation; to them it is freedom from bondage. They believe that man's real nature is perfect, and that cause and effect controls all except God. Religion was aptly illustrated by the story of the blind men who each felt of a portion of a huge elephant, and each thought the animal like the particular part he felt of it; so with religion each of the various sects have a part of the whole truth, while truth itself is infinite and no man can say "I have seen it all."

The Hindoo belief was shown to be one of the most charitable of beliefs. Persecution is something unknown in India; there is no such word in their language. The lecturer challenged the world to show an instance in Hindoo progress, of a Christian missionary being persecuted. A Greek historian, writing of them said: "No Hindoo man is dishonest, no Hindoo woman unchaste."

Viva Kananda came to this country from India in the interest of the world's congress of religions, and his lecture last evening on the "Religions of India," was an inspiration to all who heard him. He has a pleasant, clear-cut, dusky face, and a decidedly impressive manner and bearing. His voice is low and pleasant, with a secret something which rivets your attention at the start.

ALL RELIGIONS ARE TRUE SUCH IS THE MESSAGE BROUGHT FROM INDIA

By a Hindu Monk[3]

Daily Iowa Capitol, November 28, 1893.

Swami Vivekananda Tells of Ancient Faith Speaks again Tonight.[4]

It was a rare as well as an odd treat which the people of Des Moines enjoyed last evening at the Central Church of Christ. A monk, of the ancient faith of Brahma, made a happy presentation of that faith, not so much of its peculiarities as of its underlying principles. The audience was a good sized one, perhaps 500 or 600 persons being present. The main floor being well filled and there were perhaps a couple of hundred in the gallery.

The speaker opened by saying that all religious

---

1. *New Discoveries*, Vol. 1, p. 191.

2. Of which there is no verbatim transcript available. Cf. *Complete Works*, III: 481 for a less comprehensive report of the same lecture.

3. *New Discoveries*, Vol. 1, pp. 200-202.

4. The lecture was "The Hindu Religion", delivered November 27, 1893, of which there is no verbatim transcript available. Cf. *Complete Works*, III: 482-84, for different highlights of the same lecture.

systems were an attempt to answer the question What am I? This and the kindred ones, Whence Come I? and Whither Am I Going? are constantly recurring. Without following the speaker throughout the entire lecture, suffice it to say, that underlying the Hindu religion according to the speaker is the belief that "We are all divine". In each is a conscious spirit that survives the body and the mind and is a part of the absolute. The speaker very ably defended religion against the attacks of science. The latter can use only the five senses, and unless a thing can be proven to be by these senses [it] is disposed to doubt its existence. But does science know that there are only five senses? The speaker contended for the existence of a supersensuous sense; through which man obtains revelations of spiritual truths. The Hindu word for revelation is "Veda". Hence the "Vedas" are the revelations. These writings are not confined to those of the Hindus, but include those of all peoples; because said the speaker, all religions are true.

When "revelations" undertake to tell of material things they enter upon a domain which belongs to science and are not to be accepted. There was an ancient superstition that because Moses gave a revelation of the will of God, therefore everything Moses wrote must be true. There is a modern superstition that, because there are mistakes in the writings of Moses, therefore nothing Moses wrote is true. When Moses wrote the tables of the law he was inspired. When he told of the creation what he said was merely the speculations of Moses the Jew.

The speaker was not favorably impressed with the efforts to make Hindu converts—perverts he calls them—to Christianity, nor the converse. All religions being true, such perversions serve no good end. The Hindu religion the speaker claimed is not disposed to antagonize any belief; it absorbs them. As for tolerating different beliefs, the language of the Hindu has no word corresponding with the English word "intolerance". That language had a word for religion and one for sect. The former embraced all beliefs. The conception of the latter the speaker illustrated by telling the story of the frog, who had no idea there was any world outside the well in which he had always lived.

The speaker urged his hearers to cultivate the divine within them and to discard the "nonsense" of sects.

The lecturer is an able, dignified and forcible speaker. His mastery of English is perfect, there being only the faintest indications of a foreign accent. The lecturer was followed with closest attention by the audience. After the lecture, the speaker consented to answer questions to a portion of the audience that remained for that purpose. In the course of the answers he said that the Hindus were altogether opposed to the destruction of the life of any animal. He admitted the worship of the sacred cow. He said further that the Hindus had nothing answering to our church organizations. He was his own priest, bishop and pope...

A MESSAGE FROM INDIA[5]

Vive Kananda, the Famous Hindoo Monk and Scholar, Appears in Des Moines

Iowa State Register, November 28, 1893.

A Young Man of Thirty Years and a Big, Active Brain and True Heart.

The people of Des Moines had a glimpse of Oriental life and thought at its best yesterday, from the lips of the famous Hindoo monk, Swami Vive Kananda. A central figure in the great Parliament of Religions at Chicago this summer, where he coped with some of the greatest minds of the country with honor to himself and his people, he gave those who heard him, and especially those who met him at Dr. Breeden's, something new to think about. It was a message from over the sea, from another people of wholly different surroundings, training, customs and traditions, but as the monk says, the basic principles are the same in all religions. It is his doctrine that there is good in all religions and he preaches it with great power...

Yesterday afternoon he met a large number of the brightest women in Des Moines, members of the various literary clubs, at the invitation of Mrs. H.

---

5. *New Discoveries*, Vol. 1, pp. 204-6.

O. Breeden, at her home, 1318 Woodland avenue,[1] and he talked to them for two or three hours about his religion, his view of Christianity, in which he heartily concurs, and of the manners and customs of his people. The thing which Vive Kananda most strongly insists upon is that the Hindoo religion is not to be blamed for all that is bad in India any more than Christianity is to be blamed for all that is bad in America. And he insists that it is absurd to give Christianity credit for all the marvelous undertakings and achievements of the people who cherish it. He joins in the praise of the sublime things in the bible [sic], but says that when Moses undertook to speak of the creation of the world, he was merely Moses, the Jew and nothing more.

This view from the other side, and a sympathetic side at that, is a most helpful and instructive and intensely interesting one. Vive Kananda uses the purest English, for he was well educated in the English university, Calcutta.

He praises the American women most enthusiastically.

I do not know what would have become of me if it had not been for your women, he said to a reporter for The Register last night.

They took me up and took care of me and made all necessary arrangements for me. They are the best women in the world. They have been so kind to me, [the Swami said] with a grateful smile...

REINCARNATION[2]

Daily Iowa Capitol, November 29, 1893.

Swami Vivekananda last night talked of reincarnation.[3] It is based, he contended, on the fact that there never has been a new creation; that creation has existed coevally with God from all eternity. Departed souls find bodies to inhabit either better or worse than their former tenement, according as they made them fit for one or the other. The lecturer will speak again on Thanksgiving evening at the same place on the manners and customs of India.

AN INTELLECTUAL FEAST[4]

Iowa State Register, November 30, 1893.

The remarkable discussions started by the famous Hindu monk, Vive Kananda, were the topic of interest in intellectual circles yesterday.[5] Especially so was his comment on the work of American missionaries in India, and his strong defense of his own people and morals and religion. His position is that the people of India do not need any more religion, but training in the practical things of life that will enable them to cope with the English who have occupied India. Vive Kananda was the guest of Mr. F. W. Lehman and Mr. O. H. Perkins yesterday and in their company visited the state house, which he very much admired. He took a special interest in the portraits of the American Indians that he saw there...

A PRAYER MEETING[6]

Des Moines Daily News, November 30, 1893.

Vivekananda attended a prayer meeting Wednesday evening and witnessed the baptism of two young women. The service impressed him very much. He said:

I see. The sentiment is ennobling and the ceremony beautiful. It is the more impressive that the minister is honest, earnest and believes what he says.

ON AMERICAN WOMEN[7]

Daily Iowa Capitol, November 30, 1893.

The now celebrated Hindu monk, Swami Vivekananda will lecture for the last time in Des Moines tonight. He will speak on "Life in India" ["Manners and Customs of India"] a most interesting theme.

---

1. An informal talk of which there is no verbatim transcript available.

2. *New Discoveries*, Vol. 1, p. 206-7.

3. Of which there is no verbatim transcript available.

4. *New Discoveries*, Vol. 1, p. 208.

5. Of the Swami's discussions, talks and lectures in Des Moines, Iowa, lasting from November 27 until December 1, there are no available verbatim transcripts.

6. *New Discoveries*, Vol. 1, p. 207.

7. *New Discoveries*, Vol. 1, p. 208.

The renowned Hindu is a brilliant man about 30 years old. He says American women are lovely, but American men are entirely too practical.

ON THE BRAHMO SAMAJ[8]

Iowa State Register, December 1, 1893.

Before he left the city [Des Moines, Iowa], Vive Kananda took occasion to say a warm word of praise for the Bramo-somaj [sic], the work it is doing in India, especially for the women, and of its representative in this country. The visit of Vive Kananda, stirring as it did the intellectual centers of the city to their depths and starting a lively religious discussion, prepared the way for the present visitor [Nagarkar] from the Orient and heightened public interest in whatever he might have to say.

A WITTY HINDU[9]

Minneapolis Journal, December 15, 1893.

Swami Vivekananda Entertains Another Large Audience.

A large number of people assembled at the Unitarian church last evening for the purpose of listening to Swami Vivekananda of India. The customs and manners of the people of that country were described,[10] and during his lecture the Brahmin took occasion to show up some of the rough points of America. He is of the humorist order and his quick replies and witty sallies rarely failed to evoke applause. He would not admit that his people were wrong in everything, but there were a great many things peculiar to India which the Americans did not approve of and yet which might be all right. He had never seen husband and wife go before a magistrate to tell their troubles. They grew up with the idea that they were to be married and they loved each other as brothers and sisters.

---

8. Ibid., p. 215.

9. Ibid., pp. 216-17.

10. The lecture was "The Manners and Customs of India", of which there is no verbatim transcript available. Cf. the following American newspaper report, "The Manners and Customs of India", for other highlights of the lecture.

He described the customs of his country, the temples, the art of the juggler and all of the other peculiarities of oriental countries in a manner that was charming. Following the address a number of questions were asked by persons in the audience.

THE MANNERS AND CUSTOMS OF INDIA[11]

Minneapolis Tribune, December 15, 1893.

Swami Vive Kananda, the Brahmin priest, was greeted by a packed house last evening at the First Unitarian Church, when he appeared before his second Minneapolis audience. Vive Kananda is a bright, quick witted talker, ready at all points to attack or defend, and inserts a humor into his speeches that is not lost upon his auditors. He spoke last evening under the auspices of the Kappa Kappa Gammas of the University, and the audience embraced a large number of earnest thinking men and women, pleased to be enlightened upon the "Manners and Customs of India," which was his chosen subject.[12]

Robed in his native garb, with his hands for the most part clasped behind his back, Kananda paces back and forth the narrow platform, talking as he paces, with long pauses between his sentences, as if willing that his words should sink into the deepest soil. His talk is not so weighty that the frivolous mind may not appreciate some of his sayings, but he also speaks a philosophy that carries gravest truth. He tells of the manners and customs of India, of the divided life between the male and female, of the reverence for and holiness of women, and again of their degeneracy; of the calm and peaceful life, that yet is not true life because it is not liberty; he speaks of the Mohammedans, who form one-fifth of the Indian population, and that 65,000,000, equal to the entire population of the United States. He describes the magnificence of the temples, the art of the jugglers, who are the gypsies of the Indian race,

---

11. *New Discoveries*, Vol. 1, pp. 217-19.

12. Of which there is no verbatim transcript available. Cf. the preceding American newspaper report, "A Witty Hindu", for other highlights of the lecture.

and he touches upon the superstitions of the people, of how they fill the water jars and stand them in the doorway before starting on a journey; he speaks of the metaphysical knowledge of the plowman, who yet only knows that he "pays taxes to the government"; he admits the reverence of the Hindu for the river Ganges, and his ever lingering wish that he shall die on its banks; he tells all these things in a quiet, half supercilious voice that presently leads to some remark on the American way of doing things, and then his audience is in a ripple of laughter, and a tremor of clapping expresses amused acknowledgement of his sarcasm...

When some one at the close of his lecture asked him "What class of people are reached and converted by the missionaries?" he quickly replied, "You know as much about that, the American sees the reports, we never do", he has turned the query into a cause for smiling, and while the house regains its composure he paces quietly to and fro. The address was followed with the closest attention and was supplemented by several questions and answers among the audience, from whom he invited interrogation.

HINDU PHILOSOPHY[1]

Detroit Tribune, February 18, 1894.

Its Recent Expression by Vive Kananda—His Mission Worthy the Serious Attention of Americans—The Two Remarkable Things in the United States Which Gratifies the Distinguished Pagan—What Environment Will Do for Any People—Rap at Missionaries.

There has seldom been such a sensation in cultured circles in Detroit, as that created by the advent of Swami Vive Kananda, the learned Hindu monk, whose exceptional command of our own language has enabled us to receive impressions concerning ourselves from an oriental standpoint and to acquire knowledge of a people of whose peculiar civilization and philosophy we have heard so much.

Both in public and private the Hindu brother has talked freely and frankly. He acknowledges that the masses in India are very poor, very ignorant and are

[1]. *New Discoveries*, Vol. 1, pp. 366-69.

divided into a diversity of sects, with forms of worship varying from downright idolatry to the broadest and most liberal form of divine conception based on the brotherhood of man and the oneness of God. His mission, he says, is not to proselyte us—to try and make us think as he does—but to get means to start a college in India for the education of teachers who are to go among the common people and work a reform of existing evils, of which there are many. He states that India is priest-ridden to a harrowing degree. It is priest-craft that distorts truth and perpetuates ignorance. It is priest-craft that substitutes its own crude and narrow interpretations for truth, which perverts the people and prevents their moral progression. The Swami regards all sects and creeds from a broad basis. He even sees good in idolatry. It is an ideal, he thinks, for the ignorant whose mental capacity is insufficient to grasp abstract ideas, and who require a direct personification in some material form. He frankly states that we of the occident are also retarded in our progression by too much priest-craft, and that we are not free from idolatrous practices, in that some of our sects worship shrines, figures and pictures and even the sanctity with which the rostrum and pulpit of a modern church is regarded is an ideal idolatry.

Two Remarkable Things in This Country

The Swami notes two most remarkable things in this country, when asked his frank opinion of us: First, the superiority of our women, as regards influence in position and intellect. Second, in our charities and treatment of the poor, he says, we have almost solved the problem as to what shall be done with them. Not only in this, in the direction of hospitals and charitable institutions, but in our tremendous development of labor-saving machinery. He has no admiration for our material progress, as it does not make man better, nor for our boasted civilization, as we only ape and imitate the customs and manners of the English—sometimes to a very ridiculous extent. We are yet too young, to have a distinctive civilization; we have yet to assimilate the human sewerage of Europe we have allowed to be poured upon us, before we produce a distinct American type. [The writer goes on to say that the Swami's Indian background makes it difficult for him to understand that Western competitiveness is not undesirable but a primal law of nature itself—the survival of the fittest—and that inasmuch as "the dreamy and sentimental philosophy of the Hindoos" accounts for their poverty, degradation, and domination by a "mere handful of Englishmen," the Swami would do well neither to ignore nor to despise the materialism of the West. Having thus editorialized, he continues:]

His Criticism of Missionaries

If what he states is true about the results accomplished by foreign missions in India, the various boards of these various organizations would do well to consult him and follow his advice. It is for the betterment of his people he is here. But he says missionary work does no good; only adds additional sects and creeds to an already sect-ridden country; that the teachings of the Vedas, with which every Hindoo is familiar, is identical with the teachings of Christ. He makes the reasonable plea that foreign creeds and dogmas are not consonant with their inherited proclivities or civilization, and are consequently difficult to propagate.

The mission of Kananda is, however, one that should commend it[self] to every lover of humanity. He hopes to see the best of our material philosophy and progress infused into Hindoo civilization, and that, also, we may take lessons from them, until we shall all become, as we once were in ages past, brother Aryans, possessing a common civilization—the exalted philosophy of non-self, being alike without sect or creed in oneness with God.

Fred H. Seymour.[2]

A GOD EVERY DAY[3]

Detroit Tribune, February 19, 1894.

Rabbi Grossman is Refreshed by Swami Vive Kananda.

"I take your Jesus," Kananda said last Saturday evening [February 17].[4]

I take him to my heart as I take all the great and good of all lands and of all times. But you, will you take my Krishna to your heart? No—you cannot, you dare not—still you are the cultured and I am the heathen...

VIVE KANANDA LEAVES[5]

Detroit Journal, February 23, 1894.

He Tells Something About the Conditions of Hindoo Laborers.

Swami Vive Kananda repaid the admiration of his lady acquaintances by writing verses, at the same time religious and semi-sentimental, yesterday afternoon.[6] He departed this morning for Ada, O. [Ohio].

In a conversation concerning the material condition of the Hindu workingmen, the learned monk said that the poor lived on porridge alone. The laborer ate a breakfast of porridge, went off to his daily toil and returned in the evening to another breakfast of porridge and called it dinner. In most of the provinces the farmers were so poor that they could not afford to eat any of the wheat raised. A day laborer on a farm received only 12 pence a day, but a dollar in India brought 10 times as much as it would in this country. Cotton was raised, but its fiber was so short it had to be woven by hand, and even then it was necessary to import American and Egyptian cotton to mix with it.

---

2. One of the guests at Charles L. Freer's dinner party given in honour of Swami Vivekananda, on Saturday, February 17, 1894.

3. Vide: *New Discoveries*, Vol. 1, p. 348. This extract is from a sermon by Rabbi Grossman, "What Vive Kananda Has Taught Us", delivered February 18, 1894.

4. Vide "The Divinity of Man" (*Complete Works*, III: 496-501) and "Is India a Benighted Country?" (*Complete Works* IV: 198-202).

5. *New Discoveries*, Vol. 1, p. 380.

6. At the small farewell tea which Mrs. John J. Bagley held for her departing guest.

CULTURE AT HOME[1]

Detroit Evening News, February 25, 1894.
Anecdotes of Swami Vive Kananda's Visit to Detroit.

Anecdotes of Swami Vive Kananda's visit are numerous and amusing—at least they must have been amusing to him, although a little humiliating to the American self-love. One lady said: "I really was ashamed at the contrast between the knowledge possessed by him and by some of our Detroit men who consider themselves gentlemen of culture. At one dinner party a gentleman asked Kananda what books he would advise him to read on chemistry, whereupon the Hindu monk responded with a long list of English works on this science, which one would naturally expect an American to know more about than a Hindu. Another gentleman followed by a request as to books on astronomy, to which Kananda obligingly answered with another equally good list of English astronomical works. But his growing astonishment reached its climax when a lady spoke of 'The Christ,' and said, 'What do those words mean?' He again furnished the desired information, but in a tone growing slightly sarcastic."

Probably the choicest example of nineteenth century civilization and culture was given by a lady, who asked Kananda if he liked the English. He very naturally responded that he did not. Then she continued, with fine tact, to pursue the subject still further by touching references to that pleasant event, the Sepoy rebellion. As the Hindu grew excited she smiled at him ironically and said: "I thought I could disturb your philosophical Eastern calm."

KANANDA, THE PAGAN[2]

Detroit Tribune, March 11, 1894.
Attacked Christian Missions in Last Night's Lecture.
And his Words were Warmly Applauded by the Audience.

Christian Nations Kill and Murder, He Said, and Import Disease into Foreign Countries, then Add Insult to Injury by Preaching of a Crucified Christ.

Swami Vive Kananda lectured to a very large audience at the Detroit Opera House last night on "Christian Missions in India."[3] One could believe that the lecture was intended as an answer to the many statements of missionaries which have been aimed at Kananda during the past two weeks in this city.

Kananda was introduced by Honorable Thomas W. Palmer last night, who recited a fable by way of preface. "Two knights of honor once met on the field," he said, "and seeing a shield hanging on a tree they halted. One said: 'What a very fine silver shield.' The other replied that it was not silver but copper. Each disputed the other's statement until at last they got off their horses, tied them to the tree, and drawing their swords fought for several hours. After they were both well spent by the loss of blood they staggered against each other and fell on the opposite sides from where they had been fighting. Then one glanced up at the pendant shield and said: 'You were right, my friend. The shield is copper.' The other looked up and said: 'It is I who was mistaken. The shield is silver.' If they had looked at both sides of the shield in the first place it would have saved the loss of much blood. I think that if we looked at both sides of every question there would be less argument and fighting. "We have with us tonight a gentleman who, from the christian standpoint is, I suppose, a pagan. But he belongs to a religion which was old long before ours was thought of by men. I am sure that it will be pleasant to hear from the copper side of the shield. We have looked at it only from the silver side. Ladies and Gentlemen, Swami Vive Kananda."

Kananda, who had remained seated on the stage during Mr. Palmer's remarks, stepped to the front, clad in the orange robe and unique turban of the Brahman [sic] priest, bowed in acknowledgement of the welcoming applause, and launched at once into his subject.

---

1. *New Discoveries*, Vol. 1, p. 365.
2. *New Discoveries*, Vol. 1, pp. 410-16.

3. Cf. "Christianity in India", *Complete Works*, VIII: 214-9, for a somewhat less comprehensive report of the same lecture.

What India Is

[The Swami said:]

I do not know about the efforts of christian missionaries in China and Japan except through reading the books and literature on the subject, but I can speak about the efforts of christianizing India. But before I go into this I want to place before you an idea of what India is.

Then he explained in detail how the 300,000,000 inhabitants of India are divided into castes, between which there can be no affiliation, how the natives of the south cannot understand the language of the ones of the north, and vice versa. He told how the lower caste lived on the flesh of dead animals, and never bathed their bodies, and how impossible it would be for the higher class to mingle with them, although they were granted the protection of the same laws.

He referred to the first appearance of the christians in an attempt to evangelize the followers of Buddah [Buddha]. They were Spaniards, he said, and they discovered a temple near Ceylon, in which was presented a tooth of Buddah as a sacred relic. "The Spaniard christians thought that their God commanded them to go and fight and kill and murder," he said, and so they seized the tooth of Buddah and destroyed it. By the way, it was not a tooth of Buddah at all, but a relic manufactured by the priests—it was a foot long. (Laughter)

Every religion has its miracles; you needn't laugh because the tooth was a foot long. Well, after the Spaniards took away the tooth they converted a few hundred and killed a few thousands; and there Spain stops in the history of missionary efforts among the Buddhists.

The Portugese [sic] christians, he said, discovered the great temple at Bombay, built in the form of a body with three heads, in representation of the trinity as the Hindoo believes in a trinity. "The Portugese saw it and couldn't explain it," said Kananda, with a sarcastic ring in his voice, and so they concluded that it was of the devil, and gathered their forces and knocked off the three heads of the temple. The devil is such a handy man. I am sorry to see him so fast disappearing.

Then Kananda outlined the various stages of christian evangelization in India, and paid very high tribute to two or three missionaries, who, he said, had been great exceptions to the rule, and lived among the people to uplift and minister to their needs.

Antagonize Native Interests

The Hindoo priest told how as soon as the land came into possession of the English people every village had its white colony, which huddled itself together and withdrew from all association with the natives. Then when the missionaries reached the country, he said, they would naturally go at once among the English people, who sympathized with them and with whom they could converse. The missionaries know nothing of the native language, he says, and so they cannot dwell with the people. Most of them are married and for the sake of getting their wives into the English society they identify themselves with all their interests, and in doing so directly antagonize the interests of the natives, and make it impossible to get in touch with them. "We sometimes have famines in India," he said.

And so the young missionaries will hang about the fag end of a famine and give a starving native 5 shillings, and there you have him, a ready-made christian; take him. That was probably a baptist missionary, and so when a methodist missionary comes along he gives the same native 5 shillings, and his name is again registered as a convert. The only band of converts around each missionary is composed of those dependent upon him for a living. They have to be christians or starve. And they are dwindling as the money supply decreases. I am glad if you want to make christians in India by giving work and bread to the poor. God speed you to do that. There is one benefit that must be credited to the missionary movement. It makes education cheap. The missionaries bring some money with them from the people who send them, and the Indian government appropriates some, so that there are some very good colleges and schools available to the natives through missionaries. But I will be frank with you. There are no conversions from the schools to the christian religion. The Hindoo boy is very clever. He takes the bait, but never gets the hook.

The speaker said that the lady missionary goes into certain houses, gets four shillings a month, reads the Bible, while the native girls give indifferent attention, and teaches them to knit while they pay very keen attention. The girls, like the boys, he said are always alert to learn practical things, but they will give little heed to the christian religion, although they will espouse it if necessary to get the other advantages.

Most Missionaries Incompetent

"The most of the men whom you send us as missionaries are incompetent," he said.

I have never known of a single man who has studied Sanscrit [sic] before going to India as a missionary and yet all our books and literature are printed in it.

He suggested as an explanation of the visits of the missionaries that "perhaps the atheism and scepticism at home is pushing the missionaries out all over the world." When in India he said he had thought the sole business of christianity [was] to send all people to the fires of hell, but since coming to America he has found that there are a great many liberal men. He referred to the parliament of religions, and told how a certain editor of a presbyterian paper had written an article at the close of the parliament entitled "The Lying Hindoo," in which he had scored him very severely.

In the article the editor said that "while in the parliament he was here as our guest, but now that it is over we ought to make an enthusiastic attack against him and his false doctrines."

In referring to the medical missionaries in India Kananda said:

India requires health, but it must be health for people. And how can you help our people if you do not get in touch with them? When you come to us as missionaries you ought to throw over all idea of nationality. Jesus didn't go about among the English officials attending champagne suppers. He didn't care to have his wife get into high European society. If your missionary does not follow Christ what right has he to call himself a christian? We want missionaries of Christ. Let such come to India by the hundreds and thousands. Bring Christ's life to us and let it permeate the very core of society. Let Him be preached in every village and corner of India. But don't have your missionaries choose their profession as a means of livelihood. Let them have the call of Christ. Let them feel within that they were born for that work.

As far as converting India to christianity is concerned, there is no hope. If it were possible it ought not to be done. It would be dangerous; it would mark the destruction of all religions. If the whole universe should come to have the same temperament, physical or mental, destruction would immediately result. Why couldn't you convert the Jew? Why couldn't you make the Persians christians? Why is it that to every African who becomes a christian 100 become followers of Mohammed? Why can't you make an impression on India and China, and Japan? Because oneness of mental temperament all over the world would be death. Nature is too wise to allow such things.

Filled the World with Bloodshed

[The Swami said:]

The christian nations have filled the world with bloodshed and tyranny. It is their day now. You kill and murder and bring drunkenness and disease in our country, and then add insult to injury by preaching Christ and Him crucified. What christian voice goes through the land protesting against such horrors? I have never heard any. You drink the idea in your mothers' milk that you are angels and we are devils. It is not enough that there be sunlight; you must have the eyes to see it. It is not only necessary that there be goodness in people; you must have the appreciation of goodness within yourselves in order to distinguish it. This is in every heart until it has been murdered by superstition and hideous blasphemy.

Then Kananda drew a very beautiful simile to illustrate that the essential truths of all religions are [the] same, and all else is but incidental and unimportant environment. He told how the savage man might find a few jewels, and prizing them, tie them with a rude thong and string them about his neck. As he became slightly civilized he would perhaps exchange the thong for a string. Becoming still more enlightened he would fasten his jewels with a silken cord; and when possessed of a high civilization he would make an elaborate gold setting for his treasures. But throughout all the changes in settings the jewels—the essentials—would remain the same.

If the Hindoo wishes to criticize the christian religion he talks of the fables and miracles, and all the nonsense of the Bible, but he does not say one word in disparagement of the sermon on the mount, or of the beautiful life of Jesus. And so when the christian criticizes the Hindoo religion he talks about the dogmas and the temples, but he says nothing [should say nothing] against the morality and philosophy of the Hindoo. Help the Jew and let him help you. Help the Hindoo and let him help you. I deny that any human being has the faculty of seeing good at all who cannot see it in all places. There is the same beauty in the character of Christ and the character of Buddah. It is not an assimilation that we want, but adjustment and harmony. I ask the preachers to give up, first, the idea of nationality; and second, the idea of sects. God's children have no sects.

Much has been said about the ladies of India, and of their faults and condition. There are faults; God help us to make them right. We are thankful for your criticism of our women. But while you are speaking of them I will say that I should be glad to see a dozen spiritual women in America. Nice dress, wealth, brilliant society, operas, novels—. Even intellectuality is not all that there is for a man or woman. There should be also spirituality, but that side is entirely absent from christian countries. They live in India.

Vive Kananda's large audience listened very respectfully to his remarks last night, and once or twice applauded heartily.

AS THE WAVE FOLLOWS WAVE[1]

Detroit Tribune, March 20, 1894.
So Soul Follows Soul, According to Kananda.

Vive Kananda lectured to an audience of about 150 [according to the Journal, 500] at the Auditorium last night upon "Buddhism, the Religion of the Light of Asia."[2] Honorable Don M. Dickinson introduced him to the audience. "Who shall say that this system of religion is divine and that doomed?" asked Mr. Dickinson in his introductory remarks. "Who shall draw the mystic line?"

He also said that at one time the followers of Buddha were the unwilling allies of the christian religion. Kananda appeared in a robe of orange yellow with a sash-like cord about the waist, and a turban draped out of some eastern cloth of silken texture, the flowing end of which was brought in front over one shoulder.

Vive Kananda reviewed at length the early religions of India. He told of the great slaughter of animals on the altar of sacrifice; of Buddha's birth and life; of his puzzling questions to himself over the causes of creation and the reasons for existence; of the earnest struggle of Buddha to find the solution of creation and life; of the final result.

Buddha, he said, stood head and shoulders above all other men. He was one, he said, [of] whom his friends or enemies could never say that he drew a breath or ate a crumb of bread but for the good of all. "He never preached transmigration of the soul," said Kananda, except he believed one soul was to its successor like the wave of the ocean that grew and died away, leaving naught to the succeeding wave but its force. He never preached that there was a God, nor did he deny there was a God. "Why should we be good?" his disciples asked of him.

"Because," he said, "you inherited good. Let you in your turn leave some heritage of good to your successors. Let us all help the onward march of accumulated goodness, for goodness' sake."

---

1. *New Discoveries*, Vol. 1, pp. 441-43.

2. Of which there is no verbatim report available.

He was the first prophet. He never abused any one or arrogated anything to himself. He believed in our working out our own salvation in religion. "I can't tell you," he said, on his death bed, "nor any one. Depend not on any one. Work out your own religion [salvation]."

He protested against the inequality of man and man, or of man and beast. All life was equal, he preached. He was the first man to uphold the doctrine of prohibition in liquors. "Be good and do good," he said. "If there is a God you have him by being good. If there is no God, being good is good. He is to be blamed for all he suffers. He is to be praised for all his good."

He was the first who brought the missionaries into existence. He came as a savior to the downtrodden millions of India. They could not understand his philosophy, but they saw the man and his teachings and they followed him.

In conclusion Kananda said that Buddhism was the foundation of the christian religion; that the catholic church came from Buddhism.

WAYSIDE STORIES[1]

Detroit Evening News, March 21, 1894.

Curiosity, says our Hindoo visitor, is the most conspicuous trait of the American people, but he added that it is the way to knowledge. This has long been the European estimate of the American, or more strictly the Yankee character, and perhaps the Hindoo's comment was an echo of what he had heard the Englishmen in India say of the Hindoo monk.

A HINDOO MONK[2]

Bay City Times Press, March 21, 1894

He gave an interesting lecture at the Opera House last evening. It is rarely that Bay City people have the opportunity of listening to a lecture similar to the one given last evening by Swami Vive Kananda.

The gentleman is a native of India, having been born at Calcutta about 30 years ago. The lower floor of the Opera house was about half filled when the speaker was introduced by Dr. C. T. Newkirk. During his discourse, he scored the people of this country for their worship of the almighty dollar. It is true that there is caste in India. There, a murderer can never reach the top. Here, if he gets a million dollars he is as good as any one. In India, if a man is a criminal once, he is degraded forever. One of the great factors in the Hindoo religion is its tolerance of other religions and beliefs. Missionaries are much more severe on the religions of India than upon that of other Oriental countries, because the Hindoos allow them to be, thus carrying out one of their cardinal beliefs, that of toleration. Kananda is a highly educated and polished gentleman. It is said that he was asked in Detroit if the Hindoos throw their children into the river. Whereupon, he replied that they do not, neither do they burn witches at the stake. The speaker lectures in Saginaw tonight.

KANANDA ARRIVES[3]

Saginaw Evening News, March 21, 1894.

Swami Vive Kananda, the Hindu Monk, arrived this afternoon from Bay City and is registered at the Vincent. He dresses like a well to do American and speaks excellent English. He is slightly above the medium height, is stoutly built and his complexion resembles that of an Indian. In answer to a question by a NEWS representative, he said he learned English from private tutors, and by contact with Europeans, who visited Hindustan. He further stated that his talk tonight would be explanatory of the religion of the Hindoo and to show that they are not heathen but believe in a future state.

THE MANNERS AND CUSTOMS OF INDIA[4]

The Lynn Daily Evening Item, (date?).

---

1. *New Discoveries*, Vol. 1, p. 436.

2. *New Discoveries*, Vol. 2, pp. 6 7. Cf. "Swami Vivekananda on India", *Complete Works*, II: 479 81.

3. *New Discoveries*, Vol. 2, p. 11.

4. *The Vedanta Kesari*, 1987 Annual Issue, pp. 445 46 and *New Discoveries*, Vol. 2, pp. 37 39.

NORTH SHORE CLUB

The Meeting, Tuesday Afternoon, Addressed by Suami Vive Kananda, a Learned Monk from India—Description of the Manners and Customs of His Country[5]

At the meeting of the North Shore Club, Tuesday afternoon, the audience was a large and brilliant one, representing the highest culture, and including many distinguished guests. Suami Vive Kananda, from India, a learned monk, who speaks English with ease and fluency, gave an intensely interesting description of the manners and customs of his country. Suami Vive Kananda, who wore the yellow robe and turban of his order, began by saying that India is divided into two parts, the northern and the southern. In each the language and customs are so different that the speaker who was from the northern portion on meeting a fellow countryman at the Parliament of Religions from the southern, was obliged to converse with him in English, neither being able to understand the other's native language. Throughout the entire country there are nine languages and 100 dialects spoken.

There is some uniformity of religion, yet each sect is a religion and a law unto itself. Many erroneous descriptions have been written about India, based on imperfect knowledge from which inferences have been drawn that have been most prejudicial. With the Hindoo everything is subservient to religion and he gives up all that is antagonistic to it, his creed being that he is not to enjoy life but to conquer it and gain a supreme mastery over self, which is the highest type of civilization. Caste distinctions which are being obliterated are simply the Aryans and the un Aryans—the Brahmins and the Sudras. The Brahmin, who is the child of a thousand years' culture, must lead a life of rigid discipline; but the Sudra, who is ignorant, is allowed great latitude.

Woman in the position of mother is accorded universal reverence in India. When a son who has become a monk returns to his home, his father, when greeting him, must kneel and touch his forehead to the earth; but the monk must kneel before his mother. Women in India do not throw their children into the rivers to be devoured by crocodiles. Widows are not burned on the funeral pyre of their husband unless it is a voluntary act of self immolation.

There is no divorce allowed for the high class; a woman who leaves her husband, even if she be most degraded, holds still an interest in his property. Suami Vive Kananda recited a beautiful passage from the Legend of the Ramayana, one of the grandest poems of India, which showed what the love of a wife for her husband should be. The love of Sita for Rama. He added, "Much is said in these days of the 'survival of the fittest,'" and western nations use it as an argument against India, reasoning that their own wealth, prosperity and power show them to be greater and their religion higher and purer.

But India has seen mighty nations rise and fall whose aim has been only the power of conquest and the glory of this life. India has been repeatedly despÛoiled, has worn the yoke of the conqueror and borne the burden of oppression with indomitable patience and has shown tolerance to all, because she has possessed the knowledge that her people hold fast to a religion that stands securely on a high spirituality and not on the shifting sand of present enjoyment.

A LECTURE ON "INDIA AND HINDUISM"[6]

New York Daily Tribune, April 25, 1894.

Swami Vivekananda lectured before Mrs. Arthur Smith's conversation circle last evening at the Waldorf on "India and Hinduism."[7] Miss Sara Humbert, contralto, and Miss Annie Wilson, soprano, sang several selections. The lecturer wore an orange colored coat and the accompanying yellow turban, which is called a beggar's suit. This is worn when a Buddhist has given up "everything for God and humanity." The theory of reincarnation was discussed. The speaker said that many clergymen who

---

5. Delivered April 17, 1894, of which there is no verbatim transcript available.

6. *New Discoveries*, Vol. 2, p. 42.

7. Of which no verbatim transcript is available.

were more aggressive than learned asked: "Why one is unconscious of a former life if such a thing had been?" The reply was that "It would be childish to lay a foundation for consciousness, as man is unconscious of his birth in this life, and also of much that has transpired."

The speaker said that "no such thing" as "a Judgment Day" existed in his religion, and that his god neither punished nor rewarded. If wrong was done in any way, the natural punishment was immediate. The soul, he added, passed from one body to another, until it had become a perfect spirit, able to do without the limitations of a body...

AT SMITH COLLEGE, NORTHAMPTON, MASSACHUSETTS[1]

Smith College Monthly, May 1894.

On Sunday, April 15, Swami Vivekananda, the Hindoo monk whose scholarly exposition of Brahmanism caused such favorable comment at the Congress of Religions, spoke at Vespers.[2] —We say much of the brotherhood of man and the fatherhood of God, but few understand the meaning of these words. True brotherhood is possible only when the soul draws so near to the All Father that jealousies and petty claims of superiority must vanish because we are so much above them. We must take care lest we become like the frog of the well in the old Hindoo story, who, having lived for a long time in a small place, at last denied the existence of a larger space.

A LECTURE ON INDIA AND REINCARNATION[3]

New York Daily Tribune, May 3, 1894.

Swami Virekanmda [sic] lectured on "India and Reincarnation" last evening at the home of Miss Mary Phillips, No. 19 West Thirty eighth st.[4] He mentioned among other salient points regarding Hindooism, or Brahminism, that their religion bore no distinctive name; that it was considered that a belief in the truth of all creeds was religion, and that the belief that one certain dogma was the real and only religion was sect. The Karmic law of cause and effect was explained, also the external and internal natures in their close relations to each other. The actions in this world, as governed by a previous life and the change to still another life, were dwelt upon in detail.

LECTURE BY HINDOO MONK[5]

Swami Vivekananda Tells About the Religion of High Caste Indians[6]

Lawrence, Massachusetts, Evening Tribune, May 16, 1894.

Liberty hall was comfortably filled last evening, on the oc casion of the lecture by Swami Vivekananda, the noted Brahmin monk, who was a prominent personality at the world's parlia

ment of religions at Chicago last summer, and who is spending some time in this country, studying its manners and customs. The lecture was under the auspices of the woman's club, and was a novel and interesting occasion. The noted Hindu was pleasantly introduced by the president of the club, Miss Wetherbee, who alluded to the great antiquity of India, its wonderful history and the high intellectual qualities of the Hindu race.

The speaker of the evening was attired in native costume, namely, a bright scarlet robe, confined at the waist by a long scarf of the same color, and wore a picturesque white silk turban wound round his head. At the first glance one saw the swarthy complexion, the dark and dreamy eyes and introspective manner of a high caste Brahmin, whose life is devoted to religion and who is also a celibate. That he is a finely educated person, appeared in his wonderful command of English and his power of

---

1. *New Discoveries*, Vol. 2, pp. 36 37.
2. Of which no verbatim transcript is available.
3. *New Discoveries*, Vol. 2, p. 45.
4. Of which no verbatim transcript is available.
5. *New Discoveries*, Vol. 2, pp. 65 68.
6. Of which there is no verbatim transcript available.

argument, while an occasional quotation from Milton and Dickens, showed that he was appreciative of the great English classics.

He first spoke of that striking peculiarity of the social condition of the Hindu's caste, affirming that it is not now as strict an institution as in the past, although even now everything goes by heredity. Mixture of castes, though not absolutely forbidden, entails disadvantage on the children. The Brahmin or high caste person devotes the first part of his life to the study of the Vedas or sacred books and the latter part to meditating on the divinity, being supposed to have overcome the human in himself, and to be only a soul.

The speaker did not hesitate to criticise adversely some western customs, especially some connected with the position of woman. He affirmed that we worship women in the wife, while all women to the Hindu represent the mother element. In America when a woman ceases to be young and beautiful, she has a hard time of it, but in India kings must step aside for an aged woman to pass, so great is the respect in which they are held. He affirmed that some of the most beautiful portions of the Vedas, the Hindu bible, were written by women, but that there was no other bible in this world in which they had any part.

Considerable time was given to refuting the statement, which he characterized as untrue, in regard to the cruelty practised to widows in India, the speaker referring in the course of his remarks to the zenana widows, who have been for some time the objective point of Christian missionaries from other countries. Marriage is an institution very safely guarded and, in addition to the law that a Brahmin must not marry a relative, none are allowed to marry who are known to have such a disease as consumption or any incurable physical ill. The strict rules of caste which prevent a person from drinking from the same glass as another, and other kindred regulations, although [not] part of the religion, were excellent in their result on the physical condition of a country, numbering 285 millions, in the prevention of the spread of contagious diseases. The speaker was horrified, as he might well be, at the promiscuous water drinking seen in railroad trains and stations in this country. The children are, first of all, taught kindness to all living beings and so thoroughly is this training that the smallest child instinctively turns aside from stepping on a worm. A strange thought that among these so called heathen there is no need of the society with the long name which often fails in its mission in Christian lands.[7] The guest of a house, that is, a man who comes to the door and says, "I am hungry," is God's own image to the Hindu and is treated with the utmost kindness and consideration, being fed before the master and mistress of the establishment.

The speaker alluded sadly to the poverty of his country, for, while the upper caste live in comfort, there are millions whose only food is dried flowers, and who are so low in the scale of existence that they have hardly an identity, and are pitiful objects in the plane of existence. He hinted quite forcibly that food and education would be better than the sermons which Christians and Mohammedans had been throwing at them for the last hundred years. Many of the simple and primitive customs of this peculiar people were told with naivete and innocence that was refreshing in this age when words are used to conceal thoughts. He said there was no flirting or coquetting between their young men and maids, and that the latter did not strut forth into public places with all their bravery [finery?] on for the purpose of securing a husband, all of which made the inhabitants of this great and glorious republic wonder if something were not slightly rotten in the state of Denmark. It is well to see both sides of the shield in order to be able to decide with an unprejudiced eye, and many of the listeners went away quite puzzled in mind at hearing some of their pet American customs arraigned by a Hindu and a heathen.

The address was a most interesting one and was listened to with deep attention by all present. At the close many [questions] were presented to the thoughtful monk, who wasted very few words in social flourishes or unmeaning talk. He seemed much interested in Dr. Bowker, the only one in the audi-

---

7. Swami Vivekananda may have been referring to the American Society for the Prevention of Cruelty to Animals.

ence who had ever visited the strange land which was centuries old before this republic was born.

THE BRAHMAN MONK[1]

Swami Vivekananda the Guest of the Woman's Club[2]
Lawrence American and Andover Advertiser,
May 18, 1894.

He Points Out the Better Phases of Brahmanism. And Delivers a Pointed Message to Christians.

Swami Vivekananda, the Brahman monk addressed a most interested audience Tuesday night in Library Hall under the auspices of the Lawrence Woman's Club.

Miss Wetherbee introduced the speaker and prepared the way for a cordial reception which American courtesy rarely fails to give a distinguished visitor from another nation.

Miss Wetherbee wisely referred to him as a prominent personality at the World's Parliament of Religions, also to the strong impression made by him at the World's fair...

His Iterations

In his own country, in his own class, he addresses all women as mother. The Brahmin is educated thus to think of women as mother and a man may not marry his mother. In that country the mother instinct is developed in woman; in this he thought the wife instinct was cultivated, and the most beautiful thing in his lecture was his tribute to the mother, and not unnoticed was the reference to the kindness of heart of the little Hindoo child which would instinctively cause him to turn aside from his path rather than crush a worm.

The Subject of Marriage formed a large part of his lecture. Among the high classes, called Aryans, women think of marriage as indecent [?]. A widow is not expected to ever marry again. A man who never marries, is highly praised, and indeed worshipped, but should he marry then in the minutes all would be changed. He who does not marry is looked upon as high minded, as holy and spiritual.

Among the Aryans no money is paid in marriage [?], and as female children are largely in the majority it is one of most difficult things for a father to marry his daughter, and from the time of her birth he racks his brains to find her a husband.

With the two lower classes the rules in regard to marriage are all different. Widows marry again and wives and husbands if desirous become divorced. When a child is born an astrologer comes and casts a horoscope of the child, he delineates the future character of the boy or girl—it is decided whether he is manly or a devilish child; if devilish—he is married to one next in caste, and thus is obtained a minute chance of bettering the condition of the devilish child.

The matter of marriage is not left to the decision of the child as in that case he might marry because [he was] in love with a good nose or good eyes and so in having his own way would spoil the whole thing. The fact was emphasised that only the higher classes think of a True Spiritual Life and of worshiping God instead of thinking of marriage. He spoke of the pitiful condition of the lower classes, their poverty and their ignorance. Millions and millions are [un]able to write their name and yet he said:

We are all preaching sermons into them, when their hands are reaching out for bread. Poverty is so extreme in the lower classes that fifty cents a month is the average income of a Hindoo. Millions live on one poor meal a day and millions subsist on wild flowers for food.

He spoke of the idea being prevalent that there were no scholars among the women of India and stated that this was an error as many women of the Brahmins were married but became scholars, and with evident pride he referred to the fact that in no nation could one line be found in Any Bible that had been written by a woman excepting his own country alone where many beautiful things in their Bible had been written by women.

Swami Vivekananda did not fail to inform the

---
1. *New Discoveries*, Vol. 2, pp. 68 71.
2. Of which there is no verbatim transcript available. Cf. the preceding American newspaper report, "Lecture by Hindoo Monk" of the Lawrence Evening Tribune (pp. 463 66), for other highlights of the same lecture.

audience in English words which could not be misunderstood, that the effort to raise his people by teaching them the Christian religion was a thankless task. He said:

We have seen the Greek and the Persian come to us—we have seen the Spaniard with guns come to make us Christians, still we are Hindoos and thus we shall remain.

Had Vivekananda used all the power of his flashing eyes and his expressive voice it would have been a most dramatic speech when he said:

I dare here in America to say that we of India shall stand by our religion.

He said our customs were good for us and we were welcome to them. He stood before us as he has before many a cultured American audience—he, the learned exponent of the Brahman religion, the only Hindoo who has ever come to this country to tell us—as forcibly as he dared and as politely as he could and yet be forcible,—to say no more to the poor Hindoo but to be so very kind as to mind our own business.

After the lecture many of the audience gladly availed themselves of the opportunity offered by Mr. and Mrs. Young to meet Vivekananda at their residence where he has been entertained and has proven himself to be a most delightful guest.

SWAMI VIVEKANANDA[3]

Mrs. Ole Bull submitted to the Boston Evening Transcript the following report of Swami Vivekananda's public lecture at Greenacre, Maine, delivered Friday, August 3, 1894, of which there is no verbatim transcript available. Vide the notes from discourses given at Greenacre, Maine, entitled "The Religion of India", in this volume of the Complete Works (pp. 267 71).

Boston Evening Transcript, August 11, 1894.

A defense of Mahomet [sic] by a Hindu to a Christian audience; the lesson that all prophets are to be revered and their teachings studied reverently; that the followers of these teachers should not confound for us by their behavior the revelation made from God to man by prophecy—was the theme at Greenacre yesterday.

Clear thought and statement patiently corrected the crude and superficial adverse criticism and comment that had been made concerning the Eastern belief—reincarnation. The statement was masterful, because simple, and was brought home by illustrations familiar and commonplace. This was followed by a nobly eloquent plea for the judicial spirit in judging the history of the time and the faith of Mahomet himself and the service done the human race by the essentials of this faith as a prophet of God. Men and women present, many of whom fear the hea then, were moved as they tell us Wendell Phillips[4] was wont to move the hard hearts to consider the sin of slavery.

Scorn, wit and intellect did noble service in all gentleness and dignity in this appeal that the defects, the horrors, of each and all religions should be put one side that the essentials common to all—the immortality of the soul, one God, the Father and his prophets sacred, each, to some division of the human family, and each having truth to give needful to all—should be recognized and reverenced to salvation.

The speaker, Swami Vivekananda, gave what only a great soul is capable of giving. It was an hour never to be forgotten. This man brought those present into the light of truth, whatever their prejudice and training, as Phillips Brooks united Unitarian and Episcopalianism, and all who love the good and true came to hold him for their bishop. So this Hindu, in his constructive thought, when he will give it, can make the power of the prophets known to us by his own presence.

NIRVANASHATKAM[5]

Swami Vivekananda's partial translation of the "Nirvâna shatkam" by Shankara, recited at Greenacre, Maine, and reported in an 1894 issue of the Greenacre Voice.[6]

---

3. *New Discoveries*, Vol. 2, pp. 144 45.

4. American orator and reformer (1811 1884).

5. *New Discoveries*, Vol. 2, pp. 149 50 (Arena, October 1899, p. 499).

6. Vide the notes from discourses delivered at Greenacre, Maine, entitled "The Religion of India", in this volume of the Complete Works

Under the Swami's famous pine at Greenacre, Vivekananda said: "I am neither body nor changes of the body; nor am I senses nor objects of the senses. I am Existence Absolute. Bliss Absolute. Knowledge Absolute. I am It. I am It. "I am neither death nor fear of death; nor was I ever born, nor had I parents. I am Existence Absolute. Bliss Absolute. Knowledge Absolute. I am It. I am It. "I am not misery nor have I misery. I am not enemy nor have I enemies. I am Existence Absolute. Bliss Absolute. Knowledge Absolute. I am It. I am It. "I am without form, without limit, beyond space, beyond time; I am in everything, I am the basis of the universe—everywhere am I. I am Existence Absolute. Bliss Absolute. Knowledge Absolute. I am It. I am It."

THE NONSENSE OF NATIONS[1]

[Boston Evening Transcript, August 15, 1894]

A short résumé is given below of the last of the talks of Vivekananda under the pines at Eliot,[2] in the temple of the gods, to paraphrase Bryant's[3] line— "The groves were God's first Temple."

What is the nation? What is law? We have laws only that we may become outlaws (above law).

There is the freedom of the soul; through this we know the freedom of law. I am of the nation of those who seek the liberty of the soul. I am of the nation of those who worship God.

The divine ones of God are all my Masters. I learn of your Christ in learning of Krishna, of Buddha, in learning of Mohamet. I worship God alone. "I am existence absolute, bliss absolute, Knowledge Absolute." I condemn nothing that I find in nation, state or religion, finding God in all. Our growth is not from evil to good, but from good to better, and so on and on. I learn from all that is called evil or good. The nation and all such nonsense may go. It is love, love, love God and my brother.

(pp. 267 71).

1. *New Discoveries*, Vol. 2, pp. 154 55.

2. Of which no verbatim transcript is available. Vide "The Religion of India"—notes from discourses delivered at Greenacre, Maine—in this volume of the *Complete Works* (pp. 267 71).

3. William Cullen Bryant (1794 1878).

A HIGH PRIEST OF INDIA[4]

Baltimore American, October 13, 1894.

SWAMI VIVEKANANDA ARRIVES IN BALTIMORE HIS VIEWS ON RELIGION

Swami Vivekananda, a Brahmin high priest of India, arrived in Baltimore last night, and is the guest of Rev. Walter Vrooman...

To an American reporter last night Swami Vivekananda said:

I have been very favorably impressed with American institutions during my stay in this country. My time has been divided between four cities—Chicago, New York, Boston and Detroit. I never heard of Chicago when in India, but I had frequently heard of Baltimore. The main criticism I have to pass on America is that you have too little religion here. In India they have too much. I think the world would be better if some of India's surplus of religion could be sent over here, while it would be to India's profit if its people could have some of America's industrial advancement and civilization. I am a believer in all religions. I think there is truth in my religion; I think there is truth in your religion. It is the same truth in all religions applying itself through various channels to the same end. I think the great need of the world is less law, and more godly men and women...

PRIEST SWAMI IN TOWN[5]

Baltimore News, October 13, 1894.

A High Caste Hindoo Visiting in Baltimore

HIS GORGEOUS GARB ATTRACTS MUCH ATTENTION IN THE LOBBY AT THE RENNERT—HE WHISTLES AND INDULGES IN EAST INDIAN WIT—HE COMES TO BALTIMORE ON A TOUR OF THE COUNTRY AND WILL SPEAK AT THE LYCEUM TOMORROW NIGHT.

Swami Vivekananda, High Priest of the Hindoos, walked into the lobby of the Hotel Rennert

---

4. *New Discoveries*, Vol. 2, pp. 191 92.

5. *New Discoveries*, Vol. 2, pp. 200 202.

this forenoon attired in a flaming red cloak and a gaudy yellow turban that made him the centre of all eyes...

His Idea of Humor

Swami Vivekananda has the sense of humor about him. He was talking this morning about the Food Show, which he intends to visit. He says he doesn't know much about food except to swallow it, and that is a very representative specimen of the wit of Ormus[6] and of Ind.

Another time he spoke of women's rights and said laughingly that women had more rights the world over than they were credited with having. When he changed his black coat, before going to the Rennert, and put on the cardinal red garment with the yellow turban he came out of his room smiling, and said: "A transformation!"

The High Priest can whistle and has enough music in his soul to start the tunes in class meeting if he were Methodist instead of Hindoo. He whistled a couple of strains in his room this morning for a reporter of The News. It was not "Daisy Bell" nor yet "Sweet Marie," and must have been some sort of a heathen Hindoo jingle...[7]

Views on Topics of the Day

Swami is traveling around the country, as he says, lecturing and studying American institutions, but he seems not to have got much into the pith of American sociology, for he knows nothing of such questions as European immigration, divorce, the race problem, etc., which are worrying the economists of the land.

He is, however, posted on Oriental immigration, and says the United States has no right to bar out the Chinese. He says the law of love must prevail and force must yield. He predicts the downfall of any nation that uses force. He says also that the United States should open her doors to the world. He believes the Southern part of the continent should be filled with Hindoos and Chinese. "There is no such thing as divorce in India," he said;

our law does not allow it. Our women are more limited in their sphere than the women of America. Some of them are as highly educated. They are entering the medical profession to some extent now. I see no reason why American women should not vote.

He evaded a question as to the position of Hindoo women in their homes and their treatment by their husbands. It may be that he does not know much about it. He is not a married man. Priests of his caste do not marry.

He mentioned two things which he said had impressed him in America. One was the absence of poverty in the country at large, and the other was the unusual prevalence of ignorance in the South.

Likes the Elevator

When he went to the elevator at the Rennert he said:

There is an American institution which we do not have to any extent in India. I like it very much.

A lady was just coming off the elevator. She was somewhat startled by the red and yellow costume of the priest, but his imperturbable countenance gave no sign of consciousness of the attention he attracted.

His address tomorrow night at the Lyceum will be mainly introductory of himself and explanatory of the Hindoo nation. He will speak briefly, but will remain in Baltimore and speak more at length a week from tomorrow night.

A WISE MAN AMONG US[8]

Baltimore Sunday Herald, October 14, 1894.

Visit of a Distinguished Hindoo Priest to This City

HE IS A GUEST OF THE VROOMAN BROTHERS AND IS INTERESTED IN THE ESTABLISHMENT OF AN INTERNATIONAL UNIVERSITY OF RELIGIONS—HIS GORGEOUS GARB

---

6. Hormuz, or Ormuz, an ancient Iranian town.

7. *New Discoveries*, Vol. 2, pp. 200 202.

8. *New Discoveries*, Vol. 2, pp. 200 202.

Mr. Vivecananda conversed with a Sunday Herald reporter, speaking English with ease and with an accent similar to that of an educated Italian. He displayed the greatest familiarity with the institutions of this country, religious, political and social.

Mr. Vivecananda came to Baltimore at the invitation of the Vrooman brothers, Hiram, Carl and Walter, and while in this city will be their guest. Rev. Hiram Vrooman was seen at his residence, 1122 North Calvert Street, yesterday, and talked freely in reference to the visit of the distinguished guest. "Mr. Vivecananda," he said, "is one of the most intelligent men I have ever met. He came to this city at our invitation, and while here will confer with us in reference to the founding of the international university, which it is proposed to establish as an outcome of the World's Congress of Religions, which was such an interesting feature of the World's Fair. This university

is one of Mr. Vivecananda's pet ideas, and has the full sympathy of myself and my brothers, and also a number of gentlemen of wealth and position, including several religions. Among its promoters are members of the Roman Catholic and Hebrew religions. The idea of the university is education in general religion…"One of Mr. Vivecananda's ideas in the establishing of the university is that it may serve to educate a superior kind of missionary for work in India. While he is steadfast to his own religious belief, he wishes that the present system of sending ignorant men as missionaries to India may be discontinued and men sent there who can teach the Christian religion from an elevated standpoint. In this wish he is animated only by a desire for the good of general religion…"Mr. Vivecananda told me that his father was a great believer in the Lord Jesus, as he called Him, and that when a boy he had read in the Gospel of St. John the thrilling description of the crucifixion of the Savior and wept over it. He will remain in this city for several weeks. To morrow evening he will deliver a brief address at our meeting at the Lyceum, and on Sunday week will speak at length at our second meeting on the university plan."

LOVE RELIGION'S ESSENCE[1]

*Vive Kananda, a Brahmin Monk,
Preaches at the People's Church*

Washington Times, Monday, October 29, 1894.

Vive Kananda, the Brahmin monk, spoke to the congregation of the People's Church, No. 423 G Street northwest, at 11:00 a.m. yesterday.[2] Dr. Kent introduced the monk…

Vive Kananda, coming forward, said as a boy at the university he studied comparative religion. In India are many religions. One fifth are Mahomedans. A million are Christians. He studied all. He listened to a great Hindoo preacher, and when he had finished, said: "My brother, have you seen God?"

The preacher looked up in surprise.

"No."

"How, then, do you know these things are true?"

"My father told me."

"Who told your father?"

"His father," and so on through his ancestors to the clouds.

He heard a Christian preacher of great eloquence. This man told the seeker for truth that if he was not immersed in water at once he was in great danger to be roasted alive. Upon further questions this Christian also, through the records of his books, went back to his ancestors, and so back to the clouds.

The Student Not Satisfied

This did not satisfy the student. He set about praying. He prayed sometimes three days and nights with much weeping and without food. He finally found a man who knew no books, not even to write his own name. This sage was preaching his religion. When asked the old question, he replied: "Yes, I see God now and I will teach you to see Him."

1. Ray and Wanda Ellis, "Swami Vivekananda in Washington D.C.", The Vedanta Kesari, 1991, pp. 370 73.

2. On Sunday, October 28, 1894, Swami Vivekananda delivered two talks at the People's Church, of which there are no verbatim transcripts available. Cf. Complete Works, II: 497 99 for an interview with the Swami given after his morning sermon.

This man bore the stamp of God in his features. It was the same certificate that came to the man of Nazareth when the dove descended upon Him at Jordan. He made his hearer to believe that God lives and religion is not a mockery.

For twelve years Kananda sat at this man's feet. He was the master. He said one day, "Take up this book." Kananda took up the book and read. It was a calendar. He read in it where the rainfall was foretold. It said that within a certain time so many tons of rain would fall in a certain district. "Now," said the teacher, "close the book and press it." He did so. "Squeeze it very hard." He obeyed. "Did any water come from the book?" "None." So are all books. The true religion is here, at the heart.

The truth is people do not want God. Far from it. Religion is largely fashionable. My lady has a fine parlor, elegant furniture, a piano, beautiful jewelry, well fitting, costly dresses, a hat that is the latest thing out. She cannot get along without a dash of religion to keep up with her set. There is much of this religion, but it is hypocrisy, and hypocrisy is the root of all evil. This sort of religion is not of God. It is only the shadow. People with such religion sometimes grow to be in earnest and talk about religious things as if they had some reality. So talking about religion without having it these people fall to quarreling and fighting. "Mine, mine," is the cry, never "thine, thine." "My religion is best." "No, mine," and so they fight as did the savage tribes about their rival gods, Mambo and Jumbo. Competition in religion, as in business, is the bane of all.

Love Abideth

Your own Paul says "all else shall perish, but love abideth." That is the great truth. That false doctrine that my nation shall be aggrandized at the cost of every other nation is not of God.

A youth went to his master and said, "I want to know God." The master paid little attention, but the youth persisted and would not be put off. Finally one day the master said: "Let us go down to the river and have a bath." So they went down and the youth plunged in. The master followed and falling upon him held him under. The youth struggled, but the master would not let him up. Finally, when he seemed to be almost dead he desisted, drew him from the water and revived him. "What did you most want when in the water?" the master asked. "Breath," was the answer. "Then you don't want God."

So it is with men, what do you want? You want breath, without it you cannot live; you want bread, without it you cannot live; you want a house, without it you cannot live. When you want God as you want these things, He manifests himself to you. It is a great thing to want God. A majority of men and women in this world want the enjoyments of sense. They have been told that there is a God afar off and if they will send him a cartload of words he will

help them get these good things of this world. But in every land there are a few persons who want God. They would be one with the essence of good and truth. Religion is not shopkeeping. Love asks no return; love begs not; love gives.

Religion is not an outgrowth of fear; religion is joyous. It is the spontaneous outburst of the songs of birds and the beautiful sight of the morning. It is an expression of the spirit. It is from within an expression of the free and noble spirit.

If misery is religion, what is hell? No man has a right to make himself miserable. To do so is a mistake; it is a sin. Every peal of laughter is a prayer sent to God.

To go back, what I have learned is this: Religion is not in books, not in forms, not in sects, not in nations; religion is in the human heart. It is engraved there. The proof of it is in ourselves.

I make two points. There are sects. Let them go on increasing in number till each is a sect by himself. None can see God exactly as another; each must believe in Him and serve Him as he sees Him. Then I want a harmonizing of the sects. Individuality is not in a fight with universality.

Let each for himself and all together fight evils. If you have a power of eight and I a power of four, and you come and destroy me, you have lost at least four. You have only four left to conquer evil. It is love alone that can conquer hatred. If there is power in hate there is infinitely more power in love.

THE HINDOO OPTIMISTIC[1]

Washington Times, November 2, 1894.
Vive Kananda Compares Religions and Talks of Reincarnation[2]

Optimism is the feature of the belief of the Aryas or Hindoos as distinguished from Western religions, according to the Brahman monk, Vive Kananda, who spoke to a fair sized audience at Metzerott Hall last night. His subject was reincarnation. Much of his lecture was devoted to comparison of Hindoo with Christian doctrine.

To illustrate the tenet of reincarnation he compared the human body to a river. Each drop of water passes on and is replaced by another. The entire body of water, he observed, changes wholly in a few moments, but we call it the same river. In the same way the particles of the body are constantly replaced by others and no two days do we have the same body, yet we preserve our identity.

The spirit remains so, the Hindoos believe, that the person may have a different and more sudden and violent change in death and yet pass on in its existence to some other place in the universe, to some other planet or star, and then take on a body of flesh again or of some other kind.

He said there ought to be no talk of sin. The mistakes of the past ought to be used only for guidance in the future, never to be moaned over. When the lesson is learned from them they should be forgotten. "Strike a light," he said, "sit not in darkness and sorrow. Do always better and be happy."…

VIVEKANANDA'S LECTURE[3]

Baltimore News, November 3, 1894.

Swami Vivekananda, Hindoo high priest, lectured last night at Harris' Academy of Music Concert Hall. His subject was "India and Its Religion."[4] He explained the belief of the various Eastern religions, including his own, which is Brahminism. He ridiculed the idea of sending missionaries of so many different faiths to heathen lands, and said that the various religions engaged in missionary work should be united. Mr. Vivekananda explained that the Hindoo religion is optimistic and not pessimistic. His main point was the doctrine of reincarnation, which means that all have existed before and will live again in other forms. The proceeds of the lecture will be applied to the work of founding an international college.

LET INDIA ALONE[5]

Daily Eagle, April 8, 1895.
Then It will Come Out All Right, Says Swami Vivekananda.

The English people were given a raking over last night by Swami Vivekananda of India, who lectured to a throng at the Pouch mansion.[6] He said that the English used three B's—Bible, brandy and bayonets—in civilizing India. The preacher went ahead with the Bible to get the lay of the fortifications. The English, he said, had exaggerated the social conditions of India in their writings. They got their ideas from the Pariahs, who were a sort of human scavenger. No self respecting Hindoo, he declared, would associate with an Englishman. The story about widows throwing themselves under the chariot of Juggernaut he declared to be a myth. Child marriage and caste he agreed were bad. Caste, he said, originated with the mechanics' guilds. What India needed was to be let alone, and it would come out all right.

---

1. Ray and Wanda Ellis, "Swami Vivekananda in Washington D.C., The Vedanta Kesari, 1991, pp. 369 70.

2. The untranscribed lecture advertised as "Karma and Reincarnation", delivered at the People's Church, Sunday, October 28, 1894.

3. *New Discoveries*, Vol. 2, p. 223.

4. Of which there is no verbatim report available.

5. New Discoveries, Vol. 2, p. 314..

6. Of which no verbatim transcript is available. Cf. the newspaper report "Some Customs of the Hindus", Complete Works, II: 515 17, for a complementary report on the same lecture.

ABOU BEN ADHEM'S IDEAL[7]

New York World, December 8, 1895.

SWAMI VIVEKANANDA THE YOGI, COMES FROM BOMBAY, PREACHING LOVE FOR HIS FELLOW MAN.

To find an ascetic of the Highest Eastern type clad in a red and flowing Hindoo cloak over unmistakable American trousers is necessarily a surprise. But in other things besides dress is Swami Vivekananda astonishing. In the first place he declares that your religion or any one else's religion is just as good as his own, and if you should happen to be a Christian or Mussulman, Baptist or Brahmin, atheist, agnostic or Catholic, it will make no difference to him. All that he asks is that you act righteously according to your lights.

The Yogi, with his peculiar notions of dress and worship, arrived Friday on the Brittanic. He went to No. 228 West Thirty ninth street. While in New York he will lecture upon metaphysics and psychology, and will also disseminate in a general way his ideas on the universal religion which asks no man to take another by the throat because his creed happens to be different. "Let me help my fellowman; that is all I seek," he says. "There are four general types of men," he says,

the rational, the emotional, the mystical and the worker. For them we must have their proper worship. There comes the rational man, who says, "I care not for this form of worship. Give me the philosophical, the rational—that I can appreciate." So for the rational man is the rational, philosophic worship.

There comes the worker. He says: "I care not for the worship of the philosopher. Give me work to do for my fellow men." So for him is made a worship, as for the mystical the emotional. In the religion for all these men are the elements of their faith. "No," said the Swami, very softly, in answer to a question,

I do not believe in the occult. If a thing be unreal it is not. What is unreal does not exist. Strange things are natural phenomena. I know them to be matters of science. Then they are not occult to me. I do not believe in occult societies. They do no good, and can never do good.

In fact, the Swami belongs to no society, cult or creed. His is a religion which compasses all worship, all classes, all beliefs.

Swami, who is a very dark featured and good looking young fellow, explained his creed yesterday in remarkably pure English. One forgot when he spoke that an orthodox choker peered over the Bombay robe which in turn scantily concealed the American trousers. One saw instead a winning smile and a pair of deep, lustrous black eyes.

Swami believes in reincarnation. He believes that with the purification of the body the soul rises to a higher condition, and as the purification through matter continues the spirit rises, until released from further migration and is joined with the universal spirit.

Such a man as the Jew baiter [Hermann?] Ahlwardt, who has just arrived in this country, the Swami cannot understand. "You say," he said, that he comes here to preach hate against his fellow men. Is he not of wrong mind? Is he allowed to spread this hate? The doctors should examine his brain to find out the wrong.

The peculiar name of the Yogi signifies, literally, "The bliss of discrimination." He is the first Indian Yogi who ever came to this country. He comes from Bombay.

THE DOCTRINE OF THE SWAMI[8]

New York Herald, January 19, 1896.

The following is a brief sketch of the Swami's fundamental teachings:[9]

Every man must develop according to his own nature. As every science has its methods so has every religion. Methods of attaining the end of our

---

7. *New Discoveries*, Vol. 3, pp. 316 18. Abou Ben Adhem, the hero of Leigh Hunt's famous poem, asked a recording angel to list him as loving his fellowmen.

8. *New Discoveries*, Vol. 3, pp. 340 41.

9. A summary of the Swami's teachings taken from what appears to be a written statement.

religion are called Yoga, and the different forms of Yoga that we teach are adapted to the different natures and temperaments of men. We classify them in the following way, under four heads: (1) Karma Yoga—The manner in which a man realizes his own divinity through works and duty. (2) Bhakti Yoga—The realization of a divinity through devotion to and love of a personal God. (3) Rajah Yoga—The realization of divinity through control of mind. (4) Gnana Yoga—The realization of man's own divinity through knowledge.

These are all different roads leading to the same center— God. Indeed, the varieties of religious belief are an advantage, since all faiths are good, so far as they encourage man to religious life. The more sects there are the more opportunities there are for making successful appeals to the divine instinct in all men.

"UNIVERSAL RELIGION"[1]

Vivekananda's Lecture on the Creeds of the World, Hartford Daily Times, February 1, 1896.

A fair house greeted the Hindu monk, Vivekananda, last night…He was introduced by Mr. C. B. Patterson, in some fitting remarks…His subject last night was "The Ideal, or Universal Religion".[2]

Throughout the universe there are two forces constantly at work, the centrifugal and centripetal, positive and negative, action and reaction, attraction and repulsion. We find love and hatred, good and evil. What plane is stronger than the spiritual plane, the plane of religion? The world furnishes no hate stronger than that engendered by religion, and no love stronger. No teachings have brought more unhappiness into the world, nor more happiness. The beautiful teachings of Buddha have been carried across the Himalayas, at a height of 20,000 feet, by his disciples. Five hundred years later came the teachings of your beautiful Christ, and these have been carried on the wings of the wind. On the other hand, look at your beautiful earth deluged in blood in the interest of propagandism and religion. As soon as a man comes into the company of those who do not believe as he does, his very nature changes. It is his own opinions he fights for, not religion. He becomes the very embodiment of cruelty and fanaticism. His religion is all right, but when he starts out to fight for his own selfish opinions he is all wrong. People are up in arms about the Armenian and the Turkish butcheries, but their consciences don't say a word when the butcheries are committed in the interest of their own religion. In human beings we find a curious mixture of God, man, and devil, and religion stirs up the latter more than anything else. When we all think alike, the God side of our nature comes out; but let there be a clash of opinions, and presto, change! the devil has the floor. This has been so from time immemorial, and will be so always. In India we know what fanaticism means, for that country for the last thousand years has been the especial field of missionaries. But above the clash of opinions, and the fight for religions, there comes the voice of peace. For 3,000 years efforts have been made to bring the different religions into harmony. But we know how this effort has failed. And it always will fail, and it ought to fail. We have a network of words about love, peace, and universal brotherhood, which were meant all right originally, but we repeat them like parrots, and to us they mean nothing. Is there a universal philosophy for the world? Not yet. Each religion has its own creeds and dogmas and insists upon propagating them. You can't make one religion for the whole world. That must not be. The Armenians say it will be all right if you will all become Armenians. And the Pope of Rome says: "O yea, it is a very easy thing. If you will all become Roman Catholics, it will be all right." And so with the Greek church, and the Protestant church, and all the rest. There can never be one religion only, it would be death to all other religions. If every one thought alike there would be no more thought to think. If everybody looked alike, what monotony! Look alike and think alike—what could we do but sit down and die in despair? We can't live like a row of chipmunks; variation belongs to human life. One God, one religion is an old

---

1. *New Discoveries*, Vol. 3, pp. 475 79.

2. "The Ideal of a Universal Religion" was delivered January 31, 1896, of which there is no verbatim transcript available.

sing song, but there's danger in it. But, thank God, it can never be. Start out with your long purse, and your guns and cannon, to push your propagandism. And suppose you succeed for a while? In ten years your so called unity would be split into fragments. That is why there are so many sects. Take the largest religion, the Buddhist. They try to help the world to be better. Next come the Christians, with [a] good many things to teach. They have three Gods in one, and one in three, and one of the three took on the sins of the world and was killed. Whoever doesn't believe in him, goes to a very hot place. And Mohammed, whoever doesn't believe in him will have his skin burnt off, and then a fresh one will be furnished to be burnt, that he may know that Allah is the all powerful. All religions came originally from the Orient. These great teachers or incarnations come in different forms. The Hindus have ten incarnations; the first was a fish, and so on, down to the fifth, and from there, they were all men. The Buddhists say: "We don't care to have so many incarnations; we want only one." The Christians say: "We will have only one, and this is Christ." And they say he is the only one. But the Buddhist says they have the start in time; their great teacher came five hundred years earlier. And the Mohammedans say theirs came last, and therefore is the best. Each one loves his own, just as a mother loves her own child. The Buddhist never sees any fault in Buddha; the Christian never sees any fault in Christ, and the Mohammedan never sees any fault in Mohammed. The Christian says their God took the form of a dove and came down, and that they say is not mythology, but history. The Hindu says his god is manifested in a cow and that he says is not superstition, but history. The Jew thinks his Holy of Holies can be contained in a box or chest, with an angel on guard on either side. But the Christian's God in the form of a beautiful man or woman, is a horrible idol. "Break it down!" they say. One man's prophet did such and such wonderful things, while others call it only superstition. So where's your unity? Then there are your rituals. The Roman Catholic puts on his robe, as I have mine. He has his bells and candles and holy water, and says these are good and necessary, but what you do, he says is only superstition. We can never upset all this and have but one religion for the very life of thought is the differentiation of thought. We must learn to love those who think exactly opposite to us. We have humanity for the background, but each must have his own individuality and his own thought. Push the sects forward and forward till each man and woman are sects unto themselves. We must learn to love the man who differs from us in opinion. We must learn that differentiation is the life of thought. We have one common goal, and that is the perfection of the human soul, the god within us. Religion is the great force to help unfold the god within man. But we have to unfold in our own way. We can't all assimilate the same kind of food. Let your aspirations be of the highest, and your inspirations will be in harmony with reason and all known laws, and the Lord will always be with you.

VIVEKANANDA'S PHILOSOPHY[3]

Tribune, March 5, 1896.

He Would Have Many Kinds of Religion

Vivekananda, the Hindoo missionary, lectured at the Hotel Richelieu last night.[4] The parlors of the private hotel were filled to overflowing with a crowd of ladies. When Vivekananda arrived at the hotel it was with difficulty he worked his way in. He went upstairs and very shortly came down again robed in a purple gown, caught about the waist with a purple cord.

Vivekananda in his talk said that there were various religions and each believer thought his religion the only true religion. It was a mistake, he said, to suppose that all should have the same religion. "If all were of the same religious opinion," said he,

there would be no religion. No sooner does a religion start than it breaks into pieces. The process is for the religion to go on dividing until each man has his own religion, until each man has thought

---

3. *New Discoveries*, Vol. 4, p. 20.

4. The class was "The Ideal of a Universal Religion", of which there is no verbatim transcript available.

out his own thoughts and carved out for himself his own religion.

Vivekananda will remain in Detroit about two weeks and will give classes every morning at 11 o'clock and every evening at 8 o'clock at the hotel...

HEARD SWAMI TALK[1]

News Tribune, March 16, 1896.

Vivekananda Lectured in Temple Beth El—Spoke on the Ideal of a Universal Religion—He Will Probably Leave Tuesday

Temple Beth El was crowded to the doors last night when Swami Vivekananda delivered his address upon "The Ideal of a universal religion."[2] The time announced for the service was 8 o'clock, but the congregation began to assemble at the temple early in the evening so that the doors had to be opened at 6:25 p.m. They were closed at 7 o'clock and the hundreds that arrived after that time had to be turned away.

We all hear about universal brotherhood, and how societies stand up and want to preach this. But to what does it amount? As soon as you make a sect you protest against equality, and thus it is no more, said Swami.

Unity in variety is the plan of the universe. Just as we are all men, yet we are all separate. We find then, that if by the idea of a universal religion is meant one set of doctrines should be believed by all mankind, it is impossible, it can never be, any more than there will be a time when all faces will be the same. We must not seek that all of us should think alike, like Egyptian mummies in a museum, looking at each other without thought to think. It is this difference of thought, this differentiation, losing of the balance of thought, which is the very soul of our progress, the soul of thought.

Swami will probably leave Tuesday [March 17]. At the close of his address last night he thanked the people of Detroit for the kind reception tendered him and his philosophy.

---

1. *New Discoveries*, Vol. 4, p. 41.
2. Of which there is no verbatim transcript available.

PHILOSOPHY OF FREEDOM[3]

Boston Evening Transcript, March 21, 1896.

Swami Vivekananda Compares Teachings of Hindu Wisdom and Western Religions

The Swami Vivekananda, who will be remembered as the Hindu delegate to the World's Parliament of Religions, is in the city as the March class lecturer at the Procopeia, 45 St. Botolph street.[4] The Swami has been doing some most valuable and successful work in systematic class lecturing in New York, with constantly increasing audiences, during the past two winters, and comes to Boston at a most opportune time.

The Swami gives the following description of his work. In explanation of the term sannyasin, he said, [Vide "The Sannyasin", Complete Works, V: 260].

In giving some idea of his work and its methods, the Swami says he left the world because he had a deep interest in religion and philosophy from his childhood, and Indian books teach renunciation as the highest ideal to which a man can aspire. The Swami['s] teaching, as he expresses it,

is my own interpretation of our ancient books in the light which my master (a celebrated Hindu sage) shed upon them. I claim no supernatural authority. Whatever in my teachings may appeal to the highest intelligence and be accepted by thinking men, the adoption of that will be my reward. All religions have for their object the teaching of devotion, or knowledge, or activity, in a concrete form. Now, the philosophy of Vedanta is the abstract science which embraces all these methods, and this is what I teach, leaving each one to apply it to his own concrete form. I refer each individual to his own experience, and where reference is made to books, the latter are procurable, and may be studied for each one by himself.

The Swami teaches no authority from hidden beings, through visible objects, any more than he claims learning from hidden books or MSS. He believes no good can come from secret societies.

---

3. *New Discoveries*, Vol. 4, pp. 56 58.
4. There are no verbatim transcripts available of these classes.

Truth stands on its own authority, and truth can bear the light of day.

He teaches only the Self, hidden in the heart of every individual, and common to all. A handful of strong men, knowing that Self, and living in its light, would revolutionize the world, even today, as has been the case of single strong men before, each in his day.

His attitude towards Western religions is briefly this. He propounds a philosophy which can serve as a basis to every possible religious system in the world, and his attitude towards all of them is one of extreme sympathy. His teaching is antagonistic to none. He directs his attention to the individual, to make him strong, to teach him that he himself is divine, and he calls upon men to make themselves conscious of divinity within. His hope is to imbue individuals with the teachings to which he has referred, and to encourage them to express these to others in their own way; let them modify them as they will; he does not teach them as dogmas; truth, at length, must inevitably prevail...

OUT OF THE EAST[5]

Boston Daily Globe, March 24, 1896.

Message Brought by the Swami Vivekananda—in His Country the Gods Are "Bright Ones" That Help

The Swami Vivekananda is enjoying as great a degree of popularity on his present visit to Boston as he did when society, fashionable, intellectual and faddist, went wild over him on his former visit…A New York paper published an interview with the Swami, in which he is reported to have expressed the opinion that in Boston "the women are all faddists, all fickle, merely bent on following something new and strange."[6] But Swami Vivekananda says that this is an exaggerated and distorted presentation of a criticism which he made upon all American women, that they were too superficial and too prone to follow the sensational and to change from one thing to another. This he says his observation has forced upon him. The American women are intellectual, but they are not steady, serious and sincere.

The first of the Swami's lectures was delivered before an audience of 400 people in the Allen gymnasium, Saturday evening on "The Science of Work," and the second one of the course on "Devotion"[7] was given in the same place, the hall being filled and a number turned away unable to gain admittance.

The lecture was exceedingly interesting and the speaker's manner was very magnetic. In his country, said the Swami, the gods were the "bright ones" who gave help to men and received help from them. The gods are only human beings who are somewhat elevated after death, but God, the highest, is never prayed to or asked for help. He is given only love and worship without anything being asked in return. There are two phases of this God, the one, the abstract God behind the substance of the universe, and the other the personal God who is seen through human intellect and given attributes by it.

The love which is given to God never takes, but always gives, and it does not depend on anything. The worshiper does not pray for health, money or any other thing, but is content with the lot apportioned to him.

People who ask about religion from mere motives of curiosity become faddists, they are always looking for some thing new and their brains degenerate until they become old rags. It is a religious dissipation with them.

It is not the place that makes heaven or hell, but the mind. Love knows no fear, there can be no love where it is. In love of any sort external objects are only suggested by something within —it is one's own ideal projected, and God is the highest ideal that can be conceived of.

Hatred of the world does not drive good men from it, but the world slips away from the great and saintly. The world, the family and social life, are all training grounds, that is all.

When one realizes that God is love, it does not matter what his other attributes are, that is the only essential.

---

5. *New Discoveries*, Vol. 4, pp. 60-62.

6. Cf. *Complete Works*, V: 413.

7. Delivered March 21 and March 23, 1896 respectively, of which there are no verbatim transcripts available.

The more a man throws himself away, the more God comes in, hence self abnegation, which is the secret of all religion and morality.

Too many people bring down their ideals. They want a comfortable religion, but there is none such. It is all self surrender and upward striving.

SAID A UNIVERSAL RELIGION IS IMPOSSIBLE[1]

Boston Evening Transcript, March 27, 1896.

Swami Vivekananda told the large audience that crowded the Allen Gymnasium to hear him speak on the "Ideal of a Universal Religion," last night,[2] that the recent Parliament of Religions at Chicago proved, to that date, that universal religion was impossible. "Nature," he said, is wiser than we have thought her to be. It is competition of ideas, the clash of thought, that keeps thought alive. Sects have always been antithetical, and always will be splitting into little varieties of themselves. And the way to get out of this fight of religions is to let the sects go on subdividing.

There is no unity in the three elements of religion— philosophy [theology?], mythology and ceremony. Each theologian wants unity, but his idea of unity is the adjustment of all other creeds to his own. I agree with the old prophets as long as they agree with me. But there is an element of religion that towers above all; that is, philosophy. The philosopher seeks truth, which is one and the same always. And it is acceptable to the four sides of every religious nature—the emotional, mystical, active and philosophical. And he who dares to seek the truth for truth's sake is greatest among men.

FOR UNIVERSAL RELIGION[3]

Boston Evening Transcript, March 30, 1896.
The Hindu Swami Lectures Before Several Societies.

The Swami Vivekananda has, during the past few days, conducted a most successful work in connection with the Procopeia. During this time he has given four class lectures for the club itself, with constant audiences of between four and five hundred people, at the Allen Gymnasium, 44, St. Botolph street, two at the house of Mrs. Ole Bull in Cambridge, and one before the professors and graduate students of the philosophical department of Harvard University.

The idea, which brought the Swami to America three years ago as Hindu delegate to the Parliament of Religions, and has been the guiding motive of all his subsequent work, both in America and England, is one which appeals strongly to the people whose creation the parliament was, but the methods which he proposes are peculiarly his own. One of his lectures during the week has been "The Ideal of a Universal Religion,"[4] but a "harmonious religion" would, perhaps, equally meet the case, if, indeed, it would not more adequately express that for which he is striving. The Swami is not a preacher of theory. If there is any one feature of the Vedanta philosophy, which he propounds, which appears especially refreshing, it is its intense capability of practical demonstration. We have become almost wedded to the idea that religion is a sublime theory which can be brought into practice and made tangible for us only in another life, but the Swami shows us the folly of this. In preaching the Divinity of Man he inculcates a spirit of strength into us which will have none of those barriers between this life and actual realization of the sublime that, to the ordinary man, appear as insurmountable.

In discussing the general lines on which it appears to him universal religion can alone be established, he claims for his plan no super authority. As he says:

I have also my little plan. I do not know whether it will work or not, and I want to present it to you for discussion. In the first place, I would ask mankind to recognize this maxim: "Do not destroy." Iconoclastic reformers do no good to the world. Help, if you can; if you cannot, fold your hands,

---

1. *New Discoveries*, Vol. 4, pp. 64 65.
2. Of which there is no verbatim report available.
3. *New Discoveries*, Vol. 4, pp. 81 86.

---

4. Though this was one of Swami Vivekananda's recurring subjects, there is no available verbatim transcript of this March 26, 1896 lecture. Cf. *Complete Works*, II: 375 96.

stand by, and see things go on. Therefore say not a word against any man's convictions, so far as they are sincere. Secondly, take man where he stands, and from thence give him a lift.[5]

Unity in variety is the plan of the universe. Just as we are all men, yet we are all separate. As humanity, I am one with you; as Mr. So and so, I am different from you. As a man you are separate from woman, but as human beings you are all one; as a living being you are one with animals and all that lives, but as man you are separate. That existence is God, the ultimate unity in this universe. In Him we are all one. We find, then, that if by the idea of a universal religion is meant that one set of doctrines should be believed by all mankind, it is impossible, it can never be, any more than all faces will be the same. Again, if we expect that there will be one universal mythology, that is also impossible; it cannot be. Neither can there be a universal ritual. When this time comes the world will be destroyed, because variety is the first principle of life. What makes us formed beings? Differentiation. Perfect balance will be destruction.[6]

What then do I mean by the ideal of a universal religion? I do not mean a universal philosophy, or a universal mythology, or a universal ritual, but I mean that this world must go on, wheel within wheel. What can we do? We can make it run smoothly, we can lessen friction, we can grease the wheels, as it were. By what? By recognizing variation.[7]

Just as we have recognized unity, by our very nature so we must also recognize variation. We must learn that truth may be expressed in a thousand ways, and each one yet be true. We must learn that the same thing can be viewed from a hundred different standpoints, and yet be the same thing.[8]

In society we see so many various natures of mankind. A practical generalization will be impossible, but for my purpose I have simply characterized them into four. First, the active man; then the emotional man; then the mystical man, and lastly the philosopher.

To be universal, religion must provide possibility of realizing truth through means suitable to any one of these minds, and a religion which says that through one alone all men must struggle, whether these minds are capable of the struggle or not, must end in agnosticism.

In his lecture on Karma Yoga,[9] the Swami dealt with the science of work. The lecture for the most part analyzed the motives men have in work, and particularly the motive of heaven as a reward for good work on earth. This, said the Swami, is shopkeeping religion. Work alone reaches its highest when it is done absolutely without hope of reward, work for work's sake, and without regard to the consequences.

In discussing Bhakti Yoga,[10] Devotion, the Swami explained the rationale of a Personal God. This idea of devotion and worship of some being who has to be loved, and who can reflect back the love to man, is universal. The lowest stage of the manifestation of this love and devotion is ritualism, when man wants things that are concrete, and abstract ideas are almost impossible. Throughout the history of the world we find man is trying to grasp the abstract through thought forms, or symbols, and the external manifestations of religion. Bells, music, rituals, books, images come under that head. Man can only think with form and word. Immediately thought comes, form and name flash into the mind with them, so that when we think of God, whether as the Personal God with human shape, or as the Divine Principle, or in any other aspect, we are always thinking of our own highest ideal with some or other form, generally human, because the form of man is the highest of which man can conceive. But, while recognizing this as a necessity of human weakness, and while making proportionate use of rituals, symbols, books and churches, we must always remember that it is very good to be born in a

---

5. Cf. *Complete Works*, II: 384.

6. Cf. *Complete Works*, II: 384.

7. Cf. *Complete Works*, II: 384.

8. Cf. *Complete Works*, II: 382 83.

9. Probably the March 21st class entitled "The Science of Work", of which there is no verbatim transcript available.

10. Probably the March 23rd class entitled "Devotion", of which there is no verbatim transcript available.

church, but it is very bad to die in a church. If a man dies within the bounds of these forms, it shows that he has not grown, that there has been no uncovering of the real, the Divinity, within him.

True love can be regarded as a triangle. The first angle is, love knows no bargain. So when a man is praying to God, "give me this, and give me that," it is not love. How can it be? "I give you my little prayer, and you give me something in return"; that is mere shopkeeping. The second angle is, love knows no fear. So long as God is regarded as a rewarder or a punisher there can be no love for him. The third angle, the apex, is, love is always the highest ideal. When we have reached the point where we can worship the ideal as the ideal, all arguments and doubts have vanished forever. The ideal can never escape, because it is part of our own nature.

In his lecture at Harvard University,[1] the Swami traced the history, so far as is known, of the Vedanta philosophy, and showed to what extent the Vedas (the Hindu scriptures) are accepted as authoritative; merely as the foundation for the philosophy in so far as they appeal to the reason. He compared the three schools, the Dualists, who acknowledge a supreme being, and a lesser being manifesting in men, but eternally separate from men. Next he described the philosophy of the Qualified nondualists, whose particular idea is that there is a God and there is nature, but that the soul and nature is simply the expansion, or the body of God, just as the body of man is to man's soul. They claim, in support of this theory, that the effect is never different from the cause, but that it is the cause repro- duced in another form, and as God, therefore, is the cause of this universe, he is also the effect. The Monists ... declare that if there is a God, that God must be both the material and the efficient cause of the universe. Not only is he the Creator; but he is also the created. He himself is this universe, apparently; but, in reality, this universe does not exist—it is mere hypnotisation. Differentiation is in name and form only. There is but one soul in the universe, not two, because that which is immaterial cannot be bounded, must be infinite; and there cannot be two infinities, because one would limit the other. The soul is pure, and the appearance of evil is just as a piece of crystal, which is pure in itself, but appears to be variously colored when flowers are placed before it.

In discussing Raja Yoga,[2] the psychological way to union with God, the Swami expanded upon the power to which the mind can attain through concentration, both in reference to the physical and the spiritual world. It is the one method that we have in all knowledge. From the lowest to the highest, from the smallest worm to the highest sage, they have to use this one method. The astronomer uses it in order to discover the mysteries of the skies, the chemist in his laboratory, the professor in his chair. This is the one call, the one knock, which opens the gates of nature and lets out the floods of light. This is the one key, the only power—concentration. In the present state of our bodies we are so much distracted, the mind is frittering away its energies upon a hundred sorts of things. By scientific control of the forces which work the body this can be done, and its ultimate effect is realization. Religion cannot consist of talk. It only becomes religion when it becomes tangible, and until we strive to feel that of which we talk so much, we are no better than agnostics, for the latter are sincere and we are not.

The Twentieth Century Club had the Swami as their guest Saturday [March 28], and heard an address from him on the "Practical Side of the Vedanta Philosophy."[3] He leaves Boston today, and will, within a few days, sail for England, en route for India.

SWAMI VIVEKANANDA[4]

Lectures on Hindoo Religion and Philosophy

Los Angeles Times, December 9, 1899.

The well known expositor of the Hindoo philosophy, dressed in the yellow robe of the Brahmin

---

1. Cf. "The Vedanta Philosophy", *Complete Works*, I: 357 65, in which there may be some omissions.

2. Actually "Realization, or the Ultimate of Religion", of which there is no verbatim transcript available.

3. Vide *Complete Works*, I: 387 92 and 310 11 respectively, for the lecture and the discussion that followed.

4. *New Discoveries*, Vol. 5, pp. 184 86.

caste, spoke in part as follows:[5]

I come before you, ladies and gentlemen, to bring no new religion. I desire simply to tell you a few points that bind together all religions. I shall touch upon some things in the thought of eastern civilization that will appear strange to you and on others that I hope will appeal to you. All the religions of the world have a backbone of unity. This is the principle of philosophy and of toleration.

Very few people in this country understand what India is. It is a country half as large as the United States and containing 300,000,000 people, speaking a number of different tongues, but all bound together by the ideas of a common religion. By these ideas the Hindoos have made their influence felt through the ages, working gently, silently, patiently, while western civilization has been conquering by force of arms. The future will show which is the more powerful—physical force or the power of ideas. The arts and sciences of the Hindoos have found their way over all the earth—their numerals, their mathematical thought, their ethics. Was it not in India, there and there alone, that the doctrine of love was first preached, and not alone the doctrine of love of one's fellow men, but of love of every living thing, yea, even of the meanest worm that crawls under our feet. When you begin to study the arts and institutions of India, you become magnetized, fascinated. You cannot get away.

In India, as elsewhere, we find the earliest condition one of division into little tribes. These different tribes had each its different god, its different ceremonial. But in coming in contact with one another, the tribes did not follow the course that western civilization has taken—they did not persecute each other because of these differences, but endeavored to find the germs of common ideas in all the religions. And from this endeavor arose the habit of toleration which is the keynote of the Indian religion. Truth is one, can be but one, though it may be expressed in different language.

Another great difference between eastern and western religion lies in the reception of a philosophical and scientific view of the universe. In the West, agnosticism has been growing in late years, and with the loss of a hope in individual immortality, which the westerner is always desiring and seeking, a note of despair has crept into western thought. Ages ago, the Hindoo realized that the universe was one of law, and that, under law, all change. Therefore, an imperishable individuality is an impossibility. But this thought is not one of despair to the Hindoo. On the contrary —and this is what the westerner can least understand of eastern thought—he longs for freedom, for release from the thralldom of the senses, from the thralldom of pain and the thralldom of pleasure.

Western civilization has sought a personal God and despaired at the loss of belief in such. The Hindoo, too, has sought. But God cannot be known to the external senses. The Infinite, the Absolute, cannot be grasped. Yet although it eludes us, we may not infer its non existence. It exists. What is it that cannot be seen by the outward eye? The eye itself. It may behold all other things, but itself it cannot mirror. This, then, is the solution. If God may not be found by the outer senses, turn your eye inward and find, in yourself, the soul of all souls. Man himself is the All. I cannot know the fundamental reality, because I am that fundamental reality. There is no duality. This is the solution of all questions of metaphysics and ethics. Western civilization has in vain endeavored to find a reason for altruism. Here it is. I am my brother, and his pain is mine. I cannot injure him without injuring myself, or do ill to other beings without bringing that ill upon my own soul. When I have realized that I myself am the Absolute, for me there is no more death nor life nor pain nor pleasure, nor caste nor sex. How can that which is absolute die or be born? The pages of nature are turned before us like the pages of a book, and we think that we ourselves are turning, while in reality we remain ever the same.

---

5. This was Swami Vivekananda's first public lecture delivered in California, entitled "The Vedanta Philosophy or Hinduism as a Religion", of which there is no verbatim transcript available.

HINDU PHILOSOPHY[1]

Conception Of The Universe In Distant India

Los Angeles Times, December 13, 1899.

Swami Vivekananda, the Hindu philosopher, addressed the regular monthly meeting of the Southern California Academy of Sciences at Unity Church last evening.[2] The audience was large and appreciative, and at the end of the lecture a number of questions were asked by members of the audience and answered by the lecturer. . .

The speaker began with a reference to the mythological tales of the Hindus in which they attempted to explain the origin of the universe, and he told also of the endeavors of the ancients to explain the mysteries which surrounded them.

According to their belief, he said, man's first idea is of himself. His will moves all his members. A child's idea of power is in its will. All movement of the universe has a will behind it. The Hindus believe, said the speaker, that there is but one God, and he a person like the rest of them, but infinitely greater. Their mind is philosophical enough not to admit the existence of two gods, one bad and one good. With them nature is a unit, unity in all existence is the universe, and God is the same as nature. "There is not a system of philosophy," said the speaker,

from that of the ancient Egyptians down to that of the Roman Catholic Church, which does not show traces of the same thought. All forces that exist in the mental and physical world have been resolved, in India, into the one word "Father" ["Prâna"?]. Whatever is, has been projected by Him.

In closing, the philosopher said that the ancient voice of India had found an echo in the 19th century in the writings of Herbert Spencer.

---

1. *New Discoveries*, Vol. 5, pp. 194 95.

2. Cf. the following December 13, 1899 Los Angeles Herald newspaper report on the same lecture (pp. 502 4).

CONCEPTION OF THE UNIVERSE[3]

Los Angeles Herald, December 13, 1899.
Swami Vivekananda's lecture before the Academy of Sciences

Unity church was filled last evening with a large audience to hear the Swami Vivekananda, a native of India, lecture on the kosmos, or the Veda conception of the universe[4] under the auspices of the Southern California Academy of Sciences. . .

In introducing his subject the speaker reviewed the mythology of the flood, which among the Babylonians, Egyptians, Assyrians and other races is similar to the story of the Hebrew scriptures, showing that all held a similar belief concerning the creation of the universe.

In the worship of the sun and the forces of nature, we see the attempts of ancient peoples to explain the mysteries surrounding them. Man's first idea of force was himself. When a stone fell he saw no force in it but the will behind it, and he conceived the idea that the whole universe was moved by force of wills. Gradually these wills became one, and science begins to rise. Gods begin to vanish, and in their place comes oneness, and now God is in danger of being dethroned by modern science. Science wants to explain things by their own nature and make the universe self sufficient.

Wills gradually began to disappear, and in their place comes will. This was the process of development in all the nations of the world, and so it was in India. Their ideas and gods were pretty much the same as those of other lands, only in India they did not stop there. They learned that life alone can produce life, and that death can never produce life. In our speculations about God we have got to monotheism. Everywhere else speculation stops there; we make it the be all and end all of everything, but in India it does not stop there. A gigantic will can

---

3. *New Discoveries*, Vol. 5, pp. 192 94.

4. This was Swami Vivekananda's second lecture in California, entitled "The Cosmos, or the Veda Conception of the Universe", of which there is no verbatim transcript available. Cf. the Swami's two New York lectures on the Cosmos, delivered in 1896, in *Complete Works*, II ("The Cosmos: The Macrocosm" and "The Cosmos: The Microcosm").

not explain all this phenomena we see around us. Even in man there is something back of the will. In so common sense a thing as the circulation of the blood, we find will is not the motive power.

We have conceived God as a person like ourselves, only infinitely greater, and because there is goodness and mercy and happiness in the world there must be a being possessing these attributes, but there is also evil. The Hindu mind is too philosophical to admit the existence of two gods, one good and one bad. India remained true to the idea of unity. What is evil to me may be good to someone else; what is good to me may be evil to others. We are all links in a chain. Hence comes the speculation of the Upanishads, the religion of 300,000,000 of the human race. Nature is a unit; unity is in all existence, and God is the same as nature. This is one of the Indian speculations known to all the world outside of India.

There is not a system of religion or philosophy in the world that does not show the influence of India's speculation, even to the Catholic church. The conservation of energy, considered a new discovery, has been known there by the name of father [Prâna?]. Whatever is comes from the father. Brahma [Prana?] must energize on something, and that they say is an invisible ether. Brahma [Prana?] vibrating on ether, the solid, the liquid, the luminous, it is all the same ether. The potentiality of everything is there. In the beginning of the next period Brahma [Prana?] will begin to vibrate more and more.

Thus this speculation of India's scriptures is very similar to modern science. The same idea is taken up by modern evolution. Even our bodies, different only in dignity, are links in the same chain. In one individual the possibilities of every other individual are there. The living entity contains the possibility of all life, but can only express that which environment demands. The most wonderful speculations are formed in modern science. The one that interests me as a preacher of religion is the oneness of all religions [life?]. When Herbert Spencer's voice says that the same life welling up in the plant is the life welling up in the individual, the Indian religion has found a voice in the nineteenth century.

TOLD ABOUT INDIA[5]

Los Angeles Herald, January 3, 1900.
Lecture last night at Blanchard Hall by Swami Vivekananda

Swami Vivekananda, member of an ancient order of Hindu monks, who is giving a series of lessons and lectures in this city, addressed an audience last night at Blanchard hall upon the "History of India" ["The People of India"].[6] The Swami appeared before his audience in American dress, losing to a great degree the peculiar and characteristic personality given him by the aesthetic silken robes and the turban worn by his order.

The speaker said India was not a country, but a continent containing a huge mass of races united by religion. India was of ancient date. It was inhabited, when through a desire to reach it by a shorter passage, Columbus discovered America, and its production of cotton, sugar, indigo and spices have enriched the world. This country inhabited by 200,000,000 of people, is full of little villages that extend through all the valleys and up the mountains thousands of feet above the sea level. The immense fertility of the soil owes much to the tremendous rainfall, which is often 1,800 inches [sic] in a season, averaging perhaps 600 inches. Many of the people, however, in spite of the abundant productions, live wholly on millet, a kind of cereal; no animal food is eaten; no meat, eggs or fish.

The country from most ancient times has kept its own customs, its own languages and its castes. It has by its religion saved itself while it has seen other sections [nations] rise and decay. The Babylonian civilization was not new, but India dates long before its rise and fall. The most ancient language, Sanskrit, is spoken by the priests, and was spoken once by all the different races. The speaker gave examples of many of our common English words coming from Sanskrit roots, and traced the old religious ideas and even mythology to the ancient Aryan races.

Many of the customs of the country were

---

5. *New Discoveries*, Vol. 5, pp. 227 29.

6. Of which there is no verbatim transcript available.

sketched, and further it was shown how this country was the seat of civilization, the center of arts, the sciences, the philosophical thought of the world. The people of India have saved themselves by making a wall around themselves by making the castes absolute. An emperor in India is glad to trace his descent from a priest, who is the highest caste. The castes do not exist as they did once, but they are divided into many divisions and sub divisions. There are hundreds of them. No people of different castes eat together, or cook together. Marriage is not legal if made outside of one's caste. The intricacy of the laws of caste is very great and branch out into the minutest detail. The poorest beggar or the viceroy of India may belong to the same caste.

Shoes are not allowed to be worn, as they are made from the skin of an animal. The women pay even more attention to these details than the men. All these customs have their philosophy. This is the true democracy, it is the socialistic idea, the development of the masses, not the individual.

The speaker closed with comparing the position of women in India with that of this country. In India the whole idea of womanhood is the mother. The mother is revered. She is the giver of life, the founder of the race.

THE RELIGIOUS LEGENDS OF INDIA[1]

Los Angeles Times, January 17, 1900.

The Swami

Clad in his maroon robe, Swami Vivekananda addressed a small audience composed mostly of women, at the Shakespeare Club this evening [January 16].[2] He gave an account of the religious legends of Brahmanism, which are embodied in the daily lives of the Hindus, of the origin of Shiva and his surrender to the pure spirit of his wife, today the mother of all India, whose worship is carried to such an extent that no female animal can be killed. Vivekananda quoted freely from the Sanskrit, translating as he went along...

---

1. *New Discoveries*, Vol. 5, p. 269.

2. Of which there is no verbatim transcript available.

THE SCIENCE OF YOGA[3]

Los Angeles Herald, January 26, 1900

Swami Vivekananda, the Oriental seer, lectured at the Shakespeare club this morning [Thursday, January 25] on "The Science of Yoga".[4] He said that there is no difference in kind between anything in nature, but that all differences are of degree merely. The mind is the supreme power, the motor of the world.

SWAMI VIVEKANANDA AT THE LOS ANGELES HOME[5]

Unity, February (?) 1900.

We had eight lectures at the Home by the Swami[6] and all were intensely interesting, though a few malcontents complained because he did not give some short cuts into the King

dom [of Heaven] and show an easy way to the attainment of mental powers; instead he would say,

Go home and promise yourself that you will not worry for a whole month even though the maid breaks all your best china.

There is combined in the Swami Vivekananda the learning of a university president, the dignity of an archbishop, with the grace and winsomeness of a free natural child. Getting on the platform without a moment's preparation he would soon be in the midst of his subject, sometimes becoming almost tragic as his mind would wander from deep metaphysics to the prevailing condition in Christian countries today who go and seek to reform Filipinos with the swords in one hand and the Bible in the other, or in South Africa allow children of the same father to cut each other to pieces. To contrast this condition of things he described what took place during the last famine in India where men would

---

3. *New Discoveries*, Vol. 5, p. 276.

4. Of which there is no verbatim transcript available.

5. *New Discoveries*, Vol. 5, pp. 218 20.

6. This newspaper report is an overview of eight class lectures delivered at the Home of Truth in December 1899 and January 1900, of which there is only one verbatim transcript, "Hints on Practical Spirituality", published in *Complete Works*, II: 24 37.

die of starvation beside their cattle rather than stretch forth a hand to kill. (Will Unity readers remember the fifty million Hindoos who are starving today and send them a blessing?)

Instead of trying to give much of what we heard from the Swami direct, I will append a few of the sayings of his master, Ramakrishna, that will better indicate the nature of his teaching. His chief aim seems to be to encourage people in living simple, quiet wholesome lives—that the life shall be the religion, not something separate and apart.

To the true mother he gives the highest place, counting her as more to be esteemed than those who simply run around teaching. "Anyone can talk," he said, but if I had to look after a baby, I could not endure existence for more than three days.

Frequently he would speak of the "mother" as we speak of the "father," and would say "the mother will take care of us," or "the mother will look after things."

We had a lecture on Christmas day from the Swami entitled, "Christ's Mission to the World," and a better one on this subject I never heard. No Christian minister could have presented Jesus as a character worthy (of) the greatest reverence more eloquently or more powerfully than did this learned Hindoo, who told us that in this country on account of his dark skin he has been refused admission to hotels, and even barbers have sometimes objected to shave him. Is it any wonder that our "heathen" brethren never fail to make mention of this fact that even "our" Master was an Oriental?

IIINDOO MONK LECTURES[7]

[San Francisco Chronicle, February 24, 1900.

*Swami Vivekananda's Topic
Is "The Idea of Universal Religion"*

At Golden Gate Hall last evening Swami Vivekananda, a Hindoo monk, entertained an audience for an hour and a half with his lecture on "The Idea of Universal Religion."...[8]

---

7. *New Discoveries*, Vol. 5, pp. 315 16.

8. Of which there is no verbatim transcript available.

Tracing religion from the commencement of history he spoke of the existence of creeds. Sects were known from the earliest time, he said. As time rolled on there began various contests for a supremacy between the various sects. History, he declared, was a mere repetition of slaughter under the guise of religion. Superstition, he thought, was fast becoming a thing of the past through the expansion of the minds of men. They had more liberality of thought now. They were deeper students of philosophy and through the principles of true philosophy only could religion in its deepest form be found. Until men could accord to others the right of free belief on all subjects, and be willing to believe truth under whatever form it might appear, no universal religion would be manifest to the world, he declared. It would never be promulgated by any society, but would grow instinctively as the intellect of man developed.

VEDANTISM, AND WHAT IT IS AND WHAT IT IS NOT[9]

Lecture of Swami Vivekananda on the Religion of the Hindoos

Oakland Tribune, February 26, 1900.

It is the Only Creed, He Says, that Can Be Taught Without Lies and Without Compromise

The claims of the Brahmin religion, or Vedantism, on the modern world were presented to night at the Congress of Religions in the First Unitarian Church by Swami Vivekananda,[10] a remarkably eloquent expounder of that faith...

To his auditors to night he explained Vedantism as the religion of the Vedas, or ancient Hindoo books, which, he asserted, is "the mother of religion." "It may seem ridiculous how a book can be without beginning or end," he said, but by the Vedas no books are meant. They signify the accumulated

---

9. *New Discoveries*, Vol. 5, pp. 329 31.

10. The lecture was entitled "The Claims of Vedanta on the Modern World", of which there is no verbatim transcript available. Cf. *Complete Works*, VIII: 231 34 for a somewhat different report, which does not include most of the Swami's direct quotes appearing in the Oakland Tribune.

treasury of spiritual laws discovered by different persons in different times. The Hindoo believes he is a spirit. Him the sword cannot pierce, him the fire cannot burn, him the water cannot melt, him the air cannot dry. He believes every soul is a circle whose circumference is nowhere, but whose center is located in a body. Death means the change of this center from body to body. We are the children of God. Matter is our servant.

Vedantism is a sort of rebellion against the mockery of the past. Some men are so practical that if they know that by chopping off their heads they could get salvation, there are many who would do so. That is all outward; you must turn your eyes inward to learn what is in your soul. Soul is spirit omnipresent. Where does the soul go after death? Where could the earth fall to? Where can the soul go? Where is it not already? The great cornerstone of Vedantism is the recognition of Self. Man, have faith in yourself. The soul is the same in every one. It is all purity and perfection and the more pure and perfect we [you] are the more purity and perfection you will see.

A man or preaching jack who cries, "Oh Lord, I'm only a crawling worm!" should be still and crawl into his hole. His cries only add more misery to the world. I was amused to read in one of your papers, "How would Christ edit a paper!" How foolish. How would Christ cook a meal? Yet you are the advanced people of the West. If Christ came here, you would shut up shop and go into the street with him to help the poor and downtrodden. Vedantism is the only religion that can be taught without lies, without stretching the texts, without compromise.

TRUE RELIGION[1]

The Alameda Encinal, April 5, 1900.
Hindu Philosopher Gives His Ideas

Last evening the Swami Vivekananda gave the first of a series of three public lectures at Tucker Hall on "The Development of Religious Ideas."[2]

The speaker dwelt briefly on the similarity of ideas in the minds of orthodox Christians, Mohammedans and Hindus with regard to the origin of their religions. Each believed his particular prophet or teacher to have been inspired in some mysterious way by a God or Gods, who as it were, regulated or influenced the affairs of this world from a distance. The modern scientific mind, on the contrary, instead of seeking for outside or supernatural causes for phenomena endeavored to find cause in the thing or condition itself.

While at first glance this method of investigation might seem to take from religion some of its vital elements, yet in reality it resulted in man finding that the spiritual attributes of deity and the states of mind producing heaven and hell were all within himself, and although the result of this rational modern inquiry might appear to contradict much that had been handed down in the old religious writings such as Bible, Koran and Vedas, yet the contradiction was more apparent than real, for the prophets and teachers of old had true perceptions, but were mistaken only in attributing their experiences to outside agencies, instead of realizing them to be the development and expression of elements in their own souls before unknown and unrecognized.

The lecturer traced some of the common beliefs regarding location of heavens and hells, of various burial rites and customs, and he spoke of the impressions made on the primitive mind that resulted in a personification of the active natural forces in the phenomena with which we are surrounded…idealist brought the bold aspiration down to earth, the realist caused it to take form through work. Love cannot be defined in positive terms, only negatively. Its nature is of the form of renunciation. In its more general sense it might be divided threefold: (1) That love which is for one's own pleasure, irrespective of pleasure or pain to others—the purely selfish, the lowest. (2) That love which exchanges—"I will love you if you love me. We will make each other mutually happy"—the partially selfish, the middle path trodden by the great majority of mankind. (3) That love which gives all and asks for nothing, without

---
1. *New Discoveries*, Vol. 6, pp. 405-6.
2. Of which there is no verbatim transcript available.

premeditation and which never regrets, unconquerable by any evil thing done to him from whom it emanates. It is the highest, the divine. Only with this last kind are we concerned here. The first is the path of the sensualist and the animal, the second the path of struggling humanity on its way to better things, the third the real path of love, trodden by those who renounce the world and set out upon that road which leads to Eternal Peace. In that love there is no fear. Love kills fear. A lion might stand over a babe and threaten its life; the mother knows no fear, she does not fly, but she opposes. At that moment love destroys terror; at other times the same woman would run from a small dog. A fierce Mahomedan [sic] warrior went to a garden to pray. In the same garden a girl had appointed to meet her lover. The warrior lay prostrate on his face according to the prescribed form of his religion. At that moment the girl espied her lover, and with joy rushing to meet him, trod upon the prostrate form. He jumped up and laying hand upon his sword would have slain the girl. "How dare you?" cried he, "vile wench, disturb my worship, my devotion to God, with your base feet." "Worship! devotion!" cried the girl, "you do not know what they are. You had no devotion, lying there, no spirit of worship. If I, a timid girl, could so forget the presence of an object of dread like you, in my worship and devotion to my earthly lover as to tread upon you and not even know it, how much more should you, if your heart had been absorbed in love and devotion to God, have been ignorant that I touched you?" The warrior was humbled and appeased and went away. Our highest ideal of love is the image.

PART II: EUROPEAN NEWSPAPER REPORTS

SWAMI VIVEKANANDA ON LOVE[3]

Maidenhead Adviser, October 23, 1895.

On Thursday the Swami Vivekananda delivered a lecture at the Town Hall, Maidenhead, taking as his subject "The Eastern Doctrine of Love."[4] Owing to other attractions in the town the attendance was not large. Many of the public also associated the lecturer with the Theosophical Society, with which, however, he has, we are informed, nothing whatever to do, nor with any other society, neither does he propose forming any society himself. He believes in expounding his views to whoever will listen to them and leaving those individuals to advocate them as a whole, or with whatever modifications they may deem fitting, or to reject them altogether, believing that out of the strife of all opinions truth at length prevails.

The chair was taken at 8 p.m. by Mr. E. Gardner, J.P., C.C., and he very briefly introduced the lecturer, who was clad in his native costume. The Swami then proceeded to express his view upon devotion to deity, or, as more commonly expressed in the East—love (Bhakti), to the following effect:—Religion may be divided into two forms, the first almost entirely superstitious and the second merely metaphysical, but if either of these is to have any force it must be accompanied by love. Work alone without this element did not satisfy. The land might be covered with hospitals, penetrated by good roads; there might be great social institutions well conducted, and good sanitation, but these were all external physical processes and by themselves brought man no nearer to Divinity. Both the realist and the idealist were necessary and complementary one of the other. The which we form for ourselves of deity. A barbarous people have a tyrannical and cruel god. A

---

3. *New Discoveries*, Vol. 3, pp. 237 40.

4. The lecture, of which no verbatim transcript is available, was delivered October 17, 1895.

wise and noble people see God in ever and ever widening potencies. God is always God, but the views which men and nations may take of Him vary. No higher view is known than that of love. The man who bears in his heart an unrelaxing love to every creature, whether he recognise that that creature is a manifestation of God, in which he is actually present, or whether he look upon it merely as fashioned by Deity, that man is on the path to Deity, on the great path of devotion and renunciation. He cannot injure the creature of God, however repulsive to his narrower view of what should or should not be. He gives in love, not in pride; in loving Deity he loves its manifestations, works with them and abides by them.

The lecture was impressively delivered, and at the close a vote of thanks was accorded the Chairman (on the proposition of Mr. E. T. Sturdy, of Caversham).

The proceedings occupied only a little over half an hour.

AN INDIAN ASCETIC[1]

Standard, October 23, 1895.

Since the days of Ramahoun [Ram Mohan] Roy, says the Standard, with the single exception of Keshub Chunder [Keshab Chandra] Sen, there has not appeared on an English platform a more interesting Indian figure than the Brahman who lectured in Princes' [Prince's] Hall last night...

The lecture[2] was a most fearless and eloquent exposition of the pantheistic philosophy of the Vedanta school, and the Swami seems to have incorporated into his system a good deal also of the moral element of the Yoga school, as the closing passage of his lecture presented in a modified form not the advocacy of mortification, which is the leading feature of the latter school, but the renunciation of all so called material comforts and blessings, as the only means of entering into perfect union with the supreme and absolute Self. The opening passages of the lecture were a review of the rise of the grosser form of Materialism in the beginning of the present century, and the later development of the various forms of metaphysical thought, which for a time swept materialism away. From this he passed on to discuss the origin and nature of knowledge. In some respects his views on this point were almost a statement of pure Fichteism, but they were expressed in language, and they embodied illustrations, and made admissions which no German transcendentalist would have used. He admitted there was a gross material world outside, but he confessed he did not know what matter was. He asserted that mind was a finer matter, and that behind was the soul of man, which was immovable, fixed, before which outward objects passed, as it were, in a procession, which was without beginning or end—in other words, which was eternal, and finally which was God. He worked out this pantheistic conception of the personal identity of man and God with great comprehensiveness and an ample wealth of illustration, and in passage after passage of great beauty, solemnity, and earnestness. "There is only one Soul in the Universe", he said:

There is no "you" or "me"; all variety is merged into the absolute unity, the one infinite existence—God.

From this, of course, followed the immortality of the soul, and something like the transmigration of souls towards higher manifestations of perfection. As already stated, his peroration of twenty minutes was a statement of the doctrine of renunciation. In the course of it he made some remorselessly disparaging criticism on the work that factories, engines and other inventions, and books were doing for man, compared with half a dozen words spoken by Buddha or Jesus. The lecture was evidently quite extemporaneous, and was delivered in a pleasing voice, free from any kind of hesitation.

NATIVE INDIAN LECTURER AT PRINCES' HALL[3]

London Morning Post, October 23, 1895.

---

1. *New Discoveries*, Vol. 3, pp. 246 47.

2. The lecture was "Self Knowledge", of which there is no verbatim transcript available.

3. *New Discoveries*, Vol. 3, p. 248.

Last night at Princes' [Prince's] Hall, Piccadilly, Swami Vivekananda, an Indian Yogi, who is at present on a visit to this country, delivered what was described as an "oration" on the subject of "Self Knowledge."[4] A Yogi, it was explained, is one who formally renounces the world and gives himself up to study and devotion. Swami Vivekananda originally left his native land for the purpose of giving his interpretation of the Vedanta philosophy at the Parliament of Religions which was held two years ago at Chicago, and since that time he has been engaged in delivering lectures on the same subject in America. In the course of his address last night he declared that there were indications in these closing days of the 19th century that the pendulum of scientific thought was swinging back, for men all over the world were rummaging in the pages of ancient records, and ancient religious forms were again coming to the fore. To many this seemed to be a case of degeneration, while others regarded it as one of those outbursts of superstition which periodically visited society, but to the scientific student there was in the present state of things a prognostication of grand future benefit. The lecturer then proceeded at considerable length to describe the peculiar system of philosophy which he teaches, and traced the three different stages of the religion which has grown out of it. He spoke with a good deal of fluency, and his remarks were listened to with attention by the somewhat small audience.

THE CHRISTIAN COMMONWEALTH[5]

Christian Commonwealth, November 14, 1895.

South Place Chapel Lecture

"The Swami Vivekananda" enlightened the congregation at South place Chapel last Sunday morning on "The Basis of Vedanta Morality."..[6]

The Swami explained that in the system of morality which he was expounding actions were not inspired by any hope of reward, here or hereafter, nor by any fear of punishment in this world or in the beyond: "We must work simply from the impetus within, work for work's sake, duty for duty's sake." This idea of morality is claimed to be superior to the religion of Jesus, and so has beguiled some so called Christians into Buddhism or other Eastern philosophies. But the essence of true Christianity is that, if your actions are inspired by the heavenly kingdom within you, Paradise will be the result, whereas, if you act in harmony with the devil's kingdom without you will land in Perdition. The genuine Christian does not, as the Swami seemed to suggest, act for the purpose of evading punishments, but at the same time he sees the ultimate consequences of all actions...

AN UNIVERSAL RELIGION[7]

The Queen, The Lady's Newspaper, November 23, 1895.

Mrs. Haweis's first autumn At home took place last Saturday at Queen's House, when the Indian Yogi, or ascetic, Swami Vive Kananda (Buddhist [sic] delegate at the Parliament of Religions at Chicago in 1893) discussed in a liberal spirit, and not without humour, the chances and the charms of an universal religion.[8] He showed that the underlying principles of all the great religions of the world resembled one another, and amongst the great prophets he placed the Christian Redeemer very high, implying, however, that His teaching was little borne out sometimes by His professed followers. There was no radical impossibility of reconciliation between sects, now biting and devouring each other from the best motives, if charity and sympathy were carried into the kiosque, the temple, and the church. Canon Basil Wilberforce and the Rev. H. R. Haweis both made interesting speeches in reply to the Swami...The guests numbered 150.

---

4. Of which no verbatim transcript is available. Cf. the preceding newspaper report "An Indian Ascetic", pp. 515 16, for another report of the same lecture, delivered October 22, 1895.

5. *New Discoveries*, Vol. 3, pp. 267 69.

6. A lecture delivered in London, England, on November 10, 1895, of which there is no verbatim transcript available.

7. *New Discoveries*, Vol. 3, pp. 276 77.

8. This London talk, of which there is no verbatim transcript available, was delivered November 16, 1895.

EDUCATION[1]

Daily Chronicle, May 14, 1896.

The Sesame Club.—At a meeting of the Sesame Club on Tuesday night [May 12], the chairman, Mr. Ashton Jonson, said he regretted to announce that Mrs. Norman was too unwell to be present to open, as announced, a debate on "Should we return to the land." An address was accordingly given by Swami Vivekananda on the subject of education,[2] in which he urged that no one could obtain intellectual greatness until he was physically pure. Morality gave strength; the immoral were always weak, and could never raise themselves intellectually, much less spiritually. Directly [as] immorality began to enter the national life its foundations commenced to rot. As the life blood of every nation was to be found in the schools, where boys and girls were receiving their education, it was absolutely essential that the young students should be pure, and this purity must be taught them.

SPIRITUALISM AND THE VEDANTA PHILOSOPHY[3]

Light, July 4, 1896.

When first we heard that the Swami Vivekananda was coming to London to expound the Vedanta Philosophy, we were hopeful that his teaching would not only confirm the faith of Spiritualists, but might also add to their number. We hoped this, because the very essence of the Hindu Philosophy is that man is a spirit, and has a body, and not that man is a body, and may have a spirit also; which is as far as many a Western mind can reach...

It has been the glorious privilege of our modern Spiritualism to prove by actual demonstration the existence of spirit apart from flesh, and it would, therefore, seem reasonable to look for co operation on the part of the exponents of the Vedanta Philosophy and the supporters of Spiritualism. We are not quite certain, however, that this desirable consummation can be attained, for observations made very recently by the Swami are calculated only to divide the two sects.[4] The Vedanta Philosophy sets before the student an ideal aim! Nothing less, in fact, than the unfolding of the God within him, and nothing could well be more impressive and inspiring than the presentation of this idea by a speaker of the force and eloquence of the Swami. We could only respect and admire, until modern Spiritualism was alluded to, and that in a manner which left upon us the impression that the Swami condemned without reservation all sitting for phenomena. He admitted having sat for observation with professional mediums, and held that one and all had practised fraud. "Spirit voices," according to the Swami, are never heard to clash! As the "sepulchral dies away the small child's voice rises up," intimating thus that ventriloquism was invariably respon sible for the sounds. "Spirit messages," he remarked, were quite worthless, for they never rose above the level of "I am well and happy," or "Give John a piece of cake."

This assertion could, of course, only be made in ignorance of the contents of "Spirit Teachings," a book which, we think, can well stand comparison even with the exalted teaching of the Swami Vivekananda. The process of making up sham materialisations and working the figure on the end of a wire was also described in detail.

We were present again the following evening,[5] when a paper of questions bearing upon the adverse criticism of the Swami was read out to the meeting. Some thirty minutes were then passed in qualifying and explaining his remarks of the night before, and, to our deep satisfaction, the Swami not only confessed his belief in the possibility of spirits communicating with mortals, but even expressed his conviction that at times spirits of a high grade visited earth in order to assist mankind. It is, however, we conceive, no part of the Vedanta Philoso-

---

1. *New Discoveries*, Vol. 4, p. 157.

2. There is no verbatim transcript available. Cf. the Indian newspaper report "On Education", p. 535.

3. *New Discoveries*, Vol. 4, pp. 229 30.

4. A Thursday evening class delivered in the summer of 1896, at St. George's Road, of which there is no verbatim transcript available.

5. Probably "Vedic Religious Ideals", delivered in London, England, on Wednesday, October 28, 1896, of which there is no verbatim transcript available.

phy to recommend the seeking of such intercourse, on account of its possible "dangers." It is commonly held that the undeveloped spirit can most easily communicate with man, consequently the Swami uttered his word of warning and withheld any word of encouragement...

AN OCTOBER CLASS REVIEW[6]

Light, October 28, 1896.

On the sixth floor of one of the dismal but convenient Victoria street houses, we lately listened to a discourse by Swami Vivekananda—one of a long series on the Hindoo Religion and Philosophy[7]...For an hour and a half he spoke, without a note. It is true that the discourse was rather a flow of remarks than a connected study, but it was all keenly interesting.

The subject, in the main, was the Vedas, but we got excursions upon Evolution, Modern Science, Idealism and Realism, the Supremacy of Spirit, &c. On the whole, we gathered that the speaker was a preacher of the universal religion of spiritual ascendency and spiritual harmony. Certain passages from the Vedas—beautifully translated and read, by the way—were charming in their bearing upon the humanness and sharp reality of a life beyond the veil. One longed for more of this.

We were much impressed with the admission that in the Vedas there were many contradictions, and that devout Hindoos never thought of denying them nor reconciling them. Everyone was free to take what he liked. At different stages and on different planes, all were true. Hence the Hindoos never excommunicated and never persecuted. The contradictions in the Vedas are like the contradictions in life—they are very real, but they are all true. This seems impossible, but there is sound sense in it. At all events, as regards excommunication and persecution, we only wish the Christians could make the Hindoo's claim.

---

6. *New Discoveries*, Vol. 4, pp. 370 71.

7. Probably "Vedic Religious Ideals", delivered in London, England, on Wednesday, October 28, 1896, of which there is no verbatim transcript available.

PART III: INDIAN NEWSPAPER REPORTS

A BENGALI SADHU[8]

Madura Mail, January 28, 1893.

(Though this extract does not mention Swami Vivekananda by name, refers to an M.A. which the Swami never received, and describes him as two years older than his actual age—still there is indubitable internal evidence that the Bengali Sâdhu was Swami Vivekananda. Furthermore, the date coincides accurately with the Swami's stay in Madras, and a back reference to this event published in the Indian Social Reformer, on July 13, 1902, is added confirmation. Incidentally, no copy of the Indian Social Reformer of 1892 1893 is available today.)

A BENGALI SADHU ON HINDU RELIGION AND SOCIOLOGY

A young Bengalee Sanyashi [Sannyâsin] of about thirty two years of age, and a Master of Arts of the Calcutta University was last week interviewed at the Triplicane Literary Society by about a hundred educated Indians among whom was Dewan Bahadur Raghunatha Rao. A summary of what was stated by the Sadhu is published by the Indian Social Reformer, from which we make the following extracts:[9]

The Vedic Religion

The perfect religion is the Vedic religion. The Vedas have two parts, mandatory and optional. The mandatory injunctions are eternally binding on us. They constitute the Hindu religion. The optional ones are not so. These have been changing and been changed by the Rishis to suit the times. The Brahmins at one time ate beef and married Sudras. [A] calf was killed to please a guest. Sudras cooked for

---

8. Basu, Sri Sankari Prasad, "Swami Vivekananda in Madras: 1892 1893 — Some New Findings", Prabuddha Bharata, 1974, pp. 296 98.

9. The only verbatim report of Swami Vivekananda's ideas at this period in his life.

Brahmins. The food cooked by a male Brahmin was regarded as polluted food. But we have changed our habits to suit the present yug[a]. Although our caste rules have so far changed from the time of Manu, still if he should come to us now, he would still call us Hindus. Caste is a social organization and not a religious one. It was the outcome of the natural evolution of our society. It was found necessary and convenient at one time. It has served its purpose. But for it, we would long ago have become Mahomedans [sic]. It is useless now. It may be dispensed with. Hindu religion no longer requires the prop of the caste system. A Brahmin may interdine with anybody, even a Pariah. He won't thereby lose his spirituality. A degree of spirituality that is destroyed by the touch of a Pariah, is a very poor quantity. It is almost at the zero point. Spirituality of a Brahmin must overflow, blaze and burn [so] as to warm into spiritual life not one Pariah but thousands of Pariahs who may touch him. The old Rishis observed no distinctions or restrictions as regards food. A man who feels that his own spirituality is so flimsy that the sight of a low caste man annihilates it need not approach a Pariah and must keep his precious little to himself.

The Hindu Ideal of Life

The Hindu Ideal of life is "Nivarti" [Nivritti].[1] Nivarti means subjugation and conquest of evil passions, of Tamasa nature of lust, revenge and avarice. It does not mean conquest of all desire. It means only the annihilation of gross desires. Every man is bound to love and sympathize with his fellow creatures. [A] Sanyasi is one who has vanquished all his selfish passions and vowed to devote his life for the good of others. He loves all. "Pravirti" [Pravritti] means love of God and all his creatures. Sanyasis ought to be fed. They are not like the Christian bishops and Archbishops who must be paid to do their work with thousands of pounds per annum; all whose earnings are spent upon their own luxury—their wife and children. [The] Sanyasi wants only a morsel of food, and then he places all his knowledge and services at the disposal of the public. He is a wandering missionary. Individuals and society have to work themselves up from "brute through man, into divine". Even the lowest of the Hindus, the Pariah, has less of the brute in him than a Briton in a similar social status. This is the result of an old and excellent religious civilization. This evolution to a higher spiritual state is possible only through discipline and education.

The Shradh [Shrâddha] Ceremony[2]

Every institution, caste, early marriage etc., that stands in the way of education, ought at once to be knocked on the head. Even "Shradh" may be given up, if the performance of it involves waste of time which might be better used for self education. But "Shradh" should not be given up. The meaning of the Mantras is very edifying. The Mantras depict the suffering and care undergone by our parents on our behalf. The performance of it is an honour paid to the memory of the sum total of the spirit of our forefathers, whose virtues we inherit. Shradh has nothing to do with one's salvation. Yet no Hindu who loves his religion, his country and his past great men should give up Shradh. The outward formalities and the feeding of the Brahmins are not essential. We have no Brahmins in these days worthy of being fed on Shradh days. The Brahmins fed ought not to be professional eaters, but Brahmins who feed disciples gratis, and teach them true Vedic doctrines. In these days, Shradh may be performed mentally.

Education of Women

The jealous guardianship of our women shows that we Hindus have declined in our national virtues, that we reverted to the "brutal state". Every man must so discipline his mind as to bring himself to regard all women as his sisters or mothers.

---

1. Nivritti and Pravritti are key concepts in Hindu philosophy, and Swami Vivekananda has frequently interpreted and elaborated on them (e.g., see *Karma Yoga*, Ch. VI) in their traditional connotations. But the interpretation of the terms here ascribed to him by the Indian Social Reformer's reporter is not in accord with what the Swami has said elsewhere.

2. A religious ceremony in which food and drink are offered to deceased relatives or ancestors.

Women must have freedom to read, to receive as good an education as men. Individual development is impossible with ignorance and slavery.

Emancipation of the Hindus

Through the slavery of a thousand years, Hindus have at present degenerated. They have forgotten their own self respect. Every English boy is taught to feel his importance, he thinks that he is a member of a great race, the conquerors of the Earth. The Hindu feels from his boyhood just the reverse that he is born to slave. We can't become a great nation unless we love our religion and try to respect ourselves, and respect our country men and society. The Hindus of modern times are generally hypocrites. They must rise, and combine the faith in the true Vedic religion, with a knowledge of the political and scientific truths of the Europeans. The evils of caste seem to be more prevalent in the South than in Bengal. In Bengal a Brahmin uses the water touched by the Sudras, but here the Sudra is kept at a great distance by the Brahmin. There are no Brahmins in [the] Kali Yug[a]. The Pariahs, our fellow beings, ought to be educated by the higher castes, must […] truths of Hindu religion and be […] Brahmins. The first duty of a Brahmin is to love all. There must first be an amalgamation of the Brahmins, then of all the Dwijas,[3] and then of the Dwijas and Sudras.

THE PARLIAMENT OF RELIGIONS[4]

By H. R. Haweis

The Indian Mirror (from The Daily Chronicle), November 28, 1893.

…Vivekananda, the popular Hindu monk, whose physiognomy bore the most striking resemblance to the classic face of the Buddha, denounced our commercial prosperity, our bloody wars, and our religious intolerance, declaring that at such a price the "mild Hindu" would have none of our vaunted civilisation…"You come," he cried, with the Bible in one hand and the conqueror's sword in the other—you, with your religion of yesterday, to us, who were taught thousands of years ago by our Rishis precepts as noble and lives as holy as your Christ's. You trample on us and treat us like the dust beneath your feet. You destroy precious life in animals. You are carnivores. You degrade our people with drink. You insult our women. You scorn our religion—in many points like yours, only better, because more humane. And then you wonder why Christianity makes such slow progress in India. I tell you it is because you are not like your Christ, whom we could honour and reverence. Do you think, if you came to our doors like him, meek and lowly, with a message of love, living and working and suffering for others, as he did, we should turn a deaf ear? Oh no! We should receive him and listen to him, and as we have done our own inspired Rishis (teachers)…

PARLIAMENT OF RELIGIONS IN CHICAGO[5]

The Indian Mirror, December 7, 1893.

Hindu Criticises Christianity

Mr. Vivekananda Says Religion of the Vedas Is Religion of Love

Vivekananda Says Christianity Is Intolerant

Dr. Noble presided at the afternoon session. The Hall of Colombus [Columbus] was badly crowded…Dr. Noble then presented Swami Vivekananda, the Hindu monk, who was applauded loudly as he stepped forward to the centre of the platform. He wore an orange robe, bound with a scarlet sash, and a pale yellow turban. The customary smile was on his handsome face and his eyes shown with animation. Said he:

We who come from the East have sat here on the platform day after day, and have been told in a patronizing way that we ought to accept Christianity because Christian nations are the most prosperous. We look about us, and we see England, the most

---

3. Lit., "twice born"—applicable to the three higher castes in Hindu society by virtue of the investiture of the sacred thread, signifying spiritual rebirth.

4. Vivekananda in Indian Newspapers, p. 4.

5. Vivekananda in Indian Newspapers, pp. 5 6.

prosperous Christian nation in the world, with her foot on the neck of 250,000,000 of Asiatics. We look back into history, and see that the prosperity of Christian Europe began with Spain. Spain's prosperity began with the invasion of Mexico. Christianity wins its prosperity by cutting the throats of its fellowmen. At such a price the Hindu will not have prosperity.[1]

I have sat here to day, and I have heard the height of intolerance. I have heard the creed of the Moslem applauded, when to day the Moslem sword is carrying destruction into India. Blood and the sword are not for the Hindu, whose religion is based on the law of love.[2]

When the applause had ceased, Mr. Vivekananda went [on] to read his paper, a summary of which follows: [Vide "Paper on Hinduism", Complete Works, I: 6 20]…

ON CHRISTIAN CONVERSION[3]

The Indian Mirror, June 14, 1894.

There has been some lively correspondence between Swami Vivekanand and a retired Christian Missionary on the work and prospects of Christianity in India. Among other things, the

Swami is reported to have said that "the way of converting is absolutely absurd";

Missionary doctors do no good, because they are not in touch with the people…They accomplish nothing in the way of converting, although they may have nice sociable times among themselves, &c.

The reverend gentleman took exception to the words, maintaining that speaking the vernaculars well, nobody of foreigners understands, and sympathises with Indians better than Missionaries. The Missionaries are undoubtedly good and well meaning people; but we think, the statement of the Swami that they are seldom in touch with the people, is not without foundation. With the revival of Hinduism, manifested in every part of the country, it is doubtful whether Christianity will have any sway over the Hindus. The present is a critical time for Christian Missions in India. The Swami thanked the Missionary for calling him his fellow countryman. "This is the first time," he wrote, any European foreigner, born in India though he be, has dared to call a detested Native by that name—Missionary or no Missionary. Would you dare call me the same in India?

THE CENTRAL IDEA OF THE VEDAS[4]

The Indian Mirror, July 20, 1894.

Swami Vivekananda explained in America the central idea of the Vedas as follows:

I humbly beg to differ from those who see in monotheism, in the recognition of a personal God, apart from Nature, the acme of intellectual development. I believe, it is only a kind of anthropomorphism which the human mind stumbles upon in its first efforts to understand the unknown. The ultimate satisfaction of human reason and custom lies in the realisation of that universal essence which is the All. And I hold an irrefragable evidence that this idea is present in the Vedas, the numerous gods and their invocations notwithstanding. This idea of formless All, the Sat, i.e., esse or being, called Atman and Brahman in the Upanishads, and further explained in the Darsans, is the central idea of the Vedas, nay, the root idea of the Hindu religion in general.[5]

SWAMI VIVEKANANDA ON THE SEA VOYAGE MOVEMENT[6]

The Bengalee, May 18, 1895.

There is not a Hindoo who is not proud of Vivekananda Swami—who would not honor him and his teachings. He has done honor to himself, to his race and his religion. If we are right in this view,

---

1. Vide "Cantakerous Remarks", *Complete Works*, III: 474.
2. This last paragraph is a heretofore unpublished extract.
3. Vivekananda in Indian Newspapers, p. 25.
4. Vivekananda in Indian Newspapers, p. 30.
5. Unidentified source.
6. Vivekananda in Indian Newspapers, pp. 260 62.

it follows that the opinions of Vivekananda are entitled to the highest consideration. This is what he says with regard to the sea voyage movement:—

Expansion is life; contraction is death. Love is life, hatred is death. We began to die the day we began to contract—to hate other races—and nothing can prevent our death, until we come back to life, to expansion. We must mix, therefore, with all the races of the earth and every Hindoo that goes out to travel in foreign parts, does more benefit to his country than hundreds of those bundles of superstition and selfishness whose one aim in life is to be the dog in the manger. Those wonderful structures of national life which the Western nations have raised are supported by pillars of character—and until we can produce such by the hundred, it is useless to fret and fume against this power or that power. Does anyone deserve liberty who is not ready to give it to others? Let us calmly and in manly fashion go to work—instead of dissipating our energies in unnecessary frettings and fumings and I, for one, thoroughly believe that no power in the universe can withhold from anyone anything he really deserves. The past was great no doubt, but I sincerely believe that the future in store is glorious still.[7]

We must mix with other nations and take from them whatever good they have to give us. It is our exclusiveness, our unwillingness to learn from foreign nations which is mainly responsible for our present degradation. We considered ourselves to be the elect of heaven, and superior to the nations of the earth in all respects. We regarded them as barbarians, their touch as pollution, their knowledge as worse than ignorance. We lived in a world of our own creation. We would teach the foreigner nothing—we would learn nothing from the foreigner. At last the disillusion came. The foreigner became our master— the arbiter of our destinies. We eagerly took to his learning. We found that there was much in it that was novel, much that was highly useful. We found that so far as the material comforts of life were concerned the foreigner vastly out distanced us—that his control over the powers of nature was far greater than any we had dreamt of. He had annihilated time and space, and had subordinated the powers of nature to the convenience of man. He had many wonderful things to teach us. We learnt them eagerly. But still we don't visit his country. If we do, we lose caste. We are under a foreign Government. We eagerly study a foreign language and literature and admire all that is good and beautiful in it. We use foreign articles for dress and consumption. But still we dare not visit the country of our rulers, for fear of excommunication. Against this unmeaning prejudice, the great Swami, who is a Hindoo of Hindoos, indignantly raises his voice of protest. The objectors, in his expressive language, are like the dog in the manger. They will not travel to foreign countries,—they will not allow others to travel. Yet the fact remains, says the Swami, that these travelled Hindoos do more benefit to their country than hundreds of those bundles of superstition and selfishness, whose one aim in life is to be like the dog in the manger.[8] …If we had our Rishis in this age, as we had them in the ages that are gone by, we are sure they would have withdrawn the interdiction to sea voyage, if indeed any such interdiction has been laid in the past. Society is an organism which obeys the immutable law of progress; and change, judicious and cautious change, is necessary for the well being, and indeed the preservation of the social system. However that may be, it is something to know that so high an authority and so good a Hindoo as Swami Vivekananda supports travel to foreign countries…

A SUMMARY OF "BUDDHISM, THE FULFILMENT OF HINDUISM"[9]

The Indian Mirror, June 29, 1895.

Swami Vivekananda's speech, delivered in Chicago at the presentation of the Buddhists on September 26, 1893, is published in MacNeely's edition of the "History of the Parliament of Religions". The following were his concluding words:—

We cannot live without you, nor you without us. Then believe that separation has shown to us, that

---
7. Vide *Complete Works*, IV: 366.

8. Vide *Complete Works*, IV: 366.

9. Vivekananda in Indian Newspapers, p. 73.

you cannot stand without the brain and the philosophy of the Brahman [sic], nor we without your heart. This separation between the Buddhist and the Brahman [Brahmin] is the cause of the downfall of India. That is why India has been the slave of conquerors for the past 1000 years. Let us then join the wonderful intellect of the Brahman [Brahmin] with the heart, the noble soul, the wonderful humanising power of the Great Master.[1]

INDIAN PHILOSOPHY AND WESTERN SOCIETY[2]

The Indian Mirror, December 1, 1895.

At the weekly meeting of the Balloon Society, an address on "Man and Society in the Light of Vedanta"[3] was given by Swami Vivekananda. The Swami who wore the red robe of his sect, spoke with great fluency and in perfect English for more than an hour without the help of a single note. He said that religion was the most wonderful factor in the social organism. If knowledge was the highest gain that science could give, what could be greater than the knowledge of God, of the soul, of man's own nature which was given by the study of religion? It was not only impossible that there should be one religion for the whole world, but it would be dangerous. If the whole of religious thought was at the same level, it would be the death of religious thought; variety was its life. There were four types of religion—(1) the worker, (2) the emotional, (3) the mystical, and (4) the philosophical. Each man unfortunately became so wedded to his own type that he had no eyes to see what existed in the world. He struggled to make others of the same type. That religion would be perfect which gave scope to all the different characters. The Vedantic religion took in all, and each could choose in what his nature required. A discussion followed.

---

1. Vide "Buddhism, the Fulfilment of Hinduism", *Complete Works*, I: 21 23, for a somewhat different summary paragraph.

2. Vivekananda in Indian Newspapers, pp. 85 86.

3. According to Swami Vivekananda, the topic was "Indian Philosophy and Western Society", of which there is no verbatim transcript available. Vide *New Discoveries*, Vol. 3, p. 262.

SWAMI VIVEKANANDA IN AMERICA[4]

The Indian Mirror (from the New York Herald), March 25, 1896.

Many well known persons are seeking to follow the teaching of Swami Vivekananda's Philosophy...

A Lecture by the Swami

Swami Vivekananda sat in the centre, clad in an ochre coloured robe. The Hindu had his audience divided on either side of him and there was between fifty and a hundred persons present. The class was in Karma Yoga, which has been described as the realisation of one's self as God through works and duty.

Its theme was:—

"That which ye sow ye reap", whether of good or evil.

Following the lecture or instruction the Swami held an informal reception, and the magnetism of the man was shown by the eager manner in which those who had been listening to him hastened to shake hands or begged for the favour of an introduction. But concerning himself the Swami will not say more than is absolutely necessary. Contrary to the claim made by some of his pupils he declares that he has come to this country alone and not so officially representing any order of Hindu monks. He belongs to the Sanyasis he will say; and is hence free to travel without losing his caste. When it is pointed out to him that Hinduism is not a proselytising religion, he says he has a message to the West as Buddha had a message to the East.[5] When questioned concerning the Hindu religion, and asked whether he intends to introduce its practices and ritual into [t]his country, he declares that he is preaching simply philosophy.

---

4. Vivekananda in Indian Newspapers, pp. 89 90.

5. Vide *Complete Works*, V: 314.

ON EDUCATION[6]

The Indian Mirror, June 19, 1896.

Swami Saradananda in a letter from London written to the Editor of the Brahmavadin says:—

Swami Vivekananda has made a very good beginning here. A large number of the people attend his classes regularly, and the lectures are most interesting. Canon Haweis, one of the leaders of the Anglican Church, came the other day, and was much interested. He saw the Swami before, in the Chicago fairs, and loved him from that time. On Tuesday last, the Swami lectured on "Education" at the Sesame Club. It is a respectable club got up by women for diffusing female education. In this he dealt with the old educational system of India, pointed out clearly and impressively that, the sole aim of the system was "man making" and not cramming and compared it with the present system. He held that, the mind of the man is an infinite reservoir of knowledge, and all knowledge, present, past or future, is within man, manifested or non manifested, and the object of every system of education should be to help the mind to manifest it. For instance, the law of gravitation was within man, and the fall of the apple helped Newton to think upon it, and bring it out from within his mind. His class days have been arranged as follows:—

Tuesdays, morning and evening; Thursdays, morning and evening; Friday, evening question classes. So the Swami has to do four lectures, and one class on questions every week. In the class lecture, he has begun with Gnan [Jnâna] Yoga. A short hand report of these lectures is being taken down by Mr. Goodwin, who is a great admirer of the Swami, and these lectures will be published later on.

---

6. Vivekananda in Indian Newspapers, p. 101

THE SWAMI VIVEKANANDA IN ENGLAND[7]

The Brahmavadin, July 18, 1896.

Sir,

I feel sure you will be glad to have an idea of the progress of the Swami's work in England, as a supplement to the letter which the Swami Saradananda sent you a few weeks ago. At that time a series of Sunday lectures was being arranged, and three of these have now been given. They are held in one of the galleries of the Royal Institute of Painters in water colours, 191 Piccadilly, and have been so far remarkably successful in attaining their object, that of reaching people who, from one reason or another, cannot attend the class talks. The first of the series was "The Necessity of Religion".[8] The Swami claimed that religion is and has been the greatest force in moulding the destinies of the human race. Concerning its origin he said that either of the two theories, (1) Spirit origin, (2) Search after the infinite, will meet the case, and, to his mind, neither contradicts the other, because the search after the departed of the Egyptians and Babylonians, and the attempt to peep behind the veil of the dawn, the evening, the thunderstorm, or other natural phenomena, of the Aryans, can both be included as a search after the super sensuous, and therefore the unlimited. This unlimited, in the course of time became abstracted, first as a person, then as a presence, and lastly as the essence of all existence. To his mind the dream state is the first suggestion of religious inquiry, and inasmuch as the awakened state has always been, and always will be accompanied by the dream state, a suggestion of existence finer than that of the awakened state yet vanishing during it, the human mind will always be predisposed in favour of spiritual existence and a future life. It is in our dream state that we really find, in a sense, our immortality. Later on, as dreams are found to be only milder manifestations of the awakened state, the search for still deeper planes of the mind be-

---

7. Vivekananda in Indian Newspapers, pp. 493 95.

8. Cf. Mr. J. J. Goodwin's published transcript "The Necessity of Religion", *Complete Works*, II: 57 69.

gin[s], the super conscious state of the mind. All religions claim to be founded on facts discovered in this state. The two important points to consider in this connection are, that all facts discovered in this way are, in the highest sense, abstractions, and secondly, that there is a constant struggle in the race to come up to this ideal, and everything which thwarts our progress towards that we feel as a limitation. This struggle soon ends in the discovery that to find infinite happiness, or power, or knowledge, or any other infinity, through the senses, is impossible, and then the struggle for other channels of expansion begins, and we find the necessity of religion. The second lecture was upon the subject "A Universal Religion",[1] when the Swami gave, in substance, the lecture which most of your readers have seen in print as it was delivered in New York. As this lecture may be termed the Swami's "plan of campaign" we always await its delivery with very great interest, and it is most encouraging to note that the impression made here in London was equally as good as was the case when the lecture was delivered in the Hardman Hall, New York. The third of the series brought us up to Sunday last, June 21st, when "The Real and the Apparent Man"[2] was the subject under discussion. In this the Swami, link by link, glanced over the thread of thought which has gradually advanced from the consideration of men as separate entities from God and the rest of the universe, up to the point at which we concede the impossibility of more than one Infinity, and the necessary consequence that which we now regard as men, as animals, as the universe of matter, cannot be the real unity; that the real must be something which is indivisible, and unchangeable; and when reason forces us to the conclusion that this phenomenal world can only be an illusion, through which we, as entities in the illusion, have to pass to discover our real nature, "That which exists is one; sages call it variously". But the Swami did not stop with the theory; he showed what would be the practical effect of such a theory, the gradual elimination from society of class distinctions, and distinctions between man and man, by greater unselfishness in the matters of money and power. Answering the objection that such a religion means loss of individuality, he argued that that which is changeful cannot be the real individuality, and that the gradual discovery of the reality behind us would mean the assumption of individuality and not its destruction.

The three lectures thus given have been so favorably received, and there have been so many wishes expressed for their continuation that three further lectures are to be given...

Sincerely yours.

63, St. George's Rd.
London, S. W. A DISCIPLE[3]
June 23, 1896 (Correspondence)

ON THE SWISS ALPS[4]

The Indian Mirror, September 22, 1896.

Swami Vivekananda writes from Lake Luzern [Lucerne] Switzerland, under date the 23rd of August last.[5] He has been walking over several parts of the Cis Alpine country, enjoying the pleasing views of nature there. He says that the scenery is in no respect less grand than that of the Himalayas. Still, he makes out two points of difference between the two mountainous regions. In the former the rapid and thick colonization has been marring the beauty of the place. In the latter, there has not yet been any such marked tendency. The former has become a resort mainly for the sanatorists and summer residents; and the latter mainly for the pilgrims and devotees. The Swami is shortly going to visit Germany, where an interview will take place with Prof. Deussen, after which, by the 24th of September, he will go back to England. To India, most likely, as he says, he is returning by the next winter. He intends to reside in the Himalayas.

---

1. No verbatim transcript available.

2. Cf. Mr. J. J. Goodwin's published transcript "The Real Nature of Man", *Complete Works*, II: 70 87.

3. Probably Mr. E. T. Sturdy.

4. Vivekananda in Indian Newspapers, p. 117.

5. Evidently an unpublished extract from one of the three letters the Swami wrote from Lucerne (Vide "Epistles", *Complete Works*, V and VI).

"THE IDEAL OF UNIVERSAL RELIGION"[6]

The Journal of the Maha Bodhi Society, November 1896

We have been presented with a copy of a booklet entitled the "Ideal of Universal Religion", published by the Brahmavadin Publishing Company, Madras. It is a lecture by Swami Vivekananda, delivered in America. The lecture is highly interesting and instructive. It is an attempt at a reconciliation between the diversity of religions. We hail the booklet as the symptom of the times, for it is evident for obvious reasons that men are beginning to awaken to the importance of this problem of religious harmony. Recently, in these countries leaders of different religious sects have attempted in their own way to reconcile this religious diversity, and have failed; they have aspired to defend their dogmas on the ground of distorted views of sectarianism. Swami Vivekananda has propounded a philosophical and at the same time a most practical solution of this problem of religious harmony. According to him, Vedanta is the bond between the ever conflicting religious differences. In the internal world, like the external world, there is also the centripetal and centrifugal action. We repel something, we attract something. Today we are attracted by some, tomorrow we are repelled by some. The same law cannot be applied at all times and in all cases. "Religion is the highest place of human thought and life, and herein the workings of these two forces have been most marked." At the outset, it apparently appears that there cannot reign unbroken harmony in this plane of mighty struggle. In every religion there are three parts, namely, philosophy, mythology and rituals. Every recognised religion [has] all these three things. But there can be no universal philosophy, mythology and rituals for the whole world. Where then the universal-ity? How is it possible then to have a universal form of religion? "We all hear," says Swami Vivekananda, about universal brotherhood, and how societies stand up practically to preach this, Universal brotherhood, that is, we shout like drunken men we are all equal, therefore, let us make a sect. As soon as you make a sect you protest against equality, and thus it is no more.[7]

Mahomedans talk of universal brotherhood, but what comes out of them in reality? Nobody who is not a Mahomedan will be admitted into the brotherhood, he will have his throat cut. We think we cannot do better than quote his own words, wherein he with his wonderful lucidity and depth of views and in a remarkably catholic mind propounds forcibly the philosophy of the uni versal religion [Vide Complete Works, II: 375 96]...

In society there are various natures of men. Some are active working men, there is the emotional man, then there is the mystic man and lastly there is the philosopher. Vivekananda strikes the key note of his whole philosophy when he declares that the attempt to help mankind to become beautifully balanced in all these four directions, is his ideal of religion and this religion is called in India, Yoga. The worker is called the Karma yogin; who seeks union through love is called Bhakti yogin; he who seeks through mysticism is called Raja yogin; and he who seeks it through philosophy is called Jnan[a] yogin. The religion which has a place for men of all these natures and a religion which satisf[ies] the thirst of men of different inclination, may be the universal religion, and that religion is Vedanta. Most cordially we recommend this admirable little book to our readers. For it contains some clear and definite expressions of views on the most vital problem that is engaging the serious attention of theologians. The price of the book is As. 3, and may be had at the Brahmavadin Office, Triplicane, Madras.

---

6. Vivekananda in Indian Newspapers, pp. 331 33.

7. Cf. the American lecture, delivered January 12, 1896 (Complete Works, II, pp. 379 80).

THE BANQUET FOR RANJIT SINJHI[1]

The Indian Mirror, December 16, 1896.

On the 21st of this month [November], the Cambridge "Indian Majlis" gave a complimentary dinner at the University Arms Hotel [in Cambridge] to Prince Ranjit sinhji and Mr. Atul Chandra Chatterjee. Mr. Hafiz G. Sarwir of St. John's College, took the chair. There were about fifty Indians present and a few Englishmen...Swami Vivekananda rose next to respond [to the toast of India] amidst loud and deafening cheers.[2] The Swami began by saying that he did not know exactly why he should be chosen to respond to the toast unless it be for the reason that he in physical bulk bore a striking resemblance to the national animal of India (laughter). He desired to congratulate the guest of the evening and he took the statement which the Chairman had made that Mr. Chatterjee was going to correct the mistake of past historians of India, to be literally true. For out of the past the future must come and he knew no greater and more permanent foundation for the future than a true knowledge of what had preceded before. The present is the effect of the infinity of causes which represent the past. They had many things to learn from the Europeans but their past, the glory of India which had passed away, should constitute even a still greater source of inspiration and instruction. Things rise and things decay, there is rise and fall everywhere in the world...[Vide the block quotation on the following page for the remaining text of this report.]

THE MAJLIS IN CAMBRIDGE[3]

The Amrita Bazar Patrika, January 8, 1897.

The gathering was a unique one, for the Indians met together to talk (in the Majlis they all talk), about the successes of Ranjit Sing[h] and Atul Chandra Chatterjee. It is a pity the name of Professor Bose was not associated with the above two; and we think, Swami Vivekananda, who was present on the occasion, also deserved a recognition. We shall, however, not commit the mistake of omitting the last two in noticing to show what the Indians have been able to achieve in the West.

What the Swamiji did was to remove the impression from the minds of the Americans that the Indians were barbarians, superstitious in their beliefs, and addicted to monstrous cruelties. The advent of the Swamiji in the West has done this service, that it has created an impression in many quarters that the Indians are not an inferior race as Sir Charles Elliot called them, and that they can, in such subjects as religion and philosophy say things which are not known even to the West. The advent of the Swamiji in the West has undoubtedly enhanced the character of the Indians in the West...

Said Swami Vivekananda:—

And though India is fallen to day she will assuredly rise again. There was a time when India produced great philosophers and still greater prophets and preachers. The memory of those days ought to fill them with hope and confidence. This was not the first time in the history of India that they were so low. Periods of depression and degradation had occurred before this but India had always triumphed in the long run and so would she once again in the future.[4]...

VIVEKANANDA IN THE WEST[5]

The Amrita Bazar Patrika, January 20, 1897.

Swami Vivekananda has received the ovation of a conquering hero, returning home. The last we heard of him in England was when he got a farewell address from his English disciples, who expressed their undying love for India...

No one has any accurate knowledge of what Swami Vivekananda was doing in the West. We hear that he has made some impression in America and

---

1. *New Discoveries*, Vol. 4, pp. 479 80.

2. There is no verbatim transcript available. Cf. the following January 8, 1897 Indian newspaper report, "The Majlis in Cambridge", p. 542.

3. Vivekananda in Indian Newspapers, pp. 310 11.

4. At this time, there is no complete verbatim transcript available. Cf. the preceding December 16, 1896 Indian newspaper report, "The Banquet to Ranjit Sinjhi", p. 541.

5. Vivekananda in Indian Newspapers, p. 312.

also in England...

The Swami is, however, well aware of the nature of the mission before him. He says that Vedantism teaches the truth, which is that man is a divine being and that the highest and the lowest are the manifestations of the same Lord. He does not, however, admit that knowledge alone is sufficient for the salvation of man. Says he:—

But his knowledge ought not to be a theory, but life. Religion is a realization, not talk, not doctrines, nor theories, however beautiful all these may be. Religion is being and becoming, not hearing or acknowledging. It is not an intellectual assent; but one's whole nature becoming changed into it. Such is religion. By an intellectual assent we can come to a hundred sort of foolish things, and change the next day, but this being and becoming is what is religion.

In the above noble sentiments, the Swami shews [shows] that he understands the situation pretty well. That which produces the rebirth of a man is religion. Under the influence of religion a man becomes a quite different being from what he was before. Unless that is the result of his religion, his religion is a myth.

BHAKTI[6]

The Indian Mirror, February 24, 1898.

Swami Vivekananda has been urging on the people of Lahore and Sialkote the need of practical work.[7] The starving millions, he urged, cannot live on metaphysical speculation; they require bread; and in a lecture he gave at Lahore on Bhakti, he suggested as the best religion for to day that everyman should, according to his means, go out into the street and search for hungry Narayans, take them into their houses, feed them and clothe them. The giver should give to man, remembering that he is the highest temple of God. He had seen charity in many countries, and the reason of its failure was the spirit, in which it was carried out. "Here take this

---
6. Vivekananda in Indian Newspapers, pp. 203 4.

7. Cf. "Bhakti" (a report from The Tribune), *Complete Works*, III: 391, for a somewhat different paraphrased passage.

and go away". Charity belied its name so long as it was given to gain reputation or applause of the world.

OUR MISSION IN AMERICA[8]

The Indian Mirror, April 24, 1898.

Swami Vivekananda, in introducing the lecturer Swami Saradananda, said:

Ladies and Gentlemen,—The speaker of tonight just comes from America. As you all know here that America is for your country, although our countrymen, specially Swami Dayananda Saraswati, used to call this country as Patal, inhabited by Laplands, Rakshas and Asurs, &c. (Laughter and loud cheers). Well, Gentlemen, whether it is Patal or not you ought to decide that by seeing those few ladies pres- ent here, who have come from the country of your so called Patal, whether they are Naga Kanyas or not. (Cheers). Now, America is perfectly a new country. It was discovered by Columbus, the Italian, and before that a prior claim is put forward by the Norwegians who say, that they have discovered the northern part of it, and then before that there is another prior claim of the Chinese, who at one time preached the noble doctrine of Buddhism in all parts of the world, and it is said that Buddhist Missionaries were also sent from India to America, and specially in Washington, where some sort[s] of records are still to be traced by any traveller going there. Well, the table has now been turned at last for a century or more and instead of America being discovered, she discovers persons that go over to her. (Loud applause). It is a phenomenon that we observe every day there, multitudes of persons coming over from every part of the country [world?] and getting themselves discovered in the United States. It is a fact, well known to you here all that several of our own countrymen have been discovered in that way. (Cheers). To day, here I present before you one of your Calcutta boys, that has been similarly discovered by the Americans. (Cheers).

---
8. Vivekananda in Indian Newspapers, p. 208.

SWAMI VIVEKANANDA AT BELUR [on education][1]

The Indian Mirror, February 15, 1901.

A correspondent writes:—"The following is an epitome of Swami Vivekananda's speech made in Belur M.E. School on the prize distribution day held on the 22nd instant, Sunday, when the Swami was invited to preside. The audience was composed chiefly of the boys of the school and some elderly gentlemen of Belur."

The modern student is not practical. He is quite helpless. What our students want is not so much muscularity of body as hardihood. They are wanting in self help. They are not accustomed to use their eyes and hands. No handicraft is taught. The present system of English education is entirely literary. The student must be made to think for himself and work for himself. Suppose there is a fire. He is the first to come forward and put on [out] the fire who is accustomed to use his eyes and hands. There is much truth in the criticism of Europeans touching the laziness of the Bengali, the slipshod way of his doing things. This can be soon remedied if the students be made to learn some handicraft apart from its utilitarian aspect, it is an education in itself.

Secondly, how many thousands of students I know who live upon the worst food possible, and live amidst the most horrible surroundings, what wonder that there are so many idiots, imbeciles and cowards among them. They die like flies. The education that is given is onesided, weakening, it is killing by inches. The children are made to cram too much of useless matter, and are incarcerated in school rooms fifty or seventy in each, five hours together. They are given bad food. It is forgotten that the future health of the man is in the child. It is forgotten that nature can never be cheated and things cannot be pushed too early. In giving education to a child the law of growth has to be obeyed. And we must learn to wait. Nothing is more important than that the child must have a strong and healthy body. The body is the first thing to attain to virtue.

I know we are the poorest nation in the world, and we cannot afford to do much. We can only work on the lines of least resistance. We should see at least that our children are well fed. The machine of the child's body should never be exhausted. In Europe and America a man with crores of rupees sends his son if sickly, to the farmers, to till the ground. After three years he returns to the father healthy, rosy and strong. Then he is fit to be sent to school. We ought not for these reasons push the present system of education any further.

Thirdly, our character has disappeared. Our English education has destroyed everything and left nothing in its place.

Our children have lost their politeness. To talk nicely is degrading. To be reverential to one's elders is degrading. Irreverence has been the sign of liberty. It is high time that we go back to our old politeness. The reformers have nothing to give in place of what they have taken away. Yet in spite of the most adverse surrounding of climate, etc., we have been able to do much, we have to do much more. I am proud of my race, I do not despair, I am seeing daily a glorious and wonderful future in my menial [mental] visions. Take greatest care of these young ones on whom our future depends.

HINDU WIDOWS[2]

The Indian Social Reformer, June 16, 1901.

A question having arisen in America as to the Swami Vivekananda's attitude towards social questions, a lady writes to an American paper as follows: "In one of his lectures at the Pouch Mansion,[3] he spoke of the Hindu widows, declaring it unjust to state that they were generally subjected to cruelty or oppression in the Indians [sic] homes. He admitted that the prejudice against remarriage, and the custom which makes the widow a member of the husband's family instead of that of her own par-

---

1. Vivekananda in Indian Newspapers, p. 215.

2. Vivekananda in Indian Newspapers, p. 458.

3. Probably "India's Gift to the World", delivered February 25, 1895, of which there is no verbatim transcript available. Cf. two American newspaper articles published in *Complete Works*, II: 510 14 for somewhat different reports of this issue.

ents inflicted some hardships upon widows in India, and favoured wise efforts for their education which would render them self supporting and in this way alleviate their condition. He emphasised his desire for the education and elevation of the women of his country, including the widows, by volunteering to give the entire proceeds of one of his lectures in support of the school of Babu Sasipada Banerjee, at Baranagar, near Calcutta, the institution of which preceded that of the Pandita Ramabai, at Poona, and where, if I am not mistaken, the Pandita herself obtained the first inspiration of her work. This lecture was given, and the proceeds were forwarded to Babu Sasipada Banerjee, and duly acknowledged."

UNPUBLISHED

YOUR HIGHNESS — I

MADRAS,
The 15th February [1893]

YOUR HIGHNESS,

Two things I am telling your Highness.

One—a very wonderful phenomenon I have seen in a village called Kumbakonam, and another about myself. In the said village lives a man of the Chetty caste, generally passing for an astrologer. I, with two other young men, went to see him. He was said to tell about anything a man thinks of. So, I wanted to put him to the test. Two months ago, I dreamt that my mother was dead and I was very anxious to know about her. My second was whether what my Guru had told me was right. The third was a test-question — a part of the Buddhistic mantra, in Tibetan tongue.

These questions I determined upon, two days before going to this Govinda Chetty. Another young man had one of his sisters-in-law given poison to, by some unknown hand, from which she recovered. But he wanted to know the author of that delivery. When we first saw him, the fellow was almost ferocious. He said that some Europeans came to see [him] with the Dewan of Mysore and that since then through their 'Dristee Dosham' he had got fever and that he could not give us a seance then and only if we paid him 10 Rs., he would consent to tell us our 'prasnas'. The young men with me of course were ready to pay down his fees. But he goes to his private room and immediately comes back and says to me that if I gave him some ashes to cure him of his fever he would consent to give us a seance. Of course I told him that I do not boast of any power of curing diseases but he said, 'That does not matter, only I want [the ash]'. So, I consented and he took us to the private room and, taking a sheet of paper, wrote something upon it and gave it over to one of us and made me sign it and keep it into the pocket of one of my companions. Then he told me point blank, 'Why you, a Sannyasi, are thinking upon your mother?' I answered that even the great Shankaracharya would take care of his mother; and he said 'She is all right and I have written her name in that paper in the possession of your friend' and then went on saying, 'Your Guru is dead. Whatever he has told you, you must believe, for he was a very very great man,' and went on giving me a description of my Guru which was most wonderful and then he said 'What more you want to know about your Guru?' I told him 'If you can give me his name I would be satisfied', and he said, 'Which name? A Sannyasi gets different sorts of names'. I answered, 'The name by which he was known to the public', and says, 'The wonderful name, I have already written that. And you wanted to know about a mantra in Tibetan, that is also written in that paper.' And, he then told me to think of anything in any language and tell him, I told him 'Om Namo Bhagavate Vasudevaya', and he said, 'That is also written in the paper in possession of your friend. Now take it out and see'. And Lo! Wonder! They were all there as he said and even my mother's name was there!! It began thus — your mother of such and such name is all right. She is very holy and good, but she is feeling your separation like death and within two years she shall die; so if you want to see her, it must be within two years. Next it was written — your Guru Ramakrishna Paramahamsa is dead but he lives in Sukshma, i.e., ethereal body, and is watching over you, etc. and then it was written 'Lamala capsechua', in Tibetan, and then at last was written 'In conformation to what I have written, I give you also this mantra which you would give me after one hour after my writing; 'Om Namo Bhagavate etc.'; and so he was equally successful with my friends. Then I saw people coming from distant villages and as soon as he sees them he says — 'Your name is such and such and you come from such and such village for this purpose'. By the time he was reading me, he toned down very much and said — 'I won't take money from you. On the other hand, you must take some "seva" from me'. And I took some milk at his house and he brought over his whole family to bow down to me and I touched some 'vibhutee' brought by him and then I asked him the source of his wonderful powers. First he would not say, but after a while he came to me [and] said — 'Maharaj, it is "siddhi of mantras" through the "sahaya" of "Devi".' Verily, there are more things on heaven and earth Horatio than your philosophy ever dreamt of — Shakespeare.

The second is regarding me. Here is a zamindar of Ramnath, now staying in Madras. He is going to send me over to Europe and, as you are already aware of, I have a great mind to see those places. So I have determined to take this opportunity of making a tour in Europe and America. But I can't do anything without asking your Highness, the only friend on Earth I have. So kindly give your opinion about it. I only want to make a short tour in those places. One thing I am certain of, that I am [an] instrument in the hands [of] a holy and superior power.

Myself, I have no peace, am burning literally day and night, but somehow or other, wherever I go hundreds and, in some [places] as in Madras, thousands would come to me day and night and would be cured of their skepticism and unbelief but I —!

I am always unhappy!! Thy will be done!! Therefore, I don't know what this power requires of me, to be done in Europe. I cannot but obey. 'Thy will be done'!! There is no escape. I congratulate your Highness on the birth of a son and heir.

May the infant prince be quiet like his most noble father and may the Lord shower his blessings always on him and his parents.

So I am going over in two or three weeks to Europe. I can't say anything as to the future of the body. Only I pray to your Highness if it be proper to take some care of my mother that she does not starve. I would be highly obliged to get a reply soon, and pray your Highness to keep the latter part of this letter, i.e., my going over to England etc., confidential.

May you be blessed all your life, you and yours, is the prayer that is day and night offered up by,

Vivekananda.

C/o. M. Bhattacharya Esq.
Assistant Accountant General
Mt. St. Thome, Madras

YOUR HIGHNESS — II

BOMBAY,
The 22nd May [18]93.

YOUR HIGHNESS,

Leaving Khetri there happened nothing particular to relate except that I had every comfort on the way, broke journey at Kharari and then [went] to Nariad [Nadiad]. Haridas Bhai was as usual very kind to me and we had many and many a talk about your Highness, so much so that he was really very anxious to see you and intends paying his respects to your Highness in his coming winter tour to the north. And I dare say your Highness would also be very much pleased to see this old man of great experience who was for twenty-five years the mentor of Kathiawad. Withal he is the only remnant of the old school of very conservative politicians. He is a man who is thoroughly able to organize and put to perfect order an existing machinery; but he would be the last man to move a step further. At Bombay I went to see my friend Ramdas, Barrister-at-Law. He is rather a sentimental gentleman and was so much impressed with your Highness' character that he told me that had it not been midsummer he would rather fly to see such a prince.

His father intends going to Chicago on the 31st; if so, we would go together for company. Today I go to buy some steel trunks etc., and am only waiting for the Madras money to come in. Although I wired to them from Jeypore, they were rather suspicious and waited for my further communications and I have again wired them and written too. On our way we had the company of Mr. Ramnath, the charan headmaster of the Jeypore noble's school. He and I had a bout on my first coming out of Khetri years ago, about vegetarianism. He had in the meantime got hold of some American writers and pounced upon me with his arguments from them. His author, he said, has proved to his satisfaction that the human digestive organs including the teeth are exactly like those of the cow. Therefore, man is designed by nature to be a vegetarian animal. He is a very good and nice gentleman and I did not want to disturb his confidence in the American hobbyist but one thing was on the tip of my tongue — If our digestive apparatus is exactly like that of a cow — we ought and must be able to eat and digest grass. In that case poor Indians are fools to die of starvation in famine times while their natural food, grass, is so abundant, and your Highness' servants are fools to serve you while they have only to get up the nearest hillock and get a bellyful of grass instead of undergoing all the trouble of serving others!!! Grand American discovery indeed!!! Only I hope the holy dungs of such human cows may become of great use to the wonderful American author and his Indian disciple. Amen. So much for the cow-human theory. Do not find anything more to advertise to your Highness, so, beg leave to stop here.

May the giver of all good bestow his choicest blessings on you and yours, I remain,

Yours in the Lord,
Vivekananda.

Discovery Publisher is a multimedia publisher whose mission is to inspire and support personal transformation, spiritual growth and awakening. We strive with every title to preserve the essential wisdom of the author, spiritual teacher, thinker, healer, and visionary artist.

www.ingramcontent.com/pod-product-compliance
Lightning Source LLC
Chambersburg PA
CBHW081126170426
43197CB00017B/2768